Pierre Esprit Radisson

The Explorations of
Pierre Esprit Radisson

From the original manuscript in the
Bodleian Library and the British Museum

ARTHUR T. ADAMS, *Editor*

LOREN KALLSEN, *Modernizer*

ROSS & HAINES, Inc.

Minneapolis, Minnesota -   -   -   -   -   -   -   -   1961

To Harold,
Margueritte,
Karen and
Marilyn

Table of Contents

Foreword

ONE MAY NATURALLY inquire: why should a book so rare and so long forgotten as *Radisson's Voyages* be recalled from the realm of obscurity and again submitted to the reading public? The writer endeavors, in this Foreword and in the appended monograph, to answer this inquiry.

The original manuscript describing the first four voyages of this unique volume was written probably in the year 1668 or 1669[1] by Pierre Esprit Radisson, who recounts his boyhood experiences among the Iroquois Indians, and also his journeys with his brother-in-law, Medard Chouart, better known as Des Groseilliers, into the North and Northwest, including the regions around and beyond Lakes Michigan and Superior. The original purpose of the narrative is not entirely clear, though many writers believe it to have been intended for the information of King Charles II in regard to the importance of the fur trade in the Hudson Bay country.[2] After passing through the hands of the well known collectors Samuel Pepys and Richard Rawlinson, the manuscript came into the possession of the Bodleian library at Oxford, England, where it has reposed for nearly three centuries.

In 1685, Radisson described his Fifth and Sixth voyages—those of 1682-83 and 1684. The original manuscripts reside in the archives of the Hudson's Bay Company and the British Museum.

In 1885 the six narratives were published by the Prince Society of Boston as *Radisson's Voyages,* in an edition of only 250 copies.[3] These are distributed chiefly among the public libraries throughout the country, and some copies are in the possession of individual owners, who value them highly. This small edition of the narratives was received with much interest among historians, and before many years a spirited controversy arose in regard to the times, duration, and order of the first four voyages narrated in the manuscript. This controversy, carried on for a number of years among eminent scholars, and as yet unsettled, has discredited, to a large degree, the work of Radisson. It has cast a cloud upon his veracity and integrity, relegated his entire chronicle to the realm of doubt, and deprived the cause of history of a most valuable original source.

As a result of recent studies of the Radisson manuscript and sources of information bearing upon certain events which Radisson mentions and describes, three distinct parts of his narratives have been found to be out of their proper places. By discovering their correct locations and reconstructing the narratives at the points affected, the entire record becomes logical, consistent, and substantially in accord with the well-known facts of history.

Some of the defects and discrepancies in the chronicle appear to be so great and so glaring that many scholars have looked upon the author as a dispenser of deliberate falsehood and, hence, have cast the book aside as unworthy of serious consideration. Other students of Radisson have been more charitable and have looked upon these apparent defects as the result of a deficient knowledge of the English language and a waning memory, due to the fact that the narratives were written from six to fifteen years after the occurrence of the events recorded. It has also been conjectured that some of the mistakes were due to the human shortcomings of a copyist or to possible disarrangement of sheets upon which original notes were made.

A critical and analytical consideration of Radisson's manuscript has led the writer to some definite conclusions which, so far as known, have never before been suggested, and because of these conclusions it seems appropriate to state, somewhat briefly, the causes of this divergence of opinion which has resulted in the long obscurity of this significant document.

Order of the Voyages

The first step in clearing away the uncertainty that has beclouded Radisson's account is the consideration of the schedule of the first four voyages as Radisson himself recorded them.

The first, or Captivity, voyage occupied two years. Radisson was captured by the Mohawks about April or May, 1652. He remained with them until October, 1653, then went to Holland and France and returned to his home at Three Rivers in May, 1654. There is no doubt or dispute as to the period of this voyage. In the manuscript the Captivity voyage is followed immediately by

ii

the narrative of the Onondaga voyage. The context indicates that the writer of the narrative believed that these two voyages took place in close succession and therefore that the Onondaga voyage was made during the year 1654-55. This in turn is followed by the Mississippi voyage, which, according to Radisson's assertions, continued for three years, thus placing the Mississippi voyage in the years 1655-58. Then follows one year "at home at rest" ending in 1659, and this, by the context of the narrative, is followed immediately by the Superior voyage of two years, which thus falls in the years 1659-61.

Radisson's schedule as above outlined would appear to be correct and in accordance with his own recollection, but this is impossible because of certain well known historic facts. These are: the Iroquois peace of 1653; the founding of the Onondaga mission by the Jesuits in 1656; the escape from the Onondaga mission in 1658; and the Dollard massacre in 1660. (At this point the reader will do well to familiarize himself with the "year chart" located in the section of illustrations. Line A of this chart represents graphically Radisson's own version of the schedule of his voyages. Lines B, C, and D represent alternative schedules discussed in the following pages. Line C is held to be the correct schedule of voyages, and this volume has been ordered in accordance with it.)

In November, 1653, peace was effected between the French and Algonquins on one side and the Iroquois on the other. This event is referred to by Radisson at the end of the Captivity voyage in the sentence, "In my absence peace was made between the French and the Iroquois, which was the reason I stayed not long in a place." In the title of the Captivity voyage Radisson states that he came to Canada in the year 1651, and in the beginning of that narrative he asserts that he was captured by the Iroquois in the year following his arrival in Canada, which would be 1652. These assertions, together with his reference to the peace of November, 1653, and his return from France in 1654, fix definitely the period of the Captivity voyage.[4]

The Onondage voyage could not possibly follow immediately the Captivity voyage as indicated by Radisson's own outline. This is because of the well known date of the escape of the French and Hurons from the Iroquois at the Onondaga mission in the early part of 1658.[5] This remarkable and almost superhuman exploit is minutely described by Radisson near the end of the Onondaga voyage.[6] This description renders it quite certain that Radisson was present on that momentous occasion and therefore during the entire journey which commenced in June, 1657. This indisputable historic fact seems to fix beyond possible doubt the period of the Onondaga voyage as 1657-58; it could not have occurred during 1654-55, as Radisson seems to recall it in his narrative.

The Mississippi voyage follows immediately the Onondaga voyage, according to Radisson's record, and at this point it will be well to observe a significant phase of Radisson's relation of the Mississippi voyage. He states specifically in two places, and impliedly in others, that this journey occupied a period of three years.[7] In view of certain fixed dates this would be impossible, and all authorities agree that two years is the limit of time for this voyage. It therefore becomes necessary to break apart his schedule at the end of the year 1654 and move all that follows it three years forward, and at the same time reduce the Mississippi voyage to two years. This places the Onondaga voyage in the year 1657-58, where we have seen that it must be, and it also advances the Mississippi voyage to the years 1658-60 and the Superior voyage to the years 1661-63. (See the year chart, line B.)

It will now be seen that there is a vacant period of three years from 1654 to 1657 during which Radisson gives no account of the doings or whereabouts of himself or Groseilliers. There is, however, in the *Jesuit Relations,* an account of a journey of two years from August, 1654, to August, 1656, by two Frenchmen whose names are not given, covering virtually the same route as that described by Radisson in the Mississippi voyage.[8] This journey will be referred to as the Unwritten voyage and will now be included in the schedule of all five voyages. (See the year chart, line C.)

Attention must now be directed to another important historic event, namely, the Dollard massacre. Radisson describes this sanguinary conflict near the end of the Superior voyage,[9] and near the close of its description he states that "It was a terrible spectacle to us, for we came there 8 days after that defeat." It is quite clear from the context of Radisson's narrative, as will appear later in this Foreword, that the Superior voyage ended in 1663. It is also a well established historic fact that the Dollard massacre occurred in May, 1660.[10]

Now, with all this data before us, let us note a remarkable series of coincidences. First, it will be seen that the Unwritten voyage of

iv

1654-56 is followed by a vacant period of one year. Also the Mississippi voyage of 1658-60 is followed by a period of one year "at home at rest." The details of the Unwritten voyage as described by the Jesuits, particularly the departure and return, are remarkably similar to the details found in Radisson's Mississippi voyage.[11] Now, if the Mississippi voyage and the one year of "rest" that follows it be lifted up and set back to the period of 1654-57, it will be observed that the Mississippi voyage coincides perfectly with the Unwritten voyage, and the year of "rest" also fits into the vacant year of 1656-57. In view of the similarity of the two accounts this apparently perfect coincidence seems to justify the change. By making this change a vacancy is created in the period from 1658-60. Now if we lift the Superior voyage up and set it back to this period we find that it fits perfectly into the two year vacancy created by removing the Mississippi voyage, and incidentally that the Dollard massacre story will now be approximately in its right historic place. (See the year chart, line D.) These coincidences are so unusual and so well nigh perfect that this arrangement seems entirely plausible. It is not surprising, therefore, that some authorities have adopted this order of the voyages, assuming that Radisson and Groseilliers were the two unnamed Frenchmen of the Unwritten voyage, and regard all inconsistencies as due to errors, deficient memory, and even deliberate and purposeful misstatements.

Several obstacles oppose this arrangement. In the first place the removal of both the Mississippi and Superior voyages back several years breaks assunder Radisson's narrative at every point between the voyages and does great violence to his own record of his experiences. A careful reading of the narrative at the points where the transition is made from one voyage to the next will disclose an unmistakable connection between them, and will show that at the end of one reference is made to the next following, and at the beginning of each reference is made to the preceding, all of which indicates that Radisson wrote the account of his first four voyages in the order that he intended and presumably in the order of their occurrence. A rearrangement of the four journeys resulting in such a complete disorganization of the entire narrative does not seem justifiable in the effort to render a fair and proper interpretation of the chronicle.

According to the revised schedule which includes the Unwritten voyage (see the year chart, line C), the Superior voyage ended in

1663, but as stated before, the Dollard massacre, which is described near the end of this voyage, occurred in 1660. Now it becomes necessary to make an adjustment which will comply with this known date, either by removing the entire Superior voyage back to the position of 1658-60, or by moving the Dollard story alone back to a corresponding position near the end of the Mississippi voyage, which ended in 1660. The latter alternative seems to be necessary, as the evidence is almost conclusive that the Superior voyage ended in 1663. Radisson's own narrative fully supports and corroborates this view, as will now be shown.

Fortunately the narrative of the Superior voyage is followed by a brief summary of their activities between their return and the year 1669. In this summary, reference is made to a few well known events, the dates of which fix beyond reasonable doubt the year of their return from the Superior voyage.

By turning to the text of this voyage it will be seen that upon their arrival at Quebec — August, 1663 — the voyageurs had trouble with the governor,[12] and as a result of this ill treatment Groseilliers went to France to obtain redress. Failing in this he secured from a Rochelle merchant a ship to make a voyage to Hudson Bay the next season. Radisson and Groseilliers embarked on this ship, the *Nonsuch,* and reached latitude 61 degrees north. The captain, becoming frightened at the icebergs, refused to go further, and they returned to Port Royal, the place of their embarkation. These events brought them into the next year, 1664.

They were now promised two ships for a second voyage, which were made fit and ready before the proper time for their departure to the North. To gain some profit they sent one of these ships on a fishing trip to the Isle of Sand, or Sable island. A storm wrecked this ship, and the voyage to the North was abandoned. Certain merchants who suffered loss brought suit in Boston against Radisson and Groseilliers for redress.[13] This lawsuit occurred during the summer of 1665, and this was the second year following their return from the Superior voyage.

In the meantime, Radisson says, the four commissioners from England arrived in that place, and he and Groseilliers sailed for England with them that summer. It is definitely known that these four commissioners came to Boston in the summer of 1665 in connection with the business of transferring Fort Orange and New Netherland to the English.[14] The year of this event being certainly established, and it being the second year following the return of the voyageurs from the Superior voyage, it follows that the year 1663 was the end of that journey. This fact is further corroborated by Radisson's references to subsequent events, namely: the plague in London, 1665,[15] the war with Holland, 1666,[16] the stoppage of the Thames, 1666,[17] and the voyage of the *Eaglet* and *Nonsuch* and the storm at sea which separated them, 1668.[18]

Not only does Radisson's reference to these well known historic events determine the year of his and Groseilliers' return from the Superior voyage, but the context of his narrative also sustains this conclusion. It will be noticed that when the two Frenchmen left Quebec at the beginning of that voyage they had trouble with the governor, who forbade their going without his leave.[19] On their return they again became involved with the governor, whose term of office was just to expire,[20] and a careful reading of the narrative will show that the governor in office when they left and when they returned two years later was one and the same man. An examination of Canadian records will show that the only governor of Quebec who could fit into these conditions was Governor D'Avaugour, whose term extended from August 31st, 1661, to July 23rd, 1663.[21] This fact also accords with Radisson's casual remark that this voyage was "less than two years." The Superior voyage could not have ended in 1660, since Governor D'Argenson's term commenced July 11th, 1658, and did not terminate until August 31st, 1661.[22]

Another evidence may be adduced from the context of the narrative bearing upon the period of this voyage. When these explorers were leaving Chequamagon Bay in the early part of the Superior voyage, the conduct of the Indians reminded Radisson of the entry into Paris of the Fench King and his Spanish wife. The marriage of Louis XIV to Maria Theresa, Infanta of Spain, took place in June, 1660.[23] Had this journey taken place during 1658-60, they would have been at Chequamagon Bay late in 1658, and thus this association in Radisson's mind could not have occurred.

The conclusion to be drawn from the context and from the historic events mentioned seems to be, certainly, that the Superior voyage commenced after August 31st, 1661, and ended prior to July 23rd, 1663, which is the period of D'Avaugour's term of office as governor of Quebec.

This brings us again to the Dollard massacre story, which is in Radisson's manuscript found near the end of the Superior voyage. Since this voyage must have ended in 1663 and this event occurred

vii

in 1660, it follows that this story is out of its historic place by three years and apparently should be near the end of the Mississippi voyage, which ended in 1660.

Transpositions

It now becomes necessary to find a place in the Mississippi narrative where this Dollard story can be inserted, and as a basis for this inquiry the reader is asked to take note of the following significant facts:

1. On each of these two journeys (Mississippi and Superior) the voyageurs returned to Quebec by way of the Ottawa river and passed through the rapids known as the Long Sault above Montreal.

2. In that part of the Superior voyage where this passage through the rapids is described, the narrative is broken in the midst of the description, and Radisson inserts the Dollard story, after which the description of the journey continues. This story begins and ends as follows: "You must know that seventeen French . . . . as that company was."[24]

3. In identically the same place in the Mississippi voyage, where the passage through the rapids is described, the narrative is also broken in the midst of the description, and the story of the hunting journey, made by Radisson in the vicinity of the Mississippi river during the summer, is inserted. This story begins and ends thus: "We were four months . . . . like those of the wildmen."[25]

4. The hunting story is followed immediately by the phrase "to our purpose," after which the passage through the rapids is resumed.

These four statements must be clearly understood and should be carefully verified before proceeding further.

It should be clear to the most casual reader that the hunting story, in the Mississippi voyage, is out of place and must be removed. In removing it, however, note particularly that the phrase "To our purpose" is left where it is and also that the vacancy created is to remain open.

Now that the hunting story is taken out, it must be reinserted at some other point, which will now be determined. At this stage of procedure it will be well to observe the three distinct parts of the Mississippi narrative: the outward journey, the landing isle paragraph, and the return journey. The landing isle paragraph consists of about fourteen lines and begins and ends as follows: "That summer I went ahunting . . . . God gave him his health again."

All that precedes this short paragraph is the outward journey, and all that follows it is the return journey.

Now it will be observed that the last thing said in the landing isle paragraph is a reference to the sickness of Groseilliers. Also the last thing said in the hunting story is a reference to Groseilliers' sickness, but it includes the significant words "as I said before."[26] These are the only references to the sickness of Groseilliers in the entire book. Now, by context, it is clear that the hunting story cannot precede the landing isle paragraph since that would contradict the clause "as I said before." It cannot be placed at any point in the return journey, since that is complete, logical, and consistent throughout. It follows that the hunting story must be inserted between the landing isle paragraph and the return journey, which begins with the words "The desire that everyone had."[27] This construction also accords with a fundamental principle of documentary interpretation, since it renders a clear and consistent meaning to all parts of the narrative.[28]

This construction also follows the natural order of procedure taken by any writer of history. When this change is made it will be seen that the narrative of the landing isle sojourn of Groseilliers and that of the hunting journey of Radisson cover identically the same period of time (four months), but two different localities. Now, in writing of these events it would be natural, logical, and even necessary to follow the description of one locality by the description of the other.

As a further evidence of the propriety of this construction it may be observed that at the beginning of the landing isle paragraph Radisson says "That summer I went ahunting," and immediately following this paragraph (as this volume is put together) he describes in detail that hunting journey. It would seem entirely natural and proper to follow closely a general reference to an event with a detailed account of it.

Turning now to the replacement of the Dollard story in the Mississippi voyage, it will be necessary first to consider, as a further basis of our inquiry, a distinctive characteristic running through all of Radisson's writing. This is a tendency to digress from the main narrative and relate a separate and independent, though pertinent, story and follow it by an appropriate phrase to reintroduce the main narrative. A few examples will make this important point clear: in the Captivity voyage, after describing his adoption into a Mohawk family, Radisson resumes his narrative with the words "But to the purpose of my history."[29] After describing the mode of making those delicious mincemeat cornballs, he continues thus: "To make a period of this, my little voyage."[30] In the Onondaga voyage, after relating a history of the Hurons, he resumes as follows: "Let us come to our purpose and follow our voyage."[31] In the Mississippi voyage, the hunting story is followed by "To our purpose,"[32] and in the Superior voyage the relation of the beliefs of the Indians is followed by "let us come to our arrival again."[33] These are all digressive stories which are followed by appropriate expressions reintroducing the main narrative, and the list of examples might be extended.

It should now be observed that the Dollard story, which is clearly digressive, *is not followed by reintroductory words;* also that the hunting story is an integral part of the main narrative, describing actual experiences, and is not digressive, but before its removal it was followed, improperly, by the words "To our purpose." (It may be stated here that this phrase — 'To our purpose" — is the key that opened the door to the entire Radisson problem.)

It will be remembered that, when the hunting story was removed, the vacancy was left open and the phrase "To our purpose" was not disturbed. We are now prepared to transpose the Dollard story by lifting it out of the Superior voyage and placing it in the vacancy left open in the Mississippi voyage, and close up the gap now made in the Superior narrative. An examination of the reconstructed narratives at all points affected by these transpositions will now disclose the following results:

1. The hunting story now follows the landing isle paragraph in logical and consistent order.

2. The Dollard story now appears in the midst of the description of the passage through the rapids as a digressive story, followed by the appropriate reintroductory words "To our purpose," in accordance with Radisson's custom.

3. By closing the vacancy in the Superior voyage, made by removing the Dollard story, this part of the narrative is found to be a consistent and uninterrupted description of the passage through the rapids.[34]

Although the transposition of these two parts of the Mississippi and Superior voyages seem to be amply justified by the general consistency and logic of the resulting narratives, we are yet confronted by a number of minor problems, which will now enlist our attention.

There are certain peculiarities to be noticed at the end of the Dollard story. Radisson says they came to the scene of this conflict "8 days after that defeat," which is manifestly impossible. The massacre occurred on May 21st,[35] and according to the *Jesuit Journal* they arrived at Montreal on August 19th,[36] ninety days after the fight. To learn the cause of this error may be impossible, but a conjecture may be ventured.

It may be reasonably assumed that they arrived at the Ottawa rapids two days earlier than at Montreal, or August 17th, thus reducing the time to eighty-eight days. Let us now note an important fact regarding Radisson's manuscript: at this point there is a distinct change in handwriting. This indicates that, even if Radisson himself wrote the preceding part of the manuscript, he did not write this sentence but probably dictated it to another. In this dictation it would be quite possible that the word "eighty-eight" was misunderstood and written as "8." This conjecture becomes more plausible when the compound word is spoken rapidly. Not only is this error proven by historical evidence but the context of the narrative also shows it. In the Mississippi voyage, just as they are preparing to leave the landing isle, about the middle of July, 1660, Radisson says, "Here comes strange news of the defeat of the Hurons."[37] This is believed to refer to the Dollard massacre, which occurred about seven weeks before.[38]

Another error is found almost immediately following the one last mentioned. After describing, in the original manuscript, the battered and broken condition of the fort and surroundings, and stating that it was "a terrible spectacle" to them, Radisson says, "We visited that place, and there was a fine fort. Three were about the other two."[39] These two references to the scene of the conflict are wholly incompatible and indicate a visit to the scene on their return from each of these voyages. The first statement doubtless refers to the visit on August 17th, 1660, when the description "A terrible spectacle" would seem to apply, while the second refers to the visit in 1663, making the "fine fort" consistent with the lapse of three years' time.

Turning again to the Mississippi voyage, notice that the phrase "To our purpose" is followed by the words "We came back to our carriage."[40] In the light of the transposition of the Dollard story and of their visit to the scene of the massacre upon their arrival at the rapids, this sentence takes on a definite meaning. Before the transpositions were made, these words had no meaning whatever, since there is nothing to indicate that they had been away. After the transpositions, however, the meaning becomes perfectly clear. After Groseilliers' boat capsized, they doubtless decided to proceed by carrying their boats around the rapids, but before doing so they visited the scene of the massacre, and of course they "came back to their carriage" and continued their journey down the Ottawa to Montreal.

The question may arise, will the construction resulting from these transpositions give sufficient time for the voyageurs to return to Montreal by August 19th? It has already been observed that, by placing the hunting story immediately after the landing isle paragraph, the time spent on the landing isle is reduced to four months, the duration of the hunting trip. Near the end of the outward journey Radisson says they "thwarted" a land of fifty leagues[41] on snowshoes and came to a riverside where, after three weeks, the buds began to "spring." They ascended the river eight days and reached an Indian village, where they obtained a sufficient supply of corn to last them till they reached the "first landing isle." We also know that they returned to Montreal on the 19th of August. Between these extreme dates, "the springing of buds" and August 19th, must be crowded the journey of about eleven days to the landing isle, about two days to get settled in camp, the four months' hunting trip, six days' delay caused by the "strange news," and the return journey to Montreal.

Before making any estimates we must determine the approximate date to correspond to "the springing of buds." This time varies, of course, with the seasons, which range from "early" to "late" spring. Since they reached the riverside on snowshoes, the springing of buds three weeks later would indicate that the spring of 1660 was early; hence it would seem reasonable to approximate this date, for our present purpose, as March 1st.

Starting now with March 1st, eleven days would bring them to the landing isle on March 12th. Allowing two days for getting settled in camp, the hunting journey would commence on March 14th. Four months would bring Radisson back to the landing isle on July 14th, and six days later, July 20th, the return journey would commence, and in thirty days they would arrive in Montreal on August 19th, the day named by the Jesuits.

Is thirty days sufficient time for a fleet of canoes loaded with beaver skins and supplies, manned by "five hundred, all stout men," to travel from Prairie island in the Mississippi river to

Montreal? Several conditions appear to support the affirmative answer to his question. (1) They realized that it was late in the season to commence such a journey; hence they were in a hurry from the start.[42] (2) They traveled downstream and across great expanses of water with favorable winds nearly all the way.[43] (3) Their corn and other food was prepared and taken with them, and plentiful fish were caught in nets provided; and therefore little time was lost in preparing meals. (4) They traveled during the long summer days and sometimes by night, always in a hurry. The approximate distance was about 1,500 miles, and under the above conditions they oculd easily average fifty miles a day.[44]

The Manuscript

Before drawing this Foreword to a close it seems appropriate to give some attention to the question: who wrote the original manuscript of the first four voyages? As a preliminary, however, we may profitably take note of some of the peculiarities and outstanding characteristics of the document.

Perhaps the most important fact to be noted is that at least two persons participated in the writing of it. A distinct change in the handwriting is found near the end of the Dollard massacre story, as it is placed in the original manuscript; hence but a small part of the entire document was written by the second scribe. All of the chronicle that precedes this change appears to have been written by the same hand, though it is lacking in uniformity. In some parts the lines are somewhat heavier than in others, this variation being due probably to the occasional need of sharpening the quill pen. Punctuation and capitalization are sadly neglected, and frequently a period must be supplied to bring out the correct meaning. Commas, colons, semi-colons, and periods are improperly used, though the context usually rectifies this imperfection. There are no paragraphs in the entire original account. Superior letters are very generally used, especially in the words "the," "that," "with," and "which," but not uniformly; "r" is frequently so used both as final letter and in the body of the word. There are many examples of flourishing, this trait being very frequent in final "d." Many letters are written without regard to uniformity, and certain words are variously spelled. There are numerous words and expressions suggesting French origin, though the manuscript is written throughout in English, and much of it is crude and grotesque. Some pages are wider than others, and the left marginal edges are straight and in some instances appear to be lightly pencil-ruled. On certain pages the left margin is quite irregular, suggesting the possibility of a different writer. The titles are written in larger and rather bold script, and there are some evidences of a different hand than that of the writer of the text.

A very significant feature of the entire manuscript is the number and character of the mistakes that were made, some of which were corrected while others were left as first written. The errors were corrected by scrolling out or otherwise obliterating them, but the original writing can usually be made out through the scroll or erasure or from the corrected context. There are also numerous instances of meaningless repetition of a word or phrase within a sentence. Sometimes the redundancy occurs directly next to a correctly used word or phrase (immediate repetition); other times, the redundancy crops up before (antecedent repetition) or after (subsequent repetition) the correctly used word or phrase.

This analysis provides a basis for the study of the difficult problem of determining who was the writer of the manuscript.

It may be urged that this manuscript is a copy of an earlier original document. The numerous mistakes in the present work, however, would seem to contravene this theory, since a copyist would not reproduce the errors of the original, and many of those errors, particularly antecedent repetitions, would hardly be made by a copyist. It is also unlikely that he would take the liberty of making changes in construction. The general crudeness of both the writing and the language, including spelling and punctuation, precludes the likelihood of this proposition. In other words, a copyist would have done a better job.

Owing to the presence of certain French elements in this work, it may be argued that the first four voyages are a translation of an original document in French, as the Fifth and Sixth in fact are. This supposition is less impressive because of the fact that Radisson was himself a Frenchman, and therefore it is neither surprising nor derogatory that French words and other expressions appear in the work.

Up to the time his chronicle was written, Radisson's knowledge of the English language had probably been acquired chiefly through contact with English sailors, and hence it was crude and imperfect. An effort to express himself through the medium of writing in this unfamiliar language would naturally result in a product not unlike the document under consideration. The apparent condition of an unsettled mind, evidenced by the errors and corrections, is also explained by this unfamiliarity with the language employed.

If the first four voyages had been written first in French* and it was desired to have them translated into English, certainly someone could have been found in London who understood the English language, and he would have been chosen to make the translation. The result of such effort would surely have been a writing less encumbered with errors and crude expressions, and generally would have been more satisfactory than the manuscript as we have it. As in the case of a copyist, the translator would have turned out a better product. In this regard, note that the Fifth and Sixth voyages, which indeed are translations from the French, are substantially different in style from the earlier voyages. What is more, the Fifth and Sixth voyages, in translation, as they are found in *Radisson's Voyages,* are free of nearly all the errors occurring in the earlier voyages.

The fact of a change in handwriting is certain proof that Radisson could not have written the whole of the document, and this tends to weaken any argument that he may have written any part of it. The general context of the narrative indicates, however, that the language used eminated from the mind of the person who actually had the experiences described. Who but a person present could have described the cruelties at the hands of the Mohawks;[45] the escape from the Onondaga mission;[46] the departure from the first landing isle;[47] or the feast and celebration at the rendezvous?[48] If this assumption be granted, it follows that Radisson must have been present at the writing, and therefore either wrote the manuscript himself or dictated it to an amanuensis.

There can be no doubt that he had the intelligence and ability to write it[49] and also that, by virtue of his association with the English, he had acquired the language to a sufficient degree to produce it. But there are certain errors in the manuscript, in addition to the change in handwriting, which oppose the theory that Radisson himself did the writing.

For example, in the manuscript description of the celebration at the rendezvous, in the Superior voyage, Radisson says, in describing the growth of wild rice, "It grows in the water twelve

---

*For this point of view see Grace Lee Nute, *Caesars of the Wilderness* (New York, 1943), pp. 29, 30, 121.

thousand three hundred and forty-five foot deep." This number is ruled out and the words "in three or four" written above it so that it reads in print, "it grows in the water in three or four foot deep."[50] It is difficult to see how Radisson would make such a glaring mistake. The anomaly confronts us, however, and it must be explained if possible. A conjecture is here offered.

Since notes were made on the western voyages,[51] Radisson was probably dictating from these notes. The particular note in hand may have been made by Groseilliers, who wrote down the varying depths in feet of water briefly by employing the numerals 1, 2, 3, 4, and 5. If this succession of digits be written out as one number (12345) the result is the original expression in the manuscript. It may be surmised now, without a great stretch of the imagination, that during a momentary absence of Radisson from the writing table the scribe took up the notebook and did a little writing on his own account and thus, unsuspectingly, made the error. A little color is given to this conjecture by the fact that at this point the scribe apparently stopped to sharpen his quill, and by the further fact that the correction is made in ink of a lighter color.

Another curious error was made at the beginning of the Onondaga voyage (in this volume transposed to the end of the Captivity voyage) where Radisson says that he embarked on "the 15th day of March" and arrived at Percé island "the 7th of May." The "ch" is obliterated and the remaining "Mar" is changed to "May." This erasure must have been made by some other hand than Radisson's, and without his knowledge, since the original word "March" is correct and should not have been altered.[52]

Another example is found in the Mississippi voyage where, in the title, appears the word "Auxoticiat,"[53] and also at the end of that voyage the word "Auxotacicac,"[54] names which are now known to mean "to the Ottawa."[55] These apparently meaningless words must have been written by some other person than Radisson, and being no part of the text of the narrative, they may not have been at his dictation. The type of script in the headings and endings of all the voyages seem to suggest another hand than that shown in any part of the text.

Of the numerous possibilities which have been considered bearing upon the writing of the manuscript, all have been eliminated but the one suggesting that Radisson, with original notes in his hand, dictated to an amanuenis. This theory appears to the writer as the most plausible.

ARTHUR T. ADAMS

Biographical Sketch [1]

PIERRE ESPRIT RADISSON and his brother-in-law Medard Chouart, better known by his assumed title of Sieur Des Grroseilliers, or simply as Groseilliers, were French explorers and traders of North America, in the grand manner of the 17th century. They submitted themselves to incredible personal danger, to isolation from their fellows, to privation—all in the interest of reaping a fortune. They were successful, but the fortune went mostly into the pockets of other persons. What was left to Radisson and Groseilliers was the modest posthumous fame of having been among the few white men of their time to travel in the regions of the Great Lakes and Hudson Bay, and of having been instrumental in the early success of the Hudson's Bay Company—one of the great enterprises based on the exploitation of the new continent. They were not, however, strictly commercial men; not many even in their remarkable age could match them for adventurousness of spirit.

Henry Colin Campbell summarizes Radisson's early life and family relations as follows: "Radisson was a mere youth when, on May 21st, 1651, he arrived in New France. He was a native of St. Malo, in Brittany, the place in which Jacques Cartier, the discoverer of New France, was born. Radisson's father was Sebastien Hayet-Radisson, and his mother was Madeline Henault. Both parents emigrated to New France, for Radisson states in his Journal that they lived at Three Rivers. Radisson had two sisters, Marguerite and Francoise. In 1646, Marguerite married Jean Veron de Grand-Menil, by whom she had three children. Veron was killed near Three Rivers by the Iroquois, August 19, 1652, and a year and five days later his widow married Groseilliers."[2]

Few youths have passed through a school of more arduous training and severe preparation for life's activities than did the young Radisson during his first few years in New France. His capture in the spring of 1652 by the Mohawks near Three Rivers was the beginning of this course of training.

During this captivity of about one and a half years, Radisson, then scarcely more than a boy, acquired to a considerable degree the ingenuity and ability to live in peace, security, and apparent contentment with—as he said in his own account—"an enemy the cruelest that ever was upon the face of the earth."

The boy possessed characteristics which appealed strongly to the indulgence and clemency of his aboriginal captors. His intuitive diplomacy, his willingness, even determination, to do his share of the labor, his matchless courage and submission to torture without complaint doubtless contributed to his survival under circumstances that would have cost the life of many another captive less versatile and resolute. These traits are exemplified throughout his chronicle of his adventures.

An outstanding event of Radisson's captivity was his adoption into a Mohawk family, to fill the place of a son who had been killed in the wars. This relationship doubtless saved his life on the occasion of his second capture, after he had effected his escape by helping murder his captor-companions while they were asleep.

At one time during the period of his captivity, Radisson joined a war party of the Mohawks and made a somewhat extensive "tour" of what is now the state of New York. Starting from their village, which was situated at Auriesville, near the present town of Fonda,[3] they visited all of the principal villages of the five nations of the Iroquois. They probably saw Niagra, and then traveled eastward by way of Lake Ontario, and at length reached Lake Champlain. From here they returned westward and arrived at their home village after a series of strange and harrowing experiences.

At the end of October, 1653, Radisson escaped the second time and reached Fort Orange, now Albany. From there he went to New Amersterdam, and then sailed to Holland. He spent the winter at Rochelle, France.

In the spring of 1654 he sailed in a "fisher boat" to Canada and reached his home at Three Rivers in May of that year. At this time he probably met his future associate, Groseilliers, who was recently married to Radisson's sister, and it is likely that the two brothers-in-law spent the next two years, 1654-56, in exploring the country west as far as the Mississippi river.[4]

In June, 1657, Radisson joined the Jesuit Fathers Ragueneau and Duperon on a perilous expedition to their mission among the Onondagas at Liverpool, near the present city of Syracuse, New

York.[5] During this journey Radisson learned much of the duplicity and perfidy of the Iroquois, who had for a long time planned to compass the ruin of the Jesuit mission. They plotted to entice their old enemies, the Hurons, into a trap by inviting them to join the Jesuits and French in this expedition to the mission.[6] It was their intent to get them all at the mission and, when the time and conditions seemed ripe, to surround and massacre the entire group.

The French got wind of the plot, but the zeal of the Jesuits drove them on. Radisson, whose motive in this enterprise was adventure, rather than the salvation of souls, may have had some part in devising the elaborate strategy which allowed the French finally to escape from the mission. His proposal to the Fathers that they take advantage of the torpor of the Iroquois and kill the "hundred beasts not able to budge" exemplifies his practical, thorough, and efficient turn of mind, which stood him in good stead on later occasions.

Upon his return from Onondaga, in March, 1658, Radisson again met his brother-in-law, Groseilliers. Groseilliers was born near Meaux, France, about the year 1621. His parents were Medard and Marie Poirier, of Charly, parish of St. Cyr. In 1641 the young man emigrated to Canada and settled at Three Rivers. He soon became interested in the work of the Jesuit Fathers and became a donne, or lay assistant, in their Huron mission near Georgian Bay. During this period of his life he doubtless became familiar with the Algonquin and Huron languages and customs, thus fitting himself well for the tasks to come.

This service he discontinued in 1646 and became for a time a soldier in the garrison at Quebec, but soon after he engaged as a pilot on the St. Lawrence river. This was followed by his entry into the fur trading business. As a result of his success in the trade, it is presumed that he acquired a tract of land near Quebec, since he assumed the title of Sieur Des Groseilliers, probably because of the abundance of gooseberries on the land, the literal translation of the name being "gooseberry bushes."[7]

On September 3, 1647, he was married at Quebec to Helene, the widow of Claude Etienne. She was the daughter of Abraham Martin, a pilot whose name is perpetuated in the famous battlefield the Plains of Abraham, now a suburb of Quebec.

Edward D. Neill gives the following information regarding the family of Groseilliers: "In 1649, he visited France. His son, Medard, was born in 1651, and Tanguay gives the same year as

xix

the date of his mother's death. After her death, the father went to Acadia, where he met the celebrated La Tour. Upon his return, on the 24th of August, 1653, he married at Quebec, another widow, Gran-Menil, only twenty-one years old, whose maiden name was Margaret Hayet Radisson, the sister of his associate in the exploration of the Sioux country."[8] The second union produced five children.

Little further is known of Groseilliers' early life until the above-mentioned return of Radisson from the Onondaga voyage, in March, 1658. At the end of his account of the events at the mission Radisson mentions his "brother" for the first time, and in August of that year, they commenced their long period of joint discovery and exploration.

The information and experience obtained by Groseilliers during his association with the Jesuit Fathers at the Mission in the Huron country stimulated him to attempt an extensive exploration and exploitation of the West. In this enterprise he sought the aid and companionship of his young brother-in-law, whom he thought "fitter and more faithful for the discovery that he was to make."

With a party of about thirty Frenchmen and many Huron and Ottawa Indians they began their journey up the Ottawa river, where, at the Long Sault, a rapid some miles above the present city of Ottawa, they met with the opposition of the Iroquois, who for many years had obstructed the passage of similar expeditions. All the Frenchmen, except the two subjects of this sketch, became disheartened and returned, but the two lone adventurers were determined to "finish the voyage or die by the way," and together with their savage "wildmen" continued their westward journey, enduring hunger, fatigue, and many other hardships imposed by the uncharted wilderness. After passing Lake Nipissing and encircling Georgian Bay, they visited the Ottawa village which had been established for some time on Great Manitoulin island, but since their "mind was not to stay in an island" they passed on through the Strait of Mackinac, Lake Michigan, and Green Bay, reaching at length the country of the Potawatomies, now the southeastern part of Wisconsin. Here they spent the winter and became acquainted with the Mascoutens and other Indian tribes, and also observed much of the wildlife in the region.

In the spring (1659) the adventurers embarked on "the delightsomest lake in the world" (Lake Michigan), which was the beginning of their "Southern" journey, taking them into some part of the country where "it never snows nor freezes there, but mighty hot." This journey occupied the greater part of a year, and in the early spring (1660), after a period of wandering over a course impossible to trace from Radisson's ambiguous narrative, we find them among the Saulteurs (Chippewas) in northern Michigan or Wisconsin. From this point they "thwarted a land of almost 50 leagues" on snowshoes, and after many hardships arrived at "a riverside." This was undoubtedly the first time the upper Mississippi river had been seen by white men, and its discovery may be regarded as the outstanding accomplishment of these two Frenchmen on their Mississippi voyage.

After making the necessary boats and canoeing up the river for some days, they arrived at "the first landing isle," which was doubtless Prairie island, between the present cities of Hastings and Red Wing, Minnesota.[9] Upon this island they found a village of Hurons who had fled from the aggressive Iroquois in Canada a few years before. These Hurons were apparently acquainted with the Hurons who had come on the French expedition, but they positively refused to return to Canada at this time, as Radisson and Groseilliers wished them to do.

At this point the two brothers-in-law parted company and were separated for a period of about four months. Radisson joined a party of Indians (probably Sioux) on a hunting trip, the itinerary of which would be difficult to trace, while Groseilliers remained at the "landing isle." During this time, the latter made some progress in converting the natives to Christianity and also succeeded in creating a "desire" in them to go back to Canada.

When Radisson returned from his four months' hunting trip, he found that Groseilliers, notwithstanding a serious illness, had gathered provisions and made other extensive preparations for their return journey to Canada. While they were busy getting ready to depart, they received news of the "defeat of the Hurons," believed to be the Dollard massacre, which had occurred about two months before at the Long Sault. This so disconcerted the Hurons living at the landing isle that they again refused to go. This incident resulted in a dramatic council meeting. The excitement was abated by the harangues and admonitions of both Groseilliers and Radisson, and in a few days the motley cavalcade was on its way to Canada, arriving at Montreal August 19th, 1660.

The year following their return from the Mississippi voyage is blank for both men, insofar as Radisson's record goes. It is quite probable, however, that in May, 1661, Groseilliers started on a voyage with the Jesuit Fathers to Hudson Bay, by way of Tadousac and the Saguenay river, but abandoned the effort because of Iroquois opposition.[10]

Early in September, 1661, Radisson and Groseilliers embarked on their last journey to the West. Although the ultimate result of this voyage was momentous, it began inauspiciously, having been forbidden by D'Avaugour, the governor. They and their company accomplished their departure at night and were soon on their way up the Ottawa, the same course taken as on the previous voyage. At the Long Sault they again encountered the Iroquois, but succeeded in escaping serious loss or injury. In due course they passed through Lake Nipissing and Georgian Bay and reached the Sault Ste. Marie. Here they rested and feasted, and all gave thanks to their respective deities for the plentiful and excellent food obtained at this "terrestrial paradise."

Skirting the south shore of Lake Superior, they arrived at Chequamegon Bay, probably early in November, and after erecting a fort and staying about two weeks, they proceeded to a village of Ottawas by "a little lake some eight leagues in circuit," now believed to be Lac Court Oreilles, Wisconsin. After agreeing upon a meeting place in the Sioux country, they journeyed from here westward in small groups, but owing to a copious fall of light snow, they were unable to secure game for food and as a result suffered severely from famine. When relief came from this famine, they went to the "rendezvous," the appointed meeting place, which was probably near the present town of Mora, Minnesota.[11] Here they celebrated the "feast of the dead," which was followed by games, sports, sham battles, and much dancing and frivolity.

Their next move was a seven weeks' visit to the Prairie Sioux country, which was probably the vicinity of southern and south-western Minnesota.

This was followed by their return to Chequamegon Bay, from which point they began their journey to James Bay, the southern part of Hudson Bay. This voyage brought to Radisson and Groseilliers the valuable and long-desired first-hand information of the fur trading possibilities in that region; it was the dissemination of this knowledge in England which ultimately led to the organization and establishment of the Hudson's Bay Company.

Upon their return to Canada in July, 1663, they again had trouble with Governor D'Avaugour, whose term of office was about to expire. They were fined, charged a heavy duty, and Groseilliers was imprisoned by the governor for embarking two years before without his leave.

This ill treatment led to Groseilliers' going to France for redress. He urged the French officials to embrace the opportunity of inaugurating the fur trade in the Hudson Bay region, but his advice fell on deaf ears. Getting no satisfaction, he contracted privately with a Rochelle merchant for a ship to be delivered at Percé island and used in a voyage to Hudson Bay in the spring of 1664. Radisson and Groseilliers prepared to carry out this plan, but the promised ship did not materialize. Shortly after, they proceeded from Percé island to St. Peter, on Cape Breton, thence to Canseau, where they were subjected to many indignities by the local French inhabitants. After being threatened by burning and other grave dangers, they escaped and arrived at length at Port Royal, Nova Scotia.

About this time their design to go to Hudson Bay was again entertained. A ship, the *Nonsuch,* was provided under command of Captain Zachariah Gillam, of Boston. They reached Hudson Strait, but Gillam, becoming frightened by the icebergs, returned to Port Royal. Thus the year 1664 passed with only a fruitless effort to reach the fur country of Hudson Bay by way of the ocean route.

In the spring of 1665 another attempt was made to accomplish this end. Two ships were provided, one of which was wrecked in a storm at Sable island before the voyage commenced. This resulted in damage to certain merchants, and litigation followed which caused the abandonment of the undertaking.

During the summer of 1665 the undaunted traders fortunately met the English commissioners who had been sent over to this country to adjust certain matters growing out of the transfer of New Amsterdam to the English. Upon the invitation of one of these commissioners, Colonel George Cartwright, they sailed with him from Boston. Their ship was captured by the Dutch, and they were landed on the coast of Spain, and early in 1666 they reached England during the inauspicious period following the London plague and the war with Holland. They were taken to Oxford, and the story of their observations and experiences in the Hudson Bay country was conveyed by Sir George Carteret to King Charles. The King made provision for their maintenance during the winter, and in the spring a ship was prepared for a voyage to Hudson Bay, but too late to sail because of the stoppage of the Thames by the Dutch. While they were planning this expedition after the audience with the King, De Witt, the Dutch ambassador at London, endeavored to induce the two Frenchmen to desert England and go to Hudson Bay under the auspices of Holland, but they declined the offer.

The year 1667 was also fruitless, though a voyage was evidently intended, as may be inferred from Radisson's statement: "We lost our second voyage, for the order was given too late for fitting another ship, which cost a great deal of money to no purpose."

The following year saw the fitting out of two ships — the *Nonsuch,* Captain Gillam, and the *Eaglet,* Captain Stannard. On June 3, 1668, the *Eaglet,* with Radisson, and the *Nonsuch,* with Groseilliers, started for Hudson Bay. The ships were separated by a storm, and the *Eaglet* was forced to return to England. The *Nonsuch* weathered the storm and reached the south end of Hudson Bay, where Fort Charles was established on Rupert river.

During this period of enforced idlesness in England, it is probable that Radisson wrote the greater part of the account of his first four voyages, at the end of which he expresses the hope that he may make another voyage resulting in greater success. During this period he was also busy interesting the leading men of London in the fur trading possibilities of the Hudson Bay country.

At this point Radisson's narrative is interrupted and not resumed until he makes his Fifth voyage, which occurred in 1682-3. Our information of the activities of the adventurers in the meantime must therefore be obtained from other sources.

The attempt of the hoped-for voyage to Hudson Bay, referred to above by Radisson, was made in the *Waveno,* Captain Stannard, before the return of Groseilliers. Again he was forced back by storm, and on his arrival at London he found that the *Nonsuch* had returned, and Groseilliers was waiting for him.

Upon the return of Groseilliers and his account of the success of the voyage, steps were immediately taken by a number of interested men, headed by Prince Rupert, to organize the Hudson's Bay Company. This was consummated by the issue of a charter in May, 1670. Later in the year Radisson and Groseilliers, under Governor Bailey, went out on a second voyage to establish trade in Hudson Bay. They returned to London in the autumn of 1671 and during the following winter received pay from the Company for their maintenance.

In 1672 the sloop *Prince Rupert,* Captain Gillam, with Radisson and Groseilliers on board, made another voyage to the North, returning in October, 1673. They wintered again in London and provision was made by the Company to allow Radisson 100 pounds per annum for his services. During the last voyage some difficulties had developed between Radisson and Captain Gillam, which foretokened further and more serious trouble for several years following.

Some writers have taken Radisson severely to task for his want of stability and his shifting allegiance between France and England. However much or little the charges may be justified, the situation was much aggravated and complicated by Radisson's marriage to an Englishwoman, the daughter of John Kirke, Esquire, one of the incorporators of the Company. Radisson's wife would not live in France, and her father also withheld his consent because of certain large debts of long standing owed him by the French government.

The activities of Radisson and Groseilliers during the period 1674-85 are summarized as follows by George Bryce: "For seven years Radisson vacillated between the two countries. Under the French he went for one season on a voyage to the West Indies, and was even promised promotion in the French marine. At one time he applied again to the Hudson's Bay Company for employment, but was refused. The fixed determination of his wife not to leave England on the one hand, and the settled suspicion of the French government on the other, continually thwarted him. At length, in 1681, Radisson and Groseilliers were sent by the French to Canada, to undertake a trading expedition to Hudson Bay. The lack of money, and also of full confidence, led to their venture being poorly provided for. In July, 1682, rendezvous was made at Ile Percé, in the lower St. Lawrence, by Radisson in a wretched old vessel of ten tons, and by Groseilliers in a rather better craft of fifteen tons burthen.

"No better could be done, however, and so, after many mishaps, including serious mutinies, dangers of ice and flood, and hairbreadth escapes, the two vessels reached the mouth of the Hayes River on Hudson Bay. They determined to trade at this point. Groseilliers undertook to build a small fort on this river, and Radisson went inland on a canoe expedition to meet the natives. In this Radisson was fairly successful, and gathered a good quantity of furs.

"The French adventurers were soon surprised to find that an English party had taken possession of the mouth of the Nelson River, and were establishing a fort. Radisson opened communication with the English, and found them in charge of Governor Bridgar, but really led by young Gillam, son of the old captain of the *Nonsuch*. The versatile Frenchman soon met a fine field for his diplomatic arts. He professed great friendship for the new comers, exchanged frequent visits with them, and became acqainted with all their affairs. Finding the English short of provisions, he supplied their lack most generously, and offered to render them any service. Matters were so arranged that Jean Baptiste Groseilliers, his nephew, was left in charge of the forts, to carry on the trade during the next winter, and with his brother-in-law, Groseilliers, and Governor Bridgar, somewhat of a voluntary prisoner, Radisson sailed away to Canada in Gillam's ship. On reaching Canada Governor De la Barre restored the ship to the English, and in it Bridgar and Gillam sailed to New England, whence in due time they departed for England. The whole affair has a Quixotic appearance, and it is not surprising that Radisson and Groseilliers were summoned to report themselves to Colbert in France and to receive his marked displeasure. Their adventure had, however, been so successful, and the prospects were so good, that the French government determined to send them out again, in two ships, to reap the fruits of the winter's work of the younger Groseilliers.

"Now occurred another of Radisson's escapades. The French expedition was ready to start in April. The day (24th) was fixed. Radisson asked for delay, pleading important private business in England. On May 10th he arrived in England, and we find him, without any compunction, entering into negotiations with the Hudson's Bay Company, and as a result playing the traitor to his engagements in France, his native country.

"The entry in the Company's minutes bearing on this affair is as follows: —

'May 12th, 1684.
'Sir James Hayes and Mr. Young, that Peter Esprit Radisson has arrived from France; that he has offered to enter their service; that they took him to Windsor and presented him to His Royal Highness; that they had agreed to give him 50L. per annum, 200L. worth of stock, and 20L. to set him up to proceed to Port Nelson; and his brother (in-law) Groseilliers to have 20s. per week, if he come from France over to Britain and be true. Radisson took the oath of fidelity to the Company.'

"A few days later Radisson took the ship *Happy Return* to Hudson Bay. Sailing immediately to Hayes River, Radisson found that his nephew, J. Baptiste Groseilliers, had removed his post to an island in the river. On his being reached, Radisson explained to him the change that had taken place, and that he proposed to transfer everything, establishment and peltry, to the Hudson's Bay Company. Young Groseilliers, being loyal to France, objected to this, but Radisson stated that there was no option, and he would be compelled to submit. The whole quantity of furs transferred to Radisson by his nephew was 20,000 — an enormous capture for the Hudson's Bay Company. In the autumn Radisson returned in the Hudson's Bay Company's ship, bringing the great store of booty.

"At a meeting of the Committee of the Company (October 7th), 'a packet was read from Pierre Radisson showing how he had brought his countrymen to submit to the English. He was thanked, and a gratuity of 100 guineas given him.' It is also stated that 'a promise having been made of 20s. per week to Groseilliers, and he not having come, the same is transferred to his son in the bay.' The minute likewise tells us that 'Sir William Young was given a present of seven musquash skins for being instrumental in inviting Radisson to leave the service of France.' From this we infer that Sir William, who, as we shall afterwards see, was a great friend and promoter of Radisson, had been the active agent in inducing Radisson to leave the service of France and enter that of the English Company.

"The Company further showed its appreciation of Radisson's service by voting him 100L. to be given to four Frenchmen left behind in Hudson Bay. Jean Baptiste Groseilliers, nephew of Radisson, was also engaged by the Company for four years in the service at 100L. a year. Radisson seems to have had some dispute with the Company as to the salary at this time. On May 6th, 1685, his salary when out of England was raised to 100L. a year, and 300L. to his wife in case of his death. Radisson refused to accept these terms. The Company for a time would not increase its offer, but the time for the ship to sail was drawing nigh, and the Committee gave way and added to the above amount 100L. of stock to be given to his wife. John Bridgar was appointed Governor of Port Nelson for three years, and Radisson superintendent of the trade there. Radisson was satisfied with the new terms, and that the Company was greatly impressed with the value of his services is seen in the following entry: 'A hogshead of claret being ordered for Mr. Radisson, such as Mr. R. shall like.' "[12]

Radisson's version of the "escapades" above outlined and his defense of his conduct will be found in the narratives of his Fifth and Sixth voyages.

In 1684 the long association of Radisson and Groseilliers came to an end. While Radisson entered the employ of the Hudson's Bay Company and transferred his allegiance from France to England, it will be observed that Groseilliers declined to "come from France over to Britain and be true." Groseilliers finally returned to Canada, where it is said that he died before 1698.

For many years after 1685 little was known of the activities of Pierre Radisson. Some years ago, however, an investigation was made by Mr. Bryce of the records of the Hudson's Bay Company, and as a result a number of facts were brought to light.

In October, 1687, Radisson returned from a voyage to Hudson Bay and was welcomed by members of the Company, and was paid 50L. as a gratuity until he should be employed by them again. In June, 1688, he sailed again to Hudson Bay and was paid 100L. as a 50% dividend on his stock. In 1689, he received 50L. as a 25% dividend and in 1690, the year of the "great dividend," Radisson received 150L. as his share of the profits.[13] Subsequently his profits varied as the prosperity of the Company waxed and waned.

In 1694 Radisson brought suit against the Company for part of his salary which was withheld. "Notwithstanding the great influence of the Company, the justice of Radisson's claims prevailed, and the Court of Chancery ordered the payment of arrears in full . . . . Radisson then received, as the minutes show, his salary regularly from this time."[14]

In 1698 the charter of the Company was renewed, and Radisson petitioned Parliament to provide for his protection in the payment of his dues. In this petition Radisson states that he had four children and only 100L. a year from the Company to live on. In 1700 he was still hard pressed and applied to the Company to be appointed warehouse-keeper for the London premises, but was refused. "Regularly during the succeeding years the quarterly amount is voted to Radisson by the Company, until January 6th, 1710, when the last quota of 12L. 10s. was ordered to be given. About this time, at the ripe age of seventy-four, passed away Pierre Esprit Radisson, one of the most daring and ingenious men of his time. We know nothing of his death, except from the fact that his pension ceased to be paid."[15]   ARTHUR T. ADAMS

A Note on Modernization

THE PROBLEM, of course, was to render Radisson's chaotic narrative palatable to the reader who would not wish to grapple with the considerable difficulties and obscurities of the original text; at the same time, it was necessary to preserve the essential flavor of the original. With this problem in mind, I have been guided by the following procedure:

Capitalization and spelling, of both English and French words, have been standardized in keeping with modern practice; similarly with punctuation and paragraphing, insofar as the oddities of Radisson's sentence structure permit.

Radisson's use (and misuse) of verbal tense has been retained, except in those cases in which it would be extremely misleading. Where I have changed the tense, the changes have been footnoted, or my insertions have been placed between brackets [ ]. The same has been done with Radisson's handling of the singular and plural.

Editorial insertions of any kind are between brackets.

Certain excessively long and complicated sentences have been broken into shorter constructions for the sake of clarity. I have done this silently.

Most structural redundancies have been silently deleted, as have unusual connectives which would be misleading and difficult had they been retained. Deletions which, however, might conceivably change the meaning of the original text have been noted, and the questionable passage from the original has been placed in the note.

Radisson's use of figures and written-out numbers has been retained.

Certain eccentric words, apparently formed because of Radisson's unfamiliarity with English, but which are perfectly clear in context, have not been tampered with.

As to vocabulary, generally speaking, any word that can be found readily in *Webster's New International Dictionary of the English Language* (second edition) has not been herein defined.

A final word, by way of distributing blame and credit for this volume. I am responsible for all things that fall under the general topic of modernization; in addition, I am the maker of all asterisked notes and those numbered footnotes marked with a triangle ($\triangle$).

LOREN KALLSEN   Minneapolis   August, 1960

CAPTIVITY VOYAGE[1]

The relation of my voyage being in bondage in the hands of the Iroquois, which was the next year after my coming into Canada, in the year one-thousand-six-hundred-fifty-one, the 24th day of May.[2]

BEING PERSUADED in the morning by two of my comrades to go and recreate ourselves in fowling, I disposed myself to keep them company. Wherefore I clothed myself the lightest way I could possible, that I might be the nimbler and not stay behind, as much for the prey that I hoped for as for to escape the danger into which we have ventured ourselves of an enemy the cruelest that ever was upon the face of the earth. It is to be observed that the French had war with a wild nation called Iroquois, who for that time were so strong and so to be feared that scarce anybody durst stir out [of] either cottage[3] or house without being taken or killed, saving that he had nimble limbs to escape their fury. Being departed, all three well armed, [we agreed] unanimiously rather [to] die than abandon one another, notwithstanding those resolutions were but young men's deboasting, being then in a very little assurance, and less security. At an offspring of a village of Three Rivers[4] we consult together that two should go [to] the waterside, the other in a wood hardby to warn us, for to advertise us if he accidentally should sight or suspect any barbarians[5] in ambush. We also [would] retreat ourselves to him if we should discover anything upon the river.

Having comed to the first river, which was a mile distant from our dwellings, we met a man who kept cattle and asked him if he had known any appearance of enemy, and likewise demanded which way he would advise us to get better fortune, and what part he spied more danger. He, guiding us the best way he could, prohibiting us by no means to render ourselves at the skirts of the mountains, said, "I discovered oftentimes a multitude of people which rose up, as it were of a sudden from the earth, and doubtless there were some enemies that way"; which sayings made us look to ourselves and charge two of our fowling pieces, with great shot the one and the other with small. Priming our pistols, we went where our fancy first lead us, being impossible for us to avoid the destinies of the heavens. No sooner turned our backs, but my nose fell ableeding without any provocation in the least. Certainly it was a warning for me of a beginning of a year and a half of hazards and of miseries that were to befall me.[6]

We did shoot sometimes and killed some ducks, which made one of my fellow travelers go no further. I seeing him taking such a resolution, I proferred some words that did not like him, giving him the character of a timorous childish humor; to this did nothing prevail with him; to the contrary, that had with him quite another issue than what I hoped for; for offending him with my words, he prevailed so much with the others that he persuaded them to do the same. I let them go, laughing them to scorn, beseeching them to help me to my fowls, and that I would tell them the discovery of my designs, hoping to kill meat to make us meat at my return.

I went my way along the wood, sometimes by the side of the river, where I find something to shoot at, though no considerable quantity, which made me go a league[7] off and more. I could not go in further than St. Peter's, which is nine miles from the plantation, by reason of the River Ovamasis,[8] which hindered me the passage. I begun to think at my return how I might transport my fowl. I hide one part in a hollow tree to keep them from the eagles and other devouring fowls.

I came back the same way where before [I] had no bad encounter, arrived within one-half a mile [of] where my comrades had left me. I rested awhile by reason that I was loaded with three geese, ten ducks, and one crane, with some teals.

After having laid down my burden upon the grass, I thought to have heard a noise in the wood by me, which made me to overlook* my arms. I found one of my girdle pistols wet. I shot it off and charged it again, went up to the wood the softliest I might to discover and defend myself the better against any surprise. After I had gone from tree to tree some 30 paces off, I espied nothing. As I came back from out of the wood to an adjacent brook, I perceived a great number of ducks. My dis-

---

*Meaning "examine," not forget or ignore.

covery emboldened me, and [because] there was [but] a little way to the fort[9] I determined to shoot once more.

Coming nigh preparing myself for to shoot, I found another work: the two young men that I left some ten hours before here were killed. Whether they came after me or were brought thither by the barbarians, I know not; however, [they] were murdered. Looking over them [I] knew them, albeit [they were] quite naked and their hair standing up, the one being shot through with three bullets,[10] and two blows of an hatchet on the head, and the other run through in several places with a sword and smitten with an hatchet.

In the same instance my nose begun to bleed, which made me afraid of my life. Withdrawing myself to the waterside to see if anybody followed me, I espied twenty or thirty heads in a long grass; mightily surprised at that view. I must needs pass through the midst of them or turn back into the wood. I slipped a bullet upon the shot and beat the paper into my gun. I heard a noise which made me look on that side, hoping to save myself, persuading myself I was not yet perceived by them that were in the meadow.

In the meanwhile some guns were set off with an horrid cry. Seeing myself compassed round about by a multitude of dogs, or rather devils, that rose from the grass, rushes, and bushes, I shot my gun — whether unawares or purposely I know not — but I shot with a pistol confidently. But was seized on all sides by a great number that threw me down, taking away my arm without giving me one blow, for afterwards I felt no pain at all, only a great giddiness in my head; from whence it come I do not remember.

In the same time they brought me into the wood, where they showed me the two heads, all bloody.

After they consulted together for a while, [we] retired into their boats, which were four or five miles from thence, and where I have been before. They laid me hither, holding me by the hair, to the embarking place.

There they began to erect their cottages, which consisted only of some sticks to boil their meat, whereof they had plenty, but [which] stunk, which was strange to me to find such an alteration so sudden. They made [me] sit down. After this, they searched me and took what I had, then stripped me naked and tied a rope about my middle, wherein I remained in the same posture the rest of the night. After this they removed me, laughing and howling like as many wolves, I knowing not the reason, if not for my skin that was so white in respect of theirs.

But their gaping did soon cease because of a false alarm that their scout who stayed behind gave, saying that the French and the wild Algonquins, friends to the French, come with all speed. They presently put out the fire and took hold of the most advantageous passages and sent twenty-five men to discover what it meant, who brought certain tidings of assurance and liberty.

In the meanwhile I was guarded by fifty men, who gave me a good part of my clothes. After kindling a fire again, they got their supper ready, which was suddenly done, for they dress their meat half boiled, mingling some yellowish meal in the broth of that infected stinking meat. Whilst this was adoing, they combed my head and with a filthy grease greased my head and dashed all over my face with red paintings. When the meat was ready, they fed me with their hodgepodge, forcing me to swallow it in a manner. My heart did so faint at this that in good deed I should have given freely up the ghost to be freed from their claws, thinking every moment they would end my life. They perceived that my stomach could not bear such victuals. They took some of this stinking meat and boiled it in clear water, then mingled a little Indian meal put to it, which meal before was tossed amongst burning sand and then made in powder betwixt two rocks. I, to show myself cheerful at this, swallowed down some of this that seemed to me very unsavory and clammy by reason of the scum that was upon the meat.

Having supped, they untied me and made me lie betwixt them, having one end of one side and one of another and covered me with a red coverlet through which I might have counted the stars. I slept a sound sleep, for they awaked me upon the breaking of the day. I dreamed that night that I was with the Jesuits at Quebec, drinking beer, which gave me hopes to be free sometimes and also because I heard those people [the Iroquois] lived among Dutch people in a place called Menada and Fort Orange,[11] where without doubt I could drink beer.

I, after this finding myself somewhat altered and my body more like a devil than anything else — after being so smeared and burst* with their filthy meat — I could not digest, but must suffer all patiently.

---

*Full, swollen, possibly vomit-covered.

Finally they seemed to me kinder and kinder, giving me of the best bits where less worms were.

Then they laid to the waterside, where there were seven and thirty boats, for each of them embarked himself. They tied me to the bar in a boat, where they took at the same instance the heads of those that were killed the day before, and for to preserve them they cut off the flesh to the skull and left nothing but skin and hair, putting of it into a little pan wherein they melt some grease, and got it dry with hot stones. They spread themselves from off the side of the river a good way and gathered together again and made a fearful noise and shot some guns off; after which followed a kind of incondite singing after notes which was an odiousom noise. As they were departing from thence, they enjoined silence, and one of the company wherein I was made three shouts, which was answered by the like manner from the whole flock; which done, they took their way, singing and leaping, and so passed the day in such like.

They offered me meat, but such victuals I regarded little, but could drink for thirst. My spirit was troubled with infinite deal of thoughts, but all to no purpose for the ease of my sickness. Sometimes despairing, now again in some hopes, I always endeavored to comfort myself, though half dead. My resolution was so mustered with fear that, every stroke of oars of those inhumans, [I] thought it to be my end.

By sunset we arrived at the Isles of Richelieu,[12] a place rather for victors than for captives most pleasant. There is to be seen three hundred wild cows[13] together, a number of elks and beavers, an infinite [number] of fowls. There we must make cottages, and for this purpose they employ altogether their wits and art, for fifteen of those islands are drowned in spring when the floods begin to rise from the melting of the snow, and that by reason of lowness of the land. Here they found a place fit enough for two hundred and fifty men that their army consisted [of]. They landed me and showed me a great kindness, saying, "Chagon," which is as much to say (as I understood afterwards), "be cheerful or merry," but for my part I was both deaf and dumb. Their behavior made me nevertheless cheerful, or at least of a smiling countenance, and constrained my aversion and fear to an assurance — which proved not ill to my thinking — for the young men took delight in combing my head, greasing and powdering out a kind of red powder, then tying my hair with a red string of leather like to a cord, which caused my hair to grow longer in a short time.

5

The day following, they prepared themselves to pass the adjacent places, and shoot to get victuals, where we stayed three days, making great cheer and fires. I more and more getting familiar with them, I had the liberty to go from [the] cottage, having one or two by me. They untied me and took delight to make me speak words of their language and were earnest that I should pronounce as they. They took care to give me meat as often as I would; they gave me salt that served me all my voyage. They also took pains to put it up safe for me, not taking any of it for themselves.[14] There was nothing else but feasting and singing during our abode. I took notice that our men decreased, for every night one other boat took his way, which persuaded me that they went to the wars to get some booty.

The fourth day, early in the morning my brother — viz., he that took me (so he called me) — embarked [with] me without tying me. He gave me an oar, which I took with good will, and rowed till I sweat again. They, perceiving, made me give over, not content with that. I made a sign of my willingness to continue that work. They consent to my desire, but showed me how I should row without putting myself into a sweat.

Our company, being considerable hitherto, was now reduced to three score.

Midday we came to the River of Richelieu, where we were not far gone but met a new gang of their people in cottages. They began to hoop and halloo as [on] the first day of my taking. They made me stand upright in the boat, as they themselves, saluting one another with all kindness and joy. In this new company there was one that had a mind to do me mischief, but [he was] prevented by him that took me. I, taking notice of the fellow, showed him more friendship. I got some meat roasted for him and, throwing a little salt and flour over it, which he finding very good [to the] taste, gave it to the rest as a rarity. None did afterwards molested me.

They took a fancy to teach me to sing and, as I had already a beginning of their hooping, it was an easy thing for me to learn, our Algonquins making the same noise. They took an exceeding delight to hear me. Often have [I] sunged in French, to which they gave ears with a deep silence.

We passed that day and night following with little rest by reason of their joy and mirth. They lead a dance and tied my

6

comrades* both their heads at the end of a stick and hopped it.

This done, everyone packed and embarked himself, some going one way, some another. Being separated, one of the boats that we met before comes back again and approaches the boat wherein I was. I wondered: a woman of the said company taking hold of my hair, signifying great kindness. She combs my head with her fingers and tied my wrist with a bracelet and sung. My wish was that she would proceed in our way. After both companies made a shout, we separated. I was sorry for this woman's departure. Having showed me such favor at her first aspect, doubtless but she might (if need required) saved my life.

Our journey was indifferent good, without any delay, which caused us to arrive in a good and pleasant harbor. It was on the side of the sand, where our people had any pain scarce to erect their cottages, being that it was a place they had sojourned before. The place round about [was] full of trees. Here they kindled a fire and provided what was necessary for their food.

In this place they cut off my hair in the front and upon the crown of the head, and turning up the locks of the hair, they dabbed me with some thick grease. So done, they brought me a looking glass. I, viewing myself, [felt] all in a pickle — smeared with red and black, covered with such a cap, and locks tied up with a piece of leather, and stunked horridly. I could not but fall in love with myself, if not that I had better instructions to shun the sin of pride.

So, after repasting themselves, they made ready for the journey with taking repose that night. This was the time I thought to have escaped, [but] in vain, for I, being alone, feared lest I should be apprehended and dealt with more violently; and moreover I was desirous to have seen their country.

At the sun rising, I awaked my brother, telling him by signs it was time to go. He called the rest, but none would stir, which made him lie down again. I rose and went to the waterside, where I walked awhile. If there were another [prisoner] we might, I dare say, escape their sight. Here I recreated myself, running a naked sword into the sand. One of them, seeing me after such an exercise, calls me and shows me his way, which made me more confident in them. They brought me a dish full of meat to the waterside. I began to eat like a bear.

---

*The two Frenchmen, now decapitated, who had gone hunting with Radisson.

In the meantime they embarked themselves. One of them took notice that I had not a knife, brings me his, which I kept the rest of the voyage; they had [not] the least fear of me. Being ready to go, saving my boat that was amending, which was soon done, the other boats were not as yet out of sight, and in the way my boat killed a stag. They made me shoot at it, and not quite dead they runned it through with their swords, and having cut it to pieces they divided it and proceeded on their way. At three of the clock in the afternoon[15] we came into a rapid stream, where we were forced to land and carry our equipages and boats through a dangerous place. We had not any encounter that day.

At night, where we found cottages ready made, there I cut wood, as the rest, with all diligence.

The morning early following, we marched without making noise or singing as accustomed. Sojourning awhile, we came to a lake six leagues wide,[16] about it a very pleasant country embellished with great forests. That day our wild people killed two bears, one monstrous for its bigness, the other a small one. We arrived to a fine sandy bank, where not long before many cabins were erected and places made where prisoners were tied.

In this place our wild people sweated after the manner following: first heated stones till they were red as fire; then made a lantern with small sticks; then, storing the place with deal[17] trees, saving a place in the middle whereinto they put the stones, and covered the place with several covers; then stripped themselves naked, went into it. They made a noise as if the devil were there. After being there for an hour, they smoked as [they] came out and then [began] throwing one another into the water. I thought verily they were incensed. It is their usual custom.[18] Being comed out of this place, they feasted themselves with the two bears, turning the outside of the tripes[19] inward, not washed. They gave everyone his share. As for my part, I found them [neither] good nor savory to the palate.

In the night they heard some shooting, which made them embark themselves speedily. In the meanwhile they made me lay down, whilst they rowed very hard. I slept securely till the morning, where I found myself in great high rushes. There they stayed without noise. From thence we proceeded, though not without some fear of an Algonquin army. We went on for some days [on] that lake. At last they endeavored to retire to the woods, everyone carrying his bundle. After a day's march, we came to a little river, where we laid that night. The day following, we proceeded on our journey, where we met two men with whom our wildmen seemed to be acquainted by some signs. Those two men began to speak a long while. After came a company of women, twenty in number, that brought us dry fish and Indian corn. These women loaded themselves, after we had eaten, like mules with our baggage. We went through a small wood, the way well beaten, until [at] evening we touched a place for fishing of fifteen cabins.

There they were well received but myself, who was strucken by a young man. My keeper made [a] sign I should [do the same] to him again. I turning to him instantly, he to me, taking hold of my hair, all the wildmen came about us, encouraging [us] with their cries and hands, which encouraged me most that none helped him more than me. We clawed one another with hands, tooth, and nails. My adversary, being offended I have gotten the best, he kicked me, but my French shoes that they left me were harder than his, which made him [give up] that game again. He took me about the wrist, where he found himself down before he was aware, [I] holding him upon the ground till some came and put us asunder. My company, seeing me free, began to cry out, giving me water to wash me and then fresh fish to relish me. They encouraged me so much, the one combing my head, the other greasing my hair. There we stayed two days, where nobody durst trouble me.

In the same cabin that I was, there has been a wildman wounded with a small shot. I thought I have seen him the day of my taking, which made me fear lest I was the one that wounded him. He, knowing it to be so, had showed me as much charity as a Christian might have given. Another of his fellows, [whom] I also wounded, came to me at my first coming there, whom I thought to have come for revenge, contrariwise showed me a cheerful countenance. He gave me a box full of red paintings, calling me his brother.

I had not as yet carried any burden, but meeting with an old man [who] gave me a sack of tobacco of 12 pounds' weight, [I bore] it upon my head, as it's their usual customs. We made several stays that day by reason of the several encounters of their people that came from villages as warriors, others from fishing and shooting. In that journey our company increased, among others a great many Hurons that had been lately taken and who for the most part are as slaves. We laid in the wood because they [the

9

Hurons] would not go into their [the Iroquois] village in the night-time.*

The next day we marched into a village[20] where, as we came in sight, we heard nothing but outcries, as [much] from one side as from the other, being a quarter of a mile from the village. They sat down, I in the middle. I saw women and men and children with staves in array, which put me in fear, and [they] instantly stripped me naked. My keeper gave me a sign to begone as fast as I could drive.[21]

In the meanwhile many of the village came about us, among which [was] a good old woman. A boy with a hatchet in his hand came near me. The old woman covered me, and the young man took me by the hand and lead me out of the company. The old woman made me step aside from those that were ready to strike at me. There I left the two heads of my comrades. [It] comforted me that I escaped the blows.

Then they brought me into their cottage. There the old woman showed me kindness. She gave me to eat. The great terror I had a little before took my stomach away from me. I stayed an hour, where a great company of people came to see me.

Here came a company of old men having pipes in their mouths. [They] sat about me. After smoking, they lead me into another cabin, where there were a company all smoking. They made me set down by the fire, which made [me] apprehend they should cast me into the said fire, but it proved otherwise, for the old woman followed me, speaking loud, whom they answered with a loud "ho!"[22] Then she took her girdle and about me she tied it.

So brought me to her cottage and made me sit down in the same place I was before. Then she began to dance and sing awhile. After, [she] brings down from her box a comb, gives it to a maid that was near me, who presently comes to grease and comb my hair and took away the paint that the fellows stuck to my face. Now the old woman gets me some Indian corn toasted in the fire. I took pains to gather it out of the fire. After this she gave me a blue coverlet, stockings and shoes, and wherewithal to make me drawers. She looked in my clothes, and if she found any lice she would squeeze them betwixt her teeth, as if they had been substantial meat. I laid with her son, who took me from my first

---

*Presumably the Hurons are afraid of being tortured by strange Iroquois during the course of an evening's frolic.

10

takers, and got at last great acquaintance with many. I did what I could to get familiarity with them, yet I suffered no wrong at their hands, taking all freedom, which the old woman enticed me to do, but still they altered my face wherever I went—a new dish to satisfy nature.*

I took all the pleasures imaginable, having a small [fowling] piece at my command, shooting partridges and squirrels, playing most part of the day with my companions. The old woman wished that I would make myself more familiar with her daughters, which were tolerable among such people. They were accustomed to grease and comb my hair in the morning. I went with them into the wilderness, and there they would be habling,[23] which I could not understand. They wanted no company but I was sure to be of the number. I brought always some gifts that I received, which I gave to my purse keeper and refuge, the good old woman.

I lived five weeks without thinking from whence I came. I learned more of their manners in six weeks than if I had been in France six months. At the end I was troubled in mind, which made her inquire if I was Anjonack, a Huron word. At this I made as if I were subported[?] for speaking in a strange language, which she liked well, calling me by the name of her son who before was killed, Ovinha, which signifies lead or stone, without difference of the words, so that it was my lordship. She inquired me whether I was Asserony, a French. I answered no, saying I was Ganugaga, that is, of their nation, for which she was pleased.

My father feasted three hundred men that day. My sisters made me clean for that purpose and greased my hair. My mother decked me with a new cover and a red and blue cap with two necklace of porcelain.[24] My sisters tied me with bracelets and garters of the same porcelain. My brother painted my face and [put] feathers on my head and tied both my locks with porcelain. My father was liberal to me, giving me a garland instead of my blue cap, a necklace of porcelain that hung down to my heels, and a hatchet in my hand. It was hard for me to defend myself against any encounter, being so laden with riches. Then my father made a speech, showing many demonstrations of valor, broke a kettle full of cagamite[25] with a hatchet. They sung, as is their usual custom. They were waited on by a sort of young men, [who] bring down dishes of meat of oriniack,[26] of castors,[27] and of red

---

*That is, the Indians contrived to paint his face.

11

deers mingled with some flowers. The order of making was thus: the corn being dried between two stones into powder, being very thick, put it into a kettle full of water, then a quantity of bear's greast. This banquet being over, they cried to me, "Chagon, Ovinha!" that is, "be hearty, stone or lead." Everyone withdrew into his quarters, and so did I.

But to the purpose of my history.[28] I went to the fields once, where I met with three of my acquaintance who had a design for hunting a great way off. They desired me to go along. I let them know in Huron language (for that I knowed better than that of the Iroquois) I was content, desiring them to stay till I acquainted my mother.

One of them came along with me and got leave for me of my kindred. My mother got me presently a sack of meal, three pair of shoes, my gun, and [she] turned back [to] where the two stayed for us. My two sisters accompanied me even out of the wilderness and carried my bundle, where they took leave.

We marched on that day through the woods till we came by a lake, where we traveled without any rest. I wished I had stayed at home, for we had sad victuals. The next day about noon, we came to a river. There we made a skiff so little that we could scarce go into it. I admired their skill in doing it, for in less than two hours they cut the tree and pulled up the rind,[29] of which they made the boat. We embarked ourselves and went to the lower end of the river, which emptied itself into a little lake of about two miles in length and a mile in breadth. We passed [from] this lake into another river, broader than the other. There we found a fresh track of a stag, which made us stay here awhile.

It was five of the clock at least when two of our men made themselves ready to look after that beast. The other and I stayed behind. Not long after, we saw the stag cross the river, which fording brought him to his ending. So done, they went on their course and came back again at ten of the clock with three bears, a castor, and the stag which was slained at our sight. How did we rejoice to see that killed which would make the kettle boil! After we have eaten, we slept.

The next day we made traps for to trap castors. Whilst we were busy—one about one thing, one about another, [and] as three of us returned homewards to our cottage—we heard a wildman singing. He made us look to ourselves, lest he should prove an enemy, but as we have seen him, called to him, who came imme-

diately, telling us that he was in pursuit of a bear since morning
and that he gave him over, having lost his two dogs by the same
bear. He came with us to our cottage, where we met our companion after [we] killed one bear, two stags, and two mountain
cats, being five in number.

Whilst the meat was aboiling, that wildman spoke to me [in]
the Algonquin language. I wondered to hear this stranger. He told
me that he was taken two years ago. He asked me concerning
Three Rivers and Quebec. [He] wished himself there, and I said
the same, though I did not intend it. He asked me if I loved the
French. I inquired him also if he loved the Algonquins. "Mary,"
quoth he, and [I said], "So do I my own nation." Then replied
he, "Brother, cheer up. Let us escape. Three Rivers are not afar
off." I told him my three comrades would not permit me and that
they promised my mother to bring me back again. Then he inquired whether I would live like the Hurons who were in bondage
or have my own liberty with the French, where there was good
bread to be eaten. "Fear not," quoth he. "We shall kill them all
three this night when they will be asleep, which will be an easy
matter with their own hatchets." At last I consented, considering
they were mortal enemies to my country, that [they] had cut the
throats of so many of my relations, burned and murdered them,
promising him to succor him in his design.

They, not understanding our language, asked the Algonquin
what is that he said, but [he] told them some other story, nor
[did] they suspected us in the least. Their belly full, their mind
without care, wearied to the utmost of the foremost day's journey,
[they] fell asleep securely, leaning their arms up and down without
the least danger.

Then my wildman pushed me, thinking I was asleep. He rises
and sits him down by the fire, beholding them one after another.
Taking their arms aside and having the hatchets in his hand,
[he] gives me one. To tell the truth, I was loathsome to do them
mischief that never did me any. Yet, for the above said reasons,
I took the hatchet and began the execution, which was soon done.
My fellow comes to him that was nearest to the fire (I dare say
he never saw the stroke) and I have done the like to another, but
I, hitting him with the edge of the hatchet, could not disengage
[it] presently, being so deep in his head. [He] rises upon his breast,
but fell back suddenly, making a great noise which almost awaked
the third, but my comrade gave him a deadly blow of a hatchet,

13

and presently after I shot him dead. Then we prepared ourselves with all speed—throwing their dead corpses, after the wildman took off their heads, into the water.

We took three guns (leaving the fourth), their two swords, their hatchets, their powder and shot, and all their porcelain. We took also some meal and meat. I was sorry for to have been in such an encounter, but too late to repent. We took our journey that night alongst the river. The break of day we landed on the side of a rock which was smooth. We carried our boat and equipage into the wood about a hundred paces from the waterside, where we stayed most sadly all that day, tormented by the maringoines.[30] We turned our boat upside down; we put us under it from the rain. The night coming, which was the fittest time to leave that place, we go without any noise for our safety. We traveled fourteen nights in that manner, in great fear, hearing boats passing by. When we have perceived any fire, [we] left off rowing and went by with as little noise as could possible. At last, with many turnings by land and by water, we came to the Lake of St. Peter's.

We landed about four of the clock, leaving our skiff in among rushes, far out of the way from those that passes that way and [might] do us injury. We retired into the wood, where we made a fire some two hundred paces from the river. There we roasted some meat and boiled meal. After, we rested ourselves awhile from the many labors of the former night.

So, having slept, my companion awakes first and stirs me, saying it was high time, that we might by day come to our dwelling, of which counsel I did not approve. [I] told him the enemies commonly were lurking about the riverside and we should do very well to stay in that place till sunset.

"Then," said he, "let us begone. We [are] passed all fear. Let us shake the yoke of a company of whelps that killed so many French and black coats[31] and so many of my nation. Nay," saith he, "brother, if you come not, I will leave you and will go through the woods till I shall be over against the French quarters. There I will make a fire for a sign that they may fetch me. I will tell to the governor that you stayed behind. Take courage, man," says he. With this he took his piece and things.

At this, I considered how if [I] were taken at the door by mere rashness. Next, the impossibility I saw to go by myself if my comrade would leave me; perhaps the wind might rise, that I could [only] come to the end of my journey in a long time and that I should be accounted a coward for not daring to hazard myself with him that had so much ventured for me. I resolved to go along through the woods, but the little constance that is to be expected in wildmen made me fear he should [take] to his heels, which approved [to me] his unfortunate advice: he hath lost his life by it, and I in great danger have escaped by the help of the Almighty. I consent to go by water with him.

In a short time we came to the lake.[32] The water very calm and clear, no likelihood of any storm. We hazarded to the other side of the lake, thinking for more security. After we passed the third part of the lake, I being the foremost, have perceived [something] as if it were a black shadow, which proved a real thing. He at this rises and tells me that it was a company of buzzards, a kind of geese in that country. We went on. We soon perceived our own fatal blindness, for they were enemies. We went back again towards the land, with all speed, to escape the evident danger, but it was too late. Before we could come to the rushes that were within half a league of the waterside, we were tired. Seeing them approaching nigher and nigher, we threw the three heads in the water. They meet with these heads, which makes them to row harder after us, thinking that we runned away from their country. We were so near the land that we saw the bottom of the water, but yet too deep to step in, when these cruel inhumans came within a musket shot of us. Fearing lest the booty should get away from them [they] shot several times at us and deadly wounded my comrade, [he] falling dead. I expected such another shot. The little skiff was [so] pierced in several places with their shooting that water runned in apace. I defended myself with the two arms. At last they environed me with their boats, took me just as I was sinking. They held up the wildman and throwed him into one of their boats, and me they brought with all diligence to land. I thought to die without mercy.

They made a great fire and took my comrade's heart out and chopped off his head, which they put on an end of a stick, and carried it to one of their boats. They cut off some of the flesh of that miserable, broiled it, and eat it. If he had not been so desperately wounded, they had done their best to keep him alive to make him suffer the more by burning him with small fires; but being wounded in the chin, and [a] bullet gone through the throat, and another in the shoulder that broke his arms, [these] made him incurable. They burned some part of his body and the rest they left there. That was the miserable end of that wretch.

15

Let us come now to the beginning of my miseries and calamities that I was to undergo. Whilst they were busy about my companion's head, the others tied me safe and fast in a strange manner. Having stripped me naked, they tied me above the elbows behind my back, and then they put a collar about me, not of porcelain as before, but a rope wrought about my middle, [and] so brought me in that pickle to the boat. As I was embarked, they asked me several questions. [I] being not able to answer, [they] gave me great blows with their fists, then pulled out one of my nails, and partly untied me. What a displeasure had I, to have seen myself taken again, being almost come to my journey's end, that I must now go back again to suffer such torments. Death was to be expected. Having lost all hopes, I resolved altogether to die, being a folly to think otherwise.

I was not the [only] one in the claws of those wolves. Their company was composed of a hundred and fifty men, [plus prisoners] took about Quebec and other places: two French men, one French woman, seventeen Hurons, men as [well as] women. They had eleven heads which they said were of the Algonquins, and I was the thirtieth [and] three victim with those cruels. The wildmen that were prisoners sang their fatal song, which was a mournful song or noise. The twelve colors (which were heads) stood out for a show.[33]

We prisoners were separated, one in one boat, one in another. As for me, I was put into a boat with a Huron whose fingers were cut and burned, and very [few] amongst them but had the marks of those inhuman devils. They did not permit me to tarry long with my fellow prisoner, lest I should tell him any news (as I imagine), but sent me to another boat, where I remained the rest of the voyage by water, which proved somewhat to my disadvantage.

In this boat there was an old man who, having examined me, I answered him as I could best: told him how I was adopted by such an one by name and [how] as I was ahunting with my companions that wildman that was killed came to us and, after he had eaten, went his way; [how] in the evening [he] came back again and found us all asleep, took a hatchet and killed my three companions, and awaked me and so embarked me and brought me to this place. That old man believed me in some measure, which I perceived in him by his kindness towards me, but he was not able to protect me from those that had a will to do me mischief. Many slandered me, but I took no notice.

16

Some four leagues thence, they erected cottages by a small river very difficult to get to, for there is little water on [a] great sand [bar] a league wide. To this very hour I took notice how they tied their captives, though at my own cost. They planted several posts of the bigness of an arm, then laid us of a length, tied us to the said posts, far asunder from one another. Then [they] tied our knees, [next] our wrists and elbows and our hairs directly upon the crown of our heads. Then [they] cut four bars of the bigness of a leg and used [them] thus: they took two for the neck, putting one of each side, tying the two ends together so that our heads were fast in a hole like a trap; likewise they did to our legs. What tormented us most was the maringoines and great flies being in abundance. [We] did all night but puff and blow that by that means we saved our faces from the sting of those ugly creatures; having no use of our hands, we are cruelly tormented.

Our voyage was laborious and most miserable, suffering every night the like misery.

When we came near our dwellings, we met several gangs of men, to our greatest disadvantage, for we were forced to sing, and those that came to see us gave porcelain to those that did us injury. One cut off a finger. Another plucked out a nail and put the end of our fingers into their burning pipes, and burned several parts in our bodies. Some took our fingers, and of a stick made a thing like a fork with which [they] gave several blows on the back of the hands, which caused our hands to swell and became at last insensible, as [if] dead. Having suffered all these cruelties, which were nothing to that they make usually suffer their prisoners, we arrived at last to the place of execution, which is at the coming-in to their village, where not [long] before I escaped very near to be soundly beaten with staves and fists. Now I must think to be no less treated, by reason of the murder of the three men. But the fear of death takes away the fear of blows.

Nineteen of us prisoners were brought thither and two left behind with the heads. In this place we had eight colors. Who would not shake at the sight of so many men, women, and children armed with all sort of instruments? — staves, hand irons, heel-skins wherein they put half a score bullets. Others had brands, rods of thorn, and all such like that the cruelties could invent to put their prisoners to greater torments. Here [was] no help, no remedy. We must pass this dangerous passage in our extremity

17

without help. He that is the fearfulest or that is observed to stay
the last gets nothing by it but more blows, and put him to more
pain: the meanest sort of people commonly is more cruel to the
fearfulest than to the others that they see fearful; [the latter]
suffer cheerfully and with constancy.

They begun to cry to both sides, we marching one after
another, environed with a number of people from all parts to
be witness to that hideous sight which seriously may be called
the image of hell in this world. The men sings their fatal song;
the women makes horrible cries. The victors cries of joy, and
their wives makes acclamations for mirth. In a word, all prepares
for the ruin of these poor victims who are so tied — having not
saving only our legs free — [and who] advance by little and little,
according [to] the will of him that leads us. As he held us by a
long rope, he stayed us to his will and often makes us fall for
to show the cruelty, abusing you so to give them pleasure and you
more torment. As our band was great, there was a greater crew
of people to see the prisoners. The report of my taking being
now made, and of the death of the three men, which afflicted the
most of that nation, [a] great many of [them] came through a
design of revenge and to molest me more than any other.

But it was altogether otherwise, for among the tumult I perceived my father and mother, with their two daughters. The
mother pushes in among the crew directly to me, and when she
was near enough she catches hold of my hair as one desperate,
calling me often by my name. Drawing me out of my rank, she
puts me into the hands of her husband, who then bid me have
courage, conducting me another way home to his cabin.

He made me sit down [and] said to me, "You senseless! Thou
was my son, and thou rendered thyself enemy. Thou rendered
thyself enemy! Thou lovest not thy mother nor thy father that
gave thee thy life, and thou notwithstanding will kill me. Be merry;
Conharrassan, give him to eat." (That was the name of one of
the sisters.)

My heart shaked with trembling and fear, which took away my
stomach. Nevertheless, [I] signify a bold countenance, knowing
well that a bold generous mind is always accounted among all
sort of nations, especially among warriors that is very presump-
tuous and haughty because of their magnanimity and victories,
opposing themselves into all dangers and encounters whatever,
running over the whole land, slaining and killing all they meet

in exercising their cruelties, or else showing mercy to whom they please to give liberty. God gave me the grace to forget nothing of my duty. I told my father the success of my voyage in the best terms I could and how all things passed, mixturing a little of their language with that of the Hurons, which I learned more fluently than theirs, being longer and more frequently with the Hurons. Everyone attentively gave ear to me, hoping by this means to save my life.

Upon this, here comes a great number of armed men, [who] enters the cabin, where finding me yet tied with my cords, sitting by my parents, [they] made their addresses to my father and spake to him very loud. After a while my father make me rise and delivers me into their hands. My mother, seeing this, cries and laments with both my sisters. I, believing in a terrible motion, [thought] to go directly on to the place of execution. I must march; I must yield where force is predominant at the public place.

I was conducted [to] where I found a good company of those miserable wretches altogether, beaten with blows, covered with blood, and burned. One miserable Frenchman, yet breathing, having now been consumed with blows of sticks, passed so through the hands of this enraged crew, and seeing he could [endure] no more [they] cut off his head and throwed it into the fire. This was the end of this execrable woeful body of this miserable.

They made me go up the scaffold, where were five men, three women, and two children captives. I made the eleventh. There were several scaffolds nigh one another, where were these wretches, who with a doleful singings replenished the heavens with their cries. I can say that an hour [passed] before the weather approved very fair, and in an instant the weather changed and rained extremely. The most part retired to avoid this hail, and now we must expect the rigor of the weather by the retiration of those perfidious, except one band of hell who stayed about us for to learn the trade of barbary. Those little devils, seeing themselves all alone, contrived a thousand inventions of wickedness. This is nothing strange, seeing that they are brought up [thus] and suck the cruelty from their mothers' breast.

I prolong a little from my purpose of my adventure for to say the torments that I have seen suffered at Coutu,[34] after they [the prisoners] have passed the sallett[35] at their entering into

19

the village and the encounters that they meet ordinarily in the way, as above said. They tie the prisoners to a post by their hands, their backs turned towards the hangman, who hath a burning fire of dry wood and rind of trees, which doth not quench easily. They put into this fire hatchets, swords, and such like instruments of iron. They take these and quench them on human flesh. They pluck out their nails for the most part in this sort: they put a red coal of fire upon it and, when it's swollen, bits it out with their teeth; after, they stop the blood with a brand, which by little and little draws the veins the one after another from off the fingers, and when they draw all as much as they can they cut it with pieces of red hot iron; they squeeze the fingers between two stones and so draw the marrow out of the bones, and when the flesh is all taken away, they put it [the fingers] in a dish full of burning sand. After, they tie the wrist with a cord, putting two for this effect, one drawing him one way, another of another way. If the sinews be not cut with a stick, putting it through and turning it, they make them come as fast as they can and cut them in the same way as the others. Some others cuts pieces of flesh from all parts of the body and broil them, gets you to eat it, thrusting them into your mouth, putting into it a stick of fire. They break your teeth with a stone or clubs. [They] uses the handle of a kettle, and upon this do hang five or six hatchets red hot, which they hang about their [victim's] neck. [They] roast your legs with brands of fire, and thrusting into it some sticks pointed, wherein they put a lead melted and gunpowder, and [they] then give it fire like unto artificial fire and make the patient gather it by the stumps of his remaining fingers. If he cannot sing they make him quackle like a hen. I saw two men tied to a rope, one at each end, and hang them so all night, throwing red coals at them or burning sand and in such like burn their feet, legs, thighs, and breech. The little ones do exercise themselves about such cruelties. They deck the bodies all over with hard straw, putting in the end of this stray thorns. [They] so leave them now, then give them a little rest, sometimes give them fresh water, and make them repose on fresh leaves. They also give them to eat of the best they have that they come to themselves again, [in order] to give them more torments. Then, when they see that the patient can no more take up his hair, they cover his head with a platter made of rind full of burning sand, and often sets the platter afire. In the next place, they

20

clothe you with a suit made of rind of a tree, and this they make burn out on your body. They cut off your stones, and the women play with them as with balls. When they see the miserable die, they open him and pluck out his heart. They drink some of his blood and wash the children's heads with the rest to make them valiant. If you have endured all the above-said torments patiently and without moans, and have defied death in singing, then they thrust burning blades all along your bones and, so ending the tragedy, cut off the head and put it on the end of a stick and draw his body in quarters, which they haul about their village. Lastly, [they] throws him into the water or leave [him] in the fields to be eaten by the crows or dogs.

Now let me come to our miserable poor captives that stayed all along [through] the rain upon the scaffold, to the mercy of two or three hundred rogues that shot us with little arrows and drew out our beards and the hair from those that had any. The shower of rain being over, all came together again and, having kindled fires, begun to burn some of those poor wretches.

That day they plucked four nails out of my fingers and made me sing, though I had no mind at that time. I became speechless oftentimes; then they gave me water wherein they boiled a certain herb that the gunsmiths use to polish their arms. That liquor brought me to my speech again. The night being come, they made me come down all naked as I was and brought [me] to a strange cottage. (I wished heartily it had been that of my parents.) They tied me to a post, where I stayed a full hour without the least molestation. A woman came there with her boy, enticed him to cut off one of my fingers with a flint stone. The boy was not four years old. This [child] takes my finger and begins to work, but in vain because he had not the strength to break my fingers; so my poor finger escaped, having no other hurt done to it but the flesh cut round about it. His mother made him suck the very blood that runned from my finger.[36] I had no other torment all that day. At night I could not sleep because of the great pain. I did eat a little and drunk much water by reason of a fever I caught by the cruel torments I suffered.

The next morning I was brought back again to the scaffold, where there were company enough. They made me sing anew, but my mother came there and made [me] hold my peace, bidding me be cheerful and that I should not die. She brought me some meat. Her coming comforted me much, but that did not last long,

21

for here comes several old people, one of which, being on the scaffold, sat him down by me, holding in his mouth a pewter pipe burning. [He] took my thumb and put it on the burning tobacco, and so smoked three pipes one after another, which made my thumb swell and the nail and flesh became as coal. My mother was always by me to comfort me, but [I] said not what I thought. That man having finished his hard work — but I am sure I felt it harder to suffer it — he trembled, whether for fear or for so much action I cannot tell. My mother tied my fingers with cloth, and when he was gone she greased my hair and combed my hair with a wooden comb [that was] fitter to comb a horse's tail than anything else. She goes back again.

That day they ended many of those poor wretches, flinging some all alive into the middle of a great fire. They burned a French woman. They pulled out her breasts and took a child out of her belly, which they broiled, and made the mother eat of it; so in short [she] died.

I was not abused all that day till the night. They burned the soles of my feet and legs. A soldier runned through my foot a sword red hot out of the fire and plucked several of my nails. I stayed in that manner all night. I neither wanted in the meanwhile meat nor drink. I was supplied by my mother and sisters. My father also came to see me and told me I should have courage. There came a little boy to gnaw with his teeth the end of my fingers. There appears a man to cut off my thumb; being about it, [he instead] leaves me instantly and did no harm, for which I was glad. I believe that my father dissuaded him from it. A while after my father was gone, three came to the scaffold who swore they would [do] me a mischief. [One] tied his legs to mine, called for a brand of fire, laid it between his legs and mine, and sings; but by good luck it was out on my side and did none other effect than burn my skin, but [it] burned him to some purpose. In this posture I was to follow him. Being not able to hold me, [he] draweth me down. One of the company cut the rope that held us with his knife and make me go up again [on] the scaffold, and then [they] went their way. There I stayed till midday alone.

There comes a multitude of people, who makes me come down and laid me into a cottage where there were a number of [about] sixty old men smoking tobacco. Here they make me sit down among them, and [they] stayed about half an hour without that

22

they asked who and why I was brought thither; nor did I much care for the great torments that I suffered; I know not whether I was dead or alive. Albeit I was in a hot fever and great pains, I rejoiced at the sight of my brother, that I had not seen since my arrivement. He comes in very sumptuously covered with several necklaces of porcelain, and a hatchet in his hand. [He] sat down by the company and cast an eye on me now and then. Presently comes in my father with a new and long cover and a new porcelain about him, with a hatchet in his hands; [he] likewise sat down with the company. He had a calumet of red stone[37] in his hands, a cake[38] upon his shoulders that hanged down his back, and so had the rest of the old men.

In that same cake are enclosed all the things in the world, as they told me often, advertising me that I should [not] disoblige them in the least nor make them angry, by reason they had in their power the sun and moon and the heavens, and consequently all the earth. You must know in this cake there is nothing but tobacco, and roots to heal some wounds or sores. Some others keep in it the bones of their deceased friends. Most of them [keep] wolves' heads, squirrels' or any other beast's head. When they have any debatement among them, they sacrifice to this tobacco; that they throw into the fire, and make smoke of that they puff out of their pipes. Whether for peace or adversity, or prosperity or war, such ceremonies they make very often.

My father, taking his place, lights his pipe and smokes as the rest. They held great silence during this. They bring prisoners: to wit, seven women and two men, more [than] ten children from the age of three to twelve years. They placed them all by me, who as yet had my arms tied, the others all at liberty, being not tied, which put me into some despair lest I should pay for all. A while after, one of the company rises and makes a long speech, now showing the heavens with his hands, and then the earth and fire. This good man put himself into a sweat through the earnest discourse. Having finished his panegyric, another begins, and also many [more], one after another.

They gave then liberty to some, but killed two children with hatchets, and a woman of fifty years old, and threw the rest out of the cottage (saving only myself) at full liberty. I was left alone for a stake.

They contested together. [Upon] which my father rise and

23

made a speech which lasted above an hour. Being naked, having nothing on but his drawers and the cover of his head, [he] put himself all in a heat; his eyes were hollow in his head; he appeared to me like mad, naming often the Algonquins, in their language Attiseruata, which made me believe he spoke in my behalf. In that very time [my mother] comes with two necklaces of porcelain, one in her arms and another about her like a belt. As soon as she came in she begun to sing and dance and fling off one of her necklaces in the middle of the place, having made many turns from one end to the other. She takes the other necklace and gives it [to] me, then goes her way. Then my brother rises and, holding his hatchet in his hand, sings a military song. Having finished, [he] departs. I feared much that he was first to knock me in the head, and happy are those that can escape so well rather than be burned. My father rises for a second time and sings. So done, [he] retired himself. I thought all their gifts, songs, and speeches should prevail nothing with me.

Those that stayed held a council and spoke one to another very low, throwing tobacco into the fire, making exclamations. Then the cottage was open[ed on] all sides by those that came to view. Some of the company retires, and place was made for them as if they were kings. Forty stays about me, and nigh two thousand about my cottage, of men, women, and children. Those that went their way returned presently. Being set down, [they] smoked again whilst my father, mother, brothers, and sisters were present. My father sings awhile [and], so done, makes a speech. Taking the porcelain necklace from off me, [he] throws [it] at the feet of an old man and cuts the cord that held me, then makes me rise. The joy that I received at that time was incomparable, for suddenly all my pains and griefs ceased, not feeling the least pain. He bids me be merry, makes me sing, to which I consented with all my heart. Whilst I did sing they whooped and hallooed on all sides. The old man bid me, "Ever be cheerful, my son." My mother, sisters and the rest of their friends [sang] and danced.

Then my father takes me by the arm and leads me to his cabin. As we went along, nothing was heard but whooping and hallooing on all parts, bidding me to take great courage. My mother was not long after me, with the rest of her friends. Now I see myself free from death.

Their care at this was to give me meat. I have not eaten a bit all that day, and the great joy I had conceived caused me to have a good stomach, so that I did eat lustily. Then my mother begins to cure my sores and wounds. Then begins my pains anew, for she cleans my wounds and scrapes them with a knife and often thrusts a stick in them and then takes water in her mouth and spouts it to make them clean. Meanwhile my father goes to seek roots, and my sister chaws them, and my mother applies them to my sores as a plaster. The next day the swelling was gone; in less than a fortnight my sores were healed, saving my feet, that kept [me] more than a whole month in my cabin. During this time my nails growed apace. I remained only lame of my middle finger that they have squeezed between two stones. Everyone was kind to me, as before said, and [I] wanted no company to be merry with.

I should keep [you] too long to tell you the particularties that befell me during my winter. I was beloved of my parents as before. My exercise was always ahunting, without that any gave me the least injury. My mother kept me most brave, and my sisters took great care for me. Every month I had a white shirt, which my father sent for from the Flemings[39] who were not afar of our village. I could never get leave to go along with my brother, who went there very often. Finally, seeing myself in the former condition as before, I constituted as long as my father and fortune would permit me to live there.

Daily there were military feasts for the South[ern] nations and others for the Algonquins and for the French. The exclamations, whoopings and cries, songs and dances signifies nothing but the murdering and killing and the intended victory that they will have the next year, which is in the beginning of spring. In those feats my father heaves up his hatchet against the Algonquins. For this effect [he] makes great preparations for his next encamping. Every night [he] never fails to instruct and encourage the young [of] age to take arms and to revenge the death of so many of [the Iroquois on] their enemy that lived among the French nation.

The desire that I had to make me beloved — for the assurance of my life — made me resolve to offer myself to serve and take part with them. But I feared much lest he should mistrust me, touching his advice to my resolution. Nevertheless, I, finding him once of a good humor and on the point of honor, encourages his son to break the kettle and take the hatchet and

25

to be gone to the foreign nations. [I said] that [it] was of courage and of great renown to see the father of one part and the son of another part and that he should not [be] mispraise[d] if he should separate from him, but that it was the quickest way to make the world tremble, and by that means have liberty everywhere by vanquishing the mortal enemy of his nation. Upon this, I venture to ask him what I was.

Presently [he] answers that I was a Iroquois, as himself.

"Let me revenge," said I, "my kindred. I love my borther. Let me die with him. I would die with you, but you will not [take me along] because you go against the French. Let me, again, go with my brother. The prisoners and the heads that I shall bring, to the joy of my mother and sisters, will make me undertake at my return to take up the hatchet against those of Quebec, of Three Rivers, and Montreal — declaring [to] them my name and that it's I that kills them — and by that you shall know I am your son, worthy to bear that title that you gave me when you adopted me."

He let a great cry, saying, "Have great courage, son Ovinha! Thy brother died in the wars, not in the cabin; he was of a courage not of a woman. I go to avenge his death. If I die, avenge you mine."

That one word was my leave, which made me hope that one day I might escape, having so great an opportunity, or at least I should have the happiness to see their country, which I heard so much recommended by the Iroquois who brought so wonderous stories and the facility of killing so many men. Thus the winter was passed in thoughts and preparing to depart before the melting of the snow, which is very soon in that country.

I began to set my wits together how I should resolve this, my voyage, for my mother opposed against it mightily, saying I should be lost in the woods and that I should get it [put] off till the next year. But at last I flattered her and dissembled. Besides, my father had the power in his hands, she daring not to deny him anything because she was not born in my father's country, but was taken little in the Hurons' country. Notwithstanding, [she was] well beloved of her husband, having lived together more than forty years, and in that space [she] brought him nine children, five males and four females.[40] Two girls died after a while; three sons [were] killed in the wars; one went three years before with a band of thirteen men to war against

26

a fiery nation[41] which is far beyond the great lake;[42] the fifth had already performed two voyages with a great deal of success.

My father was a great captain in [the] wars, having been commander in all his times, and [he had] distructed many villages of their enemy, having killed nineteen men with his own hands, whereof he has marked his right thigh. For as many he killed he should have as many more, but you must know that the commander has not amused himself to kill, but [is] in front of his army to encourage his men. If by chance he took any prisoners, he calls one of his men and gives him the captives, saying that it's honor enough to command the conquerors, and by his example shows to the young men that he has the power as much as the honor. He received two guns' shots and seven arrows' shots and was run through the shoulders with a lance. He was aged three score years old. He was tall and of excellent wit for a wildman.

When our baggage was ready, my father makes a feast to which he invites a number [of] people and declares that he was sorry he had resolved to go to wars against an enemy which was in a cold country, which hindered him to march sooner than he would [be able to] but [that he was] willing to see his sons before him and that this banquet was made for his two sons' farewell. Then he told that his adopted son was ready to go with his own son to be revenged of the death of their brothers, and desired the commander to have a care of us both. This commander loved us both [and] said that the one which [was] myself should be with him to the end; if anything should oppose he would make me fight him.

I was not at home when he spake those words, but my mother told me it at my return; I was afishing with my sisters and brother. When we came back we found all ready, but with a heart broken that our mother and sisters let us go.

[A] few days after, I was invited to a military banquet where was the captain, a young gallant of twenty years old, with a company of eight, and I made the tenth. We all did sing and made good cheer of a fat bear. We gave our things to slaves; we carried only our muskets.

Our kindred brought us a great way. My sister could not forbear crying; yet [she] told me to be of a stout heart. We at last bid them adieu.

We took [off] on our journey over great snows for to come to the great lake before the spring. We traveled seven days

27

through woods, an indifferent country, easy in some places and others difficult. The rivers were frozen, which made us cross with a great deal of ease. We arrived the seventh day in a village called Nojottga,[43] where we stayed two days. From thence came a young man with us. We arrived into another village, Nontageya,[44] where we stayed four days.

We had always great preparations [made for us] and were invited nine or ten times a day. Our bellies had not time to empty themselves because we feeded so much. What was prepared for us were [of] several sorts: stag, Indian corn, thick flour, bears, and especially eels. We have not yet searched our bags where our provision was. In this place we mended them. For my part I found in mine six pounds of powder and more than fifteen pounds of shot, two shirts, a cap, eight pair of shoes, wherewithal to make a pair of breeches, and about [a] thousand grains of black and white porcelain, and my brother as many. We had new covers — one to our body; another hung down from our shoulders like a mantle — everyone a small necklace of porcelain, and a collar made with a thread of nettles to tie the prisoners. I had a gun, a hatchet, and a dagger. That was all we had. Our slaves brought the packs after us.

After we marched three days, we came to a village, Sononteronon.[45] There we laid a night. The next day, after a small journey, we came to the last village of their confederates. Here they do differ in their speech, though of a nation. It's called Oiongoiconon.[46] Here we stay two days. [Then we] sent away our slaves and carried our bundles ourselves, going always through the woods. We found great plains of two leagues [and] a half journey without a tree. We saw there stags, but would not go out of our way to kill them. We went through three villages of this nation near one another. They admired to see a Frenchman accompanying wildmen, which I understood by their exclamations. I thought I [had] growed lean [enough] to take such [a] little voyage, but the way seemed tedious to all. The racket[47] [was] always with the feet, and sometimes with the hands, which seemed to me hard to endure; yet have I not complained. At the parting of the slaves, I made my bundle light as the rest. We found snows in few places, saving where the trees made a shadow, which hindered the snow to thaw, which made us carry the rackets with our feet, and sometime with the hands. After ten days [we completed our] march through a country covered with water, and where also are mountains and great plains. In those plains we killed stags and a great many turkeys.

Thence we came to a great river,[48] a mile wide, which was not frozen, which made us stay there ten or twelve days, making skiffs of the rind of a walnut tree. We made good cheer and wished to stay there longer. We made three skiffs to hold three men and one to hold two.

We embarked though there were ice in many places, and yet [it was] no hindrance to us going small journeys, fearing least what should befall us. In four days we came to a lake[49] much frozen, covered in some places with ice by reason of the tossing of the wind, and the ground all covered with snow. Here we did our best to save us from the rigor of the air, and must stay fifteen days. The wildmen admired that the season of the year was so backward. At the end, the wind changed southerly, which made the lake free from ice and clear over all, the skirts of it without either snow or ice. There was such a thawing that [it] made the little brooks flow like rivers, which made us embark to wander that sweet sea.

The weather [was] lovely, the wind fair, and nature satisfied. Tending forwards, singing and playing, not considering the contrary weather past, [we] continued so six days upon the lake, and rested the nights ashore. The more we proceeded on our journey, the more pleasant [was the] country, and warmer.

Ending the lake, we entered into a beautiful sweet river,[50] a stone-cast wide. After [the] half a day we rid on it, we are forced to bring both bark and equipage upon our backs to the next stream of that river.[51] This done above twenty times, hauling our boats after us all laden, we went up that river at least thirty or forty leagues. At last [it] brought us to a lake of some nine miles in length.[52] Being come to the highest place of the lake, we landed and hid our boats far enough in the woods, took our bundles.

We were three days going through a great wilderness where was no wood, not so much as would make us fire. The thickened flour did serve us instead of meat, mingling it with water. We forded many little rivers by swimming and sailing our arms, which we put upon some sticks tied together of such wood as that desolate place could afford, to keep them from the wet. The evening we came on the side of a violent river, upon which we made bridges of trees that we met to go over, we left this place after being there three days.

We went up that river in two days. There we killed stags. After we came to a mouth of another river, we made a little fort, where it was commanded by our captain to make no noise; they desired me to be very quiet, which I observed strictly. After refreshment, we embarked, though unseasonably in the night, for to make some discovery. Some went one way, some another. We went a great way, but not far of our fort. The next day we meet altogether and made some council, where it was decreed that two should go to the furthermost part of a small river in a boat to make a discovery and see if there were tracks of people there, whilst the other nine should take notices of a village that they knowed to be nigh.

Because it was less danger to make there a discovery, the youngest of the company were picked to go into the river. We took the lightest boat. It was well, [because] in some places of the river there was not water enough to carry us, [and] we were fained to draw the boat after us. I believe not that ever a wildman went that way because of the great number of trees that stops the passage of the river. After we have gone the best part of the day, we found ourselves at the end of a small lake some four mile in length.

Seeing the woods were not so thick there as where we passed, we hid our boats in some bushes, taking only our arms along, tending on still to pretend some discovery. We scarce were in the middle of the lake when we perceive two persons going on the waterside at the other side of the lake; so my comrade gets him up a tree to discern better if there were any more. After he stayed there awhile, [he] comes and tells me that he thought they were two women and that we might go kill them.

"Doubtless," said I, "if they are women, the men are not afar from them, and we shall be forced to shoot. We are alone, and should run the hazard of two women for to be discovered? Our brethren also would be in danger that knows nothing. Moreover, it's night. What doest thou intend to do?"

"You say well," replies he. "Let us hide ourselves in the wood, for we cannot go down in the river in the nighttime. At break of day we will [go] back to our companions, where we will find them in the fort."

Here we came without any provisions, where we must lie under a rotten tree. That night it rained sadly. We were wet, but a natural exercise is good fire. We were in our boat early in the morning and with great diligence we came back better than we went up, for the river growed mighty high by reason of so much that fell of rain.

I will not omit a strange accident that befell us as we came. You must know that as we passed under the trees (as before mentioned) there laid on one of the trees a snake with four feet: her head very big like a turtle, the nose very small at the end, the neck of five thumbs wide, the body about two feet, and the tail of a foot and a half [and] of a blackish color, [all] into a shell small and round, with great eyes, her teeth very white but not long.[53] That beast was asleep upon one of the trees under which we were to go. Neither of us ever seeing such a creature, [we] were astonished. We could not tell what to do. It was impossible to carry our boat for the thickness of the wood. To shoot at her, we would be discovered; besides, it would trouble our company. At last we were resolved to go through at what cost soever, and as we were under that hellish beast she started as she awaked and with that fell down into our boat. There were herbs that served us from that dreadful animal. We durst not venture to kill her for fear of breaking of our boat. There is the question [of] who was most fearful. As for me, I quaked. Now seeing she went not about to do us hurt, and that she was as fearful [as we], we let her quiet, hoping shortly to land and to turn upside down our boat to be rid of such a devil. Then my comrade begun to call it, and before we were out of the little river our fear was over, so we resolved to bring her to the fort. When once arrived at the great river,[54] nothing [remained] but [to] cross it to be near our fort. But in the meanwhile a squirrel made us good sport for a quarter of an hour. The squirrel would not leap into the water, did not [but] run (being afraid of us) from one end of the boat to the other. Every time he came nearer, the snake opened her wide mouth and made a kind of a noise and rose up, having her two forefeet upon the side of the boat, which persuaded us that she would leave us. We leaned on that side of the boat, so with our oars thrusted her out. We, seeing her swim so well, hasted to kill her with our oars, which she had for her pains. The squirrel took the flight. So we went [on], longing to be with our comrades to tell them of what we have seen.

We found one of our company watching for us at the side of the wood, for they were in fear lest we should be taken and [had] expected us all night long. As for their part, they neither have

31

seen nor heard anything; wherefore [they] resolved to go further, but the news we brought them made them alter their resolution. We laid all night in our fort, where we made good cheer and great fires, fearing nothing, being far enough in the wood.

The next day before the breaking of the day we forded the river and, leaving our three boats in the wood, went afoot straight towards the place where we have seen the two persons. Before we came to the lake, we took notice of some fresh tracks, which made up look to ourselves. [We] followed the tracks, which brought us to a small river, where [we] no sooner came but we saw [a] woman laden with wood, which made us believe that some cottage or village was not afar off. The captain alone takes notice of the place whereabout the discovery was, who soon brought us [word] that there were five men and four women afishing. We wag[er]ed at this the safest [way would be] to come unaware upon them, and like starved dogs or wolves [we] devoured those poor creatures, who in a moment were massacred. What we got by this was not much — only stags' skins, with some girdles made of goat's hair of their own making. These were in great esteem among our wildmen. Two of ours goes to the cabin, which was made of rushes, where they found an old woman. They thought it charity to send her into the other world, with two small children whom also they killed. So we left that place, giving to the fishes their bodies. Everyone of us had his head, and my brother two, our share being considerable.

[We] went on along the river till we came to a small lake. Not desiring to be discovered, we found a fair road close by a wood, withtook ourselves out of it with all haste, and went towards a village. There we came by night, where we visited the wilderness to find out a secure place to hide ourselves, but [found] no conveniences. We into the wood in a very clear place. Here we laid down upon our bellies. We did eat, among other things, the fish we got in the cabin of the fishermen. After dispatching one of the company boldly into the village, being thirsty after eating, for here we had no water, [he] bring us [news] that all were very quiet. The great desire we had to catch and take made us to control the business.[55]

Early in the morning we came to the side of the wilderness, where we laid in an ambush, but could see nobody that morning. At two of the clock in the afternoon we see twenty men and women a great way from us. We went to the wood, whence we perceived many at work in the fields. At evening [they] passed by very nigh us, but they neither see nor perceived us. They went to cut wood. Whilst they were at work there comes four men and three women that took notice of our ambush. This we could not avoid, so were forced to appear, to their ruin. We took the three women and killed two men. The other two thought to escape but were stayed with our pieces. The other two that were aworking would run away, but one was taken. The other escaped. The news was brought over all those parts.

Thence we runned away with our four prisoners and the four new heads with all speed. The women could not go fast enough, and therefore [we] killed them after they went a whole night. Their corpses we throwed into the river. Here we found a boat, which served us to go over. We marched all that day without any delay. Being comed to an open field we hid ourselves in bushes till the next day. We examined our prisoners, who told us no news. None could understand them, although many Huron words were in their language. In this place we perceived two men ahunting afar off. We thought [it] not convenient to discover ourselves, lest we should be discovered and [forced to] pass our arm. We took another way, two before and the rest after the prisoners in the middle. We speedily went the rest of the day through a burned country, and the trees blown down with some great winds; the fire overcame all over fifteen leagues in length and ten in breadth.

We hid in the very middle of that country upon a fair sandy place where we could see three or four leagues off round about us, and being secure, we made the prisoners sing, which is their acconroga[56] before death. There we made a little fire to make our kettle boil a turkey with some meal that was left. Seeing nobody pursued [us], we resolved to go thence before daylight to seek for more booty. We stayed fourteen nights before we turned back to the village, during which time we met with nothing, and having gone off [searching on] all sides with great pains without victuals, at last we came to kill two stags, but [they] did not suffice twelve of us. We were forced to gather the dung of the stags to boil it with the meat, which made all very bitter, but good stomach makes good savor. The hunger forced us to kill our prisoners, who were chargeable in eating our food, for want of which [we might] have eaten the[ir] flesh. So by that means we were freed from the trouble.

The next day we came near a village. At our coming we killed

33

a woman with her child. Seeing no more for us that way, we turned back again for fear of pursuing and resolved to go back to the first village; that was three days' journey. On the way we met with five and twenty or thirty men and women who discovered us, which made to go to it. They fought and defended themselves lustily, but no resisting to the strongest party, for our guns was a terror to them and made them give over. During the fight the women ran away. Five of the men were wounded with arrows and four escaped, but he that was sent with me at first to make a discovery was horridly wounded with two arrows and a blow of a club on the head. If he had stucked to it as we, he might proceed better. We burned him with all speed that he might not languish long [and] to put ourselves in safety. We killed two of them, and five prisoners we took, and came away [to] where we left out boats, where we arrived within two days, without resting or eating or drinking all that time, saving a little stag's meat.

We took all their booty, which was two sacks of Indian corn, stags' skins, some pipes, some red and green stones, and some tobacco in powder, with some small loaves of bread, and some girdles, garters, necklaces made of goat's hair, and some small coin of that country, some bows and arrows and clubs well wrought. The turns of their heads were of snake's skin with bears' paws.[57] The hair of some of them [was] very long, and all proper men.

We went on the other side of the river the soonest we could and came to our fort. After we looked about us, lest we should be surprised, and preceiving nothing, we went about to get meat for our want, and then to sleep. At midnight we left that place. Six of us took a boat, five another, and two the little one. We row the rest of the night with all strength, and the breaking of the day hid ourselves in very long rushes, and our boats. The little boat went at the other side of the river; those hid it in the wood. One of them went up a tree to spy about in case he could perceive anything, to give notice to his comrade, and he was to come within sight of us to warn us. We were in great danger going down the stream of that river in the nighttime. We had trouble enough to carry all our baggage without the least noise.

Being come to the end of the river, which empties itself into a lake of some eight or nine leagues in compass, we went into a small river to kill salmons; indeed we took [a] great many with staves, and so sturgeons, of which we made provision for a long while. At last finding ourselves out of all fear and danger, we went freely ahunting about the lake, where we tarried three days, and two of our company met with two women that runned away from the Sanontins'[58] country, which is of the Iroquois nation. Those poor creatures, having taken so much pains to set themselves at liberty to go [to] their native country, found themselves beset in a greater slavery than before, they being tied [and] brought to us.

The next day we went from thence with the five prisoners and the twenty-two heads. So much for the littleness of our boats as for the weight, we had to put upon them, being in danger, which made us make the more haste to the place where we intended to make new boats. For nine days we went through dangerous places, which were like so many precipices with horrible falling of waters. We were forced to carry our boats after the same manner as before, with great pains.

We came at last to a lake[59] where we contrived other boats, and there we parted our acquired booty, and then each had care of his own. We ordered the biggest boat should hold four men and two prisoners, the next three men and the two women that last were taken, the third should hold three and the other prisoner. My brother and I had a man and a woman, with four heads, to our share, and so the rest accordingly without dispute or noise.

We wandered several days on that lake. It was a most delightful place, and a great many islands. Here we killed [a] great many bear. After, we came to a most delightful place for a number of stags that were there, thence into a straight river, from thence were forced to make many carriages through many stony mountains, where we made several traps for castors. We took above two hundred castors there, and fleeced off the best skins. There were some skins so well dressed that [they] held the oil of bear as pure bottles. During that time we met several huntsmen of our country, so we heard news of our friends. Only our father was not yet [re]turned from the wars against the French and Algonquins.

We left our small boats that were purposely confected for our hunting and took our great boats that could carry us and all our luggage. We went up the same river again, not without great labor. At last, with much ado, we arrived to the landing place, where we made a stay of four days.

35

Many Iroquois women came, and among others my two sisters, that received me with great joy [and] with a thousand kindnesses and gifts, as you may think. I gave them the two heads that I had, keeping the woman for my mother to be her slave. There was nothing but singing and dancing out of mere joy of our safe return. I had twenty castors for my share, with two skins full of oil of bear, and another full of oriniack and stag's grease. I gave to each of my sisters six stags' skins to make them coats. I kept the grease for my mother, to whom [it] is convenient to give what is necessary for the family. We made our slaves carry all our booty, and went on to little journeys through woods with ease because the woods were not thick, and the earth very fair and plain. All the way the people made much of me till we came to the village, and especially my two sisters that in all they showed their respects, giving me meat every time we rested ourselves, or painting my face, or greasing my hair, or combing my head. At night they took the pains to pull off my stockings, and when I [had] supped, they made me lay down by them and covers me with their coats, as if the weather had been cold. This voyage being ended: I came to this village twice with fear and terror, and the third time notwithstanding with joy and contentment. As we came near the village, a multitude of people came to meet us with great exclamations, and for the most part for my sake bidding me to be cheerful and qualifying me dodcon — that is, devil — being of great veneration in that country to those that shows any valor. Being arrived within half a league of the village, I showed great modesty, as usually warriors use to do. The whole village prepares to give the scourge to the captives, as you heard before, under which I myself was once to undergo. My mother comes to meet me, leaping and singing. I was accompanied with both my sisters. She takes the woman slave that I had and would not [allow] that any should meddle with her, but my brother's prisoner, as the rest of the captives, were soundly beaten. My mother accepted my brother's two heads. My brother's prisoner was burned that same day. The day following I received the salary of my booty, which was of porcelain, necklaces, tons of heads, pendants, and girdles.

There was but banqueting for a while. The greatest part of both young men and women came to see me, and the women [brought] the choicest of meats and a most dainty and cordial bit, which I go to tell you [about]: it is the best that is among

36

them. First, when the corn is green, they gather so much as need requireth, of which leaves they preserve the biggest leaves for the subject that follows. A dozen more-or-less old women meets together alike, of whom the greatest part wants teeth, and see-eth not a jot, and their cheeks hangs down like an old hunting dog, their eyes full of water and bloodshot. Each takes an ear of corn, and puts it in their mouths, which is properly as milk, chaws it, and when their mouths are full spits it out in their hands, which possibly they wash not once [in] one year. Their hands are white inside by reason of the grease that they put to their hair, and rubbing of it with the inside of their hands, which keeps them pretty clean, but the outside in the rinkness of their wrinkled hands there is a quarter of an ounce of filth and stinking grease. So, their hands being full of that mince meat minced with their gums, [they] fill a dish. So, they chaw chestnuts; then they mingle this with bear's grease or oil of flower (in French we call it tourne sol)[60] with their hands. So, [having] made a mixture, they tie the leaves at one end, and make a hodgepot and cover it with the same leaves, and tie the upper end so that what is within those leaves becomes a round ball, which they boil in a kettle full of water or broth made of meat or fish. So, there is the description of the most delicious bit of the world. I leave you to taste of their salmagundy, which I hope to tell you [more of] in my following discourses of my other voyages in that country and others that I frequented [in] the span of ten years.[61]

To make a period of this, my little voyage. After I stayed awhile in this village — with all joy and mirth for feasts, dances, and plays; of mere gladness for our small victorious company's happy return — so after their heads had sufficiently danced, they begin to talk [of going] to war against the Hollanders. Most of us are treated again for the castors we bestowed on them. They resolve unanimously to go on their design.

Everything ready, we march along. The next day we arrived in a small borough of the Hollanders, where we masters them, without that those beer-bellies had the courage to frown at us, whether it was out of hope of lucre or otherwise. We with violence took the meat out of their pots, and opening their cupboards, we take and eat what we get. For drinking of their wine we were good fellows, [so] much so that they [the Iroquois] fought with swords among themselves, without the least offer of any misdeed to me. I drunk more then they, but more soberly, letting them make their quarrels without any notice.

The fourth day we come to Fort Orange,[62] where we were very well received, or rather our castors, everyone courting us. [There] was nothing but prunes and raisins and tobacco plentifully, and all for "Ho ho," which is thanks, adding, "Niauounha," thank you. We went from house to house.

I went into the fourth with my brother, and have not yet been known a French[man], but a French soldier of the fourth speaks to me in Iroquois language and demanded if I was not a stranger, and did verily believe I was French, for all that I was all dabbed over with painting and greased. I answered him in the same language, "No." Then he speaks in swearing, desiring me how I fell in the hands of those people. Hearing him speak French, amazed, I answered him, for which he rejoiced very much, as [did] I. He embraces me; he cries out with such stir that I thought him senseless. He made a shame for all that I was wild; but, to blush red, I could be no redder than what they painted me before I came there.

All came about me, French as well as Dutch, everyone making [me] drink out of the bottle, offering me their service, but my time yet was not out, so that I wanted not their service. Only rumor of my being a Frenchman was enough; the Flemish women drawed me by force into their house, striving who should give — one bread, [an]other meat, to drink and to eat, and tobacco. I wanted not for those of my nation Iroquois, who followed me in a great squadron through the streets, as if I had been a monster in nature or a rare thing to be seen.

I went to see the governor, and [he] talked with me a long time. I told him the life that I lead, of which he admired. He offered me to buy me from them at what price soever, or else should save me, which I accepted not, for several reasons. The one was for not to be beholding to them, and the other being loathsome to leave such kind of good people, for then I began to love my new parents that were so good and so favorable to me. The third reason was to watch a better opportunity for to retire to the French, rather than make that long circuit which after I was forced to do to retire to my country more than two thousand leagues [away]; and being that it was my destiny to discover many wild nations, I would not strive against destiny. I remitted myself to fortune and adventure of time as a thing ordained by God for His greatest glory, as I hope it will prove.

Our treatise being done, overladened with booties abundantly, we put ourselves in the way that we came to see again our village, and to pass that winter with our wives and to eat with them our cagamite in peace, hoping that nobody should trouble us during our wintering, and also to expect or find our fathers returning home. Leaving that place, many cried to see me among a company of wolves, as that soldier told me [who] knowed me the first hour, and the poor man made the tear come to my eye. The truth is, I found many occasions to retire for to save me, but have not yet suffered enough to have merited my deliverance.

In two days' journey[63] we were returned to our cabins, where everyone of us rendered himself to his dearest kindred or master. My sisters were charged [with the distribution] of porcelain, of which I was sure not to fail [to get more than my share], for they were too liberal to me, and I towards them.

I was not fifteen days returned but that nature itself reproached me to lead such a life, remembering the sweet behavior and mildness of the French, and [I] considered with myself what end should I expect of such a barbarous nation, enemy to God and to man. The great effect that the Flemings showed me and the little space there was from us [made me wonder]: can I make that journey [in] one day?[64] The great belief that the people had in me should make them not to mistrust me, and by that I should have greater occasion to save me without fear of being pursued. All those reasons made me deliberate to take a full resolution without further delay of saving myself to the Flemings, for I could be at no safety among such a nation full of revenge, if in case the French and Algonquins defeats that troop of theirs. Then what spite they will have; [they] will revenge it on my bones, for where is no law, no faith. To undertake to go to the French — I was once interrupted — nor have I had a desire to venture again for the second time. I should delight to be broiled as before in pitiful torments? I repented of a good occasion I let slip, finding myself in the place with offers of many to assist me, but he that is of a good resolution must be of strong hopes of what he undertakes, and if the dangers were considered which may be found in things of importancy, you ingenious men would become cooks. Finally, without expecting my father's return, putting away all fear and apprehension, I constituted to deliver myself from their hands, at whatever rate it would come to.

For this effect, I purposed to fain to go ahunting about the borough, and for to dissemble the better I cut long sticks to make handles for a kind of a sword they use, that thereby they might not have the least suspicion. One day I took but a simple hatchet and a knife, if occasion presented to cut some tree, and to have more defence, if unhappily I should be recountered, to make them believe that I was lost in the woods. Moreover, as the whole nation took me for proud, having always great care to be garnished with procelain, [not thinking] that I would fly away like a beggar, a thing very unworthy, in this deliberation I ventured: I inquired my brother if he would keep me company; I knowed that he never thought, seeing that he was courting a young woman who, by report of many, was bastard to a Flemish.* I had no difficulty to believe, seeing that the color of her hair was much more whiter than that of the Iroquois. Nevertheless, she was of a great family. I left them to their love. In short, without any provision, I took journey through the forests, guided by fortune. No difficulty if I could keep the highway which is greatly beaten with the great concourse of the people that come and go to trade with the Flemings. But to avoid all encounters, I must prolong [my escape] afar off. So, being assisted by the best hope of the world, I made all diligence in the meanwhile that my mother nor kindred should [not] mistrust me in the least.

I made my departure at eight of the clock in the morning the 29th October, 1653.[65] I marched all that journey without eating, being accustomed to that; without staying, I continued my course at night. Before the breaking of the day, I found myself uncapable because of my feebleness and faintness of spirit for want of food and repose after such constraint. But the fear of death makes virtue of necessity. The morning commanded me to go, and its fair cold air, which [was] somewhat advantageous to keep [me] more cheerful. Finally, the resolution rescuing my courage, at four of the clock at evening the next day[66] I arrived in a place full of trees cut, which made me look to myself, fearing to aboard the habitation, though my design was such. It is a strange thing that to save this life they abhor what they wish and desire that which they apprehend. Approaching nigher and nigher, I perceived an opening that was made by cutting of wood, where was one man cutting still wood.

I went nearer and called him. Incontinently leaves his work

---

*That is, Radisson knew that his Indian brother would not consider going along.

Curves run from summer to summer approximately.

Lawsuit 1665
Meeting with Eng. Comr's 1665
London Plague 1665
War with Holland 1666
Stoppage of the Thames 1666
"Eaglet" and "Nonsuch" 1668

Peace with Iroquois – Nov.
Founding of Onon. Mis. – July
Escape from Onon. Mis. – Mar.
Dollard Massacre – May

A 1652 53 54 55 56 57 58 59 60 61 62 63 64 65
Cap. Onon. Miss. Rest Sup. Dol. Mas. Sto.

B 1652 53 54 55 56 57 58 59 60 61 62 63 64 65
Cap. Onon. Miss. Rest Sup. Dol. Mas. Sto.

C 1652 53 54 55 56 57 58 59 60 61 62 63 64 65
Cap. Un. Vacant Onon. Miss. Rest Sup. Dol. Mas. Sto.

D 1652 53 54 55 56 57 58 59 60 61 62 63 64 65
Cap. Miss. Rest Onon. Sup. Dol. Mas. Sto.

Page 33 of original manuscript. See pages 42 to 45 of present text of Quebeck being there arrived they, that they of search diligently by meanes possible for to end my voyage, and render me the service very actuall parseits and meanes proper at least for an occasion to goe by some by shallops and small boats of the wildernesse when went up as far as the french habitation there to joyne with the Algontins and Montmorancies to warre against the Iroquois, from all times as their histories mention their enemies, their Iroquois et our father to him and assuredly very exact, for as much as I know, and many others have remembred. I remounted into one of their shallops, and those of wind, for 80 98 in two dayes came to Quebeck, tho I was well in place of french. I mean not to let you the great joy received in me to see their, I took that never thought to be cured, and they in like manner to me thought I was dead long time. In my absence peace was made between the french and the Iroquois, which in my greater I stayd not long in a peace, the yeare before the french began a new plantation in those verse from by of the Iroquois, which is distant from the Low Iroquois country some foure score leagues, and were prisoners and been in the warre of that country, should be great acccompt of as I mentioned in my former voyage, which made me have mind to goe thither, agame by y reason peace was concluded among them. And I must confesse, once those poore people contrary to moreover nothing was to be feared by reason of the great distance which causes a difference in their speech, yet they understand one another. At that very time the Reverend fathers / Jesuits

Page 59 of original manuscript. See Page 79 of present text

as for, the difficulties of the wayes: for this reason the thought fires fitter and more faithfull for the discouery that he was to make. he plainly follow me hunnes. Knowing it hough his see my selfe in a boat. there weare seuerall companies of fishermen expected from seuerall places, because they promise the yeare before and take the aduantage of the spring thawes to because the Irocquois who are allwayes in wait for to destroy them and the rivers, it is by reason of the meltening of the great snows, it is onely that times, for that runs no passibility was to come that way, because for the swift streames that runs in summer. in other places the want of water to that no boat can come though, we soone sees the performances of those people. for a company came to the 3 rivers where we weare. they fancies that another company was driues att Mountroyall, and that two more weare to come shortly one to the three rivers the other to fabrique a zurer of Tadousack who a resued to th

two dayes after, they diuide themselues because of the scant of prouision, for if they weare together they could not haue victualls enough. many goes and comes to Quebuc for to know the resolution of Mr Gouerns who together with the Fathers thought fitt to find a company of french, to be my back of possibility of wildmen the next yeare, or others being that it is the best manna of the Countrey by w'ch the inhabitants doe subsist and make the french resolue to come there and goe back loaden to Quebuc for the traffique of beuers.

that time we made feasts at a high rate. So we refreshed our selves from our labo.
in that time we tooke notice that the budds of trees began to spring wch made us
to make more hast and begone. we went up ye River eight dayes till we came
to a Nation called pouoronatenick and matouenock, that is, the Scratchers
there we gott some Indian meale and Corne from those two nations wch lasted us,
till we came to the first landing Isle. There we weare well received againe.
we made guifts to the Elders to encourage the yong people to bring us downe to
the ffrench, but mightily mistaken ffor they would reply, should you bring us
to be killed. The Iroquoits are every where about the River, and undoubtedly will
destroy us if we goe downe; and afterwards our wives and those that stayed behinde
be wise breethren and offer not to goe downe this yeare to the ffrench. Lett us keep
our lives. we made many private suits but all in vaine. that vexed us most
that we had given away most of our merchandises, and swapped a great deale for
Castors. moreover they made no great harvest, being but newly there, besides they
weare no great huntsmen. our Journey was broaken till ye next yeare, and must
per force. yt summer I went a hunting, and my brother stayed where he was welcome
and putt up a great deale of Indian Corne that was given him. he intended to

Page 73 of original manuscript. See page 97 of present text

for our use. the weather proved in every way in good correspondence one to the another, and
sent ambassadors to the nations that used to goe downe to ye french, in hopes
them the more and made us hope that yeare to a greater pleasure, saying that
my brother fell into the falling sickness, and many yeares sorry for it that
for occured easily off so long stay in a new discovered countrey, and the phisissians constituted unto it. there is nothing comparable to exercise, that is only remedy
of such diseases. after he languished a while he gave him his health againe. the
sence that every one has to goe downe to the french made them earnestly looke out
for actors. they have not so many there as in the north part, so in the beginning of
sowing many came to our side, there weare no less, those few honors
when that weare willing to venture themselves. the come that my brother kept
so as a world of service. the wild men brought a quantity of ... in a byeld
when we weare ready to part here comes strong news of the great ...
of the hurons, in others, thought would put off the voyage. there was a council
held, and most of them weare against the going downe to the french saying that
the iroquois weare to leave this yeare and the best way was to stay till the ...
yeare. and now the enemy seeing himself frustrate of his expectation would not
stay longer, thinking there of that we weare resolute never more to goe downe
and

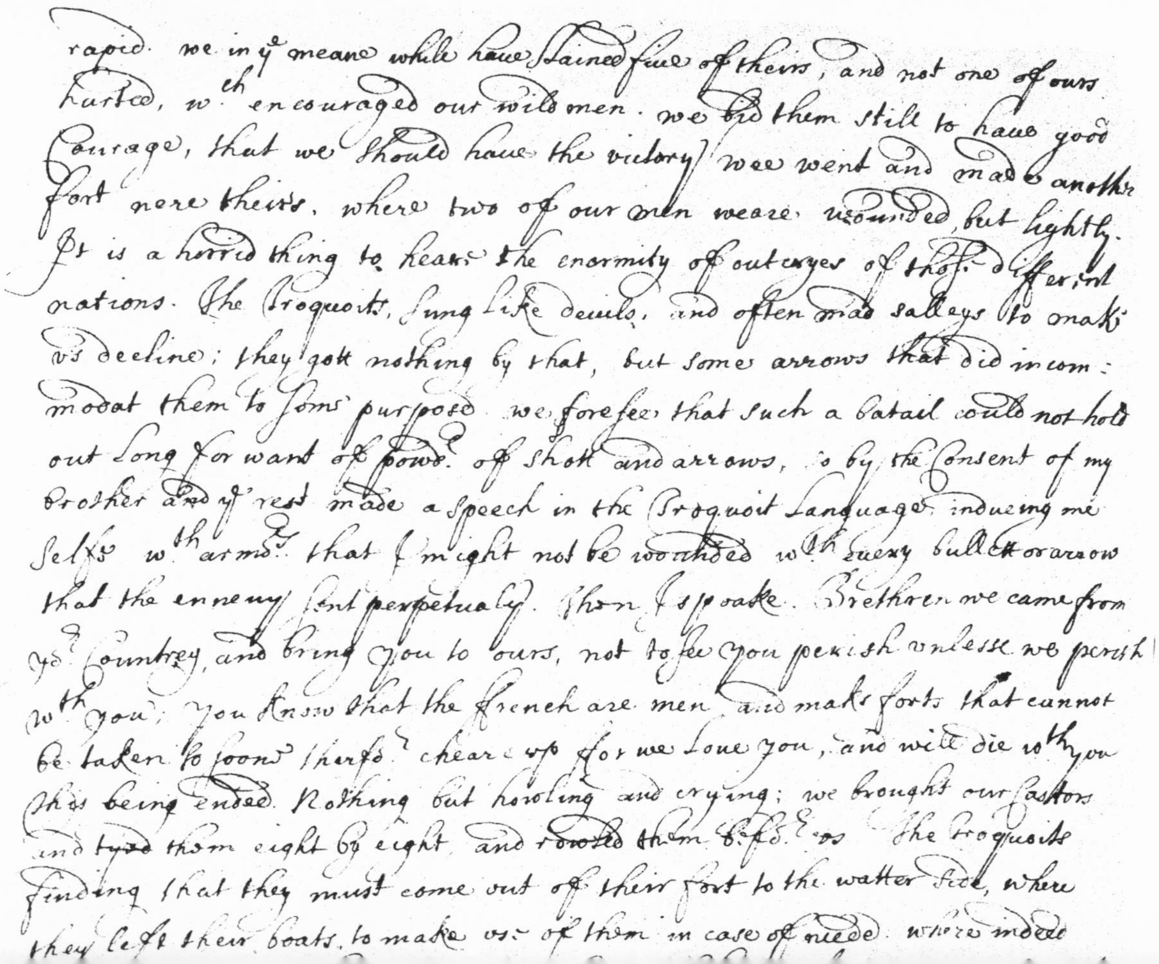
rapid. we in ye meane while have slained five of theirs, and not one of ours
hurted, wch encouraged our wildmen. we bid them still to have good
Courage, that we should have the victory. wee went and made another
fort nere theirs, where two of our men weare wounded, but lightly.
It is a horrid thing to heare the enormity of outcryes of those different
nations. The Iroquoits sung like devils, and often made salleys to make
us decline; they gott nothing by that, but some arrows that did incom-
modat them to some purpose. we foresee that such a batail could not hold
out long for want of powd. of shott and arrows, so by the Consent of my
brother and ye rest made a speech in the Iroquoit language, induceing me
selfe wth armes that I might not be wounded wth every bullett or arrow
that the ennemy sent perpetualy. Then I spoake. Brethren we came from
yor Countrey, and bring you to ours, not to see you perish unlesse we perish
wth you; you know that the French are men and make forts that cannot
be taken so soone. therfore cheare up for we love you, and will die wth you
this being ended. Nothing but howling and crying; we brought our castors
and tyed them eight by eight, and rowled them &c. &c. The Iroquoits
finding that they must come out of their fort to the watter side, where
they left their boats to make use of them in case of neede. where indeed

Page 78 of original manuscript. See page 104 of present text

kettles, broaken guns and rusty hatchets, they being gone, our postage
was free, so we made hast and endevored to come to our Journeys end
were to make the more hast, some boats went downe that sayd stream
without making any Carriag, hopeing to gett to the enemy, but the God
Looke was that whereas my brother was a boat turned in the torrent being
seaven of them togetther weare in great danger, for God was mercifull to
gue them strength to save themselves to the great admiration, for gen
can hardly do well in such a spedd when they came to lund they cutt
rocks. my brother lost his booke of annotations & by last yeare; of our
being in those foraigne nations. we lost neuer a caløe, but may be some
Gett firing & who left love all show off his life. we weare powerfreans
months in our voyage, without seeing any thing but goe from river to river
we mett seuerall sorts of people, we conuersed with them being among
for alliance with them, so the fination of some of those we went in to great
trust that sends it safe, in how where the purkous with some Ottauak, are
the wild men that had had warrs with them, has achived, there is not great
coferenc in their language, as we weare told, this nation has warrs
against those of forked nuss, it is so called because it has his bras-
ches, the ones scatters the west, the other towards the fourth
with

Page 81 of original manuscript. See page 109 of present text

mens heads that they killed at the first fight. but they left eleven of theirs in the place, & was many more that went wounded. they went straight to their Country, & we did a great service to the Islanders of our wild men, and left us not all their journey, as we heard afterwards. they went away if not today, and we stayed at home att ye next years. My brother and I considered whether we should do once what we were afeard of us, and because we had not a full and short discovery no. it was that we have not been in the Bay of the North, not knowing anything out by report of of wild Indians, we would make no mention of it, for fear that they wild men should tell us a lie. we would have made a discovery off it our selves; and have an assurance before we should is over anything of it.

The end of ye Anecdotical Voyage which is ye third Voyage.

The spring following following we were in hopes to meet with some Company, having been so fortunate the years before. now during the winter whether it was that my brother remember to his wife what we had seen in our voyage, and what we further intended, or how it came to passe it was known. so much that the he fellyth went desirous to find out away how they might get downe the Bastos from the Bay of ye North.

Page 104 of original manuscript. See page 139 of present text

prefer to kill them we should save and keep their lives, telling them for our brethren and to testify that we shot of all our artillery with was of...

hollow guns, and drew our swords, and long knives to our defence, if need should require to put the men in such a terror that they knew not what one do to our own or stay. we throw a handfull of powder in the fire, to make a greater noise and smoke. our song being finished, we began to our teeth to work...

we had show a kind of grace, much like one it grew in the water...

itself in such sorts Almighty full of ignorance and ignorance of those poore people who knoweth him not they have a particular way together...

that grain, two ladies about and two sticks by so they got of ease brains and...

get the corn out of it, their roots being full they bring it to a fit place to dry it...

and that is their food, for the most part of the year, and also ears of them, for each man a handfull of what they put in the pot, that swells so much that it can suffice a man, after the feast was over, there came two maidens bring my mess with all...

to smoke, the one the pipes, the other the fire, gave offered first to one of them...

that took some, by the, when he smoked he bid them give it to, this being...

Done

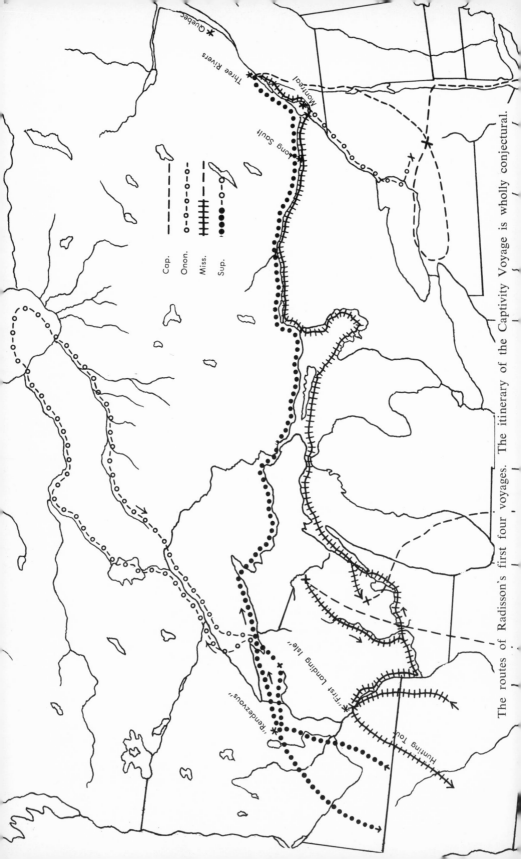

The routes of Radisson's first four voyages. The itinerary of the Captivity Voyage is wholly conjectural.

and comes to me, thinking I was Iroquois. I said nothing to him to the contrary. I kept him in that thought, promising him to treat him with all my castors at his house, if he should promise me there should be none of my brother Iroquois there, by reason we must be liberal to one another. He assured me there was none there. I told him that my castors was hidden and that I should go for it [on] the morrow.

So satisfied, [he] leads me to his cabin and sets before me what good cheer he had. Not desiring to lose time, because the affair concerned me much, I told him I was a savage but that I lived awhile among the French and that I had something [of] valeur[67] to communicate to the governor, that he would give me a piece of paper and ink and pen. He wondered very much to see that what he never saw before done by a wildman. He charges himself with my letter, with promise that he should [not] tell anybody of my being there and to return the soonest he could possible, having but two little miles to Fort Orange.

In the meanwhile of his absence, she [the white man's wife] shows me good countenance as much as she could, hoping of a better imaginary profit by me. She asked me if we had so much liberty with the French women [as] to lie with them, but I had no desire to do anything; seeing myself so insnared at death's door amongst the terrible torments, [I] must show a better countenance to a worse game. In the night we heard some wildmen singing, which redoubled my torments and apprehension, which enticed me to declare to that woman that my nation would kill [me] because I loved the French and the Flemings more than they and that I resolved hereafter to live with the Flemings. She, perceiving my reason, hides me in a corner behind a sack or two of wheat. Nothing was to me but fear.

I was scarcely there an hour in that corner but the Flemings came, four in number. Whereof that Frenchman [who] had known me the first presently gets me out and gives me a suit that they brought purposely to disguise me, if I chanced to light upon any of the Iroquois. I took leave of my landlady and landlord; yet [it] grieved me much that I had nothing to bestow upon them but thanks, being that they were very poor, but not so much as I.

I was conducted to Fort Orange, where we had not encounter in the way, where I have had the honor to salute the governor, who spoke French, and by his speech [I] thought him a Frenchman. The next day he caused another habit to be given me, with shoes and stockings and also linen. A minister that was a Jesuit[68] gave me [a] great offer, also a merchant to whom I shall ever have infinite obligations, although they were satisfied when I came to France at Rochelle. I stayed three days inclosed in the fort, and hidden.

Many came there [after I had gone] to search [for] me, and [I] doubt not but my [Indian] parents were of the party. If my father had been there [soon enough], he would [have] venture[d] hard [after me], and no doubt but [he] was troubled at it, and so was my mother: my parents who loved me as if I were their own natural son. My poor sisters cried out and lamented through the town of the Flemings, as I was told; they called me by my name, for they came there the third day after my flight. Many Flemings wondered and could not perceive how those could love me so well, but the pleasure caused it, as it agrees well with the Roman proverb "Do as they do."

I was embarked by the governor's order, after taking leave and thanks for all his favors. I was conducted to Menada, a town fair enough for a new country, where after some three weeks I embarked on one of their ships for Holland, where we arrived after many boisterous winds and ill weather, and after some six weeks' sail and some days we landed at Amsterdam [on] the 4th or 7th of January, 1654.[69] Some days after, I embarked myself for France and came to Rochelle well and safe, [but] not without blowing [on] my fingers many times, as well as I done before I arrived in Holland.

I stayed till spring, expecting the transport of a ship for New France.[70]

The 15th day of March,[71] I embarked* in a fisher boat to go for Percé island, which is six score leagues off Quebec, being there arrived the 7th of May. I search diligently [for] the means possible for to end my voyage and render myself near my natural parents and country people. At last I found an occasion to go by some shallops and small boats of the wilderness, which went up as far as the French habitation, there to join with the Algonquins and Mountaignaies to war against the Iroquois. From all times, as their histories mentions, their memory is their chroni-

*Back to North America.

42

cle for it* from father to son, and assuredly very excellent, for as much as I know, and many other has remarked. I embarked into one of their shallops, and had the wind favorable for us NE. In five days [we] came to Quebec, the first dwelling place of the French. I mean not to tell you the great joy I perceived in me to see those persons that I never thought to see more, and they in [a] like manner with me thought I was dead long since. In my absence, peace[72] was made between the French and the Iroquois, which was the reason I stayed not long in a place.[73]

---

*Conjecture: "it" refers either to the intermittent war with the Iroquois, or else to the course taken by the shallops to Quebec.

ONONDAGA VOYAGE

The second voyage made in the upper country of the Iroquois.

THE YEAR BEFORE [1656], the French began a new plantation[1] in the upper country of the Iroquois, which is distant from the low Iroquois country some four score leagues,[2] where I was prisoner and been in the wars of that country. I took great notice of it, as I mentioned in my foremost voyage, which made me have mind to go thither again, by the reason peace was concluded among them. For I must confess I loved those poor people entirely well. Moreover, nothing was to be feared by reason of the great distance which caused a difference in their speech; yet they understood one another.

At that very time the reverend Fathers Jesuits embarked themselves for a second time to dwell there and teach Christian doctrine. I offered myself to them and was (as their custom is) kindly accepted. I prepare myself for the journey, which was to be in June.

You must know that the Hurons were contained in the article of peace, but not the Algonquins,[3] which caused more difficulty; those Iroquois who embarked us durst not come down [to] Three Rivers, [from] where the French should embark, because it is the dwelling place of the Algonquins. To remedy this, the French and the barbarians that were to march must come to Montreal, the last French habitation, in shallops.

It will not be amiss to leave the following of the voyage for to repeat the reasons why those poor Hurons ventured themselves into their hands who have been enemy one to another all their lifetime (and that naturally). You must know that the Hurons (so called by the French) have a bush of hair rised up artificially upon the heads like to a cock's comb. Those people, I say, were twenty or thirty thousand, by report of many, not 20 years ago. Their dwelling is near the Upper Lake,[4] so called by name of the French. That people tell us of their pedigree; from the beginning their habitation [was] above the lake many years ago, and as they increased, many, great many, began to search out another country. To tend towards the south they durst not, for the multitude of people that was there, and besides, some of their own nations had [turned] against them.[5] Then [they] resolved to go to the North parts, for westward there was much water, which (as the report then) was without end, [and] moreover, many inhabitants monstrous for the greatness of body. We will speak about this in another place more at large,[6] where [I] will give an exact account of what came to our knowledge during our travels, and the land we have discovered since. If [they had gone] eastward, they had found the Iroquois, who possessed some parts of the River of Canada,[7] and their dwelling was where Quebec is situated, and about that place, and at the upper end of Montmorency, two leagues from Quebec, where was a great village, where now is seen a desolate country, that is, for woods and forests, nor [were there] more nor less than what small bushes [could be found] nigh the Three Rivers side, in the place called the Cape de Magdelaine. It's such a country that the French calls it "the burned country" twenty miles about, and in many places the same is [now] to be seen where there were forests. So, seeing that the North regions were not so peopled, they pursued the route that way and for the purpose provided themselves provisions for a twelve-month to live.

With all their equipage [they] embarked in the beginning of the spring. After that they passed great ways, coming to a lake which conducts them into a great river,[8] which river leads them to a great extent of salt water.[9] They, being good fishers, wants no fish. They coasted this great water for a long time, finding always some little nation whose language they knew not, [and] having great fear of one another. Finally, finding but a fearful country full of mountains and rocks, they made great boats that might hold some thirty men, to traverse with more assurance the great bay, for to decline from the tediousness of the highway which they must toe, having but small boats. Whence they came to a country full of mountains of ice, which made us believe that they descended to the golden arm.[10] Fearing the winter should come on, they made sails wherein they made great way when the wind was behind; otherwise they could not make use of their

46

sails. Many of their boats were lost, but still [they] went on, hoping of a better country. They wandered so many moons with great danger and famine.

They began to miss such plenty as they used [to have].

As last [they] got out and, coasting the skirts of the sea,[11] enters as it were into a country where the summer begins again. They were encouraged to greater hopes, insomuch that the[se] poor people became (as to say it so) from their first origin to lead another life. Being only conducted by their imaginary idea, or instinct of nature, for steering, they knewed nothing but towards the root of the sun, and likewise by some stars.

Finally the coast brings them to the great St. Lawrence, River of Canada, knowing not that it was a river till they came just opposite against the mounts of our Blessed Lady, where they then perceived [themselves] betwixt two lands. Albeit that [the] little summer was passed and that the season of the year [was] growing on somewhat sharp, which made them think to search for winter, [they] mounted always up the river.

Finding one side most beautiful for the eye, they passed it over and planted their cabins in many parts, by reason of the many streams there flowing with quantity of fish, whereof they made a good store for their wintering.

After a while upon their undertaking, they made cognizance [with] and commerced with the highlanders inhabitants of that country, who gave them notice that there were a nation higher [up the St. Lawrence] who should understand them, being that they were great travelers, that they should go on the other side and there should find another river, named Tadousac.

Seeing the winter drawing on, they made a fort and sent to discover the said place a band of their men to Tadousac. They find a nation that understands them not more than the first, but by chance; some [had] escaped the hands of their enemy the Iroquois, and doubts that there is great difference of language between the Iroquois and the Hurons. They were heard.

Further you must note that near the Lake of the Hurons, some 40 leagues eastward, there is another lake[12] belonging to the nation of the Castors, which is 30 miles about. This nation have no other traffic nor industry than huntsmen. They used to go once a year to the furthest place of the Lake of the Hurons to sell their castors for Indian corn, for some color made of nettles, for sacks, and such things, for which they were curious enough. So,

47

coming back to their small lake again, those merchandises were transported to a nation beyond that lake towards [the] N-NE. That nation [in turn] had commerce with a people called the Whitefish,[13] which is northwest to the Three Rivers some hundred and fifty leagues in the land. That nation had intelligence with the Saguenays, who are those that liveth about Tadousac. The two nation have great correspondency with one another because of their mutual language, saving that each one have a particular letter and accent.

Finding that nation of the Castors, who for the most part understands the Huron idiom, they* conversed together and were supplied with meat by that wandering nation that lives only by what they may or can get. Contrariwise, the Hurons are seditious. We shall speak of them more amply in its place.

So those miserable adventurers had aid during the winter, who doubtless should suffer without this favor. They consulted together often, seeing themselves reinforced with such a succor of people for to make wars against the Iroquois.

The next spring their war was conducted with success, for they chased the Iroquois out of their country, which they lost some winters before. They [the Hurons] march up to the furthest part of Lake Champlain to know if that was their foremost dwelling, but they speak no further of it. Those Iroquois so wander up and down and spread themselves, as you have heard, to Lake Ontario, of which I will after make mention. I heard all this from Frenchmen that knowed the Huron speech better than I myself, and after I heard it from the wildmen. It's strange—if it be so as the French [tell it], as [the] wildmen do already—that those people [the Hurons] should have made a circuit of that little world.

The Iroquois being put out of that country of Quebec, the Hurons and Algonquins made themselves masters in it; that is to say, they went up above Montmorency after they left the place of their wintering, which was over against Tadousac, at the height of the Chaudiere[14] (so called in French). After many years, they returned to live at the gap of their lake,[15] which is two hundred leagues long and fifty or sixty leagues large. Those Hurons lived in a vast country that they found uninhabited, and they in a great number builded villages, and they multiplied very many.

---

*Referring to the Castors and the traveling Hurons, the latter apparently having moved on to Castor country, though Radisson tells us nothing of the journey.

The Iroquois also got a great country, as much by sweetness as by force; they became warriors upon their own dispenses and cost. They multiplied so much, but they became better soldiers, as it's seen by the following of this discourse.

The Hurons then inhabited most advantageously in that place, for [there was] an abundance of deers and stags, from whence they have the name since of Staggy. It's certain that they have had several other callings, according as they have builded villages. Fishing they have in abundance in season of every kind; I may say, more than we have in Europe. In some places in this lake, where is an innumerable quantity of fish, in two hours they load their boat with as many as they can carry. At last [they] became so eminent strong that they were of a mind to fight against the neighboring nation.

Hearing that their sworn enemies the Iroquois retired towards the nation called Andasstoueronom,[16] which is beyond Lake Ontario between Virginia and that lake, they resolved to go and search them [out] for to war against them, but they shall find it to their ruin, which I can affirm and assure because the Iroquois in the most part of their speeches, which comes from father to son, says, "We Bears (for it's their name), whilst we scraped the earth with our claws for to make the wheat grow for to maintain our wives, not thinking that the Deer[17] shall leap over the lake to kill the Bear that slept, but they found that the Bear could scratch the Stag, for his head and legs are small to oppose." Such speeches have they commonly together, in such that they have had wars many years.

The Hollanders, being comed to inhabit Menada, furnished that nation with weapons by which means they became conquerors.[18] The French planters in New France came up to live among this nation; in effect they do live [there] now many years, but the ambition of the Fathers Jesuits [is] not willing to permit French families to go there for to converse the best to their profit, holding this pretext, that young men should frequent the wild women, so that the Christian religion by evil example could not be established. But the time came that they have forsook it themselves.

For a while after, the Iroquois came there [to] the number of seven hundred on the snow in the beginning of spring, where they make a cruel slaughter, as [in] the precedent years, where some ghostly fathers or brothers or their servants were consumed, taken or burnt, as their relation makes mention. This selfsame year [1649] they took prisoners of eleven or twelve thousand of those poor people [Hurons] in a village at sight of the Jesuits' fort, which had the name Saint, but that hour it might have the name of Fear. Here follows sickness, and famine also was got among those people flying from all parts to escape the sword. They found a more rude and cruel enemy, for some, after being taken, got their lives, but the hunger and their treachery made them kill one another, be it for booty or whatsoever. None escaped, saving some hundred came to Quebec to recover their first liberty, but contrary they found their end. So the Fathers left walls, wilderness, and all open wide to the enemy and came to Quebec.

With the rest of the poor fugitives they were placed in the wilderness near the habitation of Quebec, but [it] being not a convenient place, they were put to the Isle of Orleans, three leagues below Quebec, in a fort that they made with the succor of the French, where they lived some years, planting and sowing Indian corn for their nourishment and [making] greased robes of castors, of which grease the profit came to the Fathers the sum of ten thousand livres tournois[19] yearly. In this place they were catched when they least thought of it, not without subject of connivance, God knoweth. There were escaped that time about a hundred and fifty women and some twenty men, the rest all killed, taken, and brought away, of which for the most part were set at liberty in the country of their enemy, where they found a great number of their kindred and relations who lived with all sort of liberty and went along with the Iroquois to war as if they were natives.[20] In them was not trust to be given, for they were more cruel than the Iroquois, even to their proper country, insomuch that the rest resolved to surrender themselves than undergo the hazard to be taken by force.

The peace was made by the instancy of the Fathers Jesuits. As [I said] before, some [Jesuits] were going there to live, as they have already begunned. Seeing our departure and transporting of our goods to Montreal for to run the hazard, they [some Hurons] also must come. To let you know [if] our fortune or theirs be better or worse, it should be a hard thing for me to declare. You may judge yourself.

Let us come to our purpose and follow our voyage. Being arrived at the last French habitation,[21] where we must stay above 15 days, for to pass that place without guide was a thing impossi-

50

ble, but after the time expired our guides arrived. It was a band of Iroquois that was appointed to fetch us and conduct us into their country: one day, at ten of the clock in the morning, when we least thought of any, saw several boats coming from the point of St. Louis directly at the foot of a hill, so called, some three miles from Montreal. Then [there was] rejoicing [by] all to see coming those that they never thought to have seen again, for they promised to come at the beginning of spring and should arrive [at Montreal] 15 days before us. But, seeing them, everyone speaks [of nothing] but his embarkation. The Hurons that were present began to make speeches to encourage their wives to make ready with all their stuff, and to fear nothing, being that the heavens would have it so disposed, and that it was better to die in Iroquois country and [at] peace with their brethren than stay in the knot of their nativity — that is, their country — to be murdered, and better in the Iroquois country [than] in war for to be burned. All things so disposed, they prepare themselves to receive the Iroquois, who were no more than three thousand in number* and [who] made a halt for to hold council to know what they must say; that [was] the thought of everyone and of the Hurons. But those barbarians had another design,[22] for their destiny was to do and not to speak, but for to do this there must be a treachery, in which they are experted.

You must know that that band [of] Iroquois, descending the last stream or falling water, one of their skiffs made shipwreck in which were seven, all drowned, without none could succor them. [It was] a thing remarkable that everyone strive to help himself without that they will give aid or assistance to another.

Upon this, that untoward army, those wild barbarous, with vengeance held council, as is before said, for to be revenged of the loss of their companions. They determined, being that they came to fetch the French and the Hurons, to revenge this upon them and kill them as soon as they should be in their jurisdiction, but, considering after that we French had a fort in their country with a good strong guard[23] and that that should cause affairs, it was concluded that their furor should not be discharged but upon the poor Hurons. Upon this deliberation, they broke council and arrived at the fort [Montreal].

---

*The figure probably refers to the number of Iroquois in the vicinity of the Onondaga mission. The narrative discloses shortly that there are eighty Iroquois in the guiding party.

51

Their speech was clear contrary to their design and promises — inviolably, friendship. There was presents and gifts given of both party. But when they partook the death of their companions, they [the Hurons] must make other presents. Perhaps that prevailed somewhat in their thoughts and turn them from their perfidious undertakings, for often the liberality of those savage was soon executed. The desire [of the Iroquois] brings great booty, and observance [of the desire] causes that covetousness [which] will prove dear to the French, as to the Hurons, in few days.

Presently they procure some boats, for the Iroquois had but eleven and the Hurons none, for they came in the French shallops, so it must be contrivance [got] for the one and other, which was soon done. In less than eight days [we] parted the dwelling. We [had] found more than thirty boats, and all very great, we being also so many in company: eighty Iroquois, some hundred Huron women and some ten or twelve men, twenty French, with two Fathers Jesuits.[24] In this manner we departed Montreal, everyone loaded with his burden.

We [all] passed [along] the same tourée[25] We passed the gulf of St. Louis and made cabins in the furthermost part of the stream. That day was laborious to us, [in]somuch that the Iroquois resolved to be back [to their own people] again and make a company to fight against the Algonquins of Quebec. Upon this thirty left us.

The next day we embarked, though not without confusion, because many were not content nor satisfied. What a pleasure the two Fathers [had] to see them trot up and down the rocks to get their ménage[26] into the boat, which with much ado they got in. The boats were so loaden that many could not proceed if bad weather should happen. The journey, but small, came only to the Lake of St. Louis, 3 leagues beyond the stream. There the savage throwed the Fathers' bundle on the waterside and would take no care for them. Seeing many of their men gone, the French as well as Hurons would have disputed with them for their lives and had prevented them, if their design had been discovered. After a great debate, we must yield to the strongest party. The next embarking, the Fathers' merchandise were left behind to oblige the French to stay with it, and seven of us only embarked, one of the Fathers with six more, and the rest stayed to bring what was left behind, so that ours were diminished above 40 men. We embarked indifferently, one with another — French, Iroquois, and Hurons.

After, we came to the highest of the Isle of Montreal. We saw the separation, or rather the great two rivers,[27] that [that] of Canada are composed. The one hath its origin from the west [Ottawa] and the other [St. Lawrence] from south-southeast.[28] It was the last that we sailed. Coming to the end of that lake,[29] which is 14 or 15 leagues long and 3 in breadth, we must make carriages,[30] which are high withal, and [take] the boats by land because [there is] no other way to pass. The trainage is where the water is not so trepid; we draw the boats loaden after us. When there is not water enough, everyone [takes] his bundle by land.

Having proceeded three days' journey on that river, we entered another lake, somewhat bigger; it's called St. Francis. This is [as] delightful to the eye as the foremost. I speak not of the goodness, for there are many things to be spoken of. I am satisfied to assure you that it is a delightful and beautiful country. We wanted nothing to the view, passing those skirts killing stags, oriniacks, and fowles; as for the fish, what a thing it is to see them in the bottom of the water, and take it biting the hook, or lancing it with lance or cramp iron.[31]

In this lake the Hurons began to suspect the treachery conspirated against them, for they observed that the Iroquois always consulted privately together, not giving them the least notice. [This] made a Huron with three men and two women go away and run away to the French of Quebec; one morning after being embarked as the rest, [they] went into the middle of the river,[32] where they began to sing and take their leave, to the great astonishment of the rest and to the great discontent of the Iroquois, that saw themselves so frustrated of so much booty that they expected, but yet they made no sign at that present, but let them go without trouble for fear the rest would do the same and so be deprived of the conspiracy laid for the death of their companions. To that purpose, knowing the place where they were to land, which was in an island in the middle of the river a league long and a quarter broad, they resolved to murder them in the said place, which was promptly executed in this manner following:

They embarked both Huron men and women in their boats, and among themselves made up some twenty [Iroquois warriors] that embarked themselves in two of their [other] boats, in a posture as if they should go to the wars, and went before the break of day. We were but seven Frenchmen, and they put us [in] several boats. I find myself with three Iroquois and one Huron man. Com-

53

ing within sight of the isle where they were to play their game, one of the Iroquois in the same boat as I landed, takes his gun, and charges it. The Huron and I saw this, but neither dreamed of the tragedy that was at hand. After, [the Iroquis] goes into the wood, and the Iroquois that governed the boat takes up a hatchet and knock down the poor Huron, that never thought to be so ended, and the other that charged his musket in the wood shoots him, and [he] fell down upon my heels. My feet soon swims in the miserable Huron's blood. He did quiver as if he had an ague, and was wounded with great many wounds, that still they doubled.

Both Iroquois came to me and bid courage, for they would not hurt me; but [as] for him that was killed, he was a dog, good for nothing. The small knowledge that I have had of their speech made of a better hope, but one that could not have understood them would have been certainly in a great terror.

This murder could not be committed so but that the rest of the boats should hear it, and therefore in that very time we heard sad moans and cries horridly by Huron women. They throwed the corpse immediately into the water and went [to] the other side of the river, into the above-said isle [where the massacre was planned.]

Being landed together, the poor women went in a flock, like sheep that sees the wolves ready to devour them. There were eight Huron men that took their arms, the Iroquois not hindering them in the least, but contrarily; the captain of Iroquois appeared to defend their cause, giving sharp apprenhensions to those that hold up arms, and so far that he beat those that offered to hurt them. In this example you may perceive the dissimulation and vengeance of this cursed people.

That company reassured in some respects the affrighted company [and] made them go up to the top of the hill and there erect cottages, some forty paces from them. During the while, I walked on the side where they were hard at work, and firmly believed that the poor Huron was killed by that Iroquois out of malice, so much trust I put in the traitors' words. As I was directly coming where the Hurons were, what should I see [but] a band of Iroquois, all dabbed, rushing out of a wood, all painted, which is the sign of wars. I though they were those that I had seen in [the] morning before, as eventually they were. I came to the place where were all those poor victims. There was the good Father, comforting the poor innocent women.

The chief of them sat by a valiant Huron who all his lifetime killed many Iroquois and by his valor acquired the name of great captain at home and abroad. The Iroquois spake to him, as the Father told us, and as I myself have heard. "Brother, cheer up," says he, "and assure yourself you shall not be killed by dogs. Thou art both man and captain, as I myself am, and will die in thy defence." As the aforesaid crew showed such a horrid noise of a sudden, the captain took hold of the chain that was about him. "Thou shalt not be killed by another hand than by mine."

At that instant the cruel Iroquois fell upon those Hurons, as many wolves, with hatchets, swords, and daggers and killed as many as there were, save only one man. That Huron captain, seeing himself basely betrayed, he took hold of his hatchet that hunged down his side and struck down a Iroquois, but the infinite deal took his courage and life away.

This that was saved was an old man, who in his time had been at the defeat and taking of several Iroquois. He, in authority, by his means [had] saved some. This news [had been] brought to them, and his name as benefactor, which deed then saved his life. Here you see a good example that it is decent to be good to his enemy.

After this was done and their corpses thrown into the water, the women were brought together. I admired at them, seeing them in such a deep silence, looking on the ground with their coverlets upon their heads; not a sigh heard, where a little before they made such a lamentable noise for the loss of their companion that was killed in my boat.

Some two hours [later] all was pacified, and the kettle almost ready for [to] go to work. In this very moment there calls a council. The Father was called as a statesman to that council, where he hears their wild reasons: that what they had done was in revenge of their dear comrades that were drowned in coming for them, and also to certify the French of their good will. So done, the meat was dressed. We were invited. The Father comes to take his dish and finds us all five in arms, resolving to die valiantly, thinking the council was called to conclude our death, as the Hurons'; the sixth was not able to manage arms, being a little boy. The Father gave us a brother of his company, who had

55

[an] invincible good look and a stout heart. We waited only for his shooting; the Father could not persuade him to draw. We told him, if he would not fight, to leave our company, which [was] perceived by the Iroquois, made them look to themselves. They came and assured us of their good will. The four Frenchmen that understood not longed for the skirmish and [to] die for it. At last the Father prevailed with us and told us what was done in council. Two Iroquois came to us with weapons, who signifies there is nothing laid against you, and commended their companions to put by their arms, that they were our brethren. The agreement was made. Some went to the feast; some stayed.

Having eaten, the Father calls them again to council and for that purpose borrows some porcelain from the captain to make three gifts. All being together, the Father begins his speech, throwing the first gift into the middle of the place, desiring that it might be accepted for the conservation of the friendship that had been long between them and us, and so was accepted with a "ho ho," which is an assurance and a promise, as thanks. The second was for the lives of the women which were in their hands, and to conduct them with safety into their country, which was accepted in like manner. The third was to encourage them to bring us to their own country and carry our merchandises in such that they may not be wet nor leave them behind, which was, as above said, punctually observed. The council being ended, the captains made speeches to encourage the masters of the boats to take a bundle to his care and charge and give an account of it in the country. I wish the lots were so distributed before we came from Montreal, but it is the miserable comfort better late than never.

At night everyone to his cabin, and the women dispersed into every cabin with their children, which was a sight of compassion. The day following, being the eighth day of our departure, some went ahunting; some stayed at home.

The next day to that we embarked all asunder, a boat for each. I was more cheerful than the rest because I knowed a little of their language, and many saw me in the low country.[33] Wherefore [they] made me embark with a young man taller and properer than myself. We had pains and toils enough, especially my spirit was grieved, and [we] suffered much troubles six weeks together. I thought we should come to our journey's end, and so help one another by things past, for a man is glad to

56

drive away the time by honest ingenuous discourse, and I would rejoice very much to be always in company upon my journey. It was contrary to me all the voyage, for my boat and another, wherein were two men and a woman Iroquois, stayed behind without seeing or hearing from one another. I leave with you to think if they were troubled for me or I for them. There was a great alteration: a little before a whole fleet of boats, now to be reduced [to] two only. But patience perforce.

We wandered on that gay river[34] by the means of high and low gulfs that are in it. I made a reflection of the quantity of water that comes in that river, that comes from the top of the high mountains with such a torrent that it causes a mighty noise, which would make the boldest men afraid. We went on some journeys with a deal of pain and labor because for our weakness, and moreover, a man of the other boat fell sick of the ague, so that one of us must help him either in the carriage or drawing [of] the boat, and which was worse, my companion was childish and young as I.[35] The long familiarity we had with one another breeded contempt, so that we would take nothing from one another, which made us go together by the ears, and [we] fought very often till we were covered in blood. The rest took delight to see us fight, but when they saw us take either gun or sword then came they to put us asunder. When we were in the boat we could not fight but with our tongues [i.e., paddles], flying water at one another. I believe if the Father's packet had been there, the gift [he gave at the council] could not keep it from wetting.

As for meat, we wanted none, and we had store of large stags along the waterside. We killed some almost every day, more for sport than for need. We, finding them sometimes in islands, made them go into the water, and after we killed about a score, we clipped the ears of the rest and hung a bell to it and then let them loose. What a sport to see the rest fly from that that had the bell!

As I sat with my companion, I saw once of an evening a very remarkable thing. There comes out of a vast forest a multitude of bears, three hundred at the least together, making a horrid noise, breaking small trees, throwing the rocks down by the waterside. We shot at them, but [they] stirred not a step, which frightened us that they slighted our shooting. We knowed not whether we killed any or no because of the dark;

57

neither dare we venture to see. The wildmen told me that they never heard their father speak of so many together.[36]

We went to the other side to make cabins, where being arrived we made fire and put the kettle on. When it was ready, we eat our belly full. After supper the sick old wildman told me a story, and confirmed it to be true, which happened to him, being war in the upper country of the Iroquois near the great river that divides itself in two.[37] "Brother," says he, "it's a thing to be admired at [to] go afar to travel. You must know, although I am sick, I am [a] man and fought stoutly and invaded many. I loved always the French for their goodness, but they should have given us [guns to] kill the Algonquins. We should not war against the French, but traded with them for our castors. You shall know I am above fifty years." (Yet the fellow did not look as if he had forty.)

"I was once a captain," says he, "of thirteen men against the nation of the Fire[38] and against the Staring Hairs,[39] our enemies. We stayed three whole winters from our country, and most of that time among our enemy, but durst not appear because of the small number we had against a multitude, which made us march in the night and hide ourselves in the daytime in forests. At last [we] were weary to be so long absent from our wives and country. We resolved some more execution and [to] take the first nation that we should encounter. We have already killed many. We went some days on that river, which is bordered of fine sands, no rocks there to be seen. Being landed one morning to go out of the way, lest we should be discovered, for [to] know the place that we were [we] sent two of our men to make a discovery, who, coming back, brought us [word] that they have seen devils and could not believe that they were men. We presently put ourselves on our guards and looks to our arms. [We] thought to have been lost, but took a strong resolution to die like men and went to meet those monsters. We were close to one another, saving they that made a discovery, that went just before us [and] told us, being near the waterside, that they have seen afar off (as they thought) a great heap of stones. We, needing them mightily, we went to get some. Within two hundred paces nigh we found them converted into men, who were of an extraordinary height, lying all along the strand asleep. Brother, you must know that we were all in fear to see such a man and woman of a vast length. They were by two feet taller than I, and big accordingly. They had by them two baskets, a bow and arrows. I came nigh the place. Their arrows were not so long as ours, but bigger, and their bows the same. Each had a small stag's skin to cover their nakedness. They have no winter in their country. After being gone, we held a council to consider what was to be done. We were [in] two boats; the one did carry eight men, the other five. That of eight would go back again, but that of five would go forward into another river. So we departed.

"The night being come, as precedent nights, we saw fires in several places on the other side of the river, which made us go there at the break of day to know what it was, which was men as tall as the other man and woman, and [a] great many of them together afishing. We stealed away without any noise and resolved not to stay longer in them parts, where everything was so big; the fruits of trees are as big as the heart of an oriniack, which is bigger than that of an ox.

"The day after our return, being in cottages covered with bushes, we heard a noise in the wood, which made us speedily take our weapons, everyone hiding himself behind a tree, the better to defend himself. [We] perceived it was a beast, like a Dutch horse, that had a long and straight horn in the forehead,[40] and came towards us. We shot twice at him. [She] falls down on the ground, but on a sudden starts again and runs full boot at us and, as we were behind the trees, thrusts her horn very far into the tree, and so broke it and died. We would eat none of her flesh because the Flemings eat not their horses' flesh, but took off the skin, which proved heavy, so we left it there. Her horn [was] five foot long and bigger than the biggest part of an arm.

"We still proceeded on our journey. In seven days we overtook the boat that left us."

Now whether it was an unicorn or a fib made by that wildman, that I cannot tell, but several others told me the same who have seen several times the same beast, so that I firmly believe it. So his story ended, which lasted a great while, for having an excellent memory, [he] told me all the circumstances of his encounters.

We [went] from thence the next morning. We came to a beautiful river,[41] wide one league and a half, which was not violent nor deep, so that we made no carriages for 15 or 20 leagues. We

59

had the view of eagles and other birds taking fishes, which we ourselves have done, and [we] killed salmons with staves. One of my companions lanced a sturgeon six fathoms deep and brought it [up].

Going along the woodside, we came where a great many trees were cut, as [if] it were intended for a fort. At the end of it there was a tree left standing, but the rind taken away from it. Upon it there was painted with a coal six men hanged, with their heads at their feet, cut off. They were so well drawn that the one of them was [seen to be a] Father by the shortness of his hair, which let us know that the French that was before were executed. A little further, another was painted of two boats, one of three men, another of two, whereof one was standing with a hatchet in his hands, striking on the head. At another were represented seven boats pursuing 3 bears. A man [was] drawn as if he were on land with his gun, shooting a stag.

I considering, those things troubled me very much; yea, caused my heart to tremble within me. Those that were with me certified me of what I was too sure, telling me the six Frenchmen were dead, but told me to be cheerful, that I should not die. After I found so much treachery in them, I could but trust little in their words or promises. Yet must [I] show good countenance to a worse game than I had a mind [to], to show them that I was in no fear.

Being embarked, the wildmen told me we should go on the other side of that broad river. It was extremely hot, no wind stirring. I was ready that both should be together for the better assurance of my life. I perceived well that he alone was not able to perform the voyage; there was the other [man] sick of the other boat, that did row but very slowly. I thought to myself, They must needs bring me into their country, if they meet none by the way, and so I comforted myself with better hope. We soon came to the other side of the river. The other boat followed not.

Being nigh the land, my comrade perceived an eagle on a tree, the feathers of which are in esteem among them. He lands and takes his gun, charges it, and goes into the wood. I was in fear without blame, for I knowed not what he meant. I remembered how the poor Huron was served so a little before in his boat, and in like manner. As he went about I could not imagine what was best, but resolved to kill [rather] than to be killed. Upon this I take my gun, which the other saw. [He] desires me not to make any noise, showing me the eagle, that as yet I have not seen. To obey him, I stoop down like a monkey, visiting my weapon that she should not suspect. My eyes nevertheless followed for fear. I see at last the truth of his design. He shoots and kills the eagle.

[We] after embarked ourselves, the night drawing on, and must think to go to the other boat, or he to us, which he did. I admired, the weather [being] clear and calm, that we could scarce see him, yet that we should hear them speak, and understand, as if they were but twenty or thirty paces from us. He being come, we sought for conveniency to make cottages, which soon was done. The others sooner landed than we; they came to receive us at our landing. One took my gun, the other a little bundle of mine. I was surprised at this. Then they asked me [for] my powder and shot, and opened my bag, began to partage my combs and other things that I had. I thought it the consultest[42] way to submit to the strongest part; therefore I took [no] notice of what they did. The woman kindled the fire. Seeing myself out of care of my freight, [I] sat me down by the woman. She looked now and then upon me, which made more and more mistrust.

In the meanwhile, he that was sick calls me. I came and asked him what he pleased. "I will," said he, "that you embark yourself by me," and throws his capote[43] away, bidding me also to leave my capote. He takes his hatchet and hangs it to his wrist, goes into the boat, and I with him. I would have carried my gun; I took it from the place where they laid it. They, seeing, laughed and gave a shout, as many beasts; yet it was not in their power to make me go to the boat without my weapon, so [they] let me have it.

[We] went straight, as if we were to go on the other side of that river. About the middle, the wildman bids me go out, to which I would not consent. I bid him go. After we disputed awhile, I, not obeying, began to consider if he had a mind to drown me, that he himself would not go in the water. Being come a little better to myself, I perceived that the water was not two foot deep. It was so dark; yet one might perceive the bottom, covered with mussels. Having so much experience, I desired him to have patience. [I] got off my shirt and lept into the water and gathered about half a bushel of those shells, or mussels. I made sure that the boat should not leave me, for I fastened my girdle to it and held the end. Mistrust is the mother of safety. We came back again.

We found the kettle ready. They give me meat and a dish of broth, which exercised me awhile. Having done, the man comes and makes me pull off my shirt, having then nothing but my drawers to cover my nakedness. He puts on my shirt on his back, takes a knife, and cuts a medal that hung to my neck. He was a great while searching me and feeling if I was fat. I wished him far enough. I looked [for] an opportunity to be from him, thinking to be better sheltered by the woman. I though every foot he was to cut my throat. I could [not] bear [it]. I had rather die [at] once than be so often tormented.

I rose and sat me down by the woman, in whom was all my trust. She perceived I was in great fear, whether by color of face or other I know not. She puts her hands upon my head and combs it down with her fingers. "My son," says she, "be cheerful. It is my husband. He will not hurt thee. He loves me and knoweth that I love thee and have a mind to have thee to our dwelling." Then she rose and takes my shirt from her husband and brings it me. She gave me one of her covers. "Sleep," said she. I wanted not many persuasions, so chose rather the fatal blow sleeping than awake, for I thought never to escape.

The next morning I [awoke], finding myself freed, which made me hope for the future. I have reason to remember that day for two contrary things — first for my spirits being very much perplexed and the other that the weather was contrary, though very lovely. That morning they rendered [to me] all my things again and filled my bag with victuals.

We left this place which feared me most. Then hurt was done. Some laughed at me afterwards for the fear wherein I was, which I more and more hoped for better entertainment. The way was fair all that day, but the next we must make a wainage,[44] which [was] not very hard, but my comrade drew carelessly, and the boat slips from his hands, which turned with such force that it [would have] had me along if I had not let my hold go, choosing that [rather] than venture myself in danger. It [no] sooner got down than we got it up again, but my fortune was not hurted. Yet, it runned aground among rocks. We must go down the river.[45] I was driven to swim to it, where I found it full of water and a hole that two fists might go throught it, so that I could not drive it to land without mending it. My companion, also in the water, like a water dog, comes and takes hold of the four oars. All the wildmen swims like water dogs, not as we swim.

We mend the boat there neatly, [but] not without miscalling one another. They spoke to me a word that I understood not because of the difference between the low Iroquois and their speech, and in the anger and heat we laid the blame upon one another to have let the boat slip purposely. I took no heed of what he alleged. He comes suddenly upon me, and there [we] cuffed one another until we were all in blood. Being weary at last, out of breath, we gave over like two cocks overtired with fighting. We could not fight longer, but must find strength to draw up the boat against the stream and overtake the other, which was a good way from us.

It was impossible to overtake that day nor the next; we must lay three nights by ourselves.

The third day we arrived to a vast place full of isles,[46] which are called the Isles of Toniata, where we overtook our companions, who stayed for us. There they killed a great big and fat bear. We took some of it into our boats and went on our journey together.

We came thence to a place like a basin, made out of an isle like a half-moon. Here we caught eels five fathoms or more deep in the water, seeing clearly the bottom in abundance of fishes. We find there nine low country Iroquois in their cabins that came back from the war that was against the nation of the Cats.[47] They had with them two women, a young man of twenty-five years, and a girl of six years, all prisoners. They had a head with short hair of one of that nation that uses to have their hair turned up like the prickles of an hedgehog.[48] We cottaged ourselves by them.

Some of them knowed me and made much of me. They gave me a garland of porcelain and a girdle of goat's hair. They asked when should I visit my friends. I promised to come there as soon as I could arrive at the upper village. I gave them my hatchet to give to my father, and two dozen of brass rings and two shooting knives for my sisters, promising to bring a cover for my mother. They inquired what was it that made me go away, and how. I told them [I escaped] through woods and arrived at Three Rivers in twelve days and that I suffered much hunger by the way. I would not tell that I escaped by reason of the Dutch. They called me often devil to have undertaken such a task. I resolved to go along with them.

Here [at the island] I found certainty, and not till then, of the six Frenchmen, whom they have seen seven days before at the coming-in of the great Lake Ontario; undoubtedly the marks we have seen on the trees were done by seven other boats of their own nation that came back from the wars in the North, that met two Huron boats of eight men, who fought and killed three Iroquois and wounded others. Of the Hurons, six were slained, one taken alive, and the other escaped. Those two boats were going to the French to live there. That news satisfied much my wildmen, and much more I rejoiced at this.

We stayed with them the next day, feasting one another. They cut and burned the fingers of those miserable wretches, making them sing while they plucked out some of their nails. Which done, we parted, well satisfied for our meeting.

From that place we came to lie at the mouth of a lake in an island where we have had some tokens of our Frenchmen by the impression of their shoes on the sand that was in the said island. In that island our wildmen [had] hid two casks of Indian corn, which did us a kindness, for there was no more venison pie to be gotten.

The next day we make up our bundles in readiness to wander upon that sweet sea,[49] as is the saying of the Iroquois, who reckons [distance] by their [number of] days' journey. This was above a hundred leagues in length and thirty in breadth. Seeing the water so calm and fair, we ventured some three leagues to gain a point of the firm land, that by that means we should shorten seven or eight leagues in our way. We went on along the lake in that manner with great delight, sometimes with pain and labor. As we went along the waterside, the weather very fair, it comes in my mind to put out a cover[50] [for] a sail. My companion liked it very well, for generally wildmen are given to laziness. We, seeing that our sail made us go faster than the other boat, [did] not perceive that the wind came from the land, which carried us far in the lake. Our companions made a sign, having more experience than we, and judged of the weather that was to come. We would not hear them, thinking to have an advantage.

Soon after, the wind began to blow harder, made us soon strike sail and put our arms to work. We feel not the wind because it was in our backs, but, turning aside, we find that we had enough to do. We must get ourselves to a better element than that we were. Instantly comes a shower of rain, with a storm of wind, that was able to perish us by reason of the great

64

quantity of water that came into our boat. The lake began to vapor and make a show of his Neptune's sheep.[51] Seeing we went backwards rather than forwards, we thought ourselves utterly lost.

That rogue that was with me said, "See thy God that thou sayest He is above! Will you make me believe now that He is good, as the black coats say? (The Fathers Jesuits.) They do lie, and you see the contrary; for first you see that the sun burns us often, and rain wets us, the wind makes us have shipwreck, the thundering, the lightnings burns and kills, and all come from above, and you say that it's good to be there. For my part, I will not go there. Contrary, they say that the reprobates and guilty goeth down and burn. They are mistaken; all is good here. Do not you see the earth that nourishes all living creatures, the water the fishes—and they us—and that corn and all other seasonable fruits for our food are not so contrary to us as that from above?" As he said so, he cursed vehemently after his own manner. He took his instruments and showed them to the heavens, saying, "I will not be above! Here will [I] stay, on earth where all my friends are, and not with the French, that are to be burned above with torments."

How should one think to escape this torments and storms? But God, who through His tender mercy ceased the tempest, gave us strength to row, till we came to the side of the water. I may call it a mighty storm by reason of the littleness of the boat, that are all in water [only] to the breadth of five fingers or less. I thought upon it, and out of distress made a virtue to seek the means to save ourselves. We tied a sack full of corn in the fore end of our boat and threw it into the water, which hung down some four fathoms, and we put ourselves in the other end, so that the end that was towards the wind was higher than the other, and by that means escaped the waves. Without doubt, if we had not used that means, we had sunked.

The other boat landed to let that storm [pass] over. We found them in the evening at their cottages, and [they had] thought [it] impossible for us to escape.

After several days' travel we came to an isle where we made cottages. We went so far that evening that we might be so much the nearer to take a broader passage which should shorten our voyage about twenty leagues. At night we saw several fires upon the land. We all judged that it was our company that went before us. Before break of day we did what we could to overtake them, not without hazard, by reason [of] the wind that blowed hard, which we could not perceive before being come to the bay of the isle. We could not turn back without greater danger, so [we] resolved to proceed.

We came to the very place where we saw the fires and found that we were not mistaken in our opinions. By good luck they were there, else we had perished, for all being so near the land, for the lake swelled by reason of the great wind that blew, which [had] stayed them there above fourteen night; neither for this reason was there any landing, because of a great bank or heap of rocks, until those that were ashore came to us into the water to their oxters[52] and stopped our boats. We then cast ourselves and all that we had overboard, leaving our boats there, which were immediately in [a] thousand pieces.

Being arrived, we placed our cottages by a most pleasant delicate river,[53] where for delightfulness was what Man's heart could wish. There were woods, forests, meadow. There we stayed 3 days by reason of the weather.

One night I laid near a fair comely lass that was with us; there they take no notice, for they live in so great liberty that they are never jealous one of another. I admired of a sudden to hear new music. She was in travail and immediately delivered. I awaked, all astonished, to see her drying her child by the fireside, having done lapt the child in her bosom, and went to bed as if it had been nothing, without moan or cry as do our European women.[54] Before we left the place that babe died. I had great mind to baptize him, but feared lest they should accuse me to be the cause of his death.

Being come to the above-named place, where were the ghostly Fathers with eight other French, three came to meet us from the fort,[55] which were but thirty leagues of where I have received a censure for being so timidous, not daring to fling water on the head of that poor innocent to make him happy. We Frenchmen began to tell our adventures, having been out of hopes of ever to see one another, being exceeding glad that we were deceived in our opinions.

Some leaves us and went by land to their cabins. The rest stays for fair weather to come to our journey's end. We wanted not slaves from that place to carry our packs. We came into a river[56] towards the fort which was dangerous for its swiftness. From that river, that brought us within 30 leagues of the lake, we came into a narrow river from a small lake[57] where a French fort was built. This river was two leagues long, and the lake five in compass, about it a most pleasant country, very fruitful. Going up that same river, we meet two French that were fishing [for] a kind of fish called dab, which is excellent, and [they] have done us great kindness, having left no more provision than what we needed much.

Having come to the landing place at the foot of the fort, we found there a most fair castle, very neatly built, two great and two small ones.[58] The bottom was built with great trees, and well tied in the top with twigs of ash, strengthened with two strong walls and two bastions, which made the fort impregnable of the wildmen. There was also a fine fall of wood about it. The French corn growed there exceeding well, where was as much as covered half a league of land. The country [was] smooth like a board [for] a matter of some three or four leagues about: several fields off all sides of Indian corn, citrul,[59] of French turnips, full of chestnuts, and oaks of acorns, with [a] thousand such like fruit in abundance; a great company of hogs, so fat that they were not able to go; a plenty of all sorts of fowls, and ringdoves in such number that in a net fifteen or sixteen hundred at once might be taken. So this was not a wild country to our imagination, but plentiful in everything.

We were humanely received by the reverend Fathers Jesuits and some other forty Frenchmen, as well domestics as volunteers.

We prepared ourselves to take the country's recreation, some to hunt, some to fish, but [we were] prevented by a fever that seized on us all. Some continued a month, some more, and some less, which is the tribute that one must pay for the changement of climate.

Some days after, we had news that another company of Iroquois were arrived at Montreal. As soon we [had] went from thence, the Father and the rest of the French that did stay behind did embark themselves with them and followed us so close that ere long would be at us. As they went up to make cottages in the island of the massacre, which was 16 days before our departure, one of the company goes to shoot for his pleasure, finds a woman half starved for hunger lying on a rock by a water. He brings her to the cottages and made so much by giving her some luke warm water, which he boiled with flour and grease, that she came to

67

herself entirely again. She was examined. She told them what is above said and when it happened. She [had] hid herself in a rotten tree during the slaughter, where she remained three days. After we were gone, she came forth for to get some food, and found nothing but found only some small grapes of roots the three first days, and nothing else. She, finding herself feeble and weak, not able to sustain such, resolved for death. The Father, knowing her to be a Christian, had a singular care for her and brought her where I overtook the said Father with the eight French. Being brought, [she] was frightened again for seeing a man charging his gun to kill her, as she said, so [she] went away that night, and none knows what became of her. Being weak, not thoroughly healed, she fancied that such a thing might be done. The Father arrives that affirms this news to us, being very sorry for the loss of this poor creature that God has so long preserved without any subsistance, which shows us apparently that we ought not to despair, and that [God] keeps those that lives in His fear. We went to meet the Father, I mean those that were able, to bid the Father welcome, and his company. Being come safe and in a good disposition together, we rendered God thanks.

There were many that waited for us, desiring to turn back again to Quebec, obtaining their desire from the Fathers and the governor of the fort; they were thirteen in number, and one Father. After six weeks' end we recovered our health. So we went to bring them a part of the way [back to Quebec], some to the waterside, some to the lake's end, where we took of one another farewell, with such ceremonies as are used when friends depart.

Some days after we hear that the poor woman was in the woods (not that she knowed which way to turn, but did follow her own fancy wheresoever it lead her, and so wandered six days, getting sometimes for her substance wild garlic, young buds of trees, and roots); she was seen in an evening by a river whereby she was for three days by three Hurons, renegades. They took her, but in a sad condition. They, not considering that she was of their own nation, stripped her. It is the custom to strip whomsoever is lost in woods. They brought her to the village where the Father was that brought her from the place of murdering to that place [from] whence she runned away the second time. This Father, knowing her, brings her to our fort, that we might see her as a thing incredible, [dead] but by the mercy of God.

I was in the village* with the Father and with another Frenchman, where we see the cruelest thing in nature acted. Those Iroquois that came along the river with us, some were fishing, some ahunting. They, seeing this woman, makes her slave. One day a man of theirs was forewarned for his insolency for not referring to the governor, doing all out of his own head. The [offender him]self was to come that day, leading two women with their two children, he not intending to give an account of anything but by his own authority. The elders, hearing this, goes and meets him some 50 paces out of the village for to maintain their rights; they stayed this man. What were those beasts? [they asked.] He answered they were his. He no sooner had spoken but one one old man spoke to him thus: "Nephew, you must know that all slaves, as well men as women, are first brought before the council, and we along can dispose [of] them." So said, [he] turned to the other side and gave a sign to some soldiers that they brought for that purpose to knock those beasts in the head, who executed their office and murdered the women. One took the child, set foot on his head, taking his legs in his hands, wrought the head by often turning from off the body. Another soldier took the other child from his mother's breast, that was not yet quiet dead, by the feet and knocks his head against the trunk of a tree. This [was] a daily exercise with them, nor I can tell the one-half of their cruelties in like sorts. Those, with many others, were executed, some for not being able to serve, and the children for hindering their mothers to work. So they reckon [it] a trouble to let them live. Oh, wicked and barbarous inhumanity!

I forgot to tell that, the day the woman laid in, some hours before she and I roasted some Indian corn in the fire. [It] being ready, she pulled out the grains one by one with a stick, and as she was so doing, she made a horrid outcry, showing me a toad which was in the breadth of a dish which was in the middle of the red ashes, striving to get out. We wondered, for the like was never seen before. After he got out of the fire, we throwed stones and staves at him till it was killed. That toad lived two days in or under the fire.[60]

---

*Not the village at the Onondaga mission, but one about five miles from it. It is a characteristic of Radisson's narrative that he suddenly appears at a place without having told the reader he has gone there.

Having remained in that village six days, we have seen horrible cruelties committed. Three of us resolved to turn back to our fort, which was five miles off. We brought above a hundred women, Huron slaves and others, all loaded with corn. We were always in scarity for policy, though we had enough, for certainty is far better than the incertainty.

Before we departed this base place we perceived that the Huron who was saved by the consent of the rest in the isle of massacre, as is above said, two days after his deliverance runned away by night toward the lower country of the Iroquois, where he arrived safe; [but] not without sufferings in the way, for such long voyages cannot be performed otherwise, having gone through vast forests, finding no inn in the way, neither having the least provision. At his coming there, he spoke whatsoever the revenge, the wrath, and indignation could provoke or utter against the French, especially against the Fathers, saying that it was they that have sold and betrayed them and that he would bestow the same upon them, if ever he should meet with them. As for him, he gave heaven thanks that he was yet living, that he had his life saved by them to whom he would render like service, warning them not to let the French build a fort, as the upper Iroquois had done; that he could tell them of it by experience; that they should remember the nation of the Stags so big — as soon as the French came there, nothing but death by sorcery which brought a strange sickness amongst them. Such things can prevail much upon such a wild credulous nation. Their minds [were] all together for the wars, in which they delight most of anything in the world.

We came our way. This news troubled us very much, knowing the little fidelity that is [in] that wild nation, that have neither faith nor religion, neither law nor absolute government, as we shall hear the effect of it.

The autumn scarce began but we hear that the lower Iroquois contrived a treason against the French. So having contrived and discovered that, they were resolved to levy an army of five hundred men of their own nation, who are esteemed the best soldiers. Having the Anojot[?] to assist them, a bold rash nation, [they] thought to surprise the inhabitants of that place [Onondaga]. They were contriving, and consequently seized, upon the fort and town, thinking to execute their plot with ease, trusting (if contrary to their contrivance) to the peace, saying

70

the the French were as many hogs laid up to be fatted in their country.

But, oh Liberality, what strength hast thou! Thou art the only means whereby men know all and pierce the hearts of the most wild and barbarous people of the world. Hearing such news, we make friends by store of gifts; yea, such gifts that were able to [make certain Iroquois] betray their country. What is that that interest will not do? We discover daily new contrivances of treason by a counselor. There is nothing done or said but that we have advice of it. Their daily exercise is feasting of wars, songs, throwing of hatchets, breaking kettles. What can we do? We are in their hands. It's hard to get away from them; yea, as much as a ship in full sea without pilot, as passengers without skill. We must resolve to be upon our guard, being in the middle of our enemy. For this purpose we begin to make provisions for the future end.

We are told that a company of the Anojot nation volunteers was already in their march, to break heads and so declare open wars. This company finds enough to do at Montreal, for the French [were] being careless of themselves, working incomparably afar from their fortifications without the least apprehension. They killed two French and brought them away in triumph, their heads set up for a sign of wars.

We, seeing no other remedy but [that we] must be gone and leave a delightful country, the only thing that we wanted most was that we had not boats to carry our baggage. It's sad to tend from such a place, that is compassed with those great lakes that composes that empire, that can be named the greatest part of the known world. At last they contrived some deal boards to make ships with large bottoms, which was the cause of our destruction sooner than was expected. You have heard above said how the Fathers inhabited the Huron country to instruct them in Christian doctrine; they preach the mighty power of the Almighty, Who had drowned the world for to punish the wicked, saving only our father Noah with his family was saved in an ark. One came, bringing Indian corn, [who was] named Jaluck, who escaped the shipwreck that his countrymen had [under]gone, being slave among us. He received such instructions of those deal boards and reflected soundly upon the structure. He thought verily they were to make another ark to escape their hands, and by our inventions cause all the rest to be

71

drowned by a second deluge. They, imputing so much power to us as [to] Noah [who] had that grace of God, thought that God at least commanded us so to do. All, frighted, runs to his village. This [Jaluck] comes back, makes them all afraid. Each talks of it. The elders gathered together to consult what was to be done. In their council [it] was concluded that our fort should be visited, that our Fathers should be examined and, according to their answers, deliberation should be taken to preserve both their life and country. We had always spies of our side, which were [spies] out of zeal and obedience. The Fathers Jesuits and others voluntarily ventured their lives for the preservation of the common liberty; they remain in the village of those barbarians to spy what their intent should be, holding correspondence with some of those of the council by giving them gifts, to the end that we might know what was concluded in the council, and gave us advice with all speed. We by these means had intelligence that they were to come and visit our forts.

To take away all suspicion of our innocency, which if it had come to their knowledge had done a great prejudice to our former design (a ship then upon the dock, almost finished), we made a double floor in the hall where the ship was abuilding, so that the wildmen, being ignorant of our way of building, could not take any notice of our cunningness, which proved to our desire. So done, [the wildmen] finding nothing that was reported, all began to be quiet and out of fear. By this we were warned from thenceforth, mistrusting all that came there; so preserved ourselves, putting nothing in sight that should give the least suspicion. Both ships were accomplished. We kept them secretly and covered them with 12 boats of rind that we kept for fishing and hunting. The wildmen knowed of these small things but suspected nothing, believing that the French would never [be] susceptible to venture such a voyage for the difficulty of the way and violence of the swiftness of the rivers and length of the way.

We stayed for opportunity in some quietness, devising to contrive our game as soon as the spring should begin. The winter we pass not without apprehensions, having had several alarms, false [as well] as true, for often were we put to our arms, insomuch that one of our sentries was drawn once by force from the door of the fort. He to avoid the danger draws his sword and wounds one of them, and comes to the fort, crying, "To your arms!" This was soon appeased; some gifts healed the wound.

72

The season drawing nigh, we must think of some stratagem to escape their hands, and the rest of ours that were among them, which was a difficulty because they would have some of us by them always for the better assurance. But all their contrivances and wit were too weak to strive against our plots, which were already invented to deceive [those] that would deceive us. We let them understand that the time drew near that the French uses to treat their friends in feasting and merriment, and all should be welcome, having no greater friends than they were. They, to see our fashions as well as to fill their guts, gave consent. By that means the considerablest persons are invited, [also] the Father and two French. There they were made much of [for] two days, with great joy, with sounds of trumpets, drums, and flageolets, with songs in French as wild.

So done, they are sent away, the Father with them. He was not a mile off but [he] feigns to get a fall and sighed that his arm was broken.[61] The wild[men], being much troubled at the accident, brings the Father back and makes gifts that he may be cured. A plaster was set to his arm; which done, [he was] put into a bed. Then all the wildmen came to see him. He encouraged them that he should soon recover and see them. The French that knowed not the plot cried for the Father, which confirmed the belief of the wildmen. They all retired to their village, and we [sought] the means to embark ourselves.

We resolved once more to make another feast when we should have everything ready for our purpose (that is, when the Father should be well of his feigned sickness), for they also delight in feasting, which was to be done for the safe recovery of the Father's health. We daily had messengers from the elders of the country to know how he did, who — after the lake was opened from the ice — should be in good disposition. Many wished to have the sun shine ardently, their desire was so great to be gone. At last our patient begins to walk with a scarf about his arm. When the ships and boats were ready, we sent them word that the Father was well, and for joy would make a feast. The elders are invited. They were sure not to fail, but to be first. Being come, there are speeches made to encourage them to sing and eat. It's folly to induce them to that, for they go about it more bold than [is] welcome. They are told that the morrow should be the day of mirth. Here is but play and dances. The French by turns keep them still in exercise, showing them tricks to keep

73

them awake, as the bird catcher doth to teach the bird to sing and not to fly away, as we then intended [to do]. Not one wild-man was admitted to come into the fort that day, saying it was not our customs to show the splendor of our banquets before they should be presented at table. The wildmen have no other than the ground for their table. In the meantime we were not idle, the impotent Father exercising himself as the rest.

The evening being come, the wildmen are brought to the place destinated, not far from our fort. Everyone makes his bundle of provisions and merchandises and household stuff, guns, etc., some hid in the ground, and the rest scattered because we could not save them. We made excellent biscuits of the last year's corn, and forgot not the hogs that were afattening.

At last the trumpets blows. [We] put ourselves in order. There is nothing but outcries, clapping of hands, and capering, that they may have better stomach to their meat. There comes a dozen of great kettles full of beaten Indian corn, dressed with mince-meat. The wisest begins his speech, giving heaven thanks to have brought such generous French to honor them so. They eat as [so] many wolves, having eyes bigger than bellies; they are rare at it, without noise. The time was not yet comed to acknowledge the happiness we received from such incomparable hosts. Here comes two great kettles full of bustards, broiled and salted before the winter, with as many kettles full of ducks, as many [of] turtles [that] was taken in the season by the net. At this, nothing but whooping, to Man's admiration. Whilst one was eating, another sort comes, as divers of fish, eels, salmon, and carps gives them a new stomach. Were they to burst, here they will show their courage. The time comes on. The best is that we are sure none will forsake his place, nor man nor woman. A number of French entertains them, keeping them from sleep in dancing and sing-ing, for that is the custom. Their lutrill,[62] an instrumental music, is much here in use. Nothing is done as yet, for there comes the thickened flour, the oil of bears, venison. To this the knife is not enough; the spoons also are used. We see already several postures: the one beats his belly, the other shakes his head, others stop their mouths to keep in what they have eaten. They were in such an admiration making strange kinds of faces that [they] turned their eyes up and down. We bid them cheer up and told them it was an usual custom with the French to make much of themselves and of their friends. "They affect you, and ye must show such like to them by showing your respects to them that so splendidly treat you. Cheer up, like brave men. If the sleep overcomes you, you must awake. Come, sound [the] drum. It is not now to beat the gein.[63] Come, make a noise. Trumpet blow, and make thy cheeks swell, and make thy cheeks swell to make the bellies swell also." In the end nothing [is] spared that can be invented to the greater confusion. There is a strife between the French [over] who will make the greatest noise. But there is an end to all things. The hour is come, for all is embarked. The wildmen can hold out no longer; they must sleep. They cry out, "Skenon!" — enough. "We can bear no more." ("Let them cry skenon. We will cry hunnay! — we are agoing," says we.) They are told that the French are weary and will sleep also awhile. They say, "Be it so."

We come away. All is quiet. Nobody makes a noise after such a hurly-burly. The fort is shut up as if we had been in it. We leave a hog at the door for sentry, with a rope tied to his foot.[64] He wanted no meat for the time.

Here we make a proposition: being three and fifty French in number, to make a slaughter without any difficulty, they being but a hundred beasts not able to budge, and as many women. That done, we could go to their village at the break of the day, where we were sure there were not twenty men left, nor young nor old. It was no great matter to deal with five or six hundred women and maybe a thousand children. Besides, the huntsmen should not be ready this two months to come home. Having done so, we might have a great hole in the skirts of that untoward and perverse nation. It was in way of revenge because of their disloyalty — breaking the peace and watching [for] an opportunity to do the like to us[65] — (we should by that means [also] have a better opportunity to escape) showing by this whosoever intends to betray betrays himself.

The Fathers' answer was to this that they were sent to instruct the people in the faith of Jesus Christ, and not to destroy, that the cross must be their sword; moreover, that they are told that we were able to keep the place, having victuals for the space of four years, with other provisions;[66] so done, in the meanwhile some sixteen French should go down to the French and tell the news, for the rest they were able to oppose all the Iroquois, having such a strong fort, and before the time could be expired some succor was to be expected out of France.

75

[We replied that] with the help of some of the wildmen, their allies, [we would] make an assault and so free ourselves of such a slavery and the many miseries wherein we were daily to undergo; by that means we might save the lives of many French, and clear away from such inhumans. It was in vain [we argued] to think to convert them, but the destroying of them was to convert them, [and] so discover nations and countries. The French, finding some forty resolute brothers that would have ventured themselves, full [of] liberty and assurance of their lives, [proposed] to preserve them [the Jesuits] from the cruelest enemy that ever was found upon earth. [After] all these sayings, [we still] could prevail nothing upon people that will avoid all slaughter.

So, to be obedient to our superiors [the Jesuits], without noise of trumpet or drum, but yet with grief, we left that place. We are all embarked, and now must look for the mouth of the river.[67] [We] were put to it, for it freezed every night, and the ice of good thickness and consequently dangerous to venture our boats against it. We must all the way break the ice with great staves to make a passage. This gave us pains enough. At the break of day we were in sight at the mouth of the river,[68] where we were free from ice. If those had but the least suspicion or had looked out, they had seen us. We soon by all diligence put ourselves out of that apprehension and come at the first rising[69] of the river, where, freed from ice ten leagues from the fort, we kept a good watch.

The day following, we came to Lake Ontario. The wind being boisterous, [we] could go no further. There we sought for a place to make cottages, which was in an island very advantageous, where we stayed two days for the weather. We were not without fear, thinking that the wildmen should follow us.

They contrariwise stayed (as we heard) seven nights [at Onondaga], thinking that we were asleep, only that some rose now and then and rung the little bell which [was] stooked to the hog's foot. So mystifying [was] the business, the affair, [that they] went and brought news to the village, which made them come and look over the palisades, and saw in good earnest [that] the Anomiacks were gone.

In our journey: bad weather, high winds, snow, and every day rain on our backs. We came to the river[70] at last, where was difficulty enough by reason of the going out of the lake, which is hard to find by the many isles that are about the opening of the river. We were in a manner of sheep scattered.

After many crossing to and fro, we find ouselves at the first stream. The waters high, [we] went on without danger, but the navigation proved worse and worse because we came into a colder country and into the most dangerousest precipices. Now the river [was] covered over with ice and snow, which made the river give a terrible noise; the land also covered all over with snow, which consequently found ourselves in great perils. It was well that the river swelled, for not a mother's son of us could else escape, for where we might have made carriages we innocently did go on upon those torrents. One of our greatest vessels runned [aground] on sand, but by turnings with much ado we got it out again and by all dexterity brought [it] to a harbor, which is hard to find in that place, for the ice and the stream continually cuts the coasts steep down, and so no landing thereabouts. Here a boat of four men made shipwreck; here everyone for himself and God for all; here is no relief. There the three that could swim were drowned because they held not [to] the boat, but would swim to land. The other that held it was saved with much ado. Afterwards we came where the stream was not swift at all, but as dangerous for its ice. We cut the ice with hatchets, and we found places where [it] was rotten, so we hazarded ourselves often to sink down to our necks.

We knowed the isle of murder again because of the woman that runned away was with us. She had reason to know it, though all covered with snow. The Fathers some days before our departure [had] caused her to come to the fort to deliver her out of the hands of her enemy because she was a Christian. In [a] short time after her arrival at Quebec, [she] was married, and died in childbed.

Six weeks being expired, we came to the height of St. Louis, three leagues from Montreal, the first habitation of the French. We went all that night without making carriages, trusting to the depth of the water. God's providence made [for] us that passage free, for if we had come there the day before we could not possibly pass (by the report of the French) by reason that underneath the water was mighty swift; the river was frozen and covered with ice, and [we] could not have turned back, for the stream could bring us against our will under the ice. It was our lot to come after the ice was melted.

The French inquires who is there with astonishment, thinking that it should be the charge of the Iroquois. We thanked God

77

for our deliverance. Here we had time to rest ourselves awhile at ease, which was not permitted by the way. About the last of March we ended our great pains and incredible dangers.[71]

About fourteen nights after, we went down [to] Three Rivers, where most of us stayed.

A month after, my brother[72] and I resolves to travel and see countries. We find a good opportunity. In our voyage we proceeded three years.[73] During that time we had the happiness to see very fair countries.

The end of the second voyage made in the
upper country of the Iroquois.

MISSISSIPPI VOYAGE

Now followeth the Auxoticiat[1] voyage into the great and
filthy Lake of the Hurons, upper Sea of the East, and
Bay of the North.

BEING COME to Three Rivers, I found my brother, who the
year before[2] came back from the Lake of the Hurons, with other
French; both were upon the point of resolution to make a journey
a purpose for to discover the great lakes that they heard the wild
men speak of; yea, have seen before; for my brother made several journeys when the Fathers lived about the Lake of the Hurons,
which was upon the border of the sea.[3] So my brother, seeing
me back from those two dangerous voyages,[4] so much by the
cruelties of the barbarians as for the difficulties of the ways, for
this reason he thought I was fitter and more faithful for the discovery that he was to make. He plainly told me his mind. I,
knowing it, longed to see myself in a boat.

There were several companies of wildmen expected from several places, because they promised the year before [to] take the
advantage of the spring (this for to deceive the Iroquois, who
are always in wait to destroy them) and of the rivers, which
is [passable] by reason of the melting of the great snows, which
is only [at] that time; otherwise no possibility was to come that
way because for the want of water so that no boat can come
through. We soon see the performance of those people, for a
company came to Three Rivers, where we were. They told us
that another company was arrived at Montreal and that two more
were to come shortly, the one to Three Rivers, the other to
Saguenay, a river of Tadousac, who arrived within two days
after. They [had] divided themselves because of the scant of
provision, for if they were together they could not have victuals
enough.[5]

Many goes and come to Quebec for to know the resolution

of Mr. Governor, who together with the Fathers thought fit to send a company of French to bring back (if possible) those wildmen the next year,[6] or others, being that it is the best manna[7] of the country by which the inhabitants do subsist, and makes the French vessels to come there and go back loaded with merchandises for the traffic of furriers who come to* the remotest part of the north of America.

As soon as the resolution was made, many undertakes the voyage, for where there is lucre there are people enough to be had. They make them go up [to] Three Rivers with the band that came with the Sacs; there [they] take those that were most capable. For the purpose two Fathers[8] were chosen to conduct that company and endeavor to convert some of those foreigners of the remotest country to the Christian faith. We no sooner heard their design but saw the effects of the business, which affected in us much gladness for the pleasure we could do to one another, and so abler to oppose an enemy, if by fortune we should meet with any that would do us hurt or hinder us in our way.

About the middle of June[9] we began to take leave of our company and venture our lives for the common good. We find two and thirty men, some inhabitants, some gailliards[10] that desired but [to] do well. What a fairer bastion than a good tongue, especially when one sees his own chimney smoke, or when we can kiss our own wives, or kiss our neighbor's wife with ease and delight? It is a strange thing when victuals are wanting, work whole nights and days, lie down on the bare ground, and not always that happy — the breech in the water, the fear in the buttocks, to have the belly empty, the weariness in the bones, and drowsiness of the body by the bad weather that you are to suffer, having nothing to keep you from such calamity.

At last[11] we take our journey to see the issue of a prosperous adventure in such a dangerous enterprise. We resolved not to be the first that should complain. The French were together in order, the wildmen also. Saving my brother and I, that were accustomed to such voyages,[12] [not one of them] have foreseen what happened afterwards. Before our setting forth, we made some gifts. And by that means we were nine and twenty French in number and six wildmen.

---

*In the ms. the word is "from," not "to," but that cannot be what Radisson means. In this context "from" would suggest a non-existent phase of the fur trade.

We embarked our train in the night, because our number should not be known to some spies that might be in some ambush to know our departure, for the Iroquois are always abroad. We were two nights to get to Montreal, where eight Ottawas stayed for us and two French. If not for that company, we had passed the River of the Meadows, which makes an isle of Montreal and joins itself to the Lake of St. Louis three leagues farther than the height of that name.

We stayed no longer there than as the French got themselves ready. We took leave without noise of gun. We cannot avoid the ambush of the eagle which is like the owl that sees better in the night than in the day. We were not sooner come to the first river[13] but our wildmen sees five sorts of people of divers countries, laden with merchandise and guns which served them [better] for a show than for defense, if by chance they should be set on. The glory begins to show itself. No order being observed among them, the one sings, the other before goes in that posture. Without bad encounter we advanced three days; there was no need of such a silence among us.

Our men [being] composed only of seven score men, we had done well if we had kept together, not to go before in one river nor stay behind some two or three leagues. Some three or four boats now and then land to kill a wild beast and so put themselves into a danger of their lives; and if there were any precipice the rest should be impotent to help. We warned them to look to themselves. They laughed at us, saying we were women, that the Iroquois durst not set on them. Pride had such power that they thought themselves masters of the earth. But they will see[14] themselves soon mistaken: how that great God takes great care of the most wild creatures, and will that every man confesses his faults; and [God] gives them grace to come to obedience for the preservation of their lives, sends them a remarkable power and ordinance, which should give terror and retinue to those poor people misled* from the way of assurance.

As we wandered in the aforesaid manner all asunder, there comes a man alone out of the wood with a hatchet in his hand, with his braie,[15] and a cover over his shoulder, making signs aloud that we should come to him. The greatest part of that flock showed a palish face for fear at the sight of this man,

---

*In the ms. the phrase is ". . . poore mislead people from the way of assurance."

knowing him an enemy. They approached not without fear and apprehension of some plot. By this you may see the boldness of those buzzards that think themselves hectors[16] when they see but their shades and tremble when they see an Iroquois. That wildman, seeing us nearer, set him down on the ground and throws his hatchet away and raises again all naked to show that he hath no arms, desires them to approach nearer, for he is their friend and would save [lose] his life to save theirs. He showed indeed a right captaincy* for saving of men that runned to their ruin by their indiscretion and want of conduct. And what he did was out of mere piety, seeing well that they wanted wit, to go so like a company of bucks, everyone to his fancy, where his little experience leads him, nor thinking that danger wherein they were, showing by their march they were no men for not fearing. As for him, he was ready to die to render them service and prisoner into their hands freely. "For," saith he, "I might have escaped your sight, but that I would have saved you. I fear," saith he, "not death." So with that comes down into the water to his middle.

There comes many boats about him, takes him into one of the boats, tying a cord fast about his body. There is he fastened. He begins to sing his fatal song, that they call anouroyall. That horrid tone being finished, makes a long, a very long, speech, saying, "Brethren, the day the sun is favorable to me [it] appointed me to tell you that you are witless, before I die. Neither can they escape their enemies that are spread up and down everywhere, that watches all moments their coming [in order] to destroy them. Take great courage, brethren. Sleep not. The enemy is at hand. They wait for you. They are so near that they see you, and hear you, and are sure that you are their prey. Therefore I was willing to die to give you notice. For my part — that what I have been — I am a man and commander in the wars and took several prisoners; yet I would put myself in death's hands to save your lives. Believe me, keep you altogether. Spend not your powder in vain, thinking to frighten your enemies by the noise of your guns. See if the stones of your arrows be not bent or loose; bend your bows; open your ears; keep your hatchets sharp to cut trees to make you a fort; do not spend so much grease to grease yourselves, but keep it for your bellies. Stay not too long in the way. It's robbery to die with [such] conduct."

That poor wretch spokes the truth and gave good instructions,

---

*In the ms. the word is "capne."

but the greatest part did not understand what he said, saving the Hurons that were with him, and I, that told them as much as I could perceive. Everyone laughs, saying he himself is afraid and tells us that story. We call him a dog, a woman,[17] and a hen, which will make you know that we were men, and for his pains we should burn him when we come to our country. There you shall see the brutishness of those people that think themselves valiant to the last point. No comparison is to be made with them for valor, but quite contrary. They pass away the rest of that day with great exclamations of joy, but it will not last long.

That night we laid in our boats and made not the kettle boil because we had meat ready dressed. Every boat is tied up in the rushes, whether out of fear for what the prisoner told them or that the prisoner should escape I know not. They went to sleep without any watch. The French began to wish and moan for that place whence they came from. What will it be if we hear yet cries and sorrows after all?

Past the break of day everyone takes his oar to row. The foremost oars have great advantage. We heard the torrent rumble but could not come to the land that day, although not far from us.

Some twelve boats got afore us. There we are saluted with guns and outcries. In the meanwhile, one boat runs one way, one another. Some men lands and runs away. We are all put to it; none knows where he is, they are put to such a confusion. All those beasts gathers together again, frighted. Seeing no way to escape, got themselves all in a heap, like unto ducks that sees the eagle come to them.

That first fear being over a little, they resolved to land and to make a fort with all speed, which was done in less than two hours. The most stupidest drowsy are the nimblest for the hatchet and cutting of trees. The fort being finished, everyone maketh himself in a readiness to sustain the assault if any had attempted.

The prisoner was brought, who soon was dispatched, burned and roasted, and eaten. The Iroquois had so served them as many as they have taken. We missed twenty of our company, but some came safe to us, and lost thirteen that were killed and taken in that defeat.[18] The Iroquois, finding himself* weak,

---

*Here Radisson confuses the singular and plural pronoun. "Himself" refers to the collective Iroquois force, not to some previously unmentioned prisoner.

would not venture and was obliged to leave us, lest he should be discovered and served as the other. Neverthless, they showed good countenance, went and builded a fort as we have done, where they fortified themselves, and feed on human flesh which they got in the wars. They were afraid as much as we.

The night being come, eevryone embarks himself to the sound of a low trumpet. By the help of the darkness we went to the other side, leaving our merchandise for our ransom to the enemy that used us so unkindly. We made some carriages that night with a world of pain. We missed four of our boats, so that we must alter our equipages.

The wildmen complained much that the French could not swim; [but] for that, they might be together. The French, seeing that they were not able to undergo such a voyage, they consult together. And for conclusion resolved to give an end to such labors and dangers. Moreover, found themselves incapable to follow the wildmen, who went with all the speed possible night and day for the fear that they were in. The Fathers, seeing our weakness, desired the wildmen that they might have one or two to direct them, which by no means was granted, but bid us do as the rest. We kept still our resolution and, knowing more tricks than they, would not go back, which should be but disdainful and prejudicial. We told them so plainly that we would finish that voyage or die by the way. Besides that, the wildmen did not complain of us at all, but encouraged us. After a long arguing, everyone had the liberty to go backward, or forward if any had courage to venture himself with us. Seeing the great difficulties, all with one consent went back again, and we went on.

The wildmen were not sorry for their departure, because of their ignorance in the affairs of such navigation. It's a great alteration to see one and thirty reduced to two. We encouraged one another, both willing to live and die with one another, and that the least we could do, being brothers.

Before we [came] to the Lake of the Hurons we had crosses enough, but no encounter. We traveled only in the night in those dangerous places, which could not be done without many vexations and labors. Vanity was somewhat cooler for the example we have seen the day before. Hunger tormented us most, for we could not go seek for some wild beasts. Our chiefest food was only some few fishes, which the wildmen caught by a line, maybe two dozen a whole day, no bigger than my hand.

Being come to the place of repose, some did go along the waterside on the rocks, and there exposed ourselves to the rigor of the weather. Upon these rocks we find some shells, blackish without and the inner part whitish by reason of the heat of the sun and of the humidity. They are in a manner glued to the rock, so we must get another stone to get them off by scraping them hard.[19] When we thought to have enough [we] went back again to the cottages, where the rest were getting the little fishes ready with tripes,[20] guts and all. The kettle was full with the scraping of the rocks, which soon after it boiled became like starch, black and clammy and easily to be swallowed. I think if any bird had lighted upon the excrements of the said stuff they had stuck to it as if it were glue. In the fields we have gathered several fruits [such] as gooseberries, blackberries; in an hour we gathered above a bushel of such sorts, although not as yet full ripe.[21] We boiled it, and then everyone had his share. Here was daintiness slighted, for the belly did not permit us to get on neither shoes nor stockings[22] that the better we might go over the rocks, which did [make] our feet smart. [When] we came back our feet and thighs and legs were scraped with thorns, a heap of blood. The good God looked upon those infidels by sending them now and then a bear into the river, or if we perceived any in an isle forced them to swim, that by that means we might the sooner kill them. But the most parts there abouts is so sterile that there is nothing to be seen but rocks and sand and, on the high ways, deal trees that grow most miraculously, for that earth is not to be seen that can nourish the root, and most of them trees are very big and high.

We took a little refreshment in a place called the Lake of Castors,[23] which is some thirty leagues from the first great lake. Some of those wildmen [had] hid a rest[24] as they went down to the French, but the lake was so full of fishes we took so much that [it] served us a long while.

We came to a place where were abundance of otters, insomuch that I believe all gathered to hinder our passage. We killed some with our arrows, not daring to shoot because we discovered thereabouts some tracks, judging to be our enemy by the impression of their feet in the sand. All knows there one another by their march, for each hath his proper steps, some upon their toes, some on their heels, which is natural to them, for when they are infants the mother wrapeth them to their mode.

Here I speak not of the horrid streams we passed, nor of the falls of the water which were of an incredible height.[25]

85

[We were] in some parts most fair and delicious, where people formerly lived only by what they could get by the bow and arrow. We were come above three hundred leagues, always against the stream, and made sixty carriages, besides drawing,* besides the swift streams we overcame by the oars and poles to come to that little Lake of Castors, which may be 30 or 40 leagues in compass. The upper end of it is full of islands, where there is not time lost to wander about, finding wherewithal to make the kettle boil with venison, great bears, castors, and fishes, which are plenty in that place.

The river [26] that we go to the great lake [on] is somewhat favorable. We go down with ease and running of the water, which empties itself in that lake[27] in which we are now coming in. This river hath but eight high and violent streams, which is some 30 leagues in length.

The place where we were is a bay all full of rocks, small isles, and most between wind and water, with an infinite [number] of fishes, which are seen in the water so clear as crystal. That is the reason of so many otters, that lives only upon fish.

Each of us begins to look to his bundle and merchandise, and prepare himself for the bad weather that used to be on that great extent of water. The wildmen finds what they hid among the rocks three months before, [when] they came up to the French.

There we are stirring about in our boats as nimble as bees and divided ourselves into two companies.[28] Seven boats went towards west-northwest and the rest to the south. After we mourned enough for the death of our dear countrymen that were slained coming up, we take leave of each other with promise of amity and good correspondence one with another, as [much] for the continuance of peace as for the assistance of strength if the enemy should make an assault. [They, the Ottawas and Hurons, agreed] that they should not go to the French without giving notice one to another, and so go together.

We that were for the south went on several days merrily and saw by the way the place where the Fathers Jesuits had heretofore lived,[29] a delicious place, albeit we could but see it afar off. The coast of this lake is most delightful to the mind, the land smooth, and woods of all sorts. In many places there are many large open fields wherein, I believe, wildmen formerly lived before the de-

---

*Cordelling.

struction of the many nations which did inhabit [the fields] and [which] took more place than six hundred leagues about. I can well say that from the River of Canada[30] to the great Lake of the Hurons — which is near two hundred leagues in length and sixty in breadth, as I guess, for I have [journeyed] round about it[31] — [there are] plenty of fish. There are banks of sand five or six leagues from the waterside where [are] such an infinite deal of fish that scarcely we are able to draw our nets. There are fishes as big as children of two years old; there is sturgeon enough and other sorts that is not known to us. The south part is without isles, only in some bays where there are some. It is delightful to go along the side of the water in summer where you may pluck the ducks.

We must often stay in a place two or three days, for [if] the contrary winds were anything high we durst not venture the boats against the impetuosity of the waves, which is the reason that our voyages are so long and tedious.

A great many large deep rivers empties themselves in that lake — and an infinite number of other small rivers — that can bear boats, and all from lakes and pools which are in abundance in that country.

After we traveled many days we arrived at a large island, where we found their village, their wives, and children.[32]

You must know that we passed a strait some three leagues beyond that place. The wildmen give it a name; it is another lake, but not so big as that we passed before. We call it the Lake of the Staring Hairs[33] because those that live about it have their hair like a brush turned up. They all have a hole in their nose, which is done by a straw which is above a foot long; it bars their faces. Their ears have ordinarily five holes where one may put the end of his finger. They use those holes in this sort: to make themselves gallant, they pass throught it a screw of copper with much dexterity, and go on the lake in that posture. When the winter comes they wear no caps because of their hair turned up. They fill those screws with swan's down, and with it their ears covered; but I dare say that the people do not for to hold out the cold, but rather for pride; for their country is not so cold as the North and other lakes that we have seen since.[34]

It should be difficult to describe what variety of faces our arrival did cause — some of joy, others of sadness. Nevertheless, the number of joyful exceeded that of the sorrowful.

87

The season began to invite the lustiest to hunting. We neither desire to be idle in any place, having learned by experience that idleness is the mother of all evil, for it breeds most part of all sickness in those parts where the air is most delightful.[35]

They who had most knowledge in those quarters had familiarity with the people that live there about the last lake.

The nation that we were with[36] had wars with the Iroquois, and must trade. Our wildmen out of fear must consent to their enemy to live in their land. It's true that those who lived about the first lake had not for the most part the conveniency of our French merchandise, as [they have had] since; which obliged most of the remotest people to make peace, considering the enemy of theirs, that came as a thunderbolt upon them, so that they joined with them, and forget what was past for their own preservation.[37]

At our coming there we made large gifts to dry up the tears of the friends of the deceased; as we came there, the circumjacent neighbors came to visit us, that bid us welcome.

There comes news that there were enemy in the fields, that they were seen at the great field. There is a council called, and resolved that they should be searched [for] and set upon [as soon] as possible may be, which [was] executed speedily.

I offered my service, so went and looked for them two days, finding them the third day, gave them the assault when they least thought of it. We played the game so furiously that none escaped.

The day following, we turned to our village, with eight of our enemies dead and three alive. The dead were eaten, and the living were burned with a small fire to the rigor of cruelties, which comforted the desolate [Hurons and Ottawas] to see them[selves] revenged of the death of their relation.

We were then possessed by the Hurons and Ottawas, but our mind was not to stay in an island[38] but to be known with the remotest people. The victory that we have gotten made them consent to what we could desire, and because we showed willing[ness] to die for their defence; so we desired to go with a company of theirs that was going to the nation of the Staring Hairs.[39]

We were welcomed and much made of, saying that we were the gods and devils of the earth, that we should furnish them [supplies] and that they would bring us to their enemy to destroy them.*

---

*Radisson and company are now at Green Bay; the details of the journey there are not recorded.

We told them [we were] very well content; we [would] persuade them [the enemy] first to come peaceably, not to destroy them presently, and if they would not condescend then would we throw away the hatchet and make use of our thunders.[40]

We sent ambassadors to them with gifts. That nation, called Poutouatemick,[41] without more ado comes and meets us with the rest, and peace was concluded. Feasts were made, and dames with gifts came of each side with a great deal of mirth.

We visited them [the Potawatomies] during that winter.

By that means we made acquaintance with another nation, called Escotecke,[42] which signified fire. A fair, proper nation, they are tall and big and very strong. We came there in the spring. When we arrived there were extraordinary banquets. There they never have seen men with beards, because they pull their hairs as soon as it comes out, but much more astonished when they saw our arms, especially our guns, which they worshipped by blowing smoke of tobacco instead of sacrifice. I will not insist much upon their way of living, for of their ceremonies here you will see a patron.*

In the last voyage that we made, I will let you only know what course we runned in three years' time.[43]

We desired them [the Mascoutens] to let us know their neighboring nations. They gave us the names, which I hope to describe in the end of this most imperfect discourse,[44] at least those that I can remember. Among others they told us of a nation called Nadoueceronon,[45] which is very strong, with whom they were in wars with, and [of] another wandering nation, living only upon what they could come by. Their [the latter's] dwelling was on the side of the salt water in summertime, and in the land in the wintertime, for it's cold in their country. They call themselves Christinos.[46] Their confederates from all times, by reason of their speech, which is the same, often have joined together and have had companies of soldiers to war against that great nation [the Nadoueceronons].

Being desirous to know what they [the Mascoutens] did, they told us, if we would go with them to the great Lake of the Stinkings,[47] the time was come of their traffic, [the purpose of] which was [to get] as many knives as they could get from the French

---

*Pattern.

nation [Ottawa Indians]* which was at the coming-in of a lake called Superior.[48] But since the destruction of many neighbouring nations, they [the Ottawas] retired themselves to the height of the lake.[49] We knowed those people well; we went to them almost yearly,[50] and the company that came up with us were of the said nation,[51] but [we] never could tell punctually where they lived because they make the bars** of the Christinos, from whence they have the castors that they bring to the French. This place[52] is six hundred leagues off by reason of the circuit that we must do.

The Hurons and the Ottawas, from whence we came last,§ furnishes them [the Mascoutens] and comes to the furthest part of the Lake of the Stinkings, there to have light earthen pots and girdles made of goat's hair and small shells that grow at the seaside, with which they trim their clothes made of skin.§§

We, finding this opportunity, would not let it slip, but made gifts, telling that the other nation[s] would stand in fear of them because of us. We flattered them, saying none would dare to give them the least wrong, insomuch that many of the Ottawas were present to make the same voyage.§§§

I can assure you I liked no country as I have that wherein we wintered,[53] for whatever a man could desire was to be had in great plenty, viz., stags, fishes in abundance, and all sorts of meat, corn enough.

Those of the two nations would not come with us, but turned back to their nation. We nevertheless, [despite their friendliness, had] put ourselves in hazard, for our curiosity, [by] staying two or three years among that nation; we [had] ventured [it] for we understood some of their idiom and trusted to that.

---

*The Mascoutens, whose words Radisson is reporting, would naturally refer to the Ottawas, who traded regularly with the Frenchmen, as the "French nation."

**This seems to mean that the Ottawas stuck close to the Crees, and to some extent moved about, in order to be able to trade with them.

§At Manitoulin island.

§§Radisson, his company, and the Mascoutens apparently have now journeyed from inland Wisconsin back to Green Bay, where they meet for trade with Hurons and Ottawas from the north, as well as with the Green Bay Ottawas.

§§§Radisson is trying to recruit extra men for his journey to the South.

We embarked ourselves on the delightsomest lake of the world.[54] I took notice of their cottages and of the journeys of our navigation because the country was so pleasant, so beautiful, and fruitful that it grieved me to see that the world could not discover such enticing countries to live in. This I say because the Europeans fight for a rock in the sea against one another, or for a sterile land and horrid country that the people sent here or there by the changement of the air engenders sickness and dies thereof. Contrariwise, these kingdoms are so delicious and under so temperate a climate, plentiful of all things, the earth bringing forth its fruit twice a year, the people live long and lusty and wise in their way.

What conquest would that be at little or no cost, what labyrinth of pleasure should millions of people have, instead that millions complain of misery and poverty? What should not men reap out of the love [of] God in converting the souls? Here is more to be gained to heaven than what is by differences of nothing; there should not be so many dangers committed under the pretense of religion. Why [are] so many thresors [rewards?] hid from us by our own faults, by our negligence, covetousness, and unbelief? It's true, I confess, that the access is difficult, but must say that we are like the coxscombs of Paris when first they begin to have wings, imagining that the larks will fall in their mouths roasted;[55] but we ought [remember] that virtue is not acquired without labor and taking great pains.

We meet with several nations, all sedentary, amazed to see us, and were very civil. The further we journeyed* the delightfuller the land was to us. I can say that [in] my lifetime I never saw a more incomparable country, for all I been in Italy; yet Italy comes short of it, as I think [of] when it was inhabited and now forsaken of the wildmen.

Being about the great sea,[56] we conversed with people that dwelleth about the salt water,[57] who told us that they saw some great white thing sometimes upon the water, and [which] came towards the shore, and men in the top of it, and made a noise like a company of swans, which made me believe that they were mistaken. I could not imagine what it should be, except the Spaniard; and the reason is that we found a barrel broken as they use in Spain.

---

*In the ms. this word is "sejourned."

Those people have their hair long. They reap twice a year. They are called Tatanga,[58] that is to say, buff[alo people]. They war against Nadoueceronons* and war also against the Christinos. These two do no great harm to one another because the lake is between both.[59] They are generally stout men; they are able to defend themselves; they come but once a year to fight. If the season of the year had permitted us to stay (for we intended to go back the year following) we had endeavored to make peace between them.

We had not as yet seen the nation Nadoueceronons. We had Hurons with us; we persuaded them to come along to see their own nation that fled there,[60] but they would not by any means. We thought to get some castors there to bring down to the French, seeing [it] at last impossible to us to make such a circuit in twelve months' time.[61]

We were everywhere much made of; neither wanted victuals, for all the different nations that we met conducted us and furnished us with all necessaries.

Tending to those people, [we] went towards the south and came back by the north.

The summer passed away with admiration by the diversity of the nations that we saw [and] for the beauty of the shore of that sweet sea.[62] Here we saw fishes of divers [kinds]; some like the sturgeons and have a kind of slice at the end of their nose; some three fingers broad in the end and two only near their nose; and some eight thumbs long, all marbled of a blackish color. There are birds whose bills are two and twenty thumbs long, that swallows a whole salmon, keeps it a long time in his bill. We saw also she goats, very big.[63] There is an animal somewhat less than a cow whose meat is exceeding good. There is no want of stags nor buffs. There are so many turkeys that the boys throws stones at them for their recreation. We found no sea serpents[64] as we in other lakes have seen, especially in that of Ontario and that of the Staring Hairs. There are some in that of the Hurons, but scarce for the great cold in winter. They come not near the Upper Lake.

In that of the Staring Hairs, I saw [a] young boy [who] was bitten. He takes immediately his stony knife and a pointed stick and cuts off the whole wound, being no other remedy for it. They

*In view of note 45, this means that the different tribes of the Sioux nation sometimes battled each other.

92

[the Indians known as Staring Hairs] are great sorcerers, and turn the wheel.[65] I shall speak of this at large in my last voyage.

Most of the shores of the lake[66] is nothing but sand. There are mountains to be seen far in the land. There comes not so many rivers from that lake as from others; those that flow from it are deeper and broader. The trees are very big, but not so thick; there is a great distance from one another. And a quantity of all sorts of fruits, but small. The vines grows all by the riverside. The grape is very big, green, is seen there at all times. It never snows nor freezes there, but mighty hot; yet, for all that, the country is not so unwholesome, for we seldom have seen infirmed people.

I will speak of their manner in my last voyage which I made.[67]*

In October we came to the strait of the two Lakes of the Stinkings** and the Upper Lake,[68] where there are little isles towards [the] northwest, [a] few towards the southeast, very small. The lake towards the north, at the side of it, is full of rocks and sand, yet great ships can ride on it without danger. We, being of three nations,[69] arrived there with booty, disputed awhile, for some would return to their country — that was the nation of the Fire — and would have us back to their dwelling. We by all means would know the Christinos; to go back was out of our way. We contented[70] the Hurons to our advantage with promises, and [the] others with hope, and persuaded the Ottawas to keep his resolution, because we were but five small days[71] from those of late that lived in the sault of the coming-in of the said Upper Lake, from whence that name of [the] sault — which is Pauoestigonce in the wild language — which hereafter we will call the nation of the Sault.

---

*This sentence seems to allude to the Staring Hairs — the nearest referent of the possessive "their." Since the sentence is not omitted, as Mr. Adams suggests it might be (note 67), it would make the most sense if it were transposed to a position directly following the phrase "at large in my last voyage," which ends the second paragraph preceding. Notice the recurrence of the phrase "last voyage"; it seems to me to be merely a redundancy and not references to a pair of "last voyages." In this regard, however, see also note 68.

**Lake Michigan was not always clearly distinguished from Green Bay in the early narratives.

Not many years since, they had a cruel war against the Nadoue-ceronons. Although much inferior in number, nevertheless that small number of the Sault was a terror unto them, since they had trade with the French. They never have seen such instruments as the French furnished them. Withal, it is a proud nation; therefore would not submit, although they had to do with a bigger nation thirty times than they were.[72] They were called enemy by all those that have the accent of the Algonquin language. The wildmen call [the enemy] Nadoue, which is the beginning of their name.[73]

The Iroquois have the title of bad enemy, Maesocchy Nadoue.

Now, seeing that the Christinos had [only] hatchets and knives, they resolved to make peace with those of the Sault, that [formerly] durst not have gone [a] hundred leagues upon that Upper Lake with assurance. They [the Sault] would not [however] hearken to anything, because their [the Christinos'] general resolved [also] to make peace with another nation [probably the Iroquois] that got guns, the noise of which had frighted them more than the bullets that were in them.* The time approached. There came about one hundred of the nation of the Sault to those that lived towards the north. The Christinos got a bigger company and fought a battle. Some were slain of both sides. The captain of those of the Sault lost his eye by an arrow. The battle being over, he made a speech and said that he lost his sight of one side, [but with] the other he foresee what he would do; his courage being abject by that loss, [he said] that he himself should be ambassador and conclude the peace. He seeing that the Iroquois came too often — a visit I must confess very displeasing, being that some [of] ours looses their lives or liberty — so that we retired ourselves to the higher lake, near the nation of the Nadoueceronons, where we were well received but were mistrustd when many were seen together.

———

*In the ms. this passage reads thus: "Now seeing that the Christinos had hattchetts and knives, for that they resolved to make peace wth those of the sault, that durst not have gon hundred of leagues uppon that upper lake wth assurance. They would not hearken to any thing, because their general resolved to make peace wth those of the Sault Christinos, and an other nation that gott gunns: ye noise of wch had frighted them more then the bulletts yt weare in them." Last "Sault" crossed out in the ms.

94

We arrived then where the nation of the Sault was,[74] where we found some Frenchmen that came up with us,[75] who thanked us kindly for to come and visit them. The wild Ottawas that came with us found some of their nation slaves, who were also glad to see them. For all they were slaves, they had meat enough, which they have not in their own country so plentiful, being no huntsmen, but altogether fishers. As for those towards the north, they are most expert in hunting and live upon nothing else the most part of the year.

We were long there before we got acquaintance with those that we desired so much,[76] and they in like manner had a fervent desire to know us, as we them. Here comes a company of Christinos from the Bay of the North Sea, to live more at ease in the middle of the woods and forests; by reason they might trade with those of the Sault and have the conveniency to kill more beasts.

There we passes the winter[77] and learned the particularities that since we saw by experience. Here I will not make a long discourse. During that time [we] only made good cheer and killed stags, buff, elands,[78] and castors. The Christinos had skill in that game above the rest. The snow proved favorable that year, which caused much plenty of everything. Most of the woods and forest are very thick, so that I was in some places as dark as in a cellar, by reason of the boughs of trees. The snow that falls, being very light, hath not the strength to stop the eland, which is a mighty strong beast, much like a mule, having a tail cut off two or three or four thumbs long, the foot cloven like a stag. He has a muzzle mighty big. I have seen some that have the nostrils so big that I put into it my two fists at once with ease. Those that uses to be where the buffs be are not so big, but about the bigness of a coach horse.[79] The wildmen call them "the little sort." As for the buff, it is a furious animal. One must have a care of him, for every year he kills some Nadoueceronons. He comes for the most part in the plains and meadows. He feeds like an ox. The oriniack[80] seldom gallops; I have seen of their horns that a man could not lift them from the ground; they are branchy and flat, in the middle of which the wildmen makes dishes that can well hold three quarts. These horns fall off every year, and it's a thing impossible that they will grow again.* The horns of buffs are as those of an

---

*Radisson seems to mean it is hardly imaginable that the antlers grow again.

95

ox, but not so long, but bigger and of a blackish color. He hath a very long hairy tail; he is reddish, his hair frizzed and very fine, all the parts of his body much unto an ox. The biggest are bigger than any ox whatsoever. Those are to be found about the Lake of the Stinkings and towards the north of the same; they come not to the Upper Lake but by chance. It's a pleasure to find the place of their abode, for they turn round about, compassing two or three acres of land, beating the snow with their feet and, coming to the center, they lie down and rise again to eat the boughs of trees that they can reach. They go not out of their circle that they have made until hunger compells them.

We did what we could to have correspondence with that warlike nation[81] and reconcile them with the Christinos. We went not there that winter. Many were slained of both sides the summer last. The wound was yet fresh, wherefore it was hard to conclude peace between them. We could do nothing, for we intended to turn back to the French the summer following. Two years were expired.[82] We hoped to be at the two years' end with those that gave us over for dead, having before come back at a year's end.[83] As we are once in those remote countries, we cannot do as we would. At last we declared our mind, first to those of the Sault, [then] encouraging those of the North that we are their brethren and that we would come back and force their enemy to peace, or that we would help against them. We made gifts one to another.[84]

[We] thwarted a land of almost 50 leagues before the snow was melted. In the morning it was a pleasure to walk, for we could go without rackets; the snow was hard enough because it freezed every night. When the sun began to shine, we paid for the time past; the snow stuck so to our rackets that I believe our shoes weighed 30 pounds, which was a pain, having a burden upon our backs besides.

We arrived — some hundred and fifty of us, men and women —to a riverside[85] where we stayed three weeks making boats. Here we wanted not fish. During that time we made feasts at a high rate. So we refreshed ourselves from our labors. In that time we took notice that the buds of trees began to spring, which made us to make more haste and be gone.

We went up that river eight days, till we came to a nation called Poutouatenick and Matouenock,[86] that is, the Scratchers. There we got some Indian meal and corn from those two nations, which lasted us till we came to the first landing isle.[87]

There we were well received again.* We made gifts to the elders to encourage the young people to bring us down to the French, but [we were] mightily mistaken, for they would reply, "Would you bring us to be killed? The Iroquois are everywhere about the river[88] and undoubtedly will destroy us if we go down, and afterwards our wives and those that stayed behind. Be wise, brethren, and offer not to go down this this year to the French. Let us keep our lives." We made many private suits, but all in vain. That vexed us most that we had given away most of our merchandise and swapped a great deal for castors. Moreover, they made no great harvest, being but newly there;[89] besides, they were no great huntsmen. Our journey was broken till the next year, and must perforce.[90]

That summer I went ahunting, and my brother stayed where he was welcome and put up a great deal of Indian corn that was given him. He intended to furnish the wildmen that were to go down to the French, if they had not enough. The wildmen did not perceive this, for if they wanted any we could hardly kept it for our use. The winter passes away in good correspondence one with another, and [we] sent ambassadors to the nations that uses to go down to the French, which rejoiced them the more and made us pass that year with a greater pleasure, saving that my brother fell into the falling sickness,[91] and many were sorry for it. That [the sickness] proceeded only of a long stay in a new discovered country, and the idleness contributes much to it.[92] There is nothing comparable to exercise. It is the only remedy of such diseases. After he languished awhile, God gave him his health again.[93]

We[94] were four months in our voyage, without doing anything but go from river to river. We met several sorts of people. We conversed with them, being long time in alliance with them. By the persuasion of some of them we went into the great river that divides itself in two,[95] where the Hurons, with some Ottawa and the wildmen that had wars with them, had retired. There is no great difference in their language, as we were told. This nation have wars against those of [the] forked river;[96] it is so called because it has two branches, the one towards the west, the other towards the south, which we believe runs towards Mexico, by the tokens they gave us. Being among these people, they

---

*By the Hurons who had fled from the Iroquois.

told us the prisoners they take tells them that they have wars against a nation, against men that build great cabins and have great beards and had such knives as we have had. Moreover, they showed a decad of beads[97] and gilded pearls that they have had from that people, which made us believe they were Europeans. They showed one of that nation that was taken the year before. We understood him not. He was much more tany[98] than they with whom we were. His arms and legs were turned outside; that was the punishment inflicted upon him: so they do with them that they take, and kill them with clubs, and do often eat them. They do not burn their prisoners as those of the northern parts.

We were informed of that nation that live in the other river. There were men of an extraordinary height and bigness. That made us believe they had no communication with them. They live only upon corn and citruls[99] which are mighty big. They have fish in plenty throughout the year. They have fruit as big as the heart of an oriniack, which grows on vast trees which in compass are three armfuls. When they see little men, they are afraid and cry out, which makes many come help them. Their arrows are not of stones, as ours are, but of fish bones and other bones that they work neatly, as all other things. Their dishes are made of wood. I, having seen them, could not but admire the curiosity of their work. They have great calumets[100] of great stones, red and green. They make a store of tobacco. They have a kind of drink that makes them mad for a whole day. This I have not seen; therefore you may believe as you please.

When I came back I found my brother sick, as I said before.[101] God gave him his health, more by his courage than by any good medicine, for our bodies are not like those of the wildmen.[102]

The desire that everyone had to go down to the French made them earnestly look out for castors; they have not so many there as in the north part, so in the beginning of spring many came to our isle. There were no less, I believe, than five hundred men that were willing to venture themselves. The corn that my brother kept did us a world of service. The wildmen brought a quantity of flesh salted in a vessel. When we were ready to depart, here comes strange news of the defeat of the Hurons,[103] which news I thought would put off the voyage. There was a council held, and most of them were against going down to the French, saying that the Iroquois were to bar [the way] this year and the best was to stay till the following year; and now the enemy [the

Iroquois], seeing himself frustrated of his expectation, would not stay longer, thinking thereby that we were resolved nevermore to go down, and that next year there should be a bigger company and better able to oppose an enemy.

My brother and I — seeing ourselves all out of hopes of our voyage without our corn, which was already bestowed, and without any merchandise or scarce having one knife betwixt us both — we were in a great apprehension lest the Hurons should as they have done often, when the Fathers were in their country, kill a Frenchman. Seeing the equipage ready, and many more that thought long to depart thence for merchandise, we upon this resolved to call a public council in the place.

The elders, hearing [of it], came and advised us not to undertake it, giving many fair words, saying, "Brethren, why are you such enemies to yourselves, to put yourselves in the hands of those that wait for you? They will destroy you and carry you away captives. Will you have your brethren destroyed that loves you? Being slained, who then will come up and baptize our children?[104] Stay till the next year, and then you are like to have the number of six hundred men in company with you. Then you may freely go, without intermission. You shall take the church along with you, and the fathers and mothers will send their children to be taught in the way of truth of the Lord."

Our answer was that we would speak in public, which [was] granted.

The day appointed is come. There gathered above eight hundred men to see who should have the glory in a round. They sat down on the ground. We desired silence. The elders being in the middle, and we in their middle, my brother began to speak: "Who am I? Am I a foe or a friend? If I am a foe, why did you suffer me to live so long among you? If I am friend, and you take [me] so to be, hearken to what I shall say. You know, my uncles and brethren, that I hazarded my life going up with you. If I have no courage, why did you not tell me at my first coming here? And if you have more wit then we, why do not you use it [and] be preserving your knives, your hatchets, and your guns that you had from the French? You will see, if the enemy will set upon you, that you will be attrapped like castors in a trap. How will you defend yourselves? Like men that is not courageous, to let yourselves be catched like beasts? How will you defend your villages? With castors' skins? How will you defend your wives and children from the enemy's hands?"

Then my brother made me stand up, saying, "Show them the way to make war, if they are able to uphold it."

I took a gown of castors' skins that one of them had upon his shoulders and did beat him with it. I asked the others if I was [a] soldier. "Those are the arms that kill, and not your robes. What will your enemy say when you perish without defending yourselves? Do not you know the French way? We are used to fight with arms and not with robes. You say that the Iroquois waits for you because some of your men were killed. It is only to make you stay until you are quite out of stock,[105] that they [may] dispatch you with ease. Do you think that the French will come up here when the greatest part of you is slained by your own fault? You know that they cannot come up without you. Shall they come to baptize the dead? Shall your children learn to be slaves among the Iroquois for their fathers' cowardness? You call me Iroquois. Have not you seen me disposing my life with you? Who has given you your life, if not the French? Now you will not venture, [even though] many of your confederates are come to visit you and venture their lives with you. If you will deceive them, you must not think that they will come another time for thy words nor desire. You have spoken of it first. Do what you will. For my own part, I will venture, choosing to die like a man than live like a beggar. Having not wherewithal to defend myself, farewell! I have my sack of corn ready. Take all my castors. I shall live without you."

Then [we] departed that company.[106]

They were amazed of our proceeding. They stayed long before they spoke one to another. At last sent us considerable persons who bid us cheer up. "We see that you are in the right. The voyage is not broken. The young people took very ill that you have beaten them with the skin. All vowed to die like men, and undertake the journey. You shall hear what the council will ordain the morrow. They are to meet privately, and you shall be called to it. Cheer up and speak as you have done; that is my counsel to you. For this you will remember me when you will see me in your country, for I will venture myself with you."

Now we are more satisfied than the day before. We were to use all rhetoric to persuade them to go down, for we saw the country languish very much, for they could not subsist and, moreover, they were afraid of us.

The council is called, but we had no need to make a speech, finding them disposed to make the voyage and to submit.

"You women, get your husbands' bundles ready. They go to get wherewithal to defend themselves and you alive."

Our equipage was ready in six days; we embarked ourselves.[107] We were in number about five hundred, all stout men. We had with us a great store of castors' skins. We came to the south. We now go back to the north,[108] to overtake a band of men that went before to give notice to others. We passed the lake[109] without danger. We wanted nothing, having good store of corn and nets to catch fish, which is plentiful in the rivers. We came to a place where eight Iroquois wintered. That was the company that made a slaughter before our departure from home; our men repented now they did not go sooner, for it might be they should have surprised them. At last we are out of those lakes.[110] One hides a cache of meal, the other his camp iron and all, and all that could be cumbersome. After many pains and labors we arrived to the Sault of Calumet,[111] so called because of the stones that are there very convenient to make tobacco pipes. We are now within a hundred league of the French habitation,[112] and hitherto no bad encounter. We still found tracks of men, which made us still to have the more care and guard of ourselves.

Some thirty leagues from this place we killed wild cows,[113] and then got ourselves into cottages, where we heard some guns go off, which made us put out our fires and embark ourselves with all speed. We navigated all that night. About the break of day we made a stay, [in order] not to go through the violent stream, for fear the enemy should be there to dispute the passage. We landed and instantly sent two men to know whether the passage was free. They were not half a mile off when we saw a boat of the enemy thwarting the river, which they had not done without discovering our boats, [we] having nothing to cover our boats nor hide them. Our lightest boats showed themselves by pursuing the enemy. They did shoot, but to no effect, which made our two men come back in all haste. We, seeing ourselves but merchantmen, would not long follow a man of war because he runned swifter than ours.

We proceeded in our way with great diligence till we came to the carriage place, where the one-half of our men were in readiness, whilst the other half carried the baggage and the boats. We had a great alarms, but no hurt done. We saw but one boat, but have seen four more going up the river. Methinks they thought themselves somewhat weak for us, which persuaded us [of] two things. First, that they were afraid; secondly, that they went to warn their company, which thing warned us the more to make haste.

The second day — at evening after we landed and boiled an oriniack which we killed — we then see sixteen boats of our enemy coming. They no sooner perceived us but they went on the other side of the river. It was a good luck for us to have seen them. Our wildmen did not say what they thought, for they esteemed themselves already lost. We encouraged them and desired them to have courage and [be] not afraid. I think we were strong enough for them [and] must stoutly go and meet them, [if] they should stand still. We should be all together and put our castors' skins upon perches, which could keep us from the shot, which we did. We had four and twenty guns ready and gave them to the Hurons, who knows how to handle them better than the others. The Iroquois, seeing us come and that we were five to one, could not imagine what to do. Nevertheless, they would show their courage. Being that they must pass, they put themselves in array to fight. If we had not been with some Hurons that knowed the Iroquois' trick, I believe that our wildmen had runned away, leaving their fusiques[114] behind. We, being near one another, commanded that they should row with all their strength towards them. We kept close one to another to persecute what was our intent. We begin to make outcries and sing. The Hurons in one side, the Algonquins at the other side, the Ottawas, the Pauoestigonce, the Amickkoick, the Nadouicenago, the Ticacon,[115] and we both encouraged them all, crying out with a loud noise. The Iroquois begins to shoot, but we made ours to go on forward without any shooting. That was the only way of fighting. They indeed turned their backs, and we followed them awhile. Then was it that we were called devils, with great thanks and encouragements, attributing to us the masters of war and the only captains. We desired them to keep good watch and sentry, and if we were not surprised we should come safe and sound, without hurt, to the French. The Iroquois, seeing us go on our way, made as if they would leave us.

We made three carriages that day where the enemy could do us mischief if they had been there. The cunning knaves followed us nevertheless pretty close. We left five boats behind that were not loaded. We did so to see what invention our enemy could invent, knowing very well that his mind was to surprise us. It is enough that we are warned that they follow us. At last we perceived that he was before us, which put us in some fear, but seeing us resolute, [he] did what he could to augment his number. But we were mighty vigilant and sent some to make a discovery at every carriage through the woods. We were told that they were in an ambush and [had] builded a fort below the Long Sault,[116] where we were to pass. Our wildmen said doubtless they have got another company of their nation, so that some minded to throw their castors away and return home. We told them that we were almost at the gates of the French habitation and bid [them] therefore have courage and that our lives were in as great danger as theirs; if we were taken, we should never escape, because they knowed us: I because I runned away from their country, having slained some of their brethren,[117] and my brother [because he] long since was the man that furnished their enemy with arms.

They at last were persuaded, and landed within a mile of the landing place and sent three hundred men before, armed. We made them great bucklers that the shot could not pierce in some places; they were to be carried, if there were occasion for it. Being come near the torrent, we finding the Iroquois lying in ambush, who began to shoot. The rest of our company went about cutting trees and making a fort, whilst some brought the boats, which being come, we left as few men [guarding them] as possible might be. The rest helped to carry wood. We had about two hundred men that were gallant soldiers; most were Hurons, Pauoestigonce, and Amickkoick [who had] frequented the French for a time. The rest were skillful in their bows and arrows.

The Iroquois, perceiving our device, resolved to fight. By forcing them to let us pass with our arms, they did not know best what to do, being not so well munitioned* nor so many men above a hundred and fifty. They forsook the place and retired into the fort which was underneath the rapids.

We in the meanwhile have slained five of theirs, and not one of ours hurted, which encouraged our wildmen. We bid them still to have good courage, that we should have the victory. We went and made another fort near theirs, where two of our men were wounded, but lightly. It is a horrid thing to hear the enormity of outcries of those different nations. The Iroquois sung like devils and often made sallies to make us decline. They got nothing by that but some arrows that did incommodate them to some pur-

---

*In the ms. the phrase is ". . . not so munished . . . ."

pose. We foresee that such a battle could not hold out long for want of powder and shot and arrows, so by the consent of my brother and the rest [I] made a speech in the Iroquois language, induing myself with armors that I might not be wounded with every bullet or arrow that the enemy sent perpetually. Then I spoke: "Brethren, we came from your country, and bring you to ours, not to see you perish unless we perish with you. You know that the French are men and makes forts that cannot be taken so soon. Therefore, cheer up, for we love you and will die with you." This being ended, nothing but howling and crying.

We brought our castors, tied them eight by eight, and rolled them before us. The Iroquois — finding that they must come out of their fort to the waterside, where they left their boats to make use of them in case of need — made an escape, leaving all their baggage behind, which was not much. Neither had we enough to fill our bellies with the meat that was left. There were kettles, broken guns, and rusty hatchets.

They being gone, our passage was free, so we made haste and endeavored to come to our journey's end. To make the more haste, some boats went down that swift stream without making carriage,[118] hoping to follow the enemy. But the bad luck was where my brother was [in] the boat that turned over in the torrent. Being seven of them together, [they] were in great danger, [but] God was merciful to give them strength to save themselves, to [our] great admiration, for few can speed so well in such precipices. When they came to land, they [were] cut by rocks. My brother lost his book of annotations of the last year of our being in these foreign nations. We lost never a castor, but maybe some better thing. It's better to loose all than lose his life.[119]

You[120] must know that seventeen French made a plot with four Algonquins to make a league with three score Hurons for to go and wait for the Iroquois in the passage at their return with castors on their ground, hoping to beat and destroy them with ease, [the Iroquois] being destitute of necessary things. If one hath his gun, he wants his powder, and so the rest. The other side without doubt had notice that the travelers [Iroquois] were abroad and would not fail to come down with a company and make a valiant deed and heroic action to destroy them all, and consequently make the French tremble, as well as the wildmen, for the one could not live without the other — the one for his

104

commodities, the other for his castors. So the Iroquois, pretending to wait for us* at that passage, came thither flocking. The French and wild company, to put the Iroquois in some fear and hinder his coming there so often with such confidence, were resolved to lay a snare against him.

That company of soldiers, being come to the furthest place of the Long Sault[121] without being discovered, thought [themselves] already to be conquerors making carriage. Having abroad fifteen men to make discoveries, they met as many enemies. They assaulted one another, and the Iroquois found themselves weak, left there their lives and bodies, saving two that made the escape, went to give notice to two hundred of theirs, that made ready as they heard the guns to help their foreguard.

The French, seeing such great odds, made a retreat, and warned by four Algonquins that a fort was built not afar off — built by his nation the last year — they fled into it in an ill hour.

In the meanwhile, the Iroquois consulted what they should do. They sent to five hundred and fifty of the lower nation and fifty Anojot that were not afar off. Now they would assault the French in their fort.

The fort not holding but 20 men, the Hurons could not come in and could not avoid the shot of the enemy. Then the French pulled down the fort and closed together. They stoutly began to work. Those that the French had killed, [they] cut their heads off and put them upon long poles of their fort. This skirmish [en]dured two days and two nights. The Iroquois finds themselves plagued, for the French had a kind of bucklers and shelters.

Now arrives six hundred men that they [the French] did not think of in the least. Here is nothing but cries, fire, and flame day and night. Here is not to be doubted the one to take the other, the one to defend himself till death. The Hurons, seeing such a company, submitted to the enemies, but are like to pay for their cowardice. Being in their hands, [they] were tied, abused, smitten, and burned as if they were taken by force, for those barbarous [Iroquois] were revenged on their bones as any was wounded or killed in the battle.

In this great extremity, our small company of one and twenty did resist five days against eight hundred men, and the two fore-

---

*Meaning, of course, the Frenchmen of the story, not any group that Radisson is with.

most days against two hundred, which were seven days together without intermission, and the worst was that they had no water, as we saw, for they made a hole in the ground out of which they got but little because they were on a hill. It was to be pitied. There was not a tree but was shot with bullets.

The Iroquois come with bucklers to make a breach. The French put fire to a barrel of powder,[122] thinking to shake the Iroquois or make him go back, but did to their [own] great prejudice, for it fell again in their fort, which made an end to their combat. Upon this, the enemy enters, kills and slains all that he finds. So [not] one did make an escape, saving one that was found alive, but he stayed not long. In a short time after, his fortune was as the rest, for he was brought to one of the forts[123] of the Iroquois. As he was bid to sit down, he finds a pistolet by him and takes it at adventure, no knowing whether it was charged or no. He puts the end to the breast of him that tied him and killed him in the presence of all his comrades. Without any more ado he was burnt very cruelly. All the French, though dead, were tied to posts along the riverside, and the four Algonquins. As for the Hurons, they were burnt at their discretion. Some nevertheless escaped to bring the certain news how it happened.

It was a terrible spectacle for us, for we came there 8 days after that defeat,[124] which saved us without doubt.

I believe for certain that the Iroquois lost many men, having to do with such brave and valiant soldiers as that company was.[125]

To our purpose. We came back[126] to our carriage. Whilst we endeavored to aid our companions in their extremity, the Iroquois got a great way before, not well satisfied to have stayed for us, having lost seven of their* men; two of them were not nimble enough, for our bullets and arrows made them stay for good and all. Seven of our [men] were sick; they have been like to be drowned, and the other two were wounded by the Iroquois.

The next day we went on without any delay or encounter. I give you leave if those of Montreal were not overjoyed to see us arrived. They affirm [to] us the pitiful conditions that the country was [in] by the cruelty of those cruel barbarians that perpetually killed and slaughtered to the very gate of the French fort.

All this hindered not our going to the French at Three Rivers,

---

*In the ms. the word is "our," but that would not make sense in view of what follows.

after we refreshed ourselves three days. But like to pay dearly for our bold attempt. Twenty inhabitants came down with us in a shallop. As we doubled the point of the River of the Meadows, we were set upon by several Iroquois, but durst not come near us because of two small brass pieces that the shallop carried. We tied our boats together and made a fort about us of castors' skins, which kept us from all danger. We went down the stream in that posture. The enemy left us — and did well — for our wildmen were disposed to fight, and our shallop could not come near them for want of water.

We came to Quebec, where were saluted with the thundering of the guns and batteries of the fort and of the three ships that were then at anchor,[127] which had gone back to France without castors if we had not come. We were well treated for five days. The governor made gifts and sent two brigantines to bring us to Three Rivers, where we arrived the second day, and the fourth day they went away. This is the end of our three years' voyage and [a] few months.[128]

After so much pain and danger, God was so merciful [as] to bring us back safe to our dwelling, where the one[129] was made much of by his wife, the other[130] by his friends and kindred.

The enemy that had discovered us in our going down got more company, as many as they could, to come to the passages, and there to wait for the return of those people,* knowing well that they could not stay there long because the season of the year was almost spent. But we made them by our persuasions go down to Quebec, which proved well, for the Iroquois thought they were gone another way.

So [the Iroquois] came the next day after our arrival to make a discovery [at] Three Rivers, where, being perceived, there is care taken to receive them. The[131] French cannot go as the wildmen through the woods, but embarks themselves in small boats and went along the riverside, knowing that if the enemy was repulsed he would make his retreat to the riverside. Some Algonquins were then at the habitation who, to show their valor, disposed themselves to be the first in the pursuit of the enemy. Some of the strongest and nimblest French kept them company, with another great number of men called Ottawas.

We were soon together by the ears. There were some three

---

*The Indians that had come to Three Rivers with Radisson.

hundred men of the enemy that came in the space of a fourteen night together, but when they saw us they made use of their heels; but the better to play their game; after they runned half a mile in the wood, they turned again, where then the battle began most furiously by shooting at one another. That uppermost nation,[132] being not used to shooting nor hear such noise, began to shake off their armors and took their bows and arrows, which indeed made [more] execution than all the guns they had brought. So, seeing fifty Algonquins and fifteen French keep to it, they resolved to stick to it also, which [resolution] had not lasted long, for seeing that their arrows were almost spent, and they [the combatants] must close together, and that the Iroquois had an advantage by keeping themselves behind the trees, and we to fall upon [the Iroquois] must be without bucklers, which diminished much our company that was foremost.

We gave them, in spite [of our efforts], place to retire themselves, which they did with all speed. Having come to the waterside where their boats were, [the Iroquois] saw the French all in a row [in their boats on the river and] laid in an ambush to receive them, which they had done if God had not been for us. They [the French on the river], thinking the enemy was occupied with the other French and wildmen,* mistrusted nothing to the contrary. The French that were in the wood, seeing the evident danger where their countrymen laid, encouraged the Ottawas, who took their arms again and followed the enemy, who [was] not feared [any longer, and] arrived before the French were apprehended, by good luck. One of the Iroquois, thinking his boat would be seen, goes quickly and puts it out of sight and reveals** himself, which warned the French to hinder them to go further upon that score.

Our wildmen made a stand and fell upon them stoutly. The combat begins anew. They see the French that were upon the water come near, which reinforced them to take their boats with all haste and leave their booty behind. The few boats that the French had brought could enter but the sixty French [into the battle], who were enough. The wildmen [Iroquois] nevertheless did not go without their prey, which was three men's heads that they killed at the first fight, but they left eleven of theirs in the

---

*In the ms. the phrase is ". . . thinking yt the enemy was att hand . . . ."
**In the ms. the word is "discovers."

place, besides many more that were wounded. They went straight to their country, which did a great service to the return of our wildmen, [who] met with none all their journey, as we heard afterwards.

They[133] went away the next day, and we stayed at home at rest that year.[134] My brother and I considered whether we should discover what we have seen or no because we had not a full and whole discovery, which was that we have not been in the Bay of the North; not knowing anything but by report of the wild Christinos, we would make no mention of it for fear that those wildmen should tell us a fib. We would [rather] have made a discovery of it ourselves and have an assurance before we should discover anything of it.

The end of the Auxotacicac[135] voyage,
which is the third voyage.

SUPERIOR VOYAGE

THE SPRING FOLLOWING[1] we were in hopes to meet with some company, having been so fortunate the years before. Now, during the winter, whether it was that my brother revealed to his wife what we had seen in our voyage and what we further intended, or how it came to pass, it was [somehow] known so much that the Jesuits were desirous to find out a way how they might get down the castors from the Bay of the North by the Saguenay, and so make themselves masters of that trade. They resolved to make a trial as soon as the ice would permit them. To discover our intentions they were very earnest with me to engage myself in that voyage, to the end that my brother would give over his, which I utterly denied them, knowing that they could never bring it about; I heard the wildmen say that, although the way be easy, the wildmen that feed at their doors would have hindred them because they make a livelihood of that trade.

In my last voyage I took notice of that that goes to three hands, which is first from the people of the North to another nation that the French call Squirrels and another nation that they call Porc-épic, and from them to the Montagnais[2] and Algonquins that live in or about Quebec. But the greatest hindrance is the scant of water and the horrid torrents and want of victuals, being no way to carry more than can serve fourteen days' or three weeks' navigation on that river.[3] Nevertheless, the Fathers are gone with the governor's son of Three Rivers and six other French and twelve wildmen.[4]

During that time we made our proposition to the governor of Quebec: that we were willing to venture our lives for the good of the country and go to travel to the remotest countries with two Hurons that made their escape from the Iroquois. They wished nothing more than to be in those parts where their wives and families were, about the Lake of the Staring Hair; to that intent [they] would stay until August to see if anybody would come from thence. My brother and I were of one mind, and for more assurance my brother went to Montreal to bring these two men along. He came back, being in danger. The governor gives him leave, conditionally that he must carry two of his servants along with him and give them the moiety of the profit. My brother was vexed at such an unreasonable demand: to take inexperted men to their ruin; all our knowledge and desire depended only of this last voyage; besides, that the governor should compare two of his servants to us that have ventured ourselves so many years and maintained the country with our generosity in the presence of all; neither was there one that had the courage to undertake what we have done. We made the governor a slight answer and told him for our part we knowed what we were: discoverers before governors; we should be glad to have the honor of his company, but not of that of his servants, and that we were both masters and servants. The governor was much displeased at this and commanded us not to go without his leave.[5] We desired the Fathers to speak to him about it. Our addresses were slight because of the shame put upon them the years before of their return. Besides, they stayed for an opportunity to go there themselves, for their design is to further the Christian faith to the greatest glory of God, and indeed are charitable to all those that are in distress and needy, especially to those that are worthy or industrious in their way of honesty. This the truth; let who he will speak otherwise, for this really I know myself by experience. I hope I offend none to tell the truth. We are forced to go back without doing anything.

The month of August brings a company of the Sault,[6] who were come by the river of the Three Rivers with incredible pains, as they said. It was a company of seven boats. We wrote the news of their arrivement to Quebec. They send us word that they will stay until the two Fathers be turned from [the] Saguenay [in order] that we should go with them: an answer without reason. Necessity obliged us to go.[7] Those people [the Saulteurs] are not to be enticed, for as soon as they have done their affair they go. The governor of that place defends[8] us to go. We told him that the offense was pardonable because it was [to] everyone's interest; nevertheless, we knowed what we were to do, and he should not be blamed for us. We made gifts to the wildmen that wished with all their hearts that we might go along with them. We told them that the governor minded to send servants with them and forbids us to go along with you. The wildmen would not accept their company, but told us that they would stay for us two days in the Lake of St. Peter, in the grass, some six leagues from Three Rivers.

But we did not let them stay so long, for that very night (my brother having the keys of the borough, being captain of the place) we embarked ourselves. We [had] made ready in the morning, so that we went, three of us, about midnight. Being come opposite the fort, they ask who is there. My brother tells his name. Everyone knows what good services we had done to the country, and loved us, the inhabitants as well as the soldiers. The sentry answers him, "God give you a good voyage." We went on the rest of that night.

At six in the morning we are arrived to the appointed place, but found nobody. We were well armed and had a good boat. We resolved to go day and night to the River of the Meadows to overtake them.

Three leagues beyond the Fort of Richelieu, we saw them coming to us. We put ourselves upon our guards, thinking they were enemy, but [they] were friends and received us with joy and said that if we had not come in three days' time they would have sent their boats to know the reason of our delay. There we are in that river, waiting for the night. Being come to the River of the Meadows we did seperate ourselves, three into three boats. The man that we have taken with us was put into a boat of three men and a woman, but not of the same nation as the rest, but of one that we call Sorcerers.[9] They were going down to see some friends that lived with the nation of the Fire,[10] that now liveth with the Pouoestingonce or the Sault.

It is to be understood that this river[11] is divided much into streams, very swift and small, before you go to the River of Canada. [Because] of the great game that therein is, the enemy is to be feared, which made us go through these torrents. This could make anyone afraid who is inexperted in such voyages. We suffered much for three days and three nights without rest.

As we went we heard the noise of guns, which daunted our hearts for fear, although we had eight boats in number; but [we] were a great distance one from another, as is said in my former voyage,[12] before we could gain the height of the river.

The boat of the Sorcerers, where was one of us, albeit [had] made a voyage into the Hurons' country before with the Fathers.

The night following, [he] that was in the boat dreamed that the Iroquois had taken him with the rest. In his dream he cries out aloud. Those that were there at rest awakes of the noise. We are in alarm, and ready to be gone. Those that were with the man resolved to go back again, explicating that an evil presage. The wildmen counseled to send back the Frenchman, saying he should die before he could come to their country. It's usually spoken among the wildmen, when a man is sick or not able to do anything, to discourage him in such sayings.

Here I will give a relation of that Frenchman before I go further, and what a thing it is to have an intrigue. The next day they see a boat of their enemies, as we heard since. They presently landed; the wildmen runned away, the Frenchman also. As he went along the waterside for fear of losing himself, he finds there an arbor, very thick, lays himself down and falls asleep. The night being come, the wildmen being come to know whether the enemy had perceived them, but none pursued them, and found their boat in the same place and embarks themselves and come in good time to Montreal. They left the poor Frenchman there, thinking he had wit enough to come along the waterside, being not above ten leagues from thence. Those wildmen, after their arrivement, for fear spoke not one word of him, but went down to Three Rivers, where their habitation was. Fourteen days after, some boats ventured to go back for some oriniack, came to the same place, where they made cottages, and that within a quarter of mile where this wretch was. One of the French finds him on his back, and almost quite spent, his gun by him. He was very weak and desirous that he should be discovered by some or other. He [had] fed as long as he could on grapes and at last became so weak that he was not able [to go] any further until those French found him. After a while, being come to himself, he tends down [to] the Three Rivers. Where being arrived, the governor imprisons him. He stayed not there long. The inhabitants, seeing that the enemy, the hunger, and all other miseries tormented this poor man, and that it was by a divine providence he was alive, they would not have suffered such inhumanity, but got him out.

Three days after, we found the tracks[13] of seven boats, and five yet burning. We found out by their characters they were no enemy's, but imagined that they were Ottawas that went up into their country, which made us make haste to overtake them. We took no rest till we overtook them. They came from Montreal

114

and were gone by the great river,[14] so that we are now fourteen boats together which were to go the same way to the height of the Upper Lake.

The day following we were set upon by a company of Iroquois that [had] fortified themselves in the passage where they waited [for the] Ottawas, for they knowed of their going down. Our wildmen, seeing that there was no way to avoid them, resolved to be together, being the best way for them to make a quick expedition, for the season of the year pressed us to make [an] expedition.[15] We resolved to give a combat. We prepared ourselves with targets; now the business was to make a discovery. I doubt not but the enemy was much surprised to see us so in number. The council was held and resolution taken. I and a wildman were appointed to go and see their fort. I offered myself with a free will, to let them see how willing I was to defend them. That is the only way to gain the hearts of those wildmen. We saw that their fort was environed with great rocks, that there was no way to mine it. The mine was nothing else but to cut the nearest tree and so by his fall make a break and so go and give an assault. Their fort was nothing but trees one against another in a round, or square, without sides.

The enemy, seeing us come near, shot at us, but in vain, for we have forewarned ourselves before we came there. It was a pleasure to see our wildmen with their guns and arrows, which agreed not together. Nevertheless, we told them when they received a break their guns would be to no purpose; therefore to put them by and make use of their bows and arrows. The Iroquois saw themselves put to it, and the evident danger that they were in, but too late, except they would run away. Yet our wildmen were better footmen than they. There were Frenchmen that should give them good directions to overthrow them. [They] resolved to speak for peace, and throw necklaces of porcelain over the stakes of their fort. Our wildmen were dazzled at such gifts because the porcelain is very rare and costly in their country. Then seeing themselves flattered with fair words, to which they gave ear, we thrust them by force to put their first design in execution, but [they] feared [for] their lives and loved the porcelain, seeing they had it without danger of any life. They were persuaded to stay till the next day because now it was almost night. The Iroquois makes their escape. This occasion lost, our consolation was that we had that passage free, but [we were] vexed for having

115

lost that opportunity and, contrariwise, were contented of our side, for doubtless some of us had been killed in the battle.

The day following we embarked ourselves quietly, being upon our guard for fear of any surprise, for that enemy's danger scarcely began, who with his furor made himself so redoubted, having been there up and down to make a new slaughter. This morning passes in assurance enough. In the afternoon two boats had orders to land some two hundred paces from the landing place. One took only a small bundle very light, tends to the other side of the carriage, imagining there to make the kettle boil, having killed two stags two hours ago, and was scarce halfway when he meets the Iroquois, without doubt for that same business. I think both were much surprised. The Iroquois had a bundle of castor that he left behind without much ado; our wildmen did the same. They both run away to their partners to give them notice. By chance my brother [Groseilliers] meets them in the way. The wildmen, seeing that they all were frightened and out of breath, they asked the matter and was told "Nadoue,"[16] and so soon said he lets fall his bundle that he had upon his back into a bush, and comes back [to] where he finds all the wildmen despaired. He desired me to encourage them, which I performed with all earnestness.

We runned to the height of the carriage. As we were agoing, they took their arms with all speed. In the way we found the bundle of castors that the enemy had left. By this means we found out that they were in a fright as we and that they came from the wars of the upper country, which we told the wildmen, [and] so encouraged them to gain the waterside to discover their forces, where we no sooner came but two [Iroquois] boats were landed, and charged their guns either to defend themselves or to set upon us. We prevented this affair by our diligence and shot at them with our bows and arrows, as with our guns. They, finding such an assault, immediately forsook the place. They would have gone into their boats, but we gave them not so much time. They throwed themselves into the river to gain the other side. This river was very narrow, so that it was very violent. We had killed and taken them all if two boats of theirs had not come to their succor, which made us gave over to follow them, and look to ourselves, for we knowed not the number of their men. Three of their men nevertheless were killed. The rest is on the other side of the river, where there was a fort which was made long before. There they retired themselves with all speed.

We pass our boats to augment our victory. Seeing that they were many in number, they did what they could to hinder our passage, but all in vain, for we made use of the bundle of castors that they left, which were to us instead of gabions, for we put them at the heads of our boats and by that means got around in spite of their noses. They killed one of our men as we landed. Their number was not [enough] to resist ours. They retired themselves into the fort and brought [in] the rest of their [equipage] in hopes to save it. In this they were far mistaken, for we furiously gave an assault, not sparing time to make us bucklers, and made use of nothing else but of castors tied together. So without any more ado we gathered together. The Iroquois spared not their powder, but made more noise than hurt. The darkness covered the earth, which was somewhat favorable for us, but to overcome them the sooner we filled a barrel full of gunpowder and, having stopped the hole of it well, tied it to the end of a long pole, being at the foot of the fort. Here we lost three of our men. Our machine did play with executions. I may well say that the enemy never had seen the like. Moreover, I took three or four pounds of powder; this I put into a rind of a tree, then a fuse to have the time to throw the rind, warning the wildmen as soon as the rind made his execution that they should enter in and break the fort upside down, with the hatchet and the sword in their hands. In the meantime the Iroquois did sing, expecting death, or to their heels. At the noise of such a smoke and noise that our machines made with the slaughter of many of them, seeing themselves so betrayed, they let us go free into their fort that thereby they might save themselves. But having environed the fort, we are mingled pell-mell so that we could not know one another in that skirmish of blows. There was such an noise that should terrify the stoutest men.

Now there falls a shower of rain and a terrible storm that to my thinking there was something extraordinary: that the devil himself made that storm to give those men leave to escape from our hands to destroy another time more of these innocents. In that darkness everyone looked about for shelter, not thinking of those braves that laid down half dead to pursue them. It was a thing impossible; yet do believe that the enemy was not far. As the storm was over, we came together making a noise, and I am persuaded that many thought themselves prisoners that were at liberty. Some sang their fatal sang, albeit without any wounds, so

117

that those that had the confidence to come near the others were comforted by assuring them the victory and that the enemy was routed.

We presently make a great fire and with all haste make up the fort again, for fear of any surprise. We searched for those that were missing. Those that were dead and wounded were visited. We found eleven of our enemy slained, and two only of ours, besides seven were wounded, who in a short time passed all danger of life. While some were busy in tying five of the enemy that could not escape, the others visited the wounds of their companions, who for to show their courage sunged louder than those that were well. The sleep that we took that night did not make our heads giddy, although we had need of reposing. Many liked the occupation, for they filled their bellies with the flesh of their enemies. We broiled some of it and [filled a] kettle full of the rest. We burned our comrades, being their custom to reduce such into ashes [those] being slained in battle. It is an honor to give them such a burial.

At the break of day we cooked what could accommodate us, and fling the rest away. The greatest mark of our victory was that we had ten heads and four prisoners, whom we embarked in hopes to bring them into our country, and there to burn them at our own leisures for the more satisfaction of our wives. We left that place of massacre with horrid cries, forgetting the death of our parents. We plagued those unfortunate. We plucked out their nails one after another.

The next morning, after we slept a little in our boats, we made a sign to be gone. They prayed [me] to let off my piece, which made a great noise. To fulfill their desire I let it off. I no sooner shot but perceived seven boats of the Iroquois going from a point towards the land. We were surprised of such an encounter, seeing death before us, being not strong enough to resist such a company, for there were ten or twelve in every boat. They, perceiving us, thought that we were more in number, began in all haste to make a fort, as we received from two discoverers that we sent to know their postures. It was with much ado that those two went.

During [their absence] we persuaded our wildmen to send seven of our boats to an isle near [at] hand, and turn often again to frighten our adversaries by our show of our forces.[17] They had a mind to fortify themselves in that island, but we would not suffer it because there was time enough in case of necessity, which

118

we represent unto them, making them gather all the broken trees to make a kind of barricade, prohibiting them to cut trees, that thereby the enemy might not suspect our fear and our small number, which they had known by the stroke of their hatchets.[18] Those wildmen, thinking to be lost, obeyed us in everything, telling us every foot, "Be cheerful, and dispose of us as you will, for we are men lost." We killed our four prisoners because they embarrassed us.

They [the Iroquois] sent as soon as we were together some forty that perpetually went to and again to find out our policy and weakness.

In the meantime, we told the people that they were men—and if they must, die altogether—and for us to make a fort in the land was to destroy ourselves, because we should put ourselves in prison; to take courage; if in case we should be forced to take a retreat, the isle was a fort for us from whence we might well escape in the night; that we were strangers and they (if I must say so) in their country, and shooting ourselves in a fort all passages would be open upon us, for to save ourselves through the woods was a miserable comfort.

In the meantime, the Iroquois worked lustily, think[ing] at every step we were to give them an assault, but [they were] far deceived, for if ever blind wished the light, we wished then the obscurity of the night, which no sooner approached but we embarked ourselves without any noise and went along. It's strange to me that the enemy did not encounter us. Without question he had store of prisoners and booty. We left the Iroquois in his fort and the fear in our breeches, for without apprehension we rowed from Friday to Tuesday without intermission. We had scarce to eat [but] a bit of salt meat. It was pity to see our feet and legs in blood by drawing our boats through the swift streams, where the rocks have such sharp points that there is nothing but [fear of] death could make men do what we did. On the third day the pains and labor we took forced us to an intermission, for we were quite spent. After this we went on without an encounter whatsoever, having escaped very narrowly.

We passed a sault that falls from a vast height. Some of our wildmen went undearneath it, which I have seen, and I myself had the curiosity, but that quiver makes a man surer. The water runs over the heads with such impetuosity and violence that it's incredible. We went under this torrent a quarter of a mile that falls from the top above forty foot downwards.[19]

119

Having come to the Lake of the Castors,[20] we went about the Lake of the Castors for some victuals, being in great want, and suffered much hunger. So everyone constitutes himself: some went ahunting, some afishing. This done, we went down the River of the Sorcerers,[21] which brought us to the first great lake.[22] What joy had we to see ourselves out of that river so dangerous, after we wrought two and twenty days and as many nights, having not slept one hour on land all that while.

Now, being out of danger, safe from our enemy, perhaps we must enter into another which perhaps may give practice and trouble consequently. Our equipage and we were ready to wander upon that sweet sea, but most of that coast is void of wild beasts. So there was great famine amongst us for want. Yet the coast afforded us some small fruits. There I found the kindness and charity of the wildmen, for when they found any place of any quantity of it they called me and my brother to eat and replenish our bellies, showing themselves for gratefuller than many Christians even to their own relations. I cannot forget here the subtility of one of those wildmen that was in the same boat with me. We see a castor along the waterside that puts his head out of the water. That wildman no sooner saw him but throws him out into the water and down to the bottom, without so much time as to give notice to any, and before many knowed of anything he brings up that castor in his arms as a child, with fearing to be bitten. By this we see that hunger can do much.

Afterwards we entered into a strait[23] which had ten leagues in length, full of islands, where we wanted not fish. We came after to a rapid[24] that makes the separation of the Lake of the Hurons [from] that we call Superior or Upper, for the wildmen hold it to be longer and broader, besides a great many islands, which makes [it] appear in a bigger extent. This rapid was formerly the dwelling of those with whom we were,[25] and consequently we must not ask them if they knew where they have laid.

We made cottages at our advantages and found the truth of what those men had often [said]: that if once we could come to that place we should make good cheer of a fish that they call assickmack, which signifieth a white fish.[26] The bear, the castors, and the oriniack showed themselves often, but to their lost. Indeed, it was to us like a terrestrial paradise after so long fasting, after so great pains that we had taken, [to] find ourselves so well by choosing our diet and resting when we had a mind to it.

120

Tis here that we must taste with pleasure a sweet bit. We do not ask for a good sauce; it's better to have it naturally. It is the way to distinguish the sweet from the bitter.

But the season was far spent, and use we deligence and leave that place so wished [for], which we shall bewail to the cursed Iroquois: "What hath that poor nation [the Saulteurs] done to thee, and being so far from thy country?" Yet if they [the Iroquois] had the same liberty that in former days they have had, we poor French should not go further with our heads, except we had a strong army. [But] those great lakes had not so soon come to our knowledge if it had not been for those brutish people; two men [Radisson and Groseilliers] had not found out the truth of these seas [at] so cheap interest, and the glory could not do what terror doth at the end. We are little better come to ourselves and furnished. We left that inn without reckoning with our host; it is cheap when we are not to put the hand to the purse. Nevertheless, we must pay out of civility. The one gives thanks to the woods, the other to the river, the third to the earth, the other to the rocks that stays the fish. In a word, there is nothing but kinakouir of all sorts; the encens of our encens is not spared.[27]

The weather was agreeable when we began to navigate upon that great extent of water. Finding it so calm, and air so clear, we thwarted in a pretty broad place,[28] came to an isle most delightful for the diversity of its fruits. We called it the Isle of the Four Beggars.[29]

We arrived about five of the clock in the afternoon that we came there. We suddenly put the kettle to the fire. We reside there awhile, and seeing all this while the fair weather, and calm, we went from thence at ten of the clock the same night to gain the firm land, which was six leagues from us, where we arrived before day.

Here we found a small river.[30] I was so curious that I inquired my dearest friends the name of this stream. They named it Pauabickkomesibi, which signifieth a small river of copper. I asked him the reason. He told me, "Come, and I shall show thee the reason why." I was in a place, which is not two hundred paces in the wood, where many pieces of copper were uncovered. Further he told me that the mountains I saw was of nothing else. Seeing it so fair and pure, I had a mind to take a piece of it, but they hindered me, telling my brother there was more where we were to go. In this great lake, of mine own eyes have [I] seen [great nuggets of copper] which are admirable and can maintain of a hundred pounds [and] will not be decayed.

From this place we went along the coasts, which are most delightful and wounderous, for it's Nature that made it so pleasant to the eye, the spirit, and the belly. As we went along we saw banks of sand[31] so high that one of our wildmen went for our curiosity. Being there, [he] did show no more than a crow. That place is most dangerous when there is any storm, being no landing place so long as the sandy banks are under water, and when the wind blows that sand doth rise by a strange kind of whirling that are able to choke the passengers. One day you will see fifty small mountains at one side, and the next day [none] if the wind changes on the other side.[32] This put me in mind of the great and vast wildernesses of Turkeyland as the Turks make their pilgrimages.[33]

Some days after, we observed that there were some boats before us, but knowed not certainly what they were. We made all the haste to overtake them, fearing the enemy no more. Indeed, the faster we could go the better for us, because of the season of the year that began to be cold and freeze.[34] They were a nation that live in a land towards the south.[35] This nation is very small, being not [a] hundred in all, men and women together. As we came near them, they were surprised of our safe return and astonished to see us, admiring the rich merchandises that their confederates brought from the French, that were hatchets and knives and other utensils very commodious, rare, precious, and necessary in those countries. They told the news one to another whilst we made good cheer and great fires. They mourned for the death of their comrades. The heads of their enemy were danced.[36] Some days [later] we separated ourselves and presented gifts to those that were going another way, for which we received great store of meat, which was put up in barrels, and grease of bears and oriniack.

After this we came to a remarkable place. It's a bank of rocks[37] that the wildmen made a sacrifice to. They call it Nauitouchsinagoit, which signifies the likeness of the devil. They fling much tobacco and other things in its veneration. It is a thing most incredible that that lake should be so boisterous, that the waves if it should have the strength to do what I have to say by this my discourse. First, that it's so high and so deep that it's impossible to climb up to the point. There come many sort of birds that make their nest here: the goélands,[38] which is a white sea bird of the bigness of [a] pigeon, which makes me believe what the wildmen told me concerning the sea to be near directly to the point. It's like a great portal by reason of the beating of the waves. The lower part of that opening is as big as a tower, and grows bigger in the going up. There is, I believe, six acres of land above it. A ship of five hundred tons could pass by, so big is the arch. I gave it the name of the Portal of St. Peter because my name is so called, and that I was the first Christian that ever saw it.[39] There is in that place caves very deep, caused by the same violence. We must look to ourselves and take time with our small boats. The coast of rocks is five or six leagues, and there scarce a place to put a boat in [with] assurance from the waves. When the lake is agitated the waves goeth in these concavities with force and make a most horrible noise, most like the shooting of great guns.

Some days afterwards, we arrived to a very beautiful point of sand, where there are three beautiful islands that we called of the Trinity;[40] there be three in triangle. From this place, we discovered a bay very deep, where a river empties itself with a noise for the quantity and depth of the water. We must stay there three days to wait for fair weather to make the trainage, which was about six leagues wide.[41] So done, we came to the mouth of a small river, where we killed some oriniacks. We found meadows that were squared and ten leagues as smooth as a board. We went up some five leagues further, where we found some pools made by the castors. We must break them that we might pass. The sluice being broken, what a wonderful thing to see the industry of that animal, which had drowned more than twenty leagues in the grounds and cut all the trees, having left none to make a fire if the country should be dried up. Being come to the height, we must draw our boats over a trembling ground for the space of an hour. The ground became trembling by this means: the castor drowning great soils with dead water; herein grows moss which is two foot thick, or thereabouts; and when you think to go safe and dry, if you take not great care, you sink down to your head or to the middle of your body. When you are out of one hole you find yourself in another. This I speak [of] by experience, for I myself have been catched often, but the wildmen warned me, which saved me; that is, that when the moss should break under I should cast my whole body into the water sudden; I must with

123

my hands hold the moss and go so like a frog; then to draw my boat after me there was no danger.

Having passed that place, we made a carriage through the land for two leagues. The way was well beaten because of the comers and goers, who by making that passage shorten their passage by eight days by turning about the point that goes very far in that great lake; that is to say, five to come to the point, and three for to come to the landing of that place of carriage. In the end of that point that goeth very far, there is a isle,[42] as I was told, all of copper. This I have not seen. They say that from the isle of copper, which is a league in the lake, when they are minded to thwart it in a fair and calm weather, beginning from sunrising to sunset, they come to a great island,[43] from whence they came the next morning to firm land at the other side, so by reason of twenty leagues a day that lake should be broad of six score and ten leagues.[44] The wildmen do not much less when the weather is fair.

Five days after, we came to a place where there was a company of Christinos that were in their cottages. They were transported for joy to see us come back. They made much of us and called us men indeed to perform our promise to come and see them again.[45] We gave them great gifts, which caused some suspicion, for it* is a very jealous nation, but the short stay that we made took away that jealousy.

We went on and came to a hollow [i.e., shallow] river[46] which was a quarter of a mile in breadth. Many of our wildmen went to win the shortest way to their nation.[47] [We] were then three and twenty boats, for we met with some in that lake that joined with us and came to keep us company, in hopes to get knives from us, which they love better than we serve God, which should make us blush for shame. Seven boats stayed of the nation of the Sault.

We went on half a day before we could come to the landing place, and were forced to make another carriage — a point of two leagues long and some sixty paces broad.[48] As we came to the other side, we were in a bay of ten leagues about.[49] If we had gone in by going about that same point, we [would have]

---

*Probably meaning the Saulteurs, but, in view of the second sentence following ("their nation"), the reference might also be to some Hurons in Radisson's party.

passed a strait, for that point was very nigh the other side, which is a cape very much elevated like pyramids.[50] That point should be very fit to build [on] and advantageous for the building of a fort, as we did the spring following.[51] In that bay there is a channel where we take great store of fishes, sturgeons of a vast bigness and pikes of seven foot long. At the end of this bay we landed.[52] The wildmen gave thanks to that which they worship, we to God of Gods to see ourselves in a place where we must leave our navigation and forsake our boats to undertake a harder piece of work in hand, to which we are forced.

The men told us that we had five great days' journeys before we should arrive where their wives were. We foresee the hard task that we were to undergo by carrying our bundles upon our backs. They were used to it. Here everyone for himself and God for all. We, finding ourselves not able to perform such a task — and they could not well tell where to find their wives, fearing lest the Nadoueceronons had wars against their nation and forced them from their appointed place — my brother and I, we consulted what was best to do, and declared our will to them, which was thus: "Brethren, we resolve to say here, being not accustomed to make any carriage on our backs as ye are wont. Go ye and look for your wives. We will build us a fort here. And seeing that you are not able to carry all your merchandises at once, we will keep them for you and will stay for you fourteen days. Before the time expired you will send to us if your wives be alive, and if you find them, they will fetch what you leave here and what we have. For their pains they shall receive gifts of us. So you will see us in your country. If they be dead, we will spend all to be revenged and will gather up the whole country for the next spring for that purpose: to destroy those that were the causers of their death, and you shall see our strength and valor. Although there are seven thousand fighting men in one village, you'll see we will make them run away, and you shall kill them to your best liking by the very noise of our arms and our presence, who are the gods of the earth among those people." They wondered very much at our resolution.

The next day they went their way, and we stay for our assurance in the midst of many nations, being [all] but two[53] almost starved for want of food. We went to make a fort of stakes, which was in this manner: suppose that the waterside had been in one end; at the same end there should [then] be murtherers;

125

at need we made a bastion in triangle to defend us from an assault. The door was near the waterside. Our fire was in the middle, and our bed on the right hand, covered. There were boughs of trees all about our fort, laid across, one upon another. Besides these boughs, we had a long cord tied with some small bells, which were sentries. Finally, we made an end of that fort in two days time.

We made an end of some fish that we [had] put by for need, but as soon as we were lodged we went to fish for more whilst the other [Groseilliers] kept the house. I was the fittest to go out, being youngest.[54] I took my gun and goes where I never was before, so I choosed not one way before another. I went [in]to the wood some three or four miles. I find a small brook, where I walked by the side awhile, which brought me into meadows. There was a pool where were a good store of bustards.[55] I began to creep [as] though I might come near. The poor creatures, seeing me flat upon the ground, thought I was a beast as well as they, so they came near me, whistling like goslings, thinking to frighten me. The whistling that I made them hear was another music than theirs. There I killed three, and the rest scared, which neverthless came to that place again to see what sudden sickness befelled their comrades. I shot again; two paid for their curiosity. I think the Spaniards had no more to fulfill than [to] kill those birds that thought not of such a thunderbolt. There are yet more countries as fruitful and as beautiful as the Spaniards' to conquer, which may be done with as much ease and facility, and prove as rich, if not richer, for bread and wine and all other things are as plentiful as in any part of Europe. This I have seen, which [I] am sure the Spaniards have not in such plenty. Now I come back with my victory, which was to us more than ten thousand pistoles. We lived by it five days. I took good notice of the place in hopes to come there more frequent, but this place is not [the] only [one] so.

There we stayed still full twelve days without any news, but we had the company of other wildmen of other countries that came to us, admiring our fort and the workmanship. We suffered none to go in but one person, and [they] liked it so much the better and often durst not go in, so much they stood in fear of our arms that were in good order, which were five guns, two musketoons, three fowling pieces, three pair of great pistolets, and two pair of pocket ones, and everyone his sword and dagger; so that we might say that a coward was not well enough armed.

126

Mistrust, nevertheless, is the mother of safety, and the occasion makes the thief. During that time we had several alarms in the night. The squirrels and other small beasts, as well as foxes, came in and assaulted us. One night I forgot my braie,[56] which was wet, being up and down in those pools to fetch my fowls. One of those beasts carried it away, which did us a great deal of wrong and saved the life to great many of those against whom I declared myself an enemy. We imagined that some wildmen might have surprised us, but I may say they were far more afraid than we. Some days after, we found it one-half a mile from the fort in a hole of a tree, the most part torn.

Then I killed an oriniack. I could have killed more, but we liked the fowls better. If we had both liberty to go from our fort we should have provided in a month that should serve us a whole winter. The wildmen brought us more meat than we would [use] and as much fish as we might eat.

The 12th day we perceived afar off some fifty young men coming towards us, with some of our former companions. We gave them leave to come into our fort, but they are astonished, calling us every foot devils to have made such a machine. They brought us victuals, thinking we were half starved, but were mightily mistaken, for we had more for them than they were able to eat, having three score bustards and many sticks where was meat hanged plentifully.

They offered to carry our baggage, being come a purpose, but we had not so much merchandise as when they went from us because we [had] hid some of them that they might not have suspicion of us. We told them [the following tale] for fear the daily multitude of people that came to see us for to have our goods would kill us. We therefore took a boat and put into it our merchandises. This we brought far into the bay, where we sunk them, bidding our devil not to let them to be wet nor rustied, nor suffer them to be taken away, which he promised faithfully;[57] that we should return and take them out of his hands, at which they were astonished, believing it to be true as the Christians the Gospels. We [had] hid them in the ground on the other side of the river in a piece of ground. We told them that lie that they should not have suspicion of us.

We made good cheer. They stayed there three days, during which time many of their wives came thither, and we treated them well, for they eat not fowl at all, [which is] scarce because

127

they know not how to catch them except with their arrows. We put a great many rind about our fort, and broke all the boats that we could have, for the frost would have broken them or wildmen had stolen them away. That rind was tied all in [a] length to put the fire in it, to frighten the more those people, for they could not approach it without being discovered. If they ventured at the going out, we put the fire to all the torches, showing them how we would have defended ourselves. We were Caesars, being nobody to contradict us.

We went away free from any burden, whilst those poor miserable thought themselves happy to carry our equipage for the hope that they had that we should give them a brass ring or an awl or a needle. There came above four hundred persons to see us go away from that place, which admired more our actions [than] the fools of Paris to see enter their King and the Infanta of Spain, his spouse, for they cry out, "God save the King and Queen!"[58] Those made horrid noise and called gods and devils of the earth and heavens.

We marched four days through the woods. The country is beautiful, with very few mountains, the woods clear. At last we came within a league of the cabins, where we laid, that the next day might be for our entry. We two poor adventurers, for the honor of our country, or of those that shall deserve it, from that day the nimblest and stoutest, went before to warn the people that we should make our entry tomorrow. Everyone prepares to see what they never before have seen. We were in cottages which were near a little lake some eight leagues in circuit.[59] At the waterside there were abundance of little boats made of trees that they have hollowed, and of rind.

The next day we were to embark in them, and arrived at the village by water,[60] which was composed of a hundred cabins without palisades. There is nothing but cries. The women throw themselves backwards upon the ground, thinking to give us tokens of friendship and of welcome. We destinated three presents — one for the men, one for the women, and the other for the children — to the end that they should remember that journey, that we should be spoken of a hundred years after, if other Europeans should not come in those quarters and be liberal to them, which will hardly come to pass.

The first present was a kettle, two hatchets, and six knives, and a blade for a sword. The kettle was to call all nations that were their friends to the feast which is made for the remembrance of the death;[61] that is, they make it once in seven years; it's a renewing of friendship. I will talk further of it in the following discourse. The hatchets were to encourage the young people to strengthen themselves in all places, to preserve their wives, and show themselves men by knocking the heads of their enemies with the said hatchets. The knives were to show that the French were great and mighty, and their confederates and friends. The sword was to signify that we would be masters both of peace and wars, being willing to help and relieve them and to destroy our enemies with our arms.

The second gift was two and twenty awls, fifty needles, two graters of castors, two ivory combs and two wooden ones, with red paint, six looking glasses of tin. The awls signifieth to take good courage that we should keep their lives and that they with their husbands should come down to the French when time and season should permit; the needles for to make them robes of castor because the French loved them. The two graters were to dress the skins; the combs [and] the paint to make themselves beautiful; the looking glasses to admire themselves.

The third gift was of brass rings, of small bells, and rasades[62] of divers colors, and given in this manner. We sent a man to make all the children come together. When they were there we throw these things over their heads. You would admire what a beat was among them, everyone striving to have the best. This was done upon this consideration: that they should be always under our protection, giving them wherewithal to make them merry and remember us when they should be men.

This done, we are called to the council of welcome and to the feast of friendship, afterwards to the dancing of the heads.[63] But before the dancing we must mourn for the deceased, and then, for to forget all sorrow, to the dance. We gave them four small gifts that they should continue such ceremonies, which they took willingly; and [it] did us good, gave us authority among the whole nation. We knowed their councils and made them do whatsoever we thought best. This was a great advantage for us, you must think. Amongst such a rawish kind of people a gift is much, and bestowed, and liberality much esteemed, but prodigality is not in esteem, for they abuse it, being brutish.

We have been using such ceremonies three whole days, and were lodged in the cabin of the chiefest captain who came with

129

us from the French. We liked not the company of that kind, therefore left him. He wondered at this, but durst not speak because we were demi-gods. We came to a cottage of an ancient witty man that had a great family and many children; his wife old, nevertheless handsome. They were of a nation called Menominees, that is, the nation of Oats, grain that is much in that country. Of this [i.e., about the grain] afterwards more at large. I took this man for my father and the woman for my mother, so the children consequently brothers and sisters. They adopted me, I gave everyone a gift, and they to me.

Having so disposed of our business, the winter comes on. That warns us. The snow begins to fall,[64] so we must retire from this place to seek our living in the woods. Everyone gets his equipage ready; so away we go, but not all to the same place. Two, three at the most, went one way, and so off another. They have so done because victuals were scant for all in a [single] place. But let us where we will, we cannot escape the mighty hand of God that disposes as He pleases, and who chastises us as a good and common loving Father, and not as our sins do deserve. Finally we depart one from another. As many as we were in number, we are reduced to a small company. We appointed a rendezvous [to be held] after two months and a half, to take a new road, and [to get] an advice what we should do.

During the said term, we sent messengers everywhere to give special notice to all manner of persons and nation that within five moons[65] the feast of death was to be ceelbrated and that we should appear together and explain what the devil should command us to say, and then present them presents of peace and union. Now we must live on what God sends, and war against the bears in the meantime, for we could aim at nothing else, which was the cause that we had no great cheer. I can say that we with our comrades, who were about sixty, killed in the space of two moons and a half [enough bears to last us] a thousand moons. We wanted not bear's grease to anoint ourselves to run the better. We beated down the woods daily for to discover novelties. We killed several other beasts, as oriniacks, stags, wild cows,[66] caribou, fallow does and bucks, cats of mountains[67] (child of the devil!). In a word, we lead a good life.

The snow increased daily. There we make rackets, not to play at ball but to exercise ourselves in a game harder and more necessary. They are broad made like rackets that they may go in the snow and not sink when they run after the elend or other beast.

We are come to the small lake, [near] the place of rendezvous, where we found some company that were there before us. We cottage ourselves, staying for the rest, that came every day. We stayed fourteen days in this place most miserable, like to a church-yard. There did fall such a quantity of snow and frost, and with such a thick mist, that all the snow stuck to those trees that are there so rough, being deal trees, pousse cedars, and thorns. [It] caused darkness upon the earth; it is to be believed that the sun was eclipsed two months. After, the trees were so laden with snow that was as if it had been sifted. By that means [it was] very light and not able to bear us, albeit we made rackets six foot long and a foot and a half broad. Often thinking to turn ourselves, we felled over and over again in the snow, and if we were alone we should have difficulty enough to rise again. By the noise we made the beasts heard us a great way off, so the famine was among [a] great many that had not provided beforehand and [who] live upon what they get that day, never thinking for the next.

It grows worse and worse daily. (To augment our misery we receive news of the Ottawas,[68] who were about a hundred and fifty with their families. They had a quarrel with the Hurons in the isle[69] where we had come from some years before in the Lake of the Staring Hairs, and came purposely to make wars against them the next summer. But let us see if they brought us anything to subsist with: [they] are worst provided than we. Having no huntsmen, they are reduced to famine. But, oh cursed Covetousness, what art thou going to do? It should be far better to see a company of rogues perish than see ourselves in danger to perish by that scourge so cruel. Hearing that they have had knives and hatchets, the victuals of their poor children is taken away from them; yea, whatever they have, those dogs must have their share. They are the cursedest, unablest, the unfamous, and cowardliest people that I have seen amongst four score nations that I have frequented. Oh ye poor people, you shall have their booty, but you shall pay dearly for it.) Everyone cries out for hunger. The women become barren and dry like wood. You men must eat the cord, being you have no more strength to make use of the bow. Children, you must die. French, you called your-selves gods of the earth, that you should be feared; for your interest, notwithstanding, you shall taste of the bitterness, and [be only] too happy if you escape. Where is the time past? Where is the plentiness that ye had in all places and countries? Here comes a new family of those poor people daily to us — half dead, for they have but the skin and bones. How shall we have strength to make a hole in the snow to lay us down?—seeing we have it not to haul our rackets after us, nor to cut a little wood to make a fire to keep us from the rigor of the cold, which is extreme in those countries in its season. Oh! if the music that we hear could give us recreation. We wanted not any lamentable music nor sad spectacle. In the morning the husband looks upon his wife, the brother his sister, the cousin the cousin, the uncle the nephew, that were for the most part found dead. They languish with cries and hideous noise that it was able to make the hair stare on the heads [of those] that have any apprehension. Good God! have mercy on so many poor innocent people, and of us that acknowledge Thee; having offended, Thee punishes us. But we are not free of that cruel executioner.

Those that have any life seeketh out for roots, which could not be done without great difficulty, the earth being frozen two or three foot deep, and the snow five or six above it. The greatest subsistance that we can have is of rind tree, which grows like ivy about the trees. To swallow it, we cut the stick some two foot long, tying it in[to a] fagot, and boil it, and when it boils one hour or two the rind or skin come off with ease, which we take and dry it in the smoke, and then reduce it into powder betwixt two grain stones, and putting the kettle with the same water upon the fire, we make it a kind of broth, which nourished us. But [we] became thirstier and drier than the wood we eat. The first week we did eat our dogs. As we went back upon our step for to get anything to fill our bellies, we were glad to get the bones and carcasses of the beasts that we [had] killed, and happy was he that could get what the other did throw away, after it had been boiled three or four times to get the substance out of it. We contrived another plot: to reduce to powder those bones, the rest of crows and dogs, so put all that together half-foot within ground, and so makes a fire upon it. We covered all that very well with earth, so feeling the heat, and boiled them again, and [that] gave more froth than before. In the next place [we ate] the skins that were reserved to make us shoes, cloth, and stockings; yea, most of the skins of our cottages, the castors' skins where the children beshit them above a hundred times. We burned the hair on the coals. The rest goes down throats, eating heartily these things most abhorred. We went so eagerly to it that our gums did bleed like one newly wounded. The wood was our food the rest of [that] sorrowful time. Finally we became the very image of death. We mistook ourselves very often, taking the living for the dead and the dead for the living. We wanted strength to draw the dead out of the cabins, or if we did when we could, it was to put them four paces in the snow. At the end the wrath of God begins to appease itself, and [He] pities His poor creatures. If I should express all that befell us in that strange accidents, a great volume would not contain it. Here are above five hundred dead — men, women and children. It's time to come out of such miseries. Our bodies are not able to hold out any further. After the storm, calm comes. But storms favored us, being that calm kills us. Here comes a wind and rain that puts a new life in us. The snow falls; the forest clears itself; at which sight those that had strings left in their bows takes courage to use it. The weather continued so three days; we need no rackets more, for the snow hardened much. The small stags are [as] if they were stakes in it. After they made seven or eight capers, it's an easy matter for us to take them and cut their throats with our knives. Now we see ourselves a little furnished, but yet have not paid, for it cost many their lives. Our guts became very straight by our long fasting [so] that they could not contain the quantity that some put in them.

I cannot omit the pleasant thoughts of some of them wildmen. Seeing my brother always in the same condition, they said that some devil brought him wherewithal to eat, but if they had seen his body, they should be of another opinion; the beard that covered his face made [it appear] as if he had not altered his face. For me that had no beard,[70] they said I loved them because I lived as well as they from the second day we began to walk.

There came two men from a strange country who had a dog. The business was how to catch him cunningly, knowing well those people love their beasts. Nevertheless, we offered gifts, but they would not [take them], which made me stubborn. That dog was very lame and as hungry as we were, but the masters have not suffered so much. I went one night near that same cottage to do what discretion permits me not to speak. Those men were Nadoueceronons. They were [so] much respected that nobody durst offend them, being that we were upon their land[71] with their leave. The dog comes out not by any smell but by good like. I take him and bring him a little way. I stabbed him with my dagger. I brought him to the cottage, where [he] was broiled like a pig and cut in pieces, guts and all. So everyone of the family had his share. The snow where he was killed was not lost, for one of our company went and got it to season the kettle. We began to look better daily.

We gave the rendezvous[72] to the convenientest place to celebrate that great feast.[73]

Some two moons after, there came eight ambassadors from the nation of Nadoueceronons, that we will call now the nation of the Beef.[74] Those men each had two wives loadened of oats (corn that grows in that country), a small quantity of Indian corn, with other grains, and it was to present to us, which we received as a great favor and token of friendship. But it had been [more] welcome if they had brought it a month or two before. They made great ceremonies in greasing our feet and legs, and we painted them with red. They stripped us naked and put upon us cloth of buff and of white castors. After, they weeped upon our heads until we were wetted by their tears,[75] and made us smoke in their pipes after they kindled them. It was not in common pipes, but in pipes of peace and of the wars, that they pull out but very seldom — when there is occasion for heaven and earth. This done, they perfumed our cloths and armors one after another and, to conclude, did throw a great quantity of tobacco into the fire.

We told them that they prevented us [from] letting us know that all persons of their nation came to visit us, that we might dispose of them.

The next morning they were called by our interpreter. We understood not a word of their language, being quite contrary to those that we were with. They are arrived. They sat down. We [had] made a place for us more elevated, to be more at our ease and to appear in more state. We borrowed their calumet, saying that [we] were in their country and that it was not lawful for us to carry anything out of their country. That pipe is of a red stone, as big as a fist and as long as a hand; the small reed as long as five foot i nbreadth and of the thickness of a thumb. There is tied to it the tail of an eagle, all painted over with several colors, and open like a fan, or like that [which] makes a kind of a wheel when he shuts. Below the top, the stem is covered with feathers of ducks and other birds that are of a fine color. We took the tail of the eagle, and instead of it we hung twelve iron bows in the same manner as the feathers were, and a blade about it along the staff. A hatchet [was] planted in the ground, and that calumet over it, and all our armors about it upon forks. Everyone smoked his pipe of tobacco; they never go without it. During that while there was a great silence. We prepared some powder that was little wetted, and the good powder was precious to us.

Our interpreter told them in our name, "Brethren, we have accepted of your gifts. Ye are called here to know our will and pleasure, that is such: first, we take you for our brethren by taking you into our protection, and for to show you, we, instead of the eagle's tail, have put some of our armors, to the end that no enemy shall approach it to break the affinity that we make now with you."

Then we took the twelve iron of the bows and lift them up, telling them those points shall pass over the whole world to defend and destroy your enemies, that are [also] ours. Then we put the irons in the same place again. Then we took the sword and bade them have good courage, that by our means they should vanquish their enemy. After, we took the hatchet that was planted in the ground. We turned round about, telling them that we should kill those that would war against them and that we would make forts that they should come with more assurance to the feast of the dead.

That done, we throw powder in the fire that had more strength than we thought. It made the brands fly from one side to the other. We intended to make them believe that it was some of our tobacco, and make them smoke as they made us smoke. But, hearing such a noise and seeing that fire fled of every side, without any further delay or look for so much time as [to] look for the door of the cottage, one run one way, another another way, for they never saw a sacrifice of tobacco so violent. They went all away, and we only stayed in the place. We followed them to reassure them of their faintings. We visited them in their apartments, where they received [us] all trembling for fear, believing really by that same means that we were the devils of the earth.

There was nothing but feasting for eight days.

The time now was nigh that we must go to the rendezvous. This was betwixt a small lake and a meadow. Being arrived, most of our [Hurons] were already in their cottages in three days' time.

135

There arrived eighteen several nations, and came privately to have done the sooner. As we became to the number of five hundred we held a council. Then the shouts and cries and the encouragments were proclaimed that a fort should be builded. They went about the work and made a large fort. It was about six hundred and three score paces in length and six hundred in breadth; so that it was a square.[76] There we had a brook that came from the lake and emptied itself in those meadows, which had more than four leagues in length. Our fort might be seen afar off, and on that side [was] most delightful for the great many stags that took the boldness to be carried by quarters, where at other times they made good cheer. In two days this was finished.[77]

Some thirty young men of the nation of the Beef arrived there, having nothing but bows and arrows, with very short garments, to be the nimbler in chasing the stags. The iron of their arrows were made of stags' pointed horns very neatly. They were all proper men, and dressed with paint. They were the discoverers and the foreguard. We kept a round place in the middle of our cabin and covered it with long poles with skins over them, that we might have a shelter to keep us from the snow. The cottages were all in good order, in each ten [to] twelve companies or families. That company was brought to that place where there was wood laid for the fires. The snow was taken away, and the earth covered with deal tree bows. Several kettles were brought there full of meat. They rested and eat above five hours without speaking one to another. The considerablest of our companies went and made speeches to them. After, one takes his bow and shoots an arrow and then cries aloud, there speaks some few words, saying that they were to let them know the elders of their village were to come the morrow to renew the friendship, and to make it with the French, and that a great many of their young people came and brought them some part of their ways to take their advice, for they had a mind to go against the Christinos, who were ready for them, and they in like manner [wanted] to have their wives and children. They were scattered in many cabins that night, expecting those that were to come.

To that purpose there was a vast large place prepared some hundred paces from the fort, where everything was ready for the receiving of those persons. They were [there] to set their tents that they bring upon their backs. The perches[78] were put out and planted as we received news, the snow put aside, and the boughs of trees covered the ground.

The day following, they arrived with an incredible pomp. This made me think of the entrance that the Polanders did in Paris,[79] saving that they had not so many jewels, but instead of them they had so many feathers. The first were young people with their bows and arrows and buckler on their shoulders, upon which were represented all manner of figures according to their knowledge — as of the sun and moon, of terrestrial beasts; about it feathers very artificially painted. Most of the men, their faces were all over dabbed with several colors, their hair turned up like a crown and were cut very even, but rather so burned, for the fire is their scissors. They leave a tuft of hair upon their crown of their heads, tie it, and put at the end of it some small pearls or some turquoise stones[80] to bind their heads. They have a roll, commonly made of a snake's skin, where they tie several bears' paws, or give a form to some bits of buffs' horns and put it about the said roll. They grease themselves with very thick grease and mingle it in reddish earth which they burn as we our bricks; with this stuff they get their hair to stand up. They cut some down of swan or other fowl that hath a white feather and cover with it the crown of their heads. Their ears are pierced in five places, [and] the holes are so big that your little finger might pass through. They have yellow ware that they make with copper, made like a star or a half moon, and there hang it. Many have turquoises. They are clothed with oriniack and stags' skins, but very light. Everyone had the skin of a crow hanging at their girdles. Their stockings [were] all embroidered with pearls and with their own porc-épic work.[81] They have very handsome shoes, laced very thick all over with a piece sown at the side of the heel, which was of a hair of buff, which trailed above half a foot upon the earth, or rather on the snow. They had swords and knives of a foot and a half long, and hatchets very ingeniously done, and clubs of wood made like backswords, some made of a round head that I admired it. When they kill their enemy, they cut off the tuft of hair and tie it about their arms. After all, they have a white robe made of castors' skins painted.

Those having passed through the middle of ours, that were ranged at every side of the way, the elders came with great gravity and modesty, covered with buff coats which hung down to the ground. Everyone had in his hand a pipe of council set with precious jewels. They had a sack[82] on their shoulders, and that that holds it grows in the middle of their stomachs and on their

137

shoulders; in this sack all the world is enclosed. Their face is not painted, but their heads [are] dressed, as the foremost.

Then the women, laden like unto so many mules; their burdens made a greater show than they themselves, but I suppose the weight was not equipolent to its bigness. They were conducted to the appointed place, where the women unfolded their bundles and flung their skins whereof their tents are made, so that they had houses [in] less than half an hour.

After they rested, they came to the biggest cabin constituted for that purpose. There were fires kindled. Our captain made a speech of thanksgiving, which should be [too] long to write it. We are called to the council of [the] new come chief, where we came in great pomp, as you shall hear. First they come to make a sacrifice to the French, being gods and masters of all things, as of peace as wars, making the knives, the hatchets, and the kettles rattle, etc. [They said] that they came purposely to put themselves under their protection, [and] moreover that they came to bring them back again to their country, having by their means destroyed their enemies abroad and near. So said, they present us with gifts of castors' skins, assuring us that the mountains were elevated, the valleys risen, the ways very smooth, the bows of trees cut down to go with more ease, and bridges erected over rivers, for not to wet our feet; that the doors of their villages, cottages, of their wives and daughters were open at any time to receive us, being we kept them alive by our merchandises.

The second gift was that they would die in their alliance, and that to certify to all nations by continuing the peace; and [they] were willing to receive and assist them in their country, being well satisfied they were come to celebrate the feast of the dead.

The third gift was for to have one of the doors of the fort opened, if need required, to receive and keep them from the Christinos that come to destroy them. Being always men, and the heavens made them so, [they said] they were obliged to go before to defend their country and their wives, which is the dearest thing they had in the world, and in all times they were esteemed stout and true soldiers. They would make it appear [so] by going to meet them [the Christinos], and they would not degenerate, but show by their actions that they were as valiant as their forefathers.

The fourth gift was presented to us, which [was] robes of buff skins, to desire our assistance; for, being the masters of their

138

lives, [we] could dispose of them as we would, as well of the peace as of the wars; and we might very well see that they did well to go defend their own country, that the true means to get the victory was to have a thunder. (They meant a gun, calling it miniskoick.)

The speech being finished, they entreated us to be at the feast. We go presently back again to furnish us with wooden bowls. We made four men to carry our guns afore us, that we charged of powder alone; because of their unskillfulness they might have killed their fathers. We each of us had a pair of pistolets, a sword, a dagger, We had a roll of porc-épic about our heads, which was as a crown; and two little boys that carried the vessels that we had most need of; this was our dishes and our spoons. They [had] made a place higher and most elevated (knowing our customs) in the middle for us to sit, where we had the men lay our arms.

Presently comes four elders with the calumet kindled in their hands. They present the candles to us to smoke, and four beautiful maids went before us, carrying bears' skins to put under us. When we were together, an old man rises and throws our calumet at our feet and bids them take the kettles from off the fire, and spoke: he thanked the sun that [there] never was a day to him so happy as when he saw those terrible men whose words makes the earth quake, and sang awhile. Having ended, [he] came and covers us with his vestment, and all naked except his feet and legs, he saith, "Ye are masters over us dead or alive. You have the power over us and may dispose of us as [is] your pleasure." So done, [he] takes the calumet of the feast and brings it. A maiden brings us a coal of fire to kindle it.

So done, we rose and one of us begins to sing. We bade the interpreter to tell them we should save and keep their lives, taking them for our brethren. To testify that, we shot off all our artillery, which was twelve guns. We draw our swords and long knives to our defense, if need should requires, which put the men in such a terror that they knowed not what was best, to run or stay. We throw a handful of powder in the fire to make a greater noise and smoke.

Our songs being finished, we began our teeth to work. We had there a kind of rice, much like oats; it grows in the water in three or four foot deep.[83] There is a God that shows himself in every country, almighty, full of goodness, and the Preservator of those poor people who knoweth Him not. They have a particular way to gather up that grain: two takes a boat and two sticks by which they get the ear down and get the corn out of it; their boat being

139

full, they bring it to a fit place to dry it, and that is their food for the most part of the winter, and do dress it then. For each man a handful of that they put in the pot; that swells so much that it can suffice a man.

After the feast was over, there comes two maidens bringing wherewithal to smoke, the one the pipes, the other the fire. They offer first to one of the elders that sat down with us. When he had smoked, he bids them give it us. This being done, we went back to our fort as we came.

The day following, we made the principal persons come together to answer to their gifts. Being come with great solemnity, there we made our interpreter tell them that we were come from the other side of the great salted lake,[84] not to kill them but to make you live, acknowledging you for our brethren and children, whom we will love henceforth as our own. Then we gave them a kettle.

The second gift was to encourage them in all their undertakings, telling them that we liked men that generously defended themselves against all their enemies, and as we were masters of peace and wars, we are to dispose the affair; that we would see an universal peace all over the earth, and that this time we could not go and force the nations that were yet further to condescend and submit to our will, but that we would see the neighboring countries in peace and union; that the Christinos were our brethren, and [we] have frequented them many winters; that we adopted them for our children and took them under our protection; that we should send them ambassadors; that I myself should make them come and conclude a general peace; that we were sure of their obedience to us; that the first that should break the peace, we would be their enemies and would reduce them to powder with our heavenly fire; that we had the word of the Christinos as well as theirs, and our thunders should serve us to make wars against those that would not submit to our will and desire, which was to see them good friends, to go and make wars against the upper nations[85] that doth not know us as yet. The gift was of six hatchets.

The third was to oblige them to receive our propositions, likewise the Christinos; to lead them to the dance of union, which was to be celebrated at the death's feast and banquet of kindred. If they would continue the wars, that was not the means to see us again in their country.

The fourth was that we thanked them for making us free passage through their countries. The gift was of two dozen knives.

The last was of smaller trifles: six graters, 2 dozen of awls, two dozen of needles, 6 dozens of looking glasses made of tin, a dozen of little bells, six ivory combs, with a little vermilion. For to make a recompence to the good old man that spoke so favorably, we gave him a hatchet; and to the elders each a blade for a sword; and to the two maidens that served us two necklaces, which [were] put about their necks, and two bracelets for their arms. The last gift was in general for all the women to love us and give us to eat when we should come to their cottages.

The company gave us great ho ho ho, that is, thanks. Our wildmen made others for their interest.

A company of about 50 were dispatched to warn the Christinos of what we had done. I went myself, where we arrived the third day early in the morning.[86] I was received with great demonstration of friendship. All that day we feasted, danced, and sing. I compared that place before to the buttery of Paris for the great quantity of meat that they use to have there, but now will compare it to that of London.[87] There I received gifts of all sorts of meat, of grease more than twenty men could carry. The custom is not to deface anything that they present. There were above six hundred men in a fort, with a great deal of baggage on their shoulders, and [they] did draw it upon light slides made very neatly. I have not seen them at their entrance, for the snow blinded me.

Coming back we passed a lake[88] hardly frozen, and the sun [glared off it] for the most part, for I looked awhile steadfastly on it, so I was troubled with this seven or eight days.

The meanwhile that we were there, arrived above a thousand [Indians] that had not been there. Those two erdoubted nations[89] were to see them do what they never before had, a difference, which was executed with a great deal of mirth. (I [had] fear of being injured, I will admit.) There were plays, mirths, and battle for sport.[90] Going and coming with cries, each played his part. In the public place the women danced with melody. The young men that endeavored to get a prize endeavored to climb up a great post, very smooth and greased with oil of bear and oriniack grease. The stake was at least of fifteen foot high. The prize was a knife or [some] other thing. We laid the [prize at the top of the] stake; whoso could catch it should have it. The feast was made to eat all up. To honor the feast, many men and women did burst.*

---

*Vomit.

Those of that place, coming back, came in sight of those of the village or fort, made postures in similitude of wars. This was to discover the enemy by signs. Any that should do so, we gave orders to take him or kill him and take his head off. The prisoner [was] to be tied, to fight in retreating, to pull an arrow out of the body, to exercise and strike with a club a buckler to their feet, and take it if need requireth, and defend himself if need require from the enemy that comes near, and to hear the better lay him down on the side. These postures are played while the drums beat. This was a serious thing, without speaking, except by nodding or gestures. Their drums were earthen pots full of water, covered with stag's skin; the sticks like hammers for the purpose. The elders have bomkins to the end of their staves, full of small stones, which makes a rattle to which young men and women go in a cadence. The elders are about these pots, beating them and singing; the women also, having a nosegay in their hands, and dance very modestly, not lifting much their feet from the ground, keeping their heads downwards, making a sweet harmony.

We made gifts for that while, fourteen days' time. Everyone brings the most exquisite things to show what his country affords. The renewing of their alliances, the marriages according to their country customs are made; also the visit of the bones of their deceased friends, for they keep them and bestow them upon one another. We sang in our language, as they in theirs, to which they gave great attention. We gave them several gifts, and received many. They bestowed upon us above 3 hundred robes of castors, out of which we brought not five to the French, being far in the country. This feast ended, everyone returns to his country well satisfied.

To be as good as our words we came to the nation of the Beef, which was seven small journeys from that place.[91] We promised in like manner to the Christinos the next spring we should come to their side of the Upper Lake,[92] and there they should meet us to come into their country. We, being arrived among the nation of the Beef, we wondered to find ourselves in a town where were great cabins, most covered with skins, and other [by] close mats. They told us that there were seven thousand men. This we believed. Those have as many wives as they can keep. If anyone did trespass upon the other, his nose was cut off, and often the crown of his head.[93] The maidens have all manner of freedom, but are forced to marry when they come to the age. The more they bear children, the more they are respected. I have seen a man having fourteen wives.

There they have no wood, and make provisions of moss for their firing. This, their place, is environed with perches,[94] which are a good distance one from another, that they get in the valleys where the buff use to repair, upon which they do live. They sow corn, but their harvest is small. The soil is good, but the cold hinders it, and the grain very small. In their country are mines of copper, of pewter, and of lead.[95] There are mountains covered with a kind of stone that is transparent and tender and like to that of Venice.[96]

The people stay not there all the year. They retire in winter towards the woods of the North, where they kill a quantity of castors, and I say that there are not so good in the whole world, but not in such a store as the Christinos', but far better.[97]

We stayed there six weeks and came back with a company of people of the nation of the Sault, that came along with us, loaden with booty. We were twelve days before we could overtake our company that went to the lake [Superior]. The spring approaches, which [is] the fittest time to kill the oriniack. A wildman and I, with my brother, killed that time above six hundred, besides other beasts.[98] We came to the lakeside with much pains, for we sent our wildmen before, and we two were forced to make carriages five days through the woods. After, we met with a company that did us a great deal of service, for they carried what we had, and [we] arrived at the appointed place[99] before three days ended. Here we made a fort.[100] At our arrival we found at least twenty cottages full.

One very fair evening we went to find what we hide before, which we find in a good condition.[101] We went about to execute our resolution, foreseeing that we must stay that year there, for which we were not very sorry, being resolved to know what we heard before.

We [would have] waited until the ice should vanish, but received [news] that the Ottawas built a fort on the point that forms that bay[102] which resembles a small lake. We went towards it with all speed. We had a great store of booty which we would not trust to the wildmen, for the occasion makes the thief. We overloaded our slide on that rotten ice,[103] and the further we went the sun was stronger, which made our trainage have more difficulty. I, seeing my brother so strained, I took the slide, which was heavier than mine, and he mine. Being in the extent above four leagues[104] from the ground, we sunk down above the one-half of the leg in the ice, and must advance in spite of our [chattering] teeth. To leave our booty was to undo us. We strived so that I hurted myself insomuch that I could not stand upright, nor [go] any further.[105]

This put us in great trouble. Upon this I advised my brother to leave me with his slide. We put the two sleds one by another. I took some clothes to cover me. After I stripped myself from my wet clothes, I laid myself down on the slide. My brother leaves me [in] the keeping of that good God; we had not above two leagues more to go. He makes haste and came there[106] in time and sends wildmen for me and the slides. There we found the perfidiousness of the Ottawas. Seeing us in extremity [they] would prescribe us laws. We promised them whatever they asked. They came to fetch me. For eight days I was so tormented I thought never to recover; I rested neither day nor night. At last by means that God and my brother did use, which was by rubbing my legs with hot oil of bears and keeping my thigh and legs well tied, it came to it's former strength. After a while I came to myself.

There comes a great company of new wildmen[107] to seek a nation in that land for a weighty business. They desired me to go along, so I prepare myself to go with them.[108] I marched well two days. The third day the sore begins to break out again insomuch that I could go no further. Those left me, albeit I came for their sake. You will see the cruelties of those beasts, and I may think that those that liveth on fish[109] uses more inhumanities than those that feed upon flesh.

Nevertheless, I proceed forwards the best I could, but knowed [not] where for the most part, the sun being my only guide. There was some snow as yet on the ground which was so hard in the mornings that I could not perceive any tracks. The worst was that I had not a hatchet nor other arm, and not above the weight of ten pounds of victuals, without any drink. I was obliged to proceed five days for my good fortune. I endured much in the morning, but, a little warmed, I went with more ease. I looked betimes for some old cabins, where I found wood to make fire wherewith I melted the snow in my cap that was so greasy. One night I, finding a cottage, covered it with boughs of trees that I found ready cut. The fire came to it as I began to slumber, which

soon awaked me. In haste, as lame as I was, to save myself from
the fire: my rackets, shoes, and stockings kept me my life; I
must needs save them. I took them and flung them as far as I
could in the snow. The fire being out, I was forced to look for
them, as dark as it was, in the said snow, all naked and very
lame and almost starved, both for hunger and cold.

But what is it that a man cannot do when he seeth that it concerns his life, that one day he must loose? Yet we are to prolong
it as much as we can, and the very fear maketh us to invent new
ways.

The fifth day I heard a noise and thought it of a wolf. I stood
still and soon perceived that it was of a man. Many wildmen were
up and down looking for me, fearing lest the bears should have
devoured me. That man came near and salutes me and demands
whether it was I. We both sat down. He looks in my sack to see
if I had victuals, where he finds a piece as big as my fist. He
eats this without participation, being their usual way. He in-
quireth if I was a hungry. I told him no, to show myself stout and
resolute. He takes a pipe of tobacco, and then above twenty
pounds of victuals he takes out of his sack, and grease, and gives
it me to eat. I eat what I could and gave him the rest. He bids
me have courage, that the village was not far off. He demands
if I knowed the way, but I was not such as should say no. The
village was at hand.

The other wildmen arrived but the day before and after a
while came by boats to the lake. The boats were made of oriniacks'
skins.

I find my brother[110] with a company of Christinos that were
arrived in my absence. We resolved to cover our business better
and close our design as if we were going ahunting, and send them
before, that we would follow them the next night, which we did
and succeeded, but not without much labor and danger. Not
knowing the right way to thwart the other side of the lake,[111] we
were in danger to perish a thousand times because of the crumbs
of ice. We thwarted a place of fifteen leagues. We arrived on the
other side at night. When we came there we knowed not where
to go, on the right or left hand, for we saw nobody. At last, as
we with full sail came from a deep bay, we perceived smoke and
tents.

Then many boats from thence came to meet us. We were received with much joy by those poor Christinos.[112] They suffered

145

not that we trod on ground. They lead us into the middle of their cottages in our own boats, like a couple of cocks in a basket.

There were some wildmen that followed us, but late. We went away with all haste possible to arrive the sooner at the great river.[113] We came to the seaside,[114] where we find an old house all demolished and battered with bullets. We were told that those that came there were of two nations, one of the Wolf, the other of the Long Horned Beast; all those nations are distinguished by the representation of the beasts or animals. They tell us particularities of the Europeans.[115] We knew ourselves, and what Europe is; therefore in vain they tell us that.

We went from isle to isle all that summer.[116] We plucked [an] abundance of ducks, as of all other sort of fowls. We wanted not fish nor fresh meat. We were well beloved, and [they] were over-joyed that we promised them to come with such ships as we in-vented. This place hath a great store of cows.[117] The wildmen kill them not except for necessary use. We went further in the bay to see the place that they were to pass that summer. That river comes from the lake and empties itself in the River of Saguenay, called Tadousac, which is a hundred leagues in the great River of Canada. As we were in the Bay of the North, we left in this place our marks and rendezvous.[118] The wildmen that brought us defended* us above all things, if we would come directly to them, that we should by no means land (and so [we] go to the river to the other side, that is, to the north towards the sea), telling us that those people were very treacherous. Now whether they told us this out of policy, lest we should not come to them first and so be deprived of what they thought to get from us [I do not know]. In that you may see that envy reigns every-where amongst poor barbarous wild people, as at courts. They made us a map of what we could not see because the time was nigh to reap among the bustards and ducks. As we came to the place where these oats grows (they grow in many places), you would think it strange to see the great number of fowls, that are so fat by eating of this grain that hardly they will move from it. I have seen a wildman killing three ducks at once with one arrow. It is an ordinary thing to see five [or] six hundred swans together. I must profess I wondered that the winter there was so cold, when the sand boils at the waterside for the extreme heat of the

---

*Meaning "forbade."

146

sun. I put some eggs in that sand, and [in] less than half an hour the eggs were as hard as stones.[119] We passed that summer quietly, coasting the seaside, and as the cold began we prevented the ice.* We have the commodity of the river to carry our things in our boats to the best place, where were most beasts.

This [the Christino] is a wandering nation, and containeth a vast country. In winter they live in the land for the hunting sake, and in summer by the water for fishing. They never are many together for fear of wronging one another. They are of a good nature, and not great whoremasters, having but one wife, and are [more] satisfied than any others that I knowed. They clothe themselves all over with castors' skins in winter, in summer of stags' skins. They are the best huntsmen of all America and scorns to catch a castor in a trap. The circumjacent nations go all naked when the season permits it, but this have more modesty, for they put a piece of copper, made like a finger of a glove, which they use before their nature. They have the same tents as the nation of the Beef, and their apparel from top to toe. The women are tender and delicate and takes as much pains as slaves. They are of more acute wits than the men, for the men are fools, but diligent about their work. They kill not the young castors, but leave them in the water, being that they are sure that they will take him again, which no other nation doth. They burn not their prisoners, but knock them in the head or slain them with arrows, saying it's not decent for men to be so cruel. They have a store of turquoise from the nation of the Buff and Beef, with whom they had wars. They polish them and give them the form of pearl — long, flat, round — and [hang] them at their nose. They [find] green stones very fine at the side of the same bay of the sea, to the northwest.

There is a nation called among themselves Neuter; they speak the Beef and Christinos' speech, being friends to both. Those poor people could not tell what to give us. They were over-joyed when we said we should bring them commodities.

We went up another river to the Upper Lake.[120]

The nation of the Beef sent us gifts, and we to them by am-bassadors. In the middle of winter we joined with a company of the fort,[121] who gladly received us. They were resolved to go to the French the next spring because they were quite out of

---

*They left the bay before freeze-up.

stock; the feast of the dead [had] consumed a great deal of it. They blamed us, saying we should not trust any that we did not know. They upon this asked if [we] were where the trumpets blown are.[122] We said yea and told that they were a nation[123] not to be trusted, and if we came to that sea[124] we should war against them because they were [a] bad nation and did their endeavor to take us, to make us their slaves.

In the beginning of spring there came a company of [Sioux] men that came to see us from the elders and brought us furs to entice us to see them again. I cannot omit pleasant encounters that happened to my brother. As we were both in a cottage, two of the nation of the Beef came to see us. In that time my brother had some trade[125] in his hands. The wildmen sat near us. My brother shows unto them the image which presented the flight of Joseph and Holy Mary with the Child Jesus to avoid the anger of Herod, and the Virgin and Child were riding the ass, and Joseph carrying a long cloak; my brother showing that animal, naming it tatanga, which is a buff. The wildmen, seeing the representation of a woman, were astonished and weeps, pulls their hair, and tumbles up and down to the fire, so continued half an hour, till he was in a sweat and wetted with his tears the rest of the wildmen that were there. One of them went out of the cottage. My brother and I were surprised, thought they might have seen a vision, for instantly the man put his hands on his face, as if he should make the sign of the cross. Now, as he came to himself, he made us understand (for I began to know much of their speech) that, first, we were devils, knowing all that is and what was done, moreover that he had his desire: that was his wife and child, whom were taken by the nation of the Beef* four years ago. He took the ass for the nation of the Beef, the Virgin Mary for the picture of his wife, and Jesus for his son, and Joseph for himself, saying, "There am I with my long robe, seeking for my wife and child."

By our ambassador [from the Sioux] I came to know another lake[126] which is northerly of their country. They say that it's bigger than all the rest. The upper end is always frozen. Their fish comes from those parts. There are people that lives there

---

*Radisson apparently is confused. The Indian in question is himself a Sioux; he may possibly, of course, be talking about intra-tribal wife stealing.

and dare not trade in it towards the south. There is a river so deep and black that there is no bottom. They say that fish goes neither out nor into the river. It is very warm, and if they durst navigate in it they should not come to the end in forty days. That river comes from the lake, and the inhabitants makes wars against the birds, that defends and offends with their bills, that are as sharp as [a] sword. This I cannot tell for truth, but [it was] told me.

All the circumjacent neighbors do encourage us, saying that they would venture their lives with us, for which we were much overjoyed to see them so freely disposed to go along with us. Here, nothing but courage. "Brother, do not lie, for the French will not believe thee. All men of courage and valor, let them fetch commodities and not stand lazing and be a beggar in the cabin. It is the way to be beloved of women, to go and bring them wherewithal to be joyful." We present gifts to one and to another for to warm them. [We told them] we should make the earth quake and give terror to the Iroquois if they were so bold as to show themselves.

The Christinos made gifts that they might come with us. This was granted unto them: to send two boats to testify that they were retained slaves among the other nations, although they furnish them with castors.

The boats ready, we embark ourselves. We were seven hundred; there was not [before] seen such a company to go down to the French. There were above four hundred Christinos' boats[127] that brought us their castors, in hopes that the people should give some merchandises for them at their return; the biggest boats could carry only the man and his wife, and could scarce carry with them three castors, so little were their boats; in summertime I have seen three hundred men go to wars, and each man his [own] boat, for they are [those] that makes the least boats.* The company that we had filled above three hundred and sixty boats. There were boats that carried seven men, and the least two. It was a pleasure to see that embarking, for all the young women went in stark naked, their hairs hanging down; yet is it not their custom to do so. I though it [to] their shame, but, contrary, they think it excellent and [an] old custom good. They sing aloud and sweetly. They stood in their boats and remained in that posture

*Meaning the smallest boats.

149

half a day to encourage us to come and lodge with them again. Therefore, they are not altogether ashamed to show us all, to entice us and animate the men to defend themselves valiantly and come and enjoy them.

In two days we arrived at the River of the Sturgeon,[128] so called because of the great quantity of sturgeons that we took there. Here we were to make our provisions to pass the lake some fourteen days [later]. In the said term we dried above a million[129] of sturgeons. The women followed us close; after our abode there two days they overtook us.

We had several false alarms which put us in several troubles. They wondered to have found an oriniack dead upon the place, with a bullet in his body. There [a] thousand lies were forged. Therefore we go from thence, but before we came to the long point whereof we spoke before,[130] the wildmen call it Okiuoto-name, we perceive smoke. We go to discover what it was, and by ill luck we found it was a Iroquois boat of seven men, who doubtless [had] stayed that winter in the Lake of the Hurons and came there to discover somewhat. I cannot say that they were the first that came there; God grant that they may be the last. As they saw us, away they as swift as their heels could drive; they left their boat and all. They to the woods, and were pursued, but in vain, for they were gone before three hours. The pursuers came back. The one brings a gun, the one a hatchet, the other a kettle, and so forth. The council was called, where it was decreed to go back and shake off to go down to the French till the next year. This vexed us sore, to see such a fleet and such an opportunity come to nothing. Foreseeing that such another may be not in ten years, we were [trying] to persuade them to the contrary, but [they] checked [us] soundly, saying we were worse than enemies by persuading them to go and be slained. In this we must let their fear pass over, and we back to the River of the Sturgeons, where we found our wives very busy in killing those creatures, that come there to multiply. We daily hear some new report: all everywhere enemy, by fancy.

We in the meantime busy ourselves in the good of our country, which will recompence us badly for such toil and labor. Twelve days are passed, in which time we gained some hopes of fair words. We called a council before the company was disbanded, where we represented [that], if they [the fleeing Iroquois] were discoverers, they had not valued the loss of their kettle,

150

knowing well they were to get another where their army laid. If there should be an army, it should appear and, we in such a number, they could be well afraid and turn back. Our reasons were heard and put in execution.

The next day we embarked, saving the Christinos, that were afraid of a sight of a boat made of another stuff than theirs; they went back. As we came where the Iroquois' boat was, our words proved true, and so proceeded in our way. Being come nigh the sault,[131] we found a place where two of these men [had] sweated[132] and for want of covers buried themselves in the sand by the waterside to keep their bodies from the flies called maringoines, which otherwise had killed them with their stings. We thwarted those two great lakes[133] with great pleasure, having the wind fair with us. (It was a great satisfaction to see so many boats and so many wildmen that never had before commerce with the French. So my brother and I thought we should be welcomed. But, oh Covetousness, thou art the cause of many evils!) We made a small sail to every boat. Everyone strived to be not the last. The wind was double ways favorable to us: the one gave us rest; the other advanced us very much, which we wanted much because of the above-said delay.

We now are comed to the carriages and swift streams to get [to] the Lake of the Castors. We made them with courage, promptitude, and hunger, which made go with haste as well as the wind. We go down all the great river without any encounter till we came to the Long Sault, where my brother some years before made a shipwreck.[134] Being in that place we had work enough. The first thing we saw was several boats that the enemy had left at the riverside. This puts great fear in the hearts of our people; nor they nor we could tell what to do. Seeing nobody appeared, we sent to discover what they were. The discoverers calls us and bids us come, that those who were there [apparently Frenchmen, victims of a recent battle] could do us no harm.[135] We visited that place, and there was a fine fort. Three were about the other two.*

---

*There are two possible meanings of this ambiguous sentence. It may refer to the fort, with three bastions protecting two inner buildings; or, in view of the harmlessness of "those who were there," it might mean that there are five corpses — three about the other two.

We went down the river without making any carriage, and we adventured very much. As soon as we were at the lower end, many of our wildmen had a mind to go back and not to go any further, thinking really that all the French were killed. As for my brother and I, we did fear very much that after such a thing the pride of the enemy would make them attempt anything upon the habitations of Montreal, which is but 30 leagues from thence.[136] We did advise them to make a fort, or to put us in one of the enemies', and to send immediately two very light boats that could not be overtaken if the enemy should discover them; that, being arrived at the habitation, they should make them shoot the pieces of ordinance; and that as soon as the night should come we would embark ourselves and should hear the noise, or else we should take council of what we should do and stay for them at the height of the Isle of Montreal, which was done accordingly, without any hazard, for all the enemies were gone, despairing of our coming down and for what they had done and for what they had lost, which by the report of some Hurons was more than four score men. (If the French [mentioned one paragraph above] had had a fort flank and some water, they had resisted the enemy miraculously and forced them to leave them for want of powder and shot and also of other provisions; they were furnished for the whole summer.)[137] Our two boats did go, but the rest were so impatient that they resolved to follow them, being willing to run the same hazard, and we arrived the next morning and were in sight when the pieces were shot off with a great deal of joy to see so great a number of boats, that did almost cover the whole river.

We stayed three days at Montreal, and then we went down to Three Rivers. The wildmen did ask our advice whether it was best for them to go down farther. We told them no, because of the dangers that they may meet with at their return, for the Iroquois could have notice of their coming down and so come and lay in ambush for them, and it was in the latter season, being about the end of August.[138] Well, as soon as their business was done they went back again very well satisfied, and we very ill satisfied for our reception, which was very bad, considering the service we had done to the country, which will at another time discourage those that by our example would be willing to venture their lives for the benefit of the country, seeing a governor[139] that would grow rich by the labors and hazards of others.

152

Before I go further, I have a mind to let you know the fabulous belief of those poor people, that you may see their ignorance concerning the soul's immortality being separated from the body. The kindred and the friends of the deceased give notice to the others who [will] gather together and cry for the dead, which gives warning to the young men to take the arms to give some assistance and consolation to the deceased. Presently the corpse is covered with white skins very well tied. Afterwards all the kindred come to the cottage of the deceased and begin to mourn and lament. After they are weary of making such music, the husbands or friends of the deceased send their wives for gifts to pacify a little the widow and to dry her tears. Those gifts are of skins and of what they can get, for at such a ceremony they are very liberal. As soon as that is done and the night come, all the young men are desired to come and do what they will to have done to them, so that when darkness has covered the whole face of the earth they come, all singing, with staves in their hands for their arms and, after they are set round the cabin, begin to knock and make such a noise that one would think they have a mind to tear all in pieces and that they are possessed of some devils. All this is done to expel and frighten the soul out of that poor and miserable body, that she might not trouble his carcass nor his bones, and to make it to depart, the sooner to go and see their ancestors and to take possession of their immortal glory, which cannot be obtained but a fortnight towards the setting of the sun.

The first stop that she makes is of seven days, to begin her course, but there are many difficulties, for it is through a very thick wood full of thorns, of stones, and flints, which [are] great trouble to that poor soul. At last, having overcome all those dangers and toils, she comes to a river of about a quarter of a mile broad where there is a bridge made only of one plank, being supported by a beam pointed at one end, which is the reason that plank rises and falls perpetually, having not any rest nor stay, and when the soul comes near the side of that river she meets with a man of extraordinary stature, who is very lean and holds a dagger of very hard wood, and very keen, in his hand and speaks these words when he sees the petitioning soul come near: "Pale, pale," which signifies go, go. At every word the bridge balances, and [the man] rises his knife, and the traveler, offering herself, receives a blow by which she is cut in two, and each half is found upon that moving [bridge], and according as

153

she had lived they stay upon it; that is, if her body was valiant the passage was soon made free to her, for the two halves come together and join themselves again [and] so pass to the other side, where she finds a bladder of bear's grease to grease herself and refresh herself, which being done she finds a wood somewhat clearer and a straight road that she must go, and for 5 days neither go to the right nor to the left hand, where at last being arrived she finds a very great and clear fire through [which] she must resolve to pass. That fire is kindled by the young men that died since the beginning of the world, to know whether those that come have loved the women or have been good huntsmen. If that soul has not had any of those rare virtues she burns and broils the sole of her feet by going through the fire; but quite [the] contrary if she has had them qualities: she passes through without burning herself in the least. From that so hot place she finds grease and paint of all sorts of color, with which she daubs and makes herself beautiful to come to that place so wished for. But she has not yet all done nor made an end of her voyage. Being so dressed, she continues her course, still towards the same pole, for the space of two days in a very clear wood and where there is very high and tall trees, of which most be oaks, which is the reason that there is great store of bears. All along that way they [the journeying spirits] do nothing else but see their enemies laid all along upon the ground, that sing their fatal song for having been vanquished in this world and also in the other; not daring to be so bold as to kill one of those animals, [the enemies] feed only upon the down of those beasts.

Being arrived (if I may say) at the door of that imaginary paradise, they find a company of their ancestors, long since deceased, by whom they are received with a great deal of ceremony, and are brought by so venerable a company [to] within half a day's journey of the place of the meeting, and all along the rest of the way they discourse of things of this world that are passed. You must know they travel [the final] half a day without speaking one word, but keep a very deep silence, for, said they, it is like the goslings to confound one another with words. As soon as they are arrived they must have a time to come to themselves, to think well upon what they are to speak, without any precipitation, but with judgement, so that they are come where [are gathered] all manner of company, with drums and dried pumpkins full of stones and other such instruments.

154

The elders that have brought her there cover her with a very large white skin and color her legs with vermilion and her feet likewise, and so she is received amongst the predestinates. There is a deep silence made as soon as she is come in, and then one of the elders makes a long speech to encourage the young people to go ahunting and kill some meat to make a feast for [the] entertainment of the soul of their countryman, which is put in execution with a great deal of diligence and haste. While the meat is boiling or roasting, there is great preparations made for the feast. The young maidens set out themselves with the richest jewels and present the bosom to the newcomer.* A little while after the kettles are filled, there is feasting everywhere; comedies acted; and whatsoever is rare is then to be seen; there is dancing everywhere. Now remained nothing but to provide that poor soul of a companion, which she does presently, for she has the choice of very beautiful women and may take as many as she pleases, which makes her felicity immortal.

By this you may see the silly belief of those poor people.

I have seen right-minded Jesuits weep bitterly, hearing me speak of so many nations that perish for want of instruction, but most of them are like the wildmen, that think they offend if they reserve anything for the next day. I have seen also some of the same company say, "Alas, what pity 'tis to loose so many castors. Is there no way to go there? The fish and the sauce invite us to it. Is there no means to catch it? Oh, how happy should I be to go in those countries as an envoy, being it is so good a country." That is the relation that was made me several times by those wildmen; I thought they would never have done.

But let us come to our arrival again. The governor, seeing us come back with a considerable sum for our own particular, and seeing that his time was expired and that he was to go away,[140] made use of that excuse to do us wrong and to enrich himself with the good that we had so dearly bought, and by our means we made the country to subsist, that without us [it] had been, I believe, oftentimes quite undone and ruined. [It would have been] better to say at his last bidding, "No castors, no ship, and what [are you going] to do without necessary commodities?" He made also my brother prisoner for not having observed his orders and to be gone without his leave.[141] One of his letters made him blush

---

*That is, they embrace the newcomer.

155

for shame, not knowing what to say but that he would have some of them [beaver pelts] at what price soever, that he might the better maintain his coach and horses at Paris. He fined us four thousand pounds to make a fort at Three Rivers, telling us for all manner of satisfaction that he would give us leave to put our coat of arms upon it, and, moreover, six thousand pounds for the country, saying that we should not take it so strangely and so bad, being we were inhabitants and did intend to finish our days in the same country with our relations and friends. But the bougre[142] did grease his chops with it and, more, made us pay a custom which was the 4th part, which came to fourteen thousand pounds, so that we had left but 46 thousand pounds, and took away 24,000 [livres]. Was not he a tyrant to deal so with us, after we had so hazarded our lives and brought in less than 2 years by that voyage, as the factors of the said country said, between 40 and 50 thousand pistoles?[143] They spoke to me in this manner: "In which country have you been? From whence do you come? For we never saw the like. From whence did come such excellent castors? Since your arrival, is come into our magazine very near six hundred thousand pounds tournois[144] of that filthy merchandise which will be prized like gold in France." Them were the very words that they said to me.

Seeing ourselves so wronged, my brother did resolve to go and demand justice in France.[145] It had been better for him to have been contented with his losses and without going and spend the rest in half a year's time in France, having 10,000 [livers] that he left with his wife, and that was as good a housewife as he. There he is in France. He is paid with fair words and with promise, to make him go back from whence he came, but he, seeing no assurance of it, did engage himself with a merchant at Rochelle who was to send him a ship the next spring.[146] In that hope he come away in a fisher boat to Pierced island, some 20 leagues off from the Isle d'Eluticosty,[147] the place where the ship was to come. That [ship] was to come whilst he was going in a shallop to Quebec, where I was to go away with him to the rendezvous, being he could not do anything without me.

[He had] a great deal of difficulty, it proved. [He took so long in coming to Quebec] that I thought it possible to go taste of the pleasures of France, and by a small vessel, that I might not be idle during his absence. [But he arrived before I could depart and] he presently told me what he had done and what we should do.

156

We embarked, being nine of us. In few days we came to Pierced island, where we found several ships newly arrived, and in one of them we found a Father Jesuit that told us that we should not find what we thought to find, and that he had put a good order and that it was not well done to destroy in that manner a country, and so wrong so many inhabitants. He advised me to leave my brother, telling me that his designs were pernicious. We see ourselves frustrated of our hopes. My brother told me that we had store of merchandise that would bring much profit to the French habitations that are in Cadis.[148] I, who was desirous of nothing but new things, made no scruple.

We arrived at St. Peter in the Isle of Cape Breton at the habitation of Monsieur Denys,[149] where we delivered some merchandises for some oriniack skins. From thence to Canseau, where every day we were threatened to be burned by the French, but, God be thanked, we escaped from their hands by avoiding a surprise. In that place my brother told me of his design to come and see New England, which our servants heard, and grumbled and labored underhand against us, for which our lives were in very great danger. We sent some of them away, and at last with much labor and danger we came to Port Royal, which is inhabited by the French under the English government, where some few days after came some English ships that brought about our designs.

[They] being come, we did declare our designs. We were entertained and we had a ship promised us, and the articles drawn, and we did put to sea the next spring[150] for our discovery, and we went to the entry of Hudson's strait by the 61 degree. We had knowledge and conversation with the people of those parts, but we did see and know that there was nothing to be done unless we went further. The season of the year was far spent by the indiscretion of our master,[151] that only were accustomed to see some Barbados sugars, and not mountains of sugar candy,[152] which did frighten him [so] that he would go no further, complaining that he was furnished but for 4 months and that he had neither sails nor cord nor pitch nor tow to stay out a winter. Seeing well that it was too late, he would go no further, so brought us back to the place from whence we came,[153] where we were welcomed, although with great loss of goods and hope, but the last was not quite lost.

We were promised two ships for a second voyage. They were made fit and ready, and being the season of the year was not yet come to be gone, one of them two ships was sent to the Isle of Sand[154] —there to fish for the bass to make oil of it—where we came in very bad weather, and the ship was lost in that island, but the men were saved.

The expectation of that ship made us loose our second voyage, which did very much discourage the merchants with whom we had to do. They went to law with us to make us recant the bargain that we had made with them. After we had disputed a long time, it was found that the right was on our side, and we innocent of what they did accuse us.[155] So they endeavored to come to an agreement, but we were betrayed by our own party.

In the meantime, the commissioners of the King of Great Britain arrived in that place,[156] and one of them would have us go with him to New York, and the other advised us to come to England and offer ourselves to the King, which we did. Those of New England in general made proffers unto us of what ship we would if we would go on in our designs, but we answered them that a scalded cat fears the water though it be cold.

We are now in the passage,[157] and he that brought us, which was one of the commissioners, called Colonel George Cartwright,[158] was taken by the Hollanders, and we arrived in England at a very bad time for the plague and the wars.[159] Being at Oxford, we went to Sir George Carteret, who spoke to his matey, who gave us good hopes that we should have a ship ready for the next spring and that the King did allow us forty shillings a week for our maintenance, and we had chambers in the town by his order, where we stayed 3 months. Afterwards the King came to London and sent us to Windsor, where we stayed the rest of the winter.[160] We are sent for from that place, the season growing near, and put into the hands of Sir Peter Colleton. The ship was got ready something too late, and our master was not fit for such a design, but the Hollanders, being come to the River of Thames, had stopped the passage,[161] so we lost that opportunity.

So we were put off till the next year,[162] and a little while after, that same ship was sent to Virginia and other places to know some news of the Barbados and to be informed if that island was not in danger, which if it had been lost had taken from the English ladies the means or the pleasure of drinking French wine. Those of Bordeaux and of Rochelle were great loosers in the expectation of that ship, that was not gone to the Isle of Sand but to Holland.

We lost our second voyage, for the other was given too late for fitting another ship, which cost a great deal of money to no purpose.

The third year[163] we went out with a new company in two small vessels,[164] my brother in one and I in another, and we went together 400 leagues from the north of Ireland, where a sudden great storm did rise and put us asunder. The sea was so furious six or seven hours after that it did almost overturn our ship, so that we were forced to cut our masts rather than cut our lives, but we came back safe, God be thanked, and the other, I hope, is gone on his voyage,[165] God be with him.

I hope to embark myself by the help of God this fourth year,[166] and I beseech Him to grant me better success than I have had hitherto, and beseech Him to give me grace and to make me [a] partaker of that everlasting happiness, which is the only thing a man ought to look after.

I have here put the names of several nations amongst which I have been for the most part, which I think may extend to some nine hundred leagues, by the reckoning of my travels.

The names of the nations that live in the South

Avieronons
Aviottronons
Anontackeronons
Sononteronons
Oyongoironons
Andasstoueronoms
Konkhaderichonons
Andouauchronons
Kionontateronons
Ouendack
Khionontateronons
Oherokouauechronons
Ahondironons
Ougmarahronoms
Akrahkuaeronoms
Oneronoms
Eressaronoms
Attiouendarouks
Ekriehronoms
Tontataratouhronoms

Ariotachronoms
Oscovarahronoms
Huattochronoms
Skinchiohronoms
Attitachronons
Ontorahronons
Aoveatsiovaenhronons
Attochingochronons
Attioendarakheronons
Maingonis
Socoguis
Pacoiguis

All these nations are sedentaries and live upon corn and other grain, by hunting and fishing, which is plentiful, and by the ragouts of roots. There were many destroyed by the Iroquois, and I have seen most of those that are left.

The names of the nations that live in the North

Chisedeck
Bersiamites
Sagseggons
Attikamegues
{ Ovaouehkairiny
{ or Algonquins
Kischeripirini
Minisigons
Kotakoaveteny
Kinoncheripirini
Matouchkarini
Ountchatarounongha
Sagahigavirini
Saguitaovigama
Nipisiriniens
Tivikimi
Outimagami
Ouachegami
Mitchitamou
Orturbi
Ovasovarin
Atcheligonens
Annikouay
Otauack
Ouncisagay
Abaouicktigonions

Roguay
Mantouech
Pissings
Malhonniners
Asinipour
Trinivoick
Nasaouakouetons
Poutouatemick
Escotecke
Pauoestigonce
Nadoucenako
Titascons
Christinos
Nadoueceronons
Ouinipigoueck
Tatanga

The two last are sedentary and do reap, and all the rest are wandering people that live by their hunting and fishing, and some few of rice that they do labor for, and a great many of them have been destroyed by the Iroquois. Besides all the above-named nations, I have seen eight or nine more since my voyages.

FIFTH VOYAGE[1]

The relation of a voyage made by Peter Radisson, Esquire, to the North parts of America in the years 1682 and 1683.

IN THE FIRST place, I think myself obliged to vindicate myself from the imputation of inconstancy for acting in this voyage against the English interest, and in the year 1683 against the French interests, for which, if I could not give a very good account, I might justly lie under the sentence of capriciousness and inconstancy. But several persons of probity and good repute, being sensible [of] what my brother-in-law, Mr. Chouard Des Groseilliers, and myself performed in several voyages for the gentlemen concerned in the Hudson's Bay trade, relating to the commerce of beaver skins, and [of] the just cause of dissatisfaction which both of us had, [knew there was due cause] to make us retire into France. I have no cause to believe that I in the least deserve to be taxed with lightness or inconstancy for the employments wherein I since engaged, although they were against the interests of the [Hudson's Bay] Company, for it is sufficiently known that [neither] my brother nor myself omitted nothing that lay in our power, having both of us several times adventured our lives, and did all that was possible for persons of courage and honor to perform for the advantage and profit of the said Company ever since the year 1665 unto the year 1674.

But finding that all our advice was slighted and rejected, and the counsel of other persons embraced and made use of, which manifestly tended to the ruin of the settlement of the beaver trade, and that on all occasions we were looked upon as useless persons that deserved neither reward nor encouragement, this unkind usage made us at last take a resolution, though with very great reluctancy, to return back to France. In the main it was well known that I have a greater inclination for the interest of England than for that of France, being married at London unto an honorable family,[2] whose alliance had also the deeper engaged me in the interest of the nation. Moreover, all my friends know the tender love I had for my wife, and that I declared unto them how much I was troubled in being reduced to the necessity of leaving her. I hope these considerations will vindicate my proceedings, touching the several interests which I espoused, and what I shall relate in this ensuing narrative, touching my proceedings in regard to the English in this voyage in the river and also in Nelson's harbor in the year 1683, and will justify me against what has been reported to my prejudice to render me odious unto the nation. For it will appear that, having had the good fortune to defend my settlement against those which at that time I looked upon as my enemies, and defeated them by frustrating their designs, I improved the advantage I had over them the best I could. Yet would they [better] do me right; they must own that they had more just cause to give me thanks than to complain of me, having ever used them kindly as long as they pleased to live with me. I freely confess I used all the skill I could to compass my designs, and knowing very well what these gentlemen intended against me, I thought it better to surprise them than that they should me, knowing that if they had been aforehand with me I should have passed my time worse with them than they did with me.

I come now to discourse of my voyage, not thinking it material here to mention the campaign I made in the French fleet, since I left England, in the expeditions of Guinea, Tobaga,[3] and other occasions wherein I was concerned before I engaged in this voyage. At the time my brother-in-law and I were dissatisfied with the Hudson's Bay Company, we were several times invited by the late Monsieur Colbert[4] to return back for France, with large promises that we should be very kindly entertained. We refused a great while all the offers that were made us, but seeing our business went worse and worse with the Company, without any likelihood of finding any better usage, at last we accepted the offer that was made unto us of paying us 400 louis d'ors ready money, of discharging all our debts, and to give us good employments. These conditions being agreed upon, we passed over into France on Xber, 1674.*

---

*It will be noticed in what follows in the Fifth voyage that Radisson uses the standard names of months, as well as the constructions

As soon as we go to Paris we waited upon Monsieur Colbert. He reproached us for preferring the English interest before that of France, but having heard our defence and observed by what we said unto him of our discoveries in the northern parts of America, and of the acquaintance we had with the natives, how fit we might be for his purpose, he soon assured us of his favor and protection, and also of the King's pardon for what was past, with an entire restoration unto the same state we were in before we left France, upon condition that we should employ our care and industry for the advancement and increase of the commerce of the beaver trade in the French colonies in Canada. He also confirmed the promise [that] had been made us at London of the gratuity of 400 French pistoles, that all our debts should be discharged, and that we should be put into employments. Our letters patents of pardon and restoration were forthwith dispatched, and Monsieur Colbert would have it expressly mentioned in them for what cause the King granted them, viz., to employ the greatest of our skill and industry with the natives for the utility and advancement of the beaver trade in the French colonies. The 400 pieces of gold was paid us, and all things else promised was performed, excepting only the employment, for the which we were made to attend a great while, and all to no purpose.

But at last I perceived the cause of this delay: my marrying in England made me be suspected because my wife remained there. Monsieur Colbert having delayed us a long time with sundry excuses, one day he explained himself, saying I should bring my wife over into France if I expected that a full confidence should be put in me. I represented unto him that it was not a thing fully in my power to do, my wife's father refusing to give me liberty of bringing her over into France, but I promised him to use my best endeavors to that effect. In the meantime, Monsieur Colbert intimated that he would have my brother-in-law and myself make a voyage unto Canada to advise with the governor what was best

---

"Xber," "9ber," "8ber," etc. These latter apparently are drawn from the ancient Roman calendar; hence, "Xber" is December, "9ber" is November, "8ber" is October, etc. The reasons for the appearance of both calendars are obscure, but it is conceivable that Radisson's use of the ancient Roman has something to do with his long association with clerics more-or-less learned in the Latin.

there to be done, assuring us that he would write unto him in our behalf.

We undertook the voyage, but being arrived at Quebec, we found that jealousy and interest which some persons had over those that had the absolute command at that time of the trade in Canada, and whose creatures were employed for new discoveries, ordered things so that the Count De Frontenac, the governor, took no care to perform what we had been promised he should have done for us.

Finding myself slighted, I left my brother-in-law with his family in Canada and returned back again for France, intending to serve at sea in the fleet. Accordingly I there passed the campaigns above-mentioned until we suffered shipwreck at the Isle d'Aves, from which being escaped, I returned with the rest of the army unto Brest in the month of July, having lost all my equipage in this disaster.

The vice-admiral and the intendant wrote to court in my favor, and upon the good character they were pleased to give me I received a gratuity of 100 louis d'ors upon the King's account to renew my equipage. These gentlemen also were pleased to tell me I should ere long have the command of a man-of-war, but thinking that could not so easily be, I desired leave to make a turn over into England, under pretext of visiting my wife, and to make a further trial of bringing her over into France; whereupon I had my pass granted, with a farther gratuity of 100 louis d'ors towards the charges of my voyage. I was commanded to make what dispatch possible might be and especially to mind the business of bringing my wife along with me, and then I should not doubt of having good employments.

I set forwards and arrived in London the 4th of July and, amongst other discourse, told my father-in-law, Sir John Kirke, of what great importance it was unto me of making my fortune in France to take my wife along with me thither. Notwithstanding, he would by no means give his consent thereunto, but desired me to write to my friends in France concerning some pretention he had against the inhabitants of Canada,[5] which I did. I endeavored also during my stay at London, both by myself and by friends, to try if the gentlemen of the [Hudson's Bay] Company might conceive any better thoughts of me and whether I might not by some means or other be restored unto their good liking. But all my endeavors proved in vain; I found no likelihood of effecting what I so much desired.

Therefore I returned into France and arrived at Brest the 12th of 8ber, 1679. Having informed the vice-admiral and intendant of the little success I had in my voyage, and that it was not through any neglect of mine, they ordered me to go give an account of it unto the Marquis De Seignelay, which I did.

Telling him I could not prevail to bring my wife over along with me, he reviled me and told me he knew very well what an inclination I had still for the English interest, saying withal that I must not expect any confidence should be put in me, nor that I should not have the least employment whilst my wife stayed in England. Nevertheless, he promised to speak to his father, Monsieur Colbert, touching my affairs, which he also performed.

Afterwards, waiting upon him [Monsieur Colbert], he spoke unto me much after the same rate his son, the Marquis De Seignelay, had done before as to what concerned my wife, and ordered me to go unto Monsieur Bellinzani, his chief agent for the business of trade, who would farther inform me of his intentions.

Meeting with Monsieur Bellinzani,[6] he told me that Monsieur Colbert thought it necessary that I should confer with Monsieur De La Chesnaye,[7] a Canada merchant who managed all the trade of those parts and who was then at Paris; that with him some measures should be taken to make the best advantage of our discoveries and intrigues in the northern parts of Canada to advance the beaver trade; and as much as possible might be [done] to hinder all strangers from driving that trade to the prejudice of the French colonies. The said Monsieur Bellinzani also told me I could not more oblige Monsieur Colbert, nor take any better course to obtain his friendship by any service whatsoever, than by using all my skill and industry in drawing all the natives of those northern parts of America to traffic with and to favor the French, and to hinder and dissuade them from trading with strangers, assuring me of a great reward for the serivce I should render the state upon this account; and that Monsieur De La Chesnaye would furnish me in Canada with all things necessary for executing what designs we should conclude upon together to this intent.

According to these instructions I went unto Monsieur De La Chesnaye. We discoursed a long time together, and after several inquiries of the state of the countries that I had most frequented, having communicated unto him my observations, he proposed unto me to undertake to establish a treaty for the beaver trade in the great bay where I had been some years before upon the account of the English. We spent two days in adjusting the means of settling this business. At last it was agreed that I should make a voyage into England to endeavor to persuade my wife to come away, and also at the same time to inform myself what ships the Hudson Bay Company intended to fit out for those parts.

I performed this second voyage for England with some remainder of hopes to find the gentlemen of the Company something better inclined towards me than they had been formerly. But whether they then looked upon me as wholly unnecessary for their purpose, or as one that was altogether unable to do them any harm, I was suffered to come away without receiving the least token of kindness. All the satisfaction I had in the voyage was that Prince Rupert was pleased to tell me that he was very sorry my offers of service was so much slighted.

I resolved with myself not to be dejected at this coldness and returned into France, thinking there to have found Monsieur De La Chesnaye. But being come to Paris, I heard he was gone, and I presently resolved to follow him to Canada to execute what we had concluded upon at Paris. I went to take my leave of Monsieur Colbert, acquainting him of my design, whereof he approved very well. He wished me a good voyage, advising me to be careful. I went to visit the Society of the Jesuits at Paris, as being also concerned with De La Chesnaye in the beaver trade. They gave me some money for my voyage.

I went and took ship at Rochelle and arrived at Quebec the 25th of 7ber, 1682. As soon as I went ashore I spoke with Monsieur De La Chesnaye, who seemed to be very glad to see me, and after some discourse of what we had concluded upon at Paris, he said the business must be presently set about.

Being privy unto the court intrigues and fully acquainted with the measures we were to use in this enterprise, he took me along with him unto the governor's house and engaged me to demand his assistance and such orders as we should stand in need of from him for the carrying on our design. But the governor spoke unto us in a way as if he approved not of the business. Whereupon De La Chesnaye demanded a pass for me to return back unto Europe by the way of New England in a vessel belonging to the governor of Acadia, which was at that instant at Quebec and ready to sail in some short time.

These formalities being over, Monsieur De La Chesnaye and I spoke home to the business. We agreed upon the voyage and of all things that were to be settled relative unto our concerns and interest. He undertook to buy the goods and to furnish all things that concerned the treaty, to furnish me with a vessel well fitted and stored with good provisions. It was agreed that I should have one-fourth part of the beaver for my care and pains and the danger I exposed myself unto in making the settlement. My brother-in-law, Des Groseilliers, who was then at Quebec, made a contract with De La Chesnaye for the same voyage almost on the same terms as I had done.

All things being thus concluded, the governor was desired that I might have leave to take three men along with me. He knew very well to what intent, but he pretended to be ignorant of it, for 'tis unlikely that I would return back to France without doing something about what De La Chesnaye and I had mentioned unto him, seeing I demanded these three men to go along with me. One was my kinsman, John Baptiste Des Groseilliers, of whom I made great account, having frequented the country all his life and had contracted great familiarity and acquaintance with the natives about trade. He laid out L500 tournois of his own money in the voyage and charge, disbursed by Monsieur De La Chesnaye in the enterprise. The second was Peter Allemand, whom I took for my pilot, and the 3rd was John Baptiste Godefroy, who understood perfectly well the language of the natives and [was] one that I knew was capable of treating.

I set sail from Quebec the 4th of 9ber, 1682, with my three men, in the governor of Acadia's vessel, having my orders to be ready the spring following at the Isle Percé (Hollow isle) at the entrace of the River St. Lawrence, unto which place De La Chesnaye was to send me a vessel well equipped and fitted, according to agreement for executing the design. He also promised to send me fuller instructions in writing for my directions when I should be on the place.

We arrived at Acadia the 26th of November, 1682, and there wintered. In the spring I repaired unto Hollow island.

The vessel I expected arrived, but proved not so good as was promised, for it was only an old bark of about 50 tons, with an equipage but of 12 men, those with me being comprised in the number. There was goods enough on board to have carried on the treaty, but provisions were scant, so that had I not been so deeply engaged as I was in the business such a kind of a vessel would have quite discouraged me. But the arrival of my brother-in-law, Des Groseilliers, in a vessel of about 30 tons, with a crew of 15 men, encouraged me so that we jointly resolved not to quit our enterprise. But we had much ado to persuade our men to it, being unwilling to expose themselves to the danger of a voyage of 900 leagues in such small ordinary vessel and in such boisterous seas, where there was also danger of ice. However, they seeing us willing to run the same fortune as they did, they at length consented, and it was agreed upon betwixt my brother-in-law and myself to steer the same course and to keep as near each other as we could, the better to assist one another as occasion required. We sailed from the island the 11th July, 1682.[8]

After the space of 19 days' sailing, being past the Straits of Newfoundland, the seamen on board my brother-in-law's vessel mutinied against him, refusing to proceed any farther, pretending they feared being split with the ice, also of engaging in unknown countries where they might be reduced to want provisions in the winter. We pacified the mutineers by threatenings and by promises, and the sight of a sail in 57 degrees 30 minutes, north lat., upon the coast of Labrador, somewhat contributed thereunto, everyone desiring to shun this sail. We were twixt him and the shore, and they bore directly towards us, desirous to speak with us, but we not being in a condition of making any resistance, I thought it the best not to stand towards him, but steering the same course as he did, we recovered under the shore and so out of danger. They tacked about and stood off 2 hours before night, and we lost sight of them.

There was much ice in those seas, which drive to the southwards. We put into harbor to avoid the danger of it, as also to take in fresh water and some other provisions at the coast of the Indians called Eskimos, the most cruel of all the savages when they meet an advantage to surprise persons. Nevertheless, they came to our shipside and traded with us for some hundred of wolf skins. We stayed there 2 days, during which time there happened another mutiny, our men refusing to proceed any farther, but I pacified the seditious, and having put to sea, I ordered our men to preserve the wood and water we had taken on board the best they could, for my brother-in-law and I had resolved not to go ashore until we had gained our port, unless we were chased.

The winds proving favorable, we entered Hudson's Strait and sailed along the northern shore. There was much ice. Some of my seamen killed a white bear of extraordinary bigness. They eat of it to such excess that they all fell extremely sick with headaches and looseness; I thought they would have died out. I was forced to give my brother notice of this accident and to desire his assistance, so that by taking orvietan and sweating they escaped that danger, but all their skin peeled off. We were informed by the Indians that those white bears have a poison in the liver that diffuses itself through the whole mass of the body, which occasions these distempers unto those that eat of them.

I observed during this disorder, near Mile island, at the western point, [that] we drove NW by the compass about 8 leagues in 6 hours, towards Cape Henry. We had much ado to recover out of the ice and had like diverse times to have perished, but God was pleased to preserve us. My brother-in-law, fearing to bear too much sail, stayed behind.

I arrived before him, the 26th of August, on the western coast of Hudson's Bay, and we met the 2nd of 7ber, at the entrance of the river called Kavivvakiona[9] by the Indians, which signifies "let him that comes, go." Being entered into this river, our first care was to find a convenient place where to secure our vessels and to build us a house. We sailed up the river about 15 miles, and we stopped at a little canal, wherein we lay our vessels, finding the place convenient to reside at.

I left my brother-in-law busy about building a house, and the next day after our arrival I went up into the country to seek for Indians. To this purpose I went to a canoe with my nephew and another of my crew, being all 3 armed with firelocks and pistols, and in 8 days we went about 40 leagues up the river, and through woods, without meeting one Indian or seeing any sign where any had lately been. Finding several trees gnawed by beavers, we judged there was but few inhabitants in those parts. In our traveling we killed some deer.

But the 8th day after our departure, our canoe being drawn ashore and overturned near the waterside, reposing ourselves in a small island about evening, an Indian pursuing a deer espied our canoe. Thinking there were some of his own nation, he whistled to give notice of the beast, that passed by to the little island not far off from us. My nephew, having first spied the Indian, told me of it, not minding the deer. I presently went to the waterside and called the Indian, who was a good while before he spoke, and then said he understood me not, and presently

169

run away into the woods. I was glad of meeting this Indian, and it gave me some hopes of seeing more ere long. We stood upon our guard all night.

Next morning I caused our canoe to be carried [to] the other side of the island, to have it in readiness to use in case of danger. I caused a fire to be made a 100 paces off.

In the morning we discovered nine canoes, at the point of the island, coming towards us, and being within hearing, I demanded who they were. They returned a friendly answer. I told them the cause of my coming into their country and who I was. One of the eldest of them, armed with his lance, bow and arrows, etc., rose up and took an arrow from his quiver, making a sign from east to west and from north to south, broke it in 2 pieces and flung it into the river, addressing himself to his companions, saying to this purpose: "Young men, be not afraid. The sun is favorable unto us. Our enemies shall fear us, for this is the man that we have wished for ever since the days of our fathers."

After which they all swimmed ashore unto me, and coming out of their canoes, I invited them unto my fire. My nephew and the other man that was with him came also within 10 paces of us without any fear, although they see the Indian well armed. I asked them who was their chief commander, speaking unto him unknownst to me. He bowed the head, and another told me it was he that I talked unto. Then I took him by the hand and, making him sit down, I spoke unto him according to the genius of the Indians, unto whom, if one will be esteemed, it is necessary to brag of one's valor, of one's strength and ableness to succor and protect them from their enemies. They must also be made believe that one is wholly for their interest and have a great complaisance for them, especially in making them presents; this amongst them is the greatest band of friendship.

I would at this first interview make myself known. The chief of these savages sitting by me, I said to him in his language: "I know all the earth. Your friends shall be my friends, and I am come hither to bring you arms to destroy your enemies. You nor your wife nor children shall not die of hunger, for I have brought merchandise. Be of good cheer. I will be thy son, and I have brought thee a father. He is yonder below, building a fort where I have 2 great ships. You must give me 2 or 3 of your canoes, that your people may go visit your father."

He made a long speech to thank me and to assure me that both himself and all his nation would venture their lives in my service. I gave them some tobacco and pipes, and seeing one of them used a piece of flat iron to cut his tobacco, I desired to see that piece of iron and flung it into the fire, whereat they all wondered, for at the same time I seemed to weep and, drying up my tears, I told them I was very much grieved to see my brethren so ill-provided of all things and told them they should want for nothing whilst I was with them, and I took my sword I had by my side and gave it unto him from whom I took the piece of iron; also I caused some bundles of little knives to be brought from my canoe, which I distributed amongst them. I made them smoke and gave them to eat, and whilst they were eating I set forth the presents I brought them, amongst the rest a fowling piece with some powder and shot for their chief commander. I told him, in presenting him with it, I took him for my father. He in like manner took me to be his son in covering me with his gown. I gave him my blanket, which I desired him to carry unto his wife as a token from me, intending she should be my mother. He thanked me, as also did the rest, to the number of 26, who in testimony of their gratitude cast their garments at my feet and went to their canoes and brought all the fur skins they had. After which ceremonies we parted. They promised before noon they would send me 3 of their canoes, wherein they failed not. They put beavers in them.

We went towards the place where I left my brother-in-law. I arrived the 12th of 7ber, to the great satisfaction of all our people, having informed them [of] the happy success of my journey by meeting with the natives.

The very day I returned from this little journey, we were alarmed by the noise of some great guns. The Indians that came along with us heard them, and I told them that these guns were from some of our ships that were in the great river called Kawir-inagaw[10] 3 or 4 leagues' distance from that where we were settled. But being desirous to be satisfied what it should mean, I went in a canoe unto the mouth of our river, and seeing nothing, I supposed we were all mistaken, and I sent my nephew with another Frenchman of my crew back with the savages unto the Indians. But the same evening, they heard the guns so plain that there was no farther cause of doubt but that there was a ship. Upon which, they returned back to tell me of it.

Whereupon I presently went myself with 3 men to make the

171

discovery. Having crossed over this great River Kawirinagaw, which signifies "the dangerous," on the 16th, in the morning, we discovered a ten upon an island. I sent one of my men privately to see what it was. He came back soon after and told me they were building a house and that there was a ship. Whereupon I approached as near as I could without being discovered, and set myself with my men as it were in ambush, to surprise some of those that were there and to make them prisoners to know what or who they might be. I was as wary as might be and spent the whole night very near the place where the house stood without seeing anybody stir or speak until about noon next day, and then I see they were English, and drawing nearer them the better to observe them, I returned to my canoe with my men.

We showed ourselves a cannon-shot off and stayed as if we had been savages that wondered to see anybody there building a house. It was not long before we were discovered, and they hallowed unto us, inviting us to go unto them, pronouncing some words in the Indian tongue, which they read in a book. But seeing we did not come unto them, they came unto us along the shore, and standing right opposite unto us, I spoke unto them in the Indian tongue and in French, but they understood me not. But at last, asking them in English who they were and what they intended to do there, they answered they were Englishmen come hither to trade for beaver. Afterwards I asked them who gave them permission and what commission they had for it. They told me they had no commission and that they were of New England. I told them I was settled in the country before them for the French company and that I had strength sufficient to hinder them from trading to my prejudice; that I had a fort 7 leagues off, but that the noise of their guns made me come to see them, thinking that it might be a French ship that I expected, which was to come to a river farther north than this where they were, that had put in there by some accident contrary to my directions; that I had 2 other ships lately arrived from Canada, commanded by myself and my brother, and therefore I advised them not to make any longer stay there and that they were best begone and take along with them on board what they had landed.

In speaking I caused my canoe to draw as near the shore as could be, that I might the better discern those I talked with. Finding it was young Guillam that commanded the ship, I was very glad of it, for I was intimately acquainted with him. As soon as he knew me, he invited me ashore. I came accordingly, and we embraced each other. He invited me on board his ship to treat me. I would not seem to have any distrust but, having precautioned myself, went along with him. I caused my 3 men to come out of my canoe and to stay ashore with 2 Englishmen whilst I went on board with the captain. I see on board a New England man that I knew very well. Before I entered the ship the captain caused English colors to be set up and, as soon as I came on board, some great guns to be fired. I told him it was not needful to shoot any more, fearing lest our men might be alarmed and might do him some mischief. He proposed that we might traffic together. I told him I would acquaint our other officers of it and that I would use my endeavor to get their consent that he should pass the winter where he was without receiving any prejudice, the season being too far past to be gone away. I told him he might continue to build his house without any need of fortifications, telling him I would secure him from any danger on the part of the Indians, over whom I had an absolute sway, and secure him from any surprise on my part. I would before our parting let him know with what number of men I would be attended when I came to visit him, giving him to understand that, if I came with more than what was agreed betwixt us, it would be a sure sign our officers would not consent unto the proposal of our trading together. I also advised him he should not fire any guns and that he should not suffer his men to go out of the island, fearing they might be met by the Frenchmen that I had in the woods, [so] that he might not blame me for any accident that might ensue if he did not follow my advice. I told him also the savages advised me my ship was arrived to the northwards, and promised that I would come visit him again in 15 days and would tell him farther, whereof he was very thankful and desired me to be mindful of him. After which, we separated very well satisfied with each other, he verily believing I had the strength I spoke of, and I resolving always to hold him in this opinion, desiring to have him be gone or, if he persisted to interrupt me in my trade, to wait some opportunity of seizing his ship, which was a lawful prize, having no commission from England nor France to trade. But I would not attempt anything rashly, for fear of missing my aim. Especially I would avoid spilling blood.

Being returned with my men on board my canoe, we fell down the river with what haste we could, but we were scarce gone

173

three leagues from the island where the New England ship lay but that we discovered another ship under sail coming into the river. We got ashore to the southwards, and being gone out of the canoe to stay for ship that was sailing towards us, I caused a fire to be made. The ship being over against us, she came to anchor and sent not her boat ashore that night until next morning. We watched all night to observe what was done, and in the morning, seeing the long boat rowing towards us, I caused my 3 men, well armed, to stand at the entrance into the wood 20 paces from me, and I came alone to the waterside.

Mr. Bridgar, whom the [Hudson's Bay] Company sent [as] governor into that country, was in the boat, with 6 of the crew belonging unto the ship whereof Capt. Guillam was commander, who was father, as I understood afterwards, unto him that commanded the New England ship that I had discovered the day before. Seeing the shallop come towards me, I spoke a kind of jargon like that of the savages, which signified nothing, only to amuse those in the boat or to make them speak, the better to observe them and to see if there might be any that had frequented the Indians and that spoke their language. All were silent, and the boat coming aground 10 or 12 paces from me, seeing one of the seamen leap in the water to come to shore, I showed him my weapons, forbidding him to stir, telling him that none in the boat should come ashore until I knew who they were. Observing by the make of the ship and the habit of the sailors that they were English, I spoke in their language, and I understood that the seamen that leaped in the water, which I hindered to proceed any farther, said aloud, "Governor, it is English they spoke unto you." Upon my continuing to ask who they were, who commanded the ship, and what they sought there, somebody answered, "What has anybody to do to inquire? We are English." Upon which I replied, "And I am French, and require you to be gone," and at the same instant making sign unto my men to appear, they showed themselves at the entrance of the wood. Those of the shallop, thinking in all likelihood we were more in number, were about to have answered me in mild terms and to tell me they were of London, that the ship belonged unto the Hudson Bay Company and was commanded by Capt. Guillam. I informed them also who I was, that they came too late, and that I had taken possession of those parts in the name and behalf of the King of France. There was several other things said, which is not needful here to relate, the English asserting they had right to come into those parts, and I saying the contrary.

But at last, Mr. Bridgar saying he desired to come ashore with 3 of his crew to embrace me, I told him that I should be very well satisfied. He came ashore and, after mutual salutations, he asked of me if this was not the River Kakiwakionay. I answered it was not and that it was farther to the southward; that this was called Kawirinagaw, or "the dangerous." He asked of me if it was not the river where Sir Thomas Button, that commanded an English ship, had formerly wintered. I told him it was and showed him the place, to the northwards.

Then he invited me to go aboard. My crew, being come up, dissuaded me, especially my nephew. Yet, taking 2 hostages, which I left ashore with my men, for I suspected Capt. Guillam, having declared himself my enemy at London, being of the faction of those which were the cause that I deserted the English interest, I went aboard, and I did well to use this precaution; otherwise Capt. Guillam would have stopped me, as I was since informed, but all things passed very well. We dined together. I discoursed of my establishment in the country; that I had good numbers of Frenchmen in the woods with the Indians; that I had 2 ships and expected another; that I was building a fort; to conclude, all that I said unto young Guillam, master of the New England ship, I said the same unto Mr. Bridgar, and more too. He took all for current, and it was well for me he was so credulous, for would he have been at the trouble I was of traveling 40 leagues through woods and brakes, and lie on the cold ground to make my discoveries, he would soon have perceived my weakness. I had reason to hide it and to do what I did. Moreover, not having men sufficient to resist with open force, it was necessary to use policy. It's true I had a great advantage in having the natives on my side, which was a great strength, and that indeed whereupon I most of all depended.

Having stayed a good while on board, I desired to go ashore. Which being done, I made a sign to my men to bring the hostages, which they had carried into the woods. They brought them to the waterside, and I sent them aboard their ship. I confess I repented more than once of my going aboard. It was too rashly done, and it was happy for me that I got off as I did. Before I came ashore I promised Mr. Bridgar and the captain that in 15 days I would visit them again.

175

In the meantime, the better to be assured of their proceedings, I stayed 2 days in the woods to observe their actions; and having upon the matter seen their design, that they intended to build a fort, I passed the river to the southwards to return to my brother-in-law, who might well be in some fear for me.

But coming unto him, he was very glad of what had passed and of the good condition I had set matters. We consulted together what measures to take not to be surprised and to maintain ourselves the best we could in our settlement for carrying on our treaty. We endeavored to secure the Indians, who promised to lose their lives for us; and the more to oblige them to our side, I granted them my nephew and another Frenchman to go along with them into the country to make the several sorts of Indians to come traffic with us, and the more to encourage them I sent presents unto the chiefest of them.

During my voyage of discovering 2 English ships, there happened an ill accident for us. Our company had killed 60 deer, which had been a great help towards our winter provisions, but by an inundation of waters caused by great rains they were all carried away. Such great floods are common in those parts. The loss was very great unto us, for we had but 4 barrels of pork and 2 of beef. But our men repaired this loss, having killed some more deer and 4,000 white partridges, somewhat bigger than those of Europe. The Indians also brought us provisions they had killed from several parts at a great distance off.

Ten days after my return from discovering the English, I took 5 other men to observe what they did. I had foreseen that we should be forced to stay for fair weather to cross the mouth of the dangerous River of Kawirinagaw, which also proved accordingly, for the season began to be boisterous. But having stayed some time, at last we got safe over, although it was in the night, and 14 days after our departure we gained near the place where Mr. Bridgar lay. We presently see the ship lay aground on the ooze, a mile from the place where they built their house. Being come near the ship, we hailed several times, and nobody answered, which obliged us to go towards land, wondering at their silence.

At length a man called us and beckoned to us to come back. Going towards him and asking how all did, he said, "Something better," but that all were asleep. I would not disturb them and went alone unto the governor's house, whom I found just getting up. After the common ceremonies were past, I considered the posture of things, and finding there was no great danger and that I need not fear calling my people, we went in all together. I made one of my men pass for captain of the ship that I said was lately arrived. Mr. Bridgar believed it was so, and all that I thought good to say unto him, endeavoring all along that he should know nothing of the New England interloper. We shot off several muskets in drinking healths, those of the vessel never being concerned, whereby I judged they were careless and stood not well on their guard and might be easily surprised. I resolved to view them.

Therefore, taking leave of Mr. Bridgar, I went with my people towards the vessel. We went on board to rights without opposition. The captain was something startled at first to see us, but I bid him not fear. I was not there with any design to harm him. On the contrary, I was ready to assist and help him wherein he should command me, advising him to use more diligence than he did to preserve himself and ships from the danger I see he was in of being lost, which afterwards happened. But he was displeased at my counsel, saying he knew better what to do than I could tell him. That might be, said I, but not in the Indians' country, where I had been more frequent than he. However, he desired me to send him some refreshments from time to time during the winter season, especially some oil and candles, of which he stood in great want, which I promised to do, and performed accordingly. He made me present of a piece of beef and a few biscuits. Being full informed of what I desired to know, and that I need not fear any harm these gentlemen could do me in regard of my trade, I took leave of the captain to go see what passed on behalf of the New England interloper.

I arrived there next day in the afternoon and found they had employed the time better than the others had done, having built a fort, well fortified, with 6 great guns mounted. I fired a musket to give notice unto those in the fort of my coming, and I landed on a little beach under their guns. The lieutenant came out with another man, well armed, to see what we were. When he see me he congratulated my safe return and asked what news. I told him I had found, though with great difficulty, what I sought after and that I came to visit them, having taken other men than those I had before; that one of those with me was captain of the ship lately arrived, and the other 4 were of Canada. The lieutenant answered me very briskly: "Were they 40 devils, we will not fear.

We have built a fort and do fear nothing." Yet he invited me into his fort to treat me, provided I would go in alone, which I refused, intimating he might have spoke with more modesty, [I] coming to visit him in friendship and good will and not in a hostile manner. I told him also I desired to discourse with his captain, who doubtless would have more moderation.

Whereupon he sent to inform the captain, who came unto me well armed and told me that I need not be jealous of the fort he had caused to be built, that 'twas no prejudice to me, and that I should at any time command it, adding withal that he feared me not so much as he did the English of London, and that he built this fort to defend himself against the savages and all those that would attack him. I thanked him for his civilities unto me and assured him I came not thither to show any displeasure for his building a fort, but to offer him 20 of my men to assist him and to tell him that those he so much feared were arrived, offering my service to defend him, telling him if he would follow my counsel I would defend him from all danger, knowing very well the orders these newcomers had and also what condition they were in. I also told him that, as to the difference which was betwixt us about the trade, it was referred unto the arbitrament of both our kings; that for good luck to him, his father commanded the ship newly arrived; that he brought a governor for the English Company, whom I intended to hinder from assuming that title in the countries wherein I was established for the French company; and as for his part, I would make him pass for a Frenchman, thereby to keep him from receiving any damage.

Having said these things to the captain of the fort, I made him call his men together, unto whom I gave a charge in his presence that they should not go out of their fort nor fire any guns nor show their colors; that they should cover the head and stern of their ship; and that they should suffer neither French nor English to come near their fort, neither by land nor by water; and that they should fire on any of my people as would offer to approach without my orders.

The captain promised all should be observed that I had said and commanded his men in my presence so to do, desiring me to spare him 2 of my men as soon as I could, to guard them.

I told him that his father, captain of the Company's ship, was sick; whereat he seemed to be much troubled and desired me to put him in a way to see him without any damage. I told him of the danger and difficulty of it. Nevertheless, having private reasons that this interview of father and son might be procured by my means, I told him I would use my best endeavor to give him this satisfaction, and that I hoped to effect it, provided he would follow my directions. He agreed to do what I advised, and after some little study we agreed that he should come along with me, disguised like one that lived in the woods, and that I would make him pass for a Frenchman.

This being concluded, I sent my men next morning early to kill some fowl. They returned by 10 o'clock with 30 or 40 partridge, which I took into my canoe with a barrel of oil and some candles that I had promised the old Captain Guillam. I left one of my men hostage in the fort and embarked with young Guillam to go show him his father. The tide being low, we were forced to stop a mile short of the ship and go ashore and walk up towards the ship with our provisions. I left one of my men to keep the canoe, with orders to keep off, and coming near the ship, I placed 2 of my best men betwixt the house Mr. Bridgar caused to be built and the waterside, commanding them not to show themselves, and to suffer the governor to go to the vessel, but to seize him if they see him come back before I was got out of the ship.

Having ordered things in this manner, I went with one of my men and young Guillam aboard the ship, where we again entered without any opposition. I presented unto Capt. Guillam the provisions I had brought him, for which he gave me thanks. Afterwards, I made my 2 men go into his cabin, one of which was his son, though unknown to him. I desired Capt. Guillam to bid 2 of his servants to withdraw, having a thing of consequence to inform him of. Which being done, I told him the secret was that I had brought his son to give him a visit, having earnestly desired it of me. And having told him how necessary it was to keep it private, to prevent the damage [that] might befall them both if it should be known, I presented the son unto his father, who embraced each other very tenderly and with great joy. Yet he told him he exposed him unto a great deal of danger. They had some private discourse together; after which he desired me to save my Frenchman. I told him I would discharge myself of that trust and again advised him to be careful of preserving his ship and that nothing should be capable of making any difference betwixt us but the treaty he might make with the Indians. He told me the ship belonged to the Company; that as to the trade, I had no

179

cause to be afraid on his account; and that, though he got not one skin, it would nothing trouble him: he was assured of his wages. I warned him that he should not suffer his men to scatter abroad, especially that they should not go towards his son's fort, which he promised should be observed.

Whilst we were in this discourse, the governor, hearing I was come, came unto the ship and told me that my fort must needs be nearer unto him that he expected, seeing I returned so speedily. I told him, smiling, that I did fly when there was need to serve my friends and that, knowing his people were sick and wanted refreshments, I would not lose time in supplying them, assuring him of giving him part what our men did kill at all times. Some prying a little too narrowly, young Guillam thought he had been discovered; whereat the father and the son were not a little concerned. I took upon me and said it was not civil so narrowly to examine my people. They excused it. The tide being come in, I took leave to be gone. The governor and captain divided my provisions.

Having made a sign unto my 2 men to rise out of their ambush, I came out of the ship, and we marched all of us unto the place where we left our canoe. We got into it, and the young captain admired to see a little thing made of the rind of a tree resist so many knocks of ice as we met withal in returning. Next day we arrived at the fort, and very seasonably for us, for had we stayed a little longer on the water we had been surprised with a terrible storm at NW, with snow and hail, which doubtless would have sunk us. The storm held 2 days and hindered us from going to our pretended fort up the river, but the weather being settled, I took leave of the captain. The lieut. would fain have accompanied us unto our habitation, but I saved him that labor for good reasons and to conceal the way.

Parting from the fort, we went to the upper part of the island, but towards evening we returned back and next day were in sight of the sea, wherein we were to go to double the point to enter the river where our habitation was, but all was so frozen that it was almost impossible to pass any farther. We were also so hemmed in on all sides with ice that we could neither go forward nor get to land, yet we must get over the ice or perish. We continued 4 hours in this condition, without being able to get backwards or forwards, being in great danger of our lives. Our clothes were frozen on our backs, and we could not stir but with great pain. But at length, with much ado, we got ashore, our canoe being broke to pieces. Each of us trussed up our clothes and arms and marched along the shore towards our habitation, not having eat anything in 3 days but some crows and birds of prey that last of all retire from these parts. There was no other fowl all along the coast, which was all covered with ice and snow. At length we arrived opposite unto our habitation, which was the other side of the river. Not knowing how to get over, [it] being covered with ice, 4 of our men ventured in a boat to come unto us. They had liked to have been staved by the ice. We also were in great danger, but we surmounted all these difficulties and got unto our habitation, for which we had very great cause to give God thanks of seeing one another after having run through so great dangers.

During my traveling abroad, my brother-in-law had put our house into pretty good order. We were secure, fearing nothing from the Indians, being our allies; and as for our neighbors, their disorder and the little care they took of informing themselves of us set us safe from fearing them.

But as it might well happen that the governor, Bridgar, might have notice that the New England interloper was in the same river he was, and that in long running he might discover the truth of all that I had discoursed and concealed from him, and also that he might come to understand that we had not the strength that I boasted of, I though it fit to prevent danger. The best was to assure myself of the New England ship in making myself master of h er , for had Mr. Bridgar been beforehand with me he would have been too strong for me, and I had been utterly unable to resist him. But the question was how to effect this business wherein I see manifest difficulties, but they must be surmounted or we must perish. Therefore I made it my business wholly to follow this enterprise, referring the care of our house and of the traffic unto my brother-in-law.

Seeing the river quite froze over every other day for a fortnight, I sent my men through the woods to see in what state the Company's ship lay. At length they told me she lay aground near the shore, the creek wherein she was to have lain the winter being frozen up, which made me conjecture she would infalliby be lost. I also sent 2 of my men unto young Captain Guillam into the island, which he had desired of me for his safeguard, but I was told by my people that he intended to deceive me, having, con-

181

trary unto his promise of not receiving any into his fort but such as should come by my order, had sent his boat to receive 2 men from the Company's ship, which Mr. Bridgar had sent to discover what they could the way that I told him our fort was, and also to see if they could find any wreck of their ship. But these 2 men [of mine], seeing those of the fort begin to stir and to launch out their boat, they thought they would fire on them, as I had commanded. They [the Company men] were affrighted and run away. Being come to Mr. Bridgar, they told him there was a fort and a French ship nearer unto them than I had said. Upon this information, Mr. Bridgar sent 2 men to pass from north to south, to know if it were true that we had 2 ships besides that which was at the island.

Whereof being advised by my people, I sent out 3 several ways to endeavor to take the 2 men Mr. Bridgar had sent to make this discovery, having ordered my people not to do them any violence. My people succeeded, for they found the 2 poor men within 5 leagues of our house, almost dead with cold and hunger, so that it was no hard matter to take them. They yielded and were brought into my habitation, where, having refreshed them with such provision as we had, they seemed nothing displeased at falling into our hands. I understood by them the orders Mr. Bridgar had given them for making the discovery, which made me stand the more close on my guard and to use fresh means to hinder that the governor, Bridgar, should not have knowledge of the New England interlopers.

About this time I sent some provisions unto Mr. Bridgar, who was in great want, although he strove to keep it from my knowledge. He thanked me by his letters and assured me he would not interrupt my trade and that he would not any more suffer his men to come near the forts which he thought had been ours. I also sent to visit young Guillam, to observe his proceeding and to see in what condition he was, to make my best advantage of it.

The 2 Englishmen which my people brought told me the Company's ship was staved to pieces, and the captain left and 4 seamen drowned; but 18 of the company, being ashore, escaped that danger.

Upon this advice I went to visit Mr. Bridgar, to observe his actions. I brought him 100 partridges and gave him some powder to kill fowl and offered him my service. I asked where his ship was, but he would not own she was lost, but said she was 4 leagues lower in the river. I would not press him any farther in the business, but civilly took our leave of each other.

From thence I went unto the fort in the island also, to see what passed there and to endeavor to compass the design I had laid of taking the ship and fort, having since discovered by letters intercepted that young Guillam intended to show me a trick and destroy me. Being come to the fort in the island, I made no show of knowing the loss of his father nor of the Company's ship. Only I told young Guillam his father continued ill and did not think [it] safe to write him, fearing to discover him. Afterwards I desired he would come unto our habitation, and so I returned without affecting any more than day.

Eight days after, I returned to see Mr. Bridgar, unto whom I said that he did not take sufficient care to preserve his men; that I had 2 of them at my fort, who told me of the loss of his ship, which he owned. I told him I would assist him and would send him his 2 men and what else he desired. I also offered him one of our barks, with provisions requisite to convey him in the spring unto the bottom of the bay, which he refused. I assured him of all the service that lay in my power, treating him with all civility could be for the esteem that I ever bore unto the English nation. (As for Mr. Bridgar, I had no great cause to be over-well pleased with him, being advised that he spoke ill of me in my absence and had said publicly unto his people that he would destroy my trade, should he give 6 axes and proportionably of other goods unto the Indians for a beaver skin.[11] I have an attestation hereof to show.) I stayed 2 days on this voyage with Mr. Bridgar, having then a real intent to serve him, seeing he was not in a condition to hurt me.

Returning unto my habitation, I called at young Guillam's fort in the island, where I intended to execute my design, it being now time. When I arrived at the fort, I told young Guillam his father continued ill and that he referred all unto me. Upon which I said unto him, touching his father and of his resolution, he earnestly desired I would go back with him and take him along with me, disguised as before, that he might see him, but I dissuaded him from this and put in the head rather to come see our habitation and how we lived. I knew he had a desire to do so; therefore I would satisfy his curiosity. Having, therefore, persuaded him to this, we parted next morning betimes. He took his carpenter along with him, and we arrived at our habitation, young Guillam and his man being sufficiently tired.

183

I thought it not convenient that young Guillam should see the 2 Englishmen that was at our house. I kept them private and fitted them to be gone next morning, with 2 of my men, to go athwart the woods unto their habitation, having promised Mr. Bridgar to send them unto him. I gave them tobacco, clothes, and several other things Mr. Bridgar desired. But when they were to depart, one of the Englishmen fell at my feet and earnestly desired that I would not send him away. I would not have granted his request but that my brother-in-law desired me to do it and that it would also ease Mr. Bridgar's charge, who wanted provisions. So I suffered the other to depart along with my 2 men, having given them directions. I caused young Guillam to see them going, telling him I sent them unto our fort up the river.

I continued a whole month at quiet, treating young Guillam, my new guest, with all civility, which he abused in several particulars. For having probably discovered that we had not the strength that I made him believe we had, he unadvisedly speak threatening words of me behind my back, calling me pirate and saying he would trade with the Indians in the spring in spite of me. He had also the confidence to strike one of my men (but I connived at it). But one day, discoursing of the privileges of New England, he had the confidence to speak slightly of the best of kings. Whereupon I called him [a] pitiful dog for talking after that manner and told him that for my part, having had the honor to have been in His Majesty's service, I would pray for His Majesty as long as I lived. He answered me with harsh words that he would return back to his fort, and when he was there that [I] would not dare talk to him as I did. I could not have a fairer opportunity to begin what I designed. Upon which I told the young fool that I brought him from his fort and would carry him thither again when I pleased, not when he liked. He spoke several other impertinencies, that made me tell him that I would lay him up safe enough if he behaved not himself wiser. He asked me if he was a prisoner. I told him I would consider of it and that I would secure my trade, seeing he threatened to hinder it. After which I retired and gave him leave to be informed by the Englishman how that his father and the Company's ship were lost, and the bad condition Mr. Bridgar was in.

I left a Frenchman with them that understood English, but they knew it not. When I went out, young Guillam bid the Englishman make his escape and go tell his master that he would give

184

him 6 barrels of powder and other provisions if he would attempt to deliver him out of my hands. The Englishman made no reply, neither did he tell me of what had been proposed unto him. I understood it by my Frenchman that heard the whole matter, and I found it was high time to act for my own safety.

That evening I made no show of anything; but going to bed, I asked our men if the firelocks that we placed at night round our fort to defend us from those that would attack us were in order. At this word of firelocks young Guillam, who knew not the meaning of it, was suddenly startled and would have run away, thinking we intended to kill him. I caused him to be stayed and freed him of his fear.

But next morning I made him an unwelcome compliment. I told him that I was going to take his ship and fort. He answered very angrily that if I had 100 men I could not effect it and that his men would kill 40 before they could come near the palisade. I was nothing discouraged at his bravado, knowing very well that I should compass my design. (I [had] made account that 2 of my men would have stayed in the fort for hostages, but having what liberty they would, one of them returned to our habitation without my order. I was angry at it, but I made no show it it, having laid my design so as to make more use of skill and policy than of open force.) Seeing therefore the haughty answer young Guillam made me, that I could not take his fort with 100 men, I asked of him how many men he had in it. He said nine. I desired him to choose the like number of mine, I being one of the number, telling him I would desire no more and that in 2 days I would give him a good account of his fort and of his ship and that I would not have him to have the shame of being present to see what I should do. He chose and named such of my men as he pleased, and I would not choose any others. I suffered him to come with me to the waterside, and I made the ninth man that went upon this expeditions, with an Englishman of Mr. Bridgar's to be a witness of the business.

Being arrived within half a league of the fort, I left the Englishman and one Frenchman, ordering they should not stir without farther order. At the some time I sent 2 of my men directly to the fort, to the southward of the island, and I planted myself with my other 5 at the north point of the same island, to observe what they did that I sent to the fort. They were stopped by 3 Englishmen, armed, that asked if they had any letters from their master.

185

My people answered, according to my instructions, that he was coming along with me; that being weary, we stayed behind; that they came a little before for some brandy, which they offered to carry. The Englishmen would needs do the office, and my 2 men stayed in the fort. He that was hostage had orders to seize on the court of [the] guard door, one of them newly come to seize the door of the house, and the 3 was to go in and out, that in case the design was discovered he might stop the passage of the door with blocks of wood, to hinder it from being shut and to give me freedom to enter unto their assistance. But there needed not so much ado, for I entered into the fort before those that were appointed to defend it were aware.

The lieutenant was startled at seeing me and asked where his master was, [that] it was high time to appear and act. I answered the lieutenant [that] it mattered not where his master was, but to tell me what men he had and to call them out. My men being entered the fort and all together, I told those that were present the cause of my coming, that I intended to be master of the place, and that 'twas too late to dispute. I commanded them to bring me the keys of the fort and all their arms and to tell me if they had any powder in their chests, and how much, referring myself unto what they should say. They made no resistance, but brought me their arms, and as for powder, they said they had none. I took possession of the fort in the name of the King of France, and from thence was conducted by the lieutenant to take possession of the ship also in the same name, which I did without any resistance. Whilst I was doing all this, young Guillam's men seemed to rejoice at it rather than to be troubled, complaining of him for their ill usage and that he had killed his supercargo.

But a Scotchman, one of the crew, to show his zeal, made his escape and run through the woods towards Mr. Bridgar's house to give him notice of what passed. I sent 2 of my nimblest men to run after him, but they could not overtake him, being gone 4 hours before them. He arrived at Mr. Bridgar's house, who upon the relation of the Scotchman resolved to come surprise me.

In the meanwhile I gave my brother notice of all that passed and that I feared a Scotchman might occasion me some trouble that had got away unto Mr. Bridgar and that I feared I might be too deeply engaged, unless he presently gave me the assistance of 4 men, having more English prisoners to keep than I had Frenchmen with me.

186

I was not deceived in my conjecture. At midnight one of our dogs alarmed our sentinel, who told me he heard a noise on board the ship. I caused my people to handle their arms, and shut up the English in the cabins under the guard of 2 of my men. I, with 4 others, went out to go to the ship. I found men armed on board and required them to lay down their arms and to yield. There was 4 that submitted, and some others got away in the dark. My men would have fired, but I hindered them, for which they murmured against me. I led the prisoners away to the fort and examined them one after another. I found they were of Mr. Bridgar's people and that he was to have been of the number, but he stayed half a league behind to see the success of the business.

The last of the prisoners I examined was the Scotchman that had made his escape when I took the fort. Knowing he was the only cause that Mr. Bridgar engaged in the business, I would revenge me in making him afraid. I caused him to be tied to a stake and told that he should be hanged next day. I caused the other prisoners, his comrades, to be very kindly treated; and having no farther design but to make the Scotchman afraid, I made one advise him to desire the lieutenant of the fort to beg me to spare his life, which he did, and easily obtained his request, although he was something startled, not knowing what I meant to do with him.

The 4 men I desired of my brother-in-law arrived during these transactions, and by this supply finding myself strong enough to resist whatever Mr. Bridgar could do against me, I wrote unto him and desired to know if he did avow what his men had done, whom I detained prisoners, who had broke the 2 doors and the deck of the ship to take away the powder. He made me a very dubious answer, complaining against me that I had not been true unto him, having concealed this matter from him. He writ me also that, having sufficient orders for taking all vessels that came into those parts to trade, he would have joined me in seizing of this, but seeing the purchase was fallen into my hands, he hoped he should share with me in it.

I sent back his 3 men with some tobacco and other provisions, but kept their arms, bidding them tell Mr. Bridgar on my behalf that, had I known he would have come himself on this expedition, I would have taken my measures to have received him ere he could have had the time to get back, but I heard of it a little too late, and that in some short time I would go visit him to know what he would be at, and that, seeing he pretended to be so ignorant in what quality I lived in that country, I would go and inform him.

Before these men's departure to Mr. Bridgar's, I was informed that some Englishmen had hidden powder without the fort. I examined them all. Not one would own it. But at last I made them confess it, and 5 or 6 pound was found that had been hid. Then I took care to secure the fort.

I sent 4 of the Englishmen of the fort unto my brother-in-law, and I prepared to go discover what Mr. Bridgar was doing. I came to his house and went in before he had notice of my coming. He appeared much surprised, but I spoke to him in such a manner as showed that I had no intent to hurt him, and I told him that by his late acting he had so disobliged all the French that I could not well tell how to assist him. I told him he had much better gone a milder way to work, in the condition he was in, and that, seeing he was not as good as his word to me, I knew very well how to deal with him. But I had no intention at that time to act anything against Mr. Bridgar; I only did it to frighten him, that he should live kindly by me; and in supplying him from time to time with what he wanted my chief aim was to disable him from trading and to reduce him to a necessity of going away in the spring. Seeing Mr. Bridgar astonished at my being there with 12 men, and in a condition of ruining him if I had desire to it, I thought fit to settle his mind by sending away 6 of my men unto my brother-in-law, and kept but 6 with me, 4 of which I sent out into the woods to kill some provisions for Mr. Bridgar.

About this time I received a letter from my brother wherein he blamed me for acting after this manner with persons that but 2 days ago endeavored to surprise me; that if I did so, he would forsake all; that I had better disarm them for our greater security; and that I should not charge myself with any of them. It was also the judgement of the other Frenchmen, who were all exasperated against Mr. Bridgar. Not to displease my own people, instead of 4 Englishmen that I promised Mr. Bridgar to take along with me that he might better preserve the rest, I took but 2, one of which I put in the fort at the island and the other I brought unto our habitation.

I promised Mr. Bridgar before I left him to supply him with powder and anything else that was in my power; and demanding what store of muskets he had remaining, he told me he had ten, and of them 8 were broken. I took the 8 that were spoiled and left him mine, that was well fixed, promising to get his mended. He also offered me a pocket pistol, saying he knew well enough that I intended to disarm him. I told him it was not to disarm him, to take away his bad arms and to give him good instead of them. I offered him my pistols, but he would not accept of them. In this state I left him and went to our habitation to give my brother-in-law an account of what I had done.

Some days after, I went to the fort in the island to see if all was well there, and having given all necessary directions, I returned unto our place, taking the lieutenant of the fort along with me, unto whom I gave my own chamber and all manner of liberty, taking him to be wiser than his captain, whom they were forced to confine in my absence. He thanked me for my civilities, and desiring he might go to his captain, I consented.

About this time I had advice, by one of the men that I left to guard the fort in the island, that Mr. Bridgar, contrary to his promises, went thither with 2 of his men and that our men, having suffered them to enter into the fort, they retained Mr. Bridgar and sent the other 2 away, having given them some bread and brandy. This man also told me that Mr. Bridgar seemed very much troubled at his being stopped and acted like a madman. This made me presently go to the fort to hinder any attempts [that] might be made against me.

Being arrived, I found Mr. Bridgar in a sad condition, having drank to excess. Him that commanded the fort had much ado to hinder him from killing the Englishman that desired to stay with us. He spoke a thousand things against me in my hearing, threatening to kill me if I did not do him right. But having a long time born it, I was at length constrained to bid him be quiet; and desirous to know his designs, I asked him if any of his people were to come, because I see smoke and fires in crossing the river. He said yes and that he would shortly show me what he could do, looking for 14 men which he expected, besides the 2 my people returned back. I told him I knew very well he had not so many men, having let many of his men perish for want of meat, for whom he was to be accountable; and moreover, I was not afraid of his threats. Nevertheless, nobody appeared, and next day I ordered matters so as Mr. Bridgar should come along with me unto our habitation, whereunto he see it was in vain to resist. I assured him that neither I nor any of my people should go to his house in his absence and that, when he had recreated himself 10 or 15 days with me at our habitation, he might return with all freedom again unto his house.

Mr. Bridgar was a fortnight at our house without being overtired, and it appeared by his looks that he had not been ill-treated. But I not having leisure always to keep him company, my affairs called me abroad, I left him with my brother-in-law whilst I went unto the fort in the island to see how matters went there. At my going away I told Mr. Bridgar that if he pleased he might dispose himself for his departure home next morning, to rectify some disorders committed by his people in his absence, to get victuals; and I told him I would meet him by the way to go along with him.

Having dispatched my business at the fort of the island, I went away betimes to be at Mr. Bridgar's house before him, to hinder him from abusing his men. The badness of the weather made me go into the house before he came. As soon as I was entered, the men beseeched me to have compassion on them. I blamed them for what they had done and for the future advised them to be more obedient unto their master, telling them I would desire him to pardon them and that in the spring I would give passage unto those that would go home by the way of France. Mr. Bridgar arrived soon after me. I begged his pardon for going into his house before he came, assuring him that I had still the design of serving him and assisting him, as he should find when he pleased to make use of me, for powder and anything else he needed, which also I performed when it was desired of me, or that I know Mr. Bridgar stood in need of anything I had.

I parted from Mr. Bridgar's habitation to return unto our own. I passed by the fort in the island and put another Frenchman to command in the place of him was there before, whom I intended to take with me to work upon our ships. The spring now drawing on, the English of the fort of the island murmured because of one of Mr. Bridgar's men that I had brought thither to live with them. I was forced to send him back to give them content, not daring to send him to our habitation, our Frenchmen opposing it, we having too many already.

Arriving at our habitation, I was informed that the English captain very grossly abused one of his men that I kept with him. He was his carpenter. I was an eyewitness myself of his outrageous usage of this poor man, though he did not see me. I blamed the captain for it and sent the man to the fort of the island to look after the vessel, to keep her in good condition.

190

My nephew arrived about this time with the Frenchmen that went with him to invite down the Indians, and 2 days after, there came several that brought provisions. They admired to see the English that we had in our house, and they offered us 200 beaver skins to suffer them to go kill the rest of them, but I declared unto them I was far from consenting thereunto, and charged them on the contrary not to do them any harm. Mr. Bridgar coming at [that] instant with one of his men unto our habitation, I advised him not to hazard himself any more without having some of my men with him, and desired him, whilst he was at my house, not to speak to the Indians. Yet he did, and I could not forbear telling him my mind, which made him go away of a sudden. I attended him with 7 or 8 of my men, fearing lest the Indians who went away but the day before might do him mischief.

I came back next day, being informed that a good company of Indians, our old allies, were to come, and I found they were come with a design to war against the English, by the persuasion of some Indians that I see about 8ber last and with whom I had renewed an alliance. I thanked the Indians for their good will in being ready to make war against our enemies, but I also told them that I had no intent to do them any harm and that, having hindered them from hurting me, I was satisfied and that therefore they would oblige me to say nothing of it, [the English] having promised me they would be gone in the spring, but if they came again I would suffer them to destroy them. The Indians made great complaints unto me of the English in the bottom of the bay, which I will here omit, desiring to speak only of what concerns myself, but I ought not omit this: amongst other things, they alleged to have my consent that they might war against the English. They said this: "Thou hast made us make presents to make thine enemies become ours, and ours to be thine. We will not be found liars." By this may be seen what dependence is to be laid on the friendship of this people when once they have promised. I told them also that I loved them as my own brethren the French and that I would deal better by them than the English of the bay did and that if any of my men did them the least injury I would kill him with my own hands—adding withal that I was very sorry I was not better stored with goods to give them [as] greater tokens of my friendship, that I came this voyage unprovided, not knowing if I should meet them, but I promised to come another time better stored of all things they wanted and in a condition to help them to destroy their enemies and to send them away very well satisfied. The English admired to see with what freedom I lived with these savages. This passed in the beginning of April, 1683.

Being fair weather, I caused my nephew to prepare himself, with 3 men, to carry provisions and brandy unto our Frenchmen and to the Englishmen at the fort of the island. The ice began to be dangerous, and I see that it was not safe hazarding to go over it at this time. Therefore I said to my nephew that he would do well to proceed farther unto the Indians, unto whom he promised to give an account how we did, and to inform them also that we had conquered our enemies.

After my nephew's departure on this voyage, there happened an unlooked-for accident, the 22 or 23rd of April, at night. Having hauled our vessels as far as we could into a little slip in a wood, we thought them very secure, lying under a little hill about 10 fathom high, our houses being about the same distance off from the riverside. Yet, about 10 o'clock at night, a hideous great noise roused us all out of our sleep, and our sentinel came and told us it was the clattering of much ice and that the floods came down with much violence. We hasted unto the riverside and see what the sentinel told us, and great flakes of ice were born by the waters unto the top of our little hill. But the worst was that the ice, having stopped the river's mouth, they gathered in heaps and were carried back wih great violence and entered with such force into all our brooks that discharged into the river that 'twas impossible our vessels could resist, and they were staved all to pieces. There remained only the bottom, which stuck fast in the ice or in the mud, and had it held 2 hours longer we must have been forced to climb the trees to save our lives. But by good fortune the flood abated. The river was cleared by the going away of the ice, and 3 days after we see the disorder our vessels were in and the good luck we had in making so great a voyage in such bad vessels, for mine was quite rotten, and my brother's was not trunneled.*

This accident put us into a great fear the like mischief might be happened unto the New England ship, the Indians telling us that the river was more dangerous than ours and that they believed the vessel could not escape in the place where she lay. But Mr.

---

*A shipbuilding term; the timbers were not fastened together with pins of hardwood.

Bridgar, having heretofore related unto me a like accident happened in the River Kechechewan in the bottom of the bay, that a vessel was preserved by cutting the ice round about her, I took the same course and ordered the ice should be cut round this vessel quite to the keel, and I have reason to thank Mr. Bridgar for this advice; it saved the vessel. She was only driven ashore by the violence of the ice and there lay without much damage.

Whilst the waters decreased we consulted upon which of the 2 bottoms we should build us a ship, and it was at last resolved it should be on mine. Upon which we wrought day and night without intermission, intending this vessel should carry the English into the bay, as I had promised Mr. Bridgar.

I went down 2 or 3 times to the river's mouth to see what the floods and ice had done there and if I could pass the point into the other river, where Mr. Bridgar and the English vessel was at the fort of the island, for 'twas impossible to pass through the woods, all being covered with water. I adventured to pass, and I doubled the point in a canoe of bark, though the ice was so thick that we drew our canoe over it. Being entered the river, I marched along the south shore and got safe to the fort of the island with great difficulty. I found the ship lying dry, as I mentioned before, in a bad condition but easily remedied, the stern being only a little broke. I gave directions to have her fitted, and I encouraged the English to work, which they did perform better than the French. Having given these directions, I took the ship's boat and went down to Mr. Bridgar's habitation, and looking in what condition it was, I found that 4 of his men were dead for lack of food, and two that had been poisoned a little before by drinking some liquor they found in the doctor's chest, not knowing what it was. Another of Mr. Bridgar's men had his arm broke by an accident abroad ahunting.

Seeing all these disorders, I passed as soon as I could to the south side of the river to recover unto our houses, from whence I promised Mr. Bridgar I would send his English Curiorgion[?] that was with us, some brandy, vinegar, linen, and what provisions I could spare out of the small store we had left. Being got ashore, I sent back the boat to the fort of the isle, with orders unto my 2 men I left there to bring my canoe and to use it for fowling. In returning, I went ashore with one of Mr. Bridgar's men that I took along with me to carry back the provisions I had promised, although he did not seem to be very thankful for it, continuing his threatenings, and boasted that he expected ships would come unto him with which he would take us all. I was nothing daunted at this, but kept on my course, knowing very well Mr. Bridgar was not in a capacity of doing us any harm. (But it being impossible but that his being present on the place should hinder me, I ordered my business so as to be gone with what skins I had, and sent away Mr. Bridgar after having secured our trade.)

I made several journeys to the fort of the island about repairing of the ship. Also, I went several times to Mr. Bridgar's house to carry him provisions and to assist him and also his men with all things that I could procure, which they can testify; had it not been for me they had suffered much more misery. I had like to be lost several times in these journeys, by reason of great stores of ice, and the passage of the entrance of the river—to double the point, to enter into that where Mr. Bridgar and the New England ship lay—was always dangerous. I will not here insist upon the perils I exposed myself unto in coming and going to prepare things for our departure when the season would permit. But I cannot omit telling that, amongst other kindnesses I did Mr. Bridgar, I gave him stuff sufficient to sheathe his shallop, which was quite out of order, as also cordage and all things else necessary.

But he did not well by me, for contrary to his word which he had given me not to go the fort in the island, he attempted to go thither with his people in his shallop, and being come within musket-shot under a pretense of desiring some powder, the commander would not sufer him to come any nearer and made him cast anchor farther off. He sent his boat for Mr. Bridgar, who came alone into the fort, though he earnestly desired one of his men might be admitted along with him, but was denied. His men were ordered to lodge themselves ashore [on] the north side of the river in huts, and provisions was sent unto them. Mr. Bridgar spent that night in the fort, went away the next day. The day before, I see the shallop going full sail towards the fort, whither I was also going myself, by land, with one Englishman in whom I put a great deal of confidence, having nobody else with me. I did suspect that Mr. Bridgar had a design to make some surprise, but I was not much afraid by reason of the care and good order I had taken to prevent him. Nevertheless I feared that things went not well, for when I came near the fort, seeing the boat coming for me and that the commander did not made the signal that was agreed upon betwixt us, this startled me very much, and I appeared as a man that had cause to fear the worst. [Upon] which one of our French-men that steered the boat, wherein there was 4 Englishmen, per-ceiving, cried out all was well and made the signal. I blamed him and the commander for putting me in fear in not making the usual signs. When I came to the fort I was told Mr. Bridgar was there and that he was received, as has been recited. I was also told he had private discourse with the carpenter of the New England ship, that I had formerly engaged in a friendly manner to attend and serve him. This discourse made the commander the more nar-rowly to inspect Mr. Bridgar and to stand better upon his guard, the Scotchman telling him he was not to come thither with any good intention. So the commander of the fort sent him away in the morning, having given him some pork, peas, and powder.

Having given order at the fort, I went to Mr. Bridgar. Being come to his house, I taxed him of breach of promise, and told him there should be no quarter if he offered to do so any more and that therefore he should prepare himself to go for the bay (as soon as ever the ice did permit) in the vessel that we had left, it being so agreed on by our Frenchmen, assuring him I would furnish him with all things necessary for the voyage. He appeared much amazed at the compliment I made him, and told me in plain terms that it must be one of these 3 things that must make him quit the place—his master's orders, force, or hunger. He desired me after-wards that if the captain of the savages of the river of New Severn came that he might see him by my means, which I promised to do. Having thus disposed Mr. Bridgar for his departure, I con-tinued to assist him and his people with all that I could to enable them to work, [in order] to fit ourselves to be gone.

I left Mr. Bridgar in his house and I went unto ours, and having consulted my brother-in-law, we resolved that 'twas best to burn the fort in the island and secure Mr. Bridgar.

The crew of both our vessels made an agreement amongst them-selves to oppose our design of giving our ship unto the English for their transportation. It was necessary at the first to seem to yield, knowing that in time we should master the factions. It was the master of my bark that began the mutiny. The chief reason that made me seem to yield was that I would not have the English come to know of our divisions, who happily might have taken some advantage of it.

We had 4 amongst us unto whom I granted liberty upon their parol. But to make sure of those of New England, we caused a lodge to be built in a little island over against our house, where they were at a distance off us. We sent from time to time to visit them to see what they did. We gave them a fowling piece to divert them, but one day abusing my nephew, we took away the gun from them.

Going afterwards unto the fort of the island, I sent a boat unto Mr. Bridgar, advising him the captain he desired to see was come and that he might come with one of his men, which he did. And as soon as he was come I told him that to assure our trade I was obliged to secure him and would commit him unto the custody of my nephew, unto whom I would give orders to treat him kindly and with all manner of respect, telling him withal that when I had put all things on board the vessel that was in the fort I would go and set it [the fort] on fire. I told him he might send his man with me to his house with what orders he thought fit. (I went thither the same day.) I told Mr. Bridgar's people that, not being able to supply them any longer, but with powder only, and being ready for my departure to Canada, it was necessary that those that intended to stay should speak their minds and that those that desired to go should have their passage. I demanded their names, which they all told me except 2. I ordered them to have a great care of all things in the house. I left one Frenchman to observe them and to go fowling, Mr. Bridgar's men not being used to it.

These orders being given, I left Mr. Bridgar's house and crossed over to the south side, where I met 2 of our Frenchmen ahunting. I sent them with what fowl they had killed to the fort of the island, where they might be serviceable unto the rest in carrying down the ship and in bringing her to an anchor right against Mr. Bridgar's house, to take on board his goods, which was accordingly done.

I came by land unto the other river and met at the entrance of it several Indians, that waited impatiently for me how we might adjust and settle our trade. They would have had my brother-in-law to have rated the goods at the same prices as the English did in the bottom of the bay, and they expected also I would be more kind unto them. But this would have ruined our trade. Therefore I resolved to stand firm in this occasion, because what we now concluded upon with these savages touching commerce would have been a rule for the future.

The Indians being assembled presently after my arrival, and having laid out their presents before me, being beavers' tails, caribou tongues dried, grease of bears, deer, and elks, one of the Indians spoke to my brother-in-law and me in this wise: "You men that pretend to give us our lives, will not you let us live? You know what beaver is worth, and the pains we take to get it. You style yourselves our brethren, and yet you will not give us what those that are not our brethren will give. Accept our presents, or we will come see you no more, but will go unto others."

I was a good while silent without answering the compliment of this savage, which made one of his companions urge me to give my answer. And it being that whereon our welfare depended, and that we must appear resolute in this occasion, I said to the Indian that pressed me to answer: "To whom will thou have me answer? I heard a dog bark. Let a man speak, and he shall see I know [how] to defend myself. We love our brothers and deserve to be loved by them, being come hither a purpose to have your lives." Having said these words, I rose and drew my dagger. I took the chief of these Indians by the hair, who had adopted me for his son, and I demanded of him who he was. He answered, "Thy father." "Well," said I, "if thou art my father and dost love me, and if thou art the chief, speak for me. Thou art master of my goods. This dog that spoke but now, what doth he hear? Let him begone to his brethren, the English in the bay. But I mistake; he need not go so far; he may see them in the island," intimating unto them that I had overcome the English. "I know very well," said I, continuing my discourse to my Indian father, "what woods are and what 'tis to leave one's wife and run the danger of dying with hunger or to be killed by one's enemies. You avoid all these dangers in coming unto us, so that I see plainly 'tis better for you to trade with us than with the others. Yet I will have pity on this wretch and will spare his life, though he has a desire to go unto our enemies." I caused a sword blade to be brought me, and I said unto him that spoke: "Here, take this, and begone to your brethren, the English. Tell them my name and that I will go take them." There was a necessity I should speak after this rate in this juncture, or else our trade had been ruined forever. Submit once unto the savages and they are never to be recalled.

Having said what I had a mind to say unto the Indian, I went to withdraw with my brother-in-law, but we were both stopped by the chief of the Indians, who encouraged us, saying we were men: we force nobody; everyone was free; and that he and his nation would hold true unto us; that he would go persuade the nations to come unto us, as he had already done, by the presents we had sent them by him; desiring we would accept of his and that we would trade at our own discretion.

Thereupon the Indian that spoke, unto whom I had presented the sword, being highly displeased, said he would kill the Assempoits if they came down unto us. I answered him I would march into his country and eat sagamite in the head of his grandmother, which is a great threat amongst the savages and the greatest distaste can be given them.

At the same instant I caused the presents to be taken up and distributed, 3 fathom of black tobacco, among the savages that were content to be our friends, saying, by way of disgrace to him that appeared opposite to us, that he should go smoke in the country of the tame wolves women's tobacco. I invited the others to a feast; after which the savages traded with us for their beavers, and we dismissed them all very well satisfied.

Having ended my business with the Indians, I embarked without delay to go back, and I found the New England ship at anchor over against Mr. Bridgar's house, as I had ordered. I went into the house and caused an inventory to be taken of all that was there. Then I went to the fort of the island, having sent [an] order to my nephew to burn it. I found him there with Mr. Bridgar, who would himself be the first in setting the fort afire, of which I was glad. There being no more to do there, I went down to the ship and found they had put everything aboard. I gave [an] order to my nephew at my coming away that the next day he should bring Mr. Bridgar along with him unto our house. Where being arrived, my brother-in-law, not knowing him as well as I did, made him be sent into the island with the captain of the New England ship and his folks, of which Mr. Bridgar complained unto me next day, desiring that I would release him from thence, saying he could not endure to be with those people, which I promised to do, and in a few days after brought him unto a place I caused to be fitted on a point on the north side of our river, where he found his own men in a very good condition. I not being yet able to overcome our men's obstinacy in not yielding that I should give our vessel unto the English, Mr. Bridgar proposed that he would build a deck upon the shallop if I would but furnish him with material necessary for it, saying that if the shallop were but well decked and fitted he would willingly

198

venture to go in her unto the bay, rather than to accept of his passage for France in one of our vessels. I offered him all that he desired to that purpose and stayed with him till the ship that I caused to be fitted was arrived.

When she was come, I see a smoke on the other side of the river. I crossed over and found that it was my Indian father. I told him how glad I was to see him and invited him to go aboard, saying that, going at my request, my nephew would use him civilly, that they would fire a great gun at his arrival, would give him something to eat, would make him a present of biscuits and of 2 fathom of tobacco. He said I was a fool to think my people would do all this without [an] order. I wrote with a coal on the rind of a tree and gave it to him to carry aboard. He, seeing that all I said unto him was punctually performed, was much surprised, saying we were devils (so they call those that do anything that is strange unto them). I returned back to our houses, having done with Mr. Bridgar.

I had founded the captain of the ship that was in the island right against our house, to know of him that, being an Englishman, whether he would give a writing under his hand to consent that Mr. Bridgar should be put in possession of his ship, or if he had rather I should carry her to Quebec. But he and his men entreated me very earnestly not to deliver them unto Mr. Bridgar, believing they should receive better usage of the French than of the English. I told my brother-in-law what the captain said and that he referred himself wholly unto our discretion.

Whilst we were busy in setting things for our departure, I found myself necessitated to compose a great feud that happened betwixt my Indian father's family and another great family of the country. I had notice of it by a child, some of my Indian father's, who, playing with his comrades, who, quarreling with him, one told him that he should be killed, and all his family, in revenge of one of the family of the Martins that his father had killed, for the families of the Indians are distinguished by the names of sundry beasts. And death being very affrighting unto those people, this child came to my house weeping bitterly, and after much ado I had to make him speak he told me how his comrade had threatened him. I thought at first of something else and that the savages had quarreled amongst themselves.

Desiring, therefore, to concern myself in keeping peace amongst them, I presently sent for this chief of the Indians, my adopted

199

father, who being come according to my order, I told him the
cause of my fear and what his child had told me. I had no sooner
done speaking but he, leaning against a pillar and covering his
face with his hands, he cried more than his child had done before.
Having asked what was the matter, after having a little dried up
his tears, he told me that an Indian of another family, intending
to have surprised his wife, whom he loved very tenderly, he killed
him; and the savages that sided to revenge the other's cause having chased him, he was forced to fly; and that was it that made
him meet me about 8ber last; that he continued the fear of his
enemies' displeasure, that they would come kill him.

I told him he should not fear anything, the Frenchmen being
his fathers and I his son; that our King that had sent me thither
covered him with his hand, expecting they should all live in peace;
that I was there to settle him and that I would do it or die; that I
would require all the Indians to come in that day [that they]
might know me and that he should know my intentions. Having
thus spoke unto him, I caused [to be brought] a fowling piece and
2 kettles, 3 coats, 4 sword blades, 4 tranches,* 6 graters, 6 dozen
knives, 10 axes, 10 fathom of tobacco, 2 coverlets for women,
3 caps, some powder and shot, and said unto the savage, my
adopted father, in presence of his allies that were there present:
"Here is that [which] will cure the wound and dry away tears,
which will make men live. I will have my brethren love one
another. Let 2 of you presently go and invite the family of the
Martins to the feast of amity and make them accept my presents.
If they refuse it and seek for blood, it is just I should sacrifice
my life for my father, whom I love as I do all the rest of the
Indians, our allies, more than I do my own self. I am ready to
lay down my head to be cut off in case my presents did not serve
turn, but I would stir up all the Frenchmen, my brethren, to
carry guns to assist me to make war against that family."

The savages went to go unto the family that was enemy unto
my adopted father, to make them [an] offer of my presents and
in my name to invite them unto the feast of unity. I stayed so little
a while in the country afterwards that I could not quite determine
this difference. In due time I will relate what upon inquiry I farther
heard of it in my last voyage.

This business being upon a matter ended, I was informed that

---

*A small paring knife.

Mr. Bridgar, contrary to his promise of not speaking with the Indians, yet entered into discourse with them and said that we were ill people and told them he would come and kill us; that he would traffic with them more to their advantage than we did; that he would give them 6 axes for a beaver skin and a fowling piece for 5 skins. I taxed Mr. Bridgar with it. Also, I rated the savages, who promised they would go near him no more and that I should fear nothing.

Being desirous to make all things ready for my departure, I again crossed over the dangerous river to go burn Mr. Bridgar's house, there being nothing left remaining in it, having caused everything to be put on board the New England ship, and taken full inventory of it before. I had along with me 3 Englishmen and one Frenchman, relying more on the English, who loved me because I used them kindly, than I did on the Frenchmen. What I did at this time doth show the great confidence I put in the English, for had I in the least distrusted them I would not have ventured to have gone 11 leagues from my habitation with 3 English and but one of my own Frenchmen to have fired Mr. Bridgar's house.

We were very like to be lost in returning home. I never was in so great danger in all my life. We were surprised with a sudden storm of wind near the flats, and there was such a great mist that we knew not where we were.

Being returned unto our habitation, I found our men had brought the ship to anchor near our house, and seeing the weather beginning to come favorable, I gave my nephew instructions to carry on the trade in my absence until our return. I left 7 men with him and the absolute command and disposal of all things. Which being done, I caused our furs to be put on board and the ship to fall down to the mouth of the river, to set sail the first fair wind; it was where I left Mr. Bridgar.

His shallop being well provided and furnished with all things, he was ready to sail, but having made some trips from one river unto the other, the sight of such vast quantities of ice as was in those seas made him afraid to venture himself so great a voyage in so small a vessel to sail unto the bay, so that we, fitting things to be gone the 20 July, having sent for Mr. Bridgar to come receive his provisions, he told me he thought it too rash an action for him to venture himself so great a voyage in so small a vessel, and desired I would give him passage in our ship, supposing all

201

along that I would compel him to embark for France. I told him he should be very welcome and that I intended not to force him to anything, but only to quit the place. It was concluded that he should embark with my brother-in-law in the small vessel. He said he had rather go in the other ship, but it was but just that the captain should continue on board, and we could not with great reason take Mr. Bridgar on board, having already more English to keep than we were French.

The 27th of July we weighed anchor and passed the flats. But next day, having as yet sailed but 8 or 9 leagues, we were forced to enter into the ice and used all our endeavor not to be far from each other. The bark, tacking to come, cast her grapplers on the same ice as we fastened unto. She split to pieces, so that we were forced to send presently to their help and to take out all the goods [that] was on board her and to lay them on the ice, [in order] to career [the bark], which we did with much difficulty. We continued in this danger till the 24 of August.

We visited one another with all freedom, yet we stood on our guard, for the Englishman that we found the beginning of the winter in the snow, remembering how kindly he was used by me, gave me notice of a design the Englishmen had that were in the bark of cutting all the Frenchmen's throats, and that they only waited a fit opportunity to do it. This hint made us watch them the more narrowly. At nighttime we secured them under lock and key, and in the daytime they enjoyed their full liberty.

When we were got to the southward, in the 56 degree, Mr. Bridgar desired me to let him have the bark, along with his men. I told him I would speak to my brother-in-law about it, who was not much against it. There was only the master and some other obstinate fellows that opposed, but at length I got all to consent, and having taken the things out, we delivered the bark unto Mr. Bridgar, taking his receipt. It was in good will that I managed all this for him, and I thought he would have gone in the bark, for he knows that I offered it unto him, but having made the Englishman that belonged unto him, and since chosen to stay with us and in whom we put much confidence, to desire leave of me to go along with Mr. Bridgar, we presently supposed, and we were not deceived, that 'twas by his persuasion this seaman desired to be gone, and we had some apprehension that Mr. Bridgar might have some design to trepan us by returning unto Port Nelson before us, to surprise our people, whereunto the

202

English seaman that understood our business might have been very serviceable unto him. Having therefore conferred amongst ourselves upon this demand, we resolved to keep Mr. Bridgar and to take him along with us unto Quebec. We caused him to come out of the bark and told him our resolution. Whereat he flew into great passion, especially against me, who was not much concerned at it. We caused him to come into our vessel, and we told his people that they may proceed on their voyage without him and he should come along with us.

After which, we took in our grapple irons from off the ice, seeing the sea open to the westward and the way freed to sail. We were distant about 120 leagues from the bottom of the bay when we parted from the bark, who might easily have got there in 8 days, and they had provisions on board for above a month, viz., a barrel of oatmeal, 42 double pieces of beef, 8 or 10 salt geese, 2 pieces of pork, a powder barrel full of biscuit, 8 or 10 pounds of powder, and 50 pounds of shot. I gave over and above [this], unknown to my brother-in-law, 2 horns full of powder and a bottle of brandy, besides a barrel they drank the evening before we parted.

I made one of the New England seamen to go on board the bark to strengthen the crew, many of them being sickly.

Being got out of the ice, having a favorable wind, we soon got into the straits, where through the negligence or the ignorance of one of our French pilots and seamen, the English being confined in the night, a storm of wind and snow drove us into a bay from whence we could not get out. We were driven ashore without any hopes of getting off. But when we expected every moment to be lost, God was pleased to deliver us out of the danger, finding amongst the rocks wherein we were engaged the finest harbor that could be; 50 ships could have lain there and been preserved without anchor or cable in the highest storms.

We lay there 2 days, and having refitted our ship, we set sail and had the weather pretty favorable until we arrived at Quebec, which was the end of 8ber.

As soon as ever we arrived we went unto Monsieur La Barre, governor of Canada, to give him an account of what we had done. He thought fit we should restore the ship unto the New England merchants, in warning them they should go no more unto the place from whence she came.[12]

Mr. Bridgar embarked himself on her, with young Guillam,

203

for New England against my mind, for I advised him as a friend to embark himself on the French ships, which were ready to sail for Rochelle. I foretold him what came to pass, that he would live a long while in New England for passage. We parted good friends, and he can bear me witness that I intimated unto him at that time my affection for the English interest and that I was still of the same mind of serving the King and the nation as fully and affectionately as I had now served the French.

Eight or ten days after my arrival, Monsieur La Barre sent for me to show me a letter he had received from Monsieur Colbert by a man-of-war that had brought over some soldiers, by which he writ him that those which parted last year to make discoveries in the northern parts of America, being either returned or would soon return, he desired one of them to give the court an account of what they had done, and of what settlements might be made in those parts; and the governor told that I must forthwith prepare myself to go satisfy Monsieur Colbert in the business.

I willingly accepted the motion and left my business in the hands of Monsieur De La Chesnaye, although I had not any very good opinon of him, having dealt very ill by me. But thinking I could not be a loser by satisfying the prime minister of state, although I neglected my own private affairs, I took leave of Monsieur La Barre and embarked for France with my brother-in-law, the 11th 9ber, 1683, in the frigate that brought the soldiers, and arrived at Rochelle the 18 of Xber, where I heard of the death of Monsieur Colbert. Yet I continued my journey to Paris, to give the court an account of my proceedings.

I arrived at Paris with my brother-in-law the 15th January, where I understood there was great complaints made against me in the King's council by my Lord Preston, His [English] Majesty's envoy extraordinary, concerning what had passed in the river and Port Nelson, and that I was accused of having cruelly abused the English, robbed, stolen, and burnt their habitation, for all which my Lord Preston demanded satisfaction, and that exemplary punishment might be inflicted on the offenders to content His Majesty. This advice did not discourage me from presenting myself before the Marquis De Seignelay and to inform him of all that had passed betwixt the English and me during my voyage. He found nothing amiss in all my proceedings, whereof I made him a true relation; and so far was it from being blamed in the court of France, that I may say, without flattering myself, it was well approved, and [I] was commended.[13] I do not say that I deserved it, only that I endeavored in all my proceedings to discharge the part of an honest man and that I think I did no other. I refer it to be judged by what is contained in this narrative, which I protest is faithful and sincere; and if I have deserved the accusations made against me in the court of France, I think it needless to say aught else in my justification, which is fully to be seen in the relation of the voyage I made by His Majesty's order last year, 1684, for the Royal Company of Hudson's Bay, the success and profitable returns whereof has destroyed, unto the shame of my enemies, all the evil impressions they would have given of my actions.

SIXTH VOYAGE

Relation of the voyage of Peter Esprit Radisson, anno
1684.

(Translated from the French)[1]

I HAVE TREATED at length the narrative of my voyage in the
years 1682 and 1683, in Hudson's Bay, to the north of Canada.
Up to my arrival in the city of Paris, all things were prepared for
the fitting out of the ships with which I should make my return
to the north of Canada, pending the negotiations at court for the
return to me of every fourth beaver skin that the very Christian
King took for the customs duty — which had been promised to
me in consideration of my discoveries, voyages, and services —
by which I hope to profit over and above my share during the
first years of that establishment.

It was also at the same time that my Lord Viscount Preston,
minister extraordinary from the King [of England] at the court
of France, continued to pursue me concerning the things of which
I was accused by the account against me of the gentlemen of the
Royal Hudson's Bay Company; my enemies have taken due care
to publish the enormous crimes of which I was charged, and my
friends taking the pains to support me under it and to give me
advice of all that passed. Although at last no longer able to suffer
anyone to tax my conduct, I considered myself obliged to un-
deceive each one. I resolved at length within myself to speak to
the effect of making it appear as if my dissatisfaction had passed
away. For that effect I made choice of persons who did me the
honor of loving me, and this was done in the conversations that I
had avowed to them, on different occasions, the sorrow that I
had felt at being obliged to abandon the service of England because of the bad treatment that I had received from them, and
that I should not be sorry of returning to it, being more in a condition than I had been for it of rendering service to the King and

the nation, if they were disposed to render me justice and to remember my services. I spoke also several times to the English government: I had left my nephew, son of Sieur Des Groseilliers, my brother-in-law, with other Frenchmen near Port Nelson, who were there the sole masters of the beaver trade, which ought to be considerable at that port, and that it depended upon me to make it profitable for the English. All these things having been reported by one of my particular friends to the persons who are in the interest of the government, they judged correctly that a man who spoke freely in that manner and who made no difficulty in letting his sentiments be known and who showed by them that it was possible to be easily led back, by rendering justice to him, to a party that he had only abandoned through dissatisfaction, I was requested to have some conferences with these same persons.

I took in this matter the first step without repugnance, and upon the report that was made to my Lord Preston of things that we had treated upon in the interviews, and of that of which I claimed to be capable of doing, I was exhorted from his side of re-entering into my first engagements with the English — assuring me that if I could execute that which I had proposed I should receive from His Majesty in England, and from His Royal Highness of the Hudson's Bay Company, and from the government, all kinds of good treatment and an entire satisfaction; that, moreover, I need not make myself uneasy of that which regarded my interests, this minister being willing himself to be charged with the care of me, to preserve them, and of procuring me other advantages after I should be put in a position of rendering service to the King, his master. They represented to me again that, His Royal Highness honoring the Hudson's Bay Company with his protection, it would pass even on to me if I would employ upon it my credit, my attentions, and the experience that I had in the country of the North for the utility and the benefit of the affairs of that Company, in which His Royal Highness took great interest.

At the same time I received some letters at Paris from the Sieur Ecuyer Young, one of those interested in the Hudson's Bay Company, in which he solicited me on his part and in the name of the Company to return into England, giving me some assurances of a good reception and that I should have reason to be satisfied on my part, in regard to my particular interests, as well as for some advantages that they would make me.

These letters, joined to those in which my Lord Preston continued his urgencies against me to the very Christian King, decided me to determine, by the counsel of one of my friends, to yield myself at last to all their solicitations of passing over to England for good, and of engaging myself so strongly to the service of His Majesty and to the interests of the nation that any other consideration was never able to detatch me from it. There was only my Lord Preston, some of his household, and the friend who had counseled me to come into England who knew of my design.

I took care to save appearances from suspicion by the danger in which I exposed myself, and up to the evening of my departure I had some conferences with the ministers of the court of France, and the persons who there have the departments of the marine and commerce, upon some propositions of armament and the equipment of the ships destined for my 2nd voyage. They wished to bind me to make them upon the same footing as the preceding, which was made since then the talk of the two nations.

The day of my departure was fixed for the 24th of April, 1684. But [to the] last those with whom I was obliged to confer daily by order of the ministers of France never doubted in the least of my discontinuing to see them. I told them that I was obliged to make a little journey into the country for some family business and [that] I could be useful to them during that time by going to London, where I arrived the 10th of May.

At the moment of my arrival I had the honor of going to see the gentlemen Ecuyer Young and the Chevalier Hayes, both of whom were interested in the Hudson's Bay Company, who gave me a good reception in showing me the joy that they felt at my return and in giving me such assurances that I should receive on their part and on that of their Company all manner of satisfaction. I then explained fully to them the nature of the service that I expected to render to His Majesty, to the Company, and to the nation in establishing the beaver trade in Canada, and making those to profit by it who were interested to the extent of 15 or 20,000 beaver skins, that I hoped to find already in the hands of the French that I had left there, that would cost to them only the interest that I had in the thing and the just satisfaction that was owing to the French who had made the trade for them.

These gentlemen, having received in an agreeable manner my proposition, and wishing to give me some marks of their satisfaction, did me the honor of presenting me to His Majesty and to His Royal Highness, to whom I mad my submission, the offer of my very humble services, a sincere protestation that I would do my duty, that even to the peril of my life I would employ all my care and attention for the advantage of the affairs of the Company, and that I would seek all occasions of giving proof of my zeal and inviolable fidelity for the service of the King, of all which His Majesty and His Royal Highness appeared satisfied and did me the favor of honoring me with some evidences of their satisfaction upon my return and of giving me some marks of their protection.

After that I had several conferences in the assembled body, and in particular with the gentlemen interested in the Hudson's Bay Company, in which I made them acquainted in what manner it was necessary for them to proceed there for establishing to the best advantage the beaver trade in the northern country, the means of properly sustaining it, and of ruining in a short time the trade with foreigners; and to that end I would commence by becoming master of both the fort and the settlement of the French, as well as of all the furs that they had traded for since my departure, on the condition that my influence would serve to convert them and that my nephew, whom I had left commandant in that fort, and the other French would be paid what would be to them their legitimate due. These gentlemen, satisfied with what I had said to them, believed with justice that they would be able to have entire confidence in me. As for that, having resolved to entrust me with their orders for going with their ships, equipped and furnished with everything to found the establishment in putting into execution my projects, they gave the power of settling in my own mind and conscience the claims of my nephew and the other French, assuring me that they would be satisfied with the account that I would present to them. I accepted that commission with the greatest pleasure in the world, and I hurried with so much diligence the necessary things for my departure that in less than eight days I was in a condition to embark myself. This was done even without any precaution on my part for my own interests, for I did not wish to make any composition with these gentlemen. I said to them that since they had confidence in me, I wished also on my part to make use of it generously with them and remit everything to the success of my voyage, and on my return, in the hope that I had that they would satisfy my honesty of purpose, and that after having given to them some marks of my sincerity in executing the things to perform which I had engaged myself for their service, they would render me all the justice that I had cause for hoping from gentlemen of honor and probity.

The ships destined for Hudson's Bay and the execution of my design were ready to make sail, and myself being all prepared for embarking, I took leave of the gentlemen of the Company in giving them fresh assurances of the good success of my voyage, if God did me the favor of preserving me from the dangers to which I went to expose myself, of which they appeared so well satisfied that the Chevalier Hayes dared not flatter himself of the advantage that I promised to him: that they should get from 15 to 20,000 beavers that I hoped to find in the hands of the French; [Hayes] said, in embracing me, that the Company would be satisfied if I had only 5,000 of them there.

The event has justified that which I predicted, and the gentlemen have not been deceived in the hopes that I have given to them.

I departed from the port of Gravesend the 17th of the same month of May [1684], in the ship called *The Happy Return,* in the company of 2 others that these gentlemen sent also to Port Nelson for the same reason. The winds having been favorable for us, we arrived in a few days upon the western side of Button's bay without anything happening to us worth mentioning but the winds and the currents.

We having been made to drift to the south of Port Nelson about 40 leagues, and the ice having separated the ship in which I was from the 2 others in Hudson's Straits, I began to doubt of succeeding in my enterprise, by the apprehension that I had that the 2 ships, having arrived sooner than ours, the men who were inside would not hazard themselves to take any step which could at all do them any damage. Under this anxiety, knowing the necessity that there was that I should arrive the first, I resolved to embark myself in a shallop that we had brought to be employed in any service that might be necessary. I ordered the captain to equip it, and although but little more than 20 leagues from Port Nelson, I put myself on board with 7 men, and after 48 hours of fatigue, without having been able to take any rest because of the danger that there was to us, we found, by the breadth of Hayes river, which having recognized, at last we touched land at a point north of the river, where we landed with an Englishman who spoke good French, whom I wished to make accompany me in order that he might be the witness of all that I did.

After having come to land, I recognized by certain marks that my nephew, having heard the noise of the cannon of the English ships, had come to the place where we landed to know if his father or myself were arrived, and that he had himself [departed] after having recognized that they were English ships. These same marks gave me also to know that he had left me further away from those that I had given him since I had established him for governor in my absence,* which should inform me of his condition and the place where he was with his men. But I did not find it to the purpose of going as far as that place; I had not learned truly the condition of the English who had arrived in the country since I had departed from it.

I resolved then to embark myself afresh in the shallop to go and learn some news. I encouraged for that purpose the 7 men who were with me, who were so diligent that, in spite of a contrary wind and tide, we arrived in a very little time at the mouth of that great and frightful river of Port Nelson, where I had wished to see myself with such impatience that I had not dreamed a moment of the danger to which we had exposed ourselves. That pleasure was soon followed by another, for I saw at anchor in this same place 2 ships, of which one had the glorious flag of His Majesty hoisted upon his main mast; that I recognized to be the one that was commanded by Captain Outlaw when the one in which I was passed had been separated from the 2 others. At the same time I made the shallop approach, and I perceived the new governor,[2] with all his men under arms, upon the deck, who demanded of us where our shallop came from and who we were. Upon that I made myself known, and I went on board the ship, where I learned that the one which was alongside was an English frigate that had wintered in the Port of Nelson with the governor, which port they had abandoned to retire themselves for fear of being insulted by the French and the savages; but that, having been met with by Capt. Outlaw going out of the bay, he had returned, having learned that I had thrown myself into the service of England and that I came into the country to reestablish there everything to the advantage of the nation.

My first care after that was of making myself informed of what had passed between the English and the French since my departure and their arrival. By what the English told me I judged that it was proper to risk everything to try to join my nephew as soon

---

*That is, the nephew had moved the fort.

as possible, and the men that I had left with him; in fine, of endeavoring to reach them by kindness, or to intercept them by cunning, before they received the shock upon what design I came, for that was of extreme consequence.

Thus, without waiting for the arrival of the ship in which I had come, I resolved to embark myself upon the same shallop, which was named *The Little Adventure*; which I did not, nevertheless, on the same day because the governor found it proper to delay the party until the following day, and of giving me other men in the place of those that I had brought, who found themselves fatigued. I embarked myself on the morrow, early in the morning, with Captain Gazer. But the wind being found contrary, I had myself landed on the coast, with Captain Gazer and the Englishman who spoke French, and after having sent back the other men, I resolved to go by land as far as the place where I should find the marks of my nephew, which should make me recognize the place where he was, and his condition. We marched, all three, until the morrow morning. But being arrived at the place where I had told my nephew to leave me some marks, which having taken up, I learned that he and his men had left our old houses and that they had built themselves another of them upon an island above the rapids of the River Hayes. After that we continued our route until opposite to the houses which had been abandoned, where I hoped that we should discover something, or at least that we should make ourselves seen or heard by firing some reports of the gun and making of smoke, in which my attempt was not altogether vain, for after having rested some time in that place we perceived 10 canoes of savages, who descended the river. I believed at first that it would be probable they had there some French with them, that my nephew would be able to send to discover who were the people newly arrived, which obliged me to tell Captain Gazer that I should go down to the bank of the river to speak to them, that I prayed him to await me upon the heights without any apprehension, and that in a little while he would be able to render evidence of my fidelity for the service of the Company.

I was at the same moment met by the savages, and from the bank of the river I made them the accustomed signal, to the end of obliging them to come towards me. But having perceived that they did not put themselves to the trouble of doing it, I spoke to them in their language for to make myself known; which done, they approached the bank and, not recognizing me, they demanded of me to see the marks that I had, which having shown them, they gave evidence by their cries and postures of diversion the pleasure that they had of my arrival. I learned then from them that my nephew and the other Frenchmen were above the rapids of the river, distant about 4 leagues from the place where I was, and that they had told them that my brother-in-law, Des Groseilliers, should also come with me, which obliged me telling them that he was arrived and that they would see him in a few days. Then I told them that we had always loved them as our brothers and that I would give them some marks of my amity, for which they thanked me in begging me to not be angry for that which, by counsel, they had been trading with the English, nor of that when I found them going to meet their captain, who had gone across some woods, with 20 men, to the English ships to procure some powder and guns, which they did; that their laying over for a month, in awaiting for me, had compelled them, but that since I had arrived they would not go on farther, and that their chief, whom they went to inform of my arrival, would speak more of it to me. As I had occasion for someone among them to inform my nephew that I was in the country, I asked of all of them if they loved the son of Des Groseilliers and if he had not some relation among them; upon which there was one of them who said to me, "He is my son. I am ready to do that which thou wishest." At that moment, he having landed, I made him throw his beaver skin on the ground, and having called Captain Gazer, I spoke in these terms to this savage in the presence of all the others: "I have made peace with the English for love of you. They and I from henceforth shall be but one. Embrace this captain and myself in token of peace. He is thy new brother, and this one thy son. Go at once to him to carry this news, with the token of peace, and tell him to come to see me in this place here, whilst the savages of the Company go to attend me to the mouth of the river."

This savage did not fail to go and inform his son, my nephew, of my arrival, and of carrying to him the news of peace between the French and the English, during which we awaited with impatience his descent towards the place where we were, whom nevertheless, did not arrive until the morrow, about 9 o'clock in the morning. I saw at first appear my nephew, in a canoe with 3 other Frenchmen, accompanied by another canoe of the savages that I had sent, and which came in advance to inform me of the

214

arrival of my nephew. I promised to this savage and his comrade each one a watch coat, and returned to them their beaver skins, with the order of going to join those of their nation and to wait for me at the mouth of the river.

After that, Captain Gazer, the Englishman who spoke French, and myself waded into the water half-leg deep to land upon a little island where my nephew, with his men, would come on shore. He had arrived there before us, and he came to meet us, saluting me, greatly surprised at the union that I had made with the English. We then proceeded all together in his canoe as far as our old houses, where I had the English and French to enter, and whilst they entertained each other with the recital of their mutual hardships, I spoke privately to my nephew in these terms:

"It is within your recollection, without doubt, of having heard your father relate how many pains and fatigues we have had in serving France during several years. You have also been informed by him that the recompense we had reason to hope for from her was a black ingratitude on the part of the court, as well as on the part of the company of Canada, and that they, having reduced us to the necessity of seeking to serve elsewhere, the English received us with evidences of pleasure and of satisfaction. You know also the motives that have obliged your father and myself, after 13 years of service, to leave the English. The necessity of subsisting, the refusal that showed the bad intention of the Hudson's Bay Company to satisfy us, have given occasion to our separation and to the establishment that we have made, and for which I left you in possession in parting for France. But you ignore, without doubt, that the Prince who reigns in England had disavowed the proceedings of the Company in regard to us and that he had caused us to be recalled to his service, to receive the benefits of his royal protection and a complete satisfying of our own discontents. I have left your father in England, happier than we in this that he is assured of his subsistence and that he commences to taste some repose, whilst I come to inform you that we are now Englishmen and that we have preferred the goodness and kindness of a clement and easy King in following our inclinations, which are to serve people of heart and honor in preference of the offers that the King of France caused to be made to us by his ministers, to oblige us to work indirectly for his glory. I received an order, before leaving London, of taking care of you and of obliging you to serve the English nation. You are young

215

and in a condition to work profitably for your fortune. If you are resolved to follow my sentiments I never will abandon you. You will receive the same treatment as myself. I will participate even at the expense of my interests for your satisfaction. I will have a care also of those who remain under my control in this place with you, and I shall leave nothing undone that will be able to contribute to your advancement. I love you. You are of my blood. I know that you have courage and resolution. Decide for yourself promptly and make me see by your response, that I wait for, that you are worthy of the goodness of the clement prince that I serve. But do not forget, above all things, the injuries that the French have inflicted upon one who has given his life to you, and that you are in my power."

When my nephew had heard all that I had to say to him, he protested to me that he had no other sentiments but mine and that he would do all that I would wish of him, but that he begged me to have care of his mother. To which I answered that I had not forgotten that she was my sister, and that the confidence that he gave me evidence of had on that occasion imposed upon me a double engagement, which obliged me of having care of her and of him. With which, having been satisfied, he remitted to me the power of commandant that I had left to him, and having embraced him, I said to him that he should appear in the assembly of the English and French as satisfied as he should be, and leave the rest to my management.

After which, we reentered into the house, and I commanded one of the Frenchmen to go out immediately and inform his comrades that all would go well if they should have an entire confidence in me and obey all my orders, which doing, they should want nothing. I ordered also this same Frenchman to inform the savages to come to me and work immediately with their comrades to bring back into the house newly built the beaver skins buried in the wood, and to that end, to be able to work with more diligence, I told them I would double their rations. Then I told my nephew to cross the river with the Frenchman who served him as interpreter and go by land to the north side at the rendezvous that I had given to the savages the preceding day, whilst I would make my way by water to the same meeting place with Captain Gazer and 2 other men who remained with me.

Having embarked in my nephew's canoe, I descended the river as far as the mouth, where I found the savages, who awaited me

216

with impatience, they having been joined the following day by 30 other canoes of savages that I had warned to descend by their captain, who had come towards me. We were all together in the canoes of the savages and boarded some ships which were stranded upon Nelson's river.

This was in that strait that the chief of the savages spoke to me of many things, and who after having received from my hands one of the presents designed for the chief of these nations, he told me that he and his people would speak of my name to all the nations, to invite them to come to me to smoke the pipe of peace. But he blamed strongly the English governor for telling him that my brother had been made to die, that I was a prisoner, and that he had come to destroy the rest of the French. The chief of the savages added to the blame his complaint also. He said haughtily that the governor was unworthy of his friendship and of those of their old brothers who commenced to establish it amongst them, in telling them such falsehoods. Grumbling and passion had a share in his indignation. He offered several times to inflict injuries upon the governor, who endeavored to justify himself for these things that he had said to them through imprudence against the truth. But the chief savage would not hear anything in his defense, neither of those of the other Englishmen there, all of whom were become under suspicion.

Nevertheless I appeased this difference by the authority that I have upon the spirit of these nations. And after having made the governor and the chief embrace, and having myself embraced both of them, giving the savage to understand that it was a sign of peace, I said to him also that I wished to make a feast for this same peace, and that I had given orders what they should have to eat.

On such familiar occasions, the savages have the custom of making a speech precede the feast, which consists in recognizing for their brothers those with whom they make peace, and praise their strength. After having informed the chief of the savages of the experience, strength, valor of the English nation, he [the governor] acquitted himself with much judgment in that action, for which he was applauded by our and his own people. I said afterwards in presence of his people that the French were not good seamen, that they were afraid of the icebergs which they would have to pass across to bring any merchandise; besides, their ships were weak and incapable of resistance in the Northern seas. But

217

as to those of the English, they were strong, hardy, and enter-
prising, that they had the knowledge of all seas and an indefinite
number of large and strong ships, which carried for them merchandises in all weathers and without stoppage. Of which this chief,
having full confidence, was satisfied.

He came to dine with us whilst his people were eating together
of that which I had ordered to be given them. The repast being
finished, it was a question with me whether I should commence
to open a trade, as I had formed the design of abolishing the
custom which the English had introduced since I had left their
service, which was of giving some presents to the savages to draw
them to our side, which was opposed to that that I had practiced,
for in place of giving some presents I had myself made I said
then to the chief of the savages, in the presence of those of his
nation, that he should make me presents that I ordinarily received
on similar occasions.

Upon that they spoke between themselves, and at length they
presented me with 60 skins of beaver, asking me to accept them
as a sign of our ancient friendship and of considering that they
were poor and far removed from their country, that they had
fasted several days in coming and that they were obliged to fast
also in returning, that the French of Canada made them presents
to oblige them to open their parcels, and that the English at the
bottom of the bay gave to all the nations 3 hatchets for a beaver
skin. They added to that that the beaver was very difficult to kill
and that their misery was worthy of pity.

I replied to them that I had compassion for their condition and
that I would do all that was in my power to relieve them, but
that it was much more reasonable that they made me some presents, rather than I to them, because that I came from a country
very far more removed than they to carry to them excellent merchandise; that I spared them the trouble of going to Quebec; and
as to the difference in the trade of the English at the bottom of
the bay with ours, I told that each was the master of that which
belonged to him and at liberty to dispose of it according to his
pleasure; that it mattered very little of trading with them, since
I had for my friends all the other nations; that those there were
the masters of my merchandises who yielded themselves to my
generosity for it; that there were 30 years that I had been their
brother and that I would be in the future their father if they continued to love me, but that if they were of other sentiments, I

218

was very easy about the future; that I would cause all the nations around to be called, to carry to them my merchandises; that the gain that they would receive by the succor rendered them powerful and placed them in a condition to dispute the passage to all the savages who dwelt in the lands; that by this means they would reduce themselves to lead a languishing life and to see their wives and children die by war or by famine, of which their allies, although powerful, could not guarantee them of it, because I was informed that they had neither knives nor guns. This discourse obliged these savages to submit themselves to all that I wished.

Seeing them disposed to trade, I said to them that, as they had an extreme need of knives and guns, I would give them 10 knives for one beaver, although the master of the earth, the King, my sovereign, had given me orders to not give but 5 of them, and that as for the guns, I would give them one of them for 12 beavers, which they went to accept, when the governor, through fear or imprudence, told them that we demanded of them but 7 and up to 10 beavers for each gun, which was the reason that it was made necessary to give them to the savages at that price.

The trade was then made with all manner of tranquillity and good friendship. After which these people took their leave of us, very well satisfied according to all appearances, as much in general as in particular of our proceeding, and the chief as well as the other savages promised us to return in token of their satisfaction.

But at the moment that they went to leave, my nephew having learned from a chief of a neighboring nation who was with them that they would not return, he drew aside the savage chief and told him that he had been informed that he did not love us and that he would return no more. At which this chief seemed very much surprised in demanding who had told him that. My nephew said to him, "It is the savage called Bear's Grease." Which having heard, he made at the same time all his people range themselves in arms, speaking to one and to the other; in fine, obliging the one who was accused to declare himself with the firmness of a man of courage, without which they could do nothing with him, but Bear's Grease could say nothing in reply.

Jealousy, which prevails as much also among these nations as among Christians, had given place to this report, in which my nephew had placed belief because he knew that the conduct of the governor towards them had given to them as much of discontent against us all as he had caused loss to the Company — the genius of these people being that one should never demand whatever is just; that is to say, that which one wishes to have for each thing that one trades for, and that when one retracts, he is not a man. That makes it clear that there are, properly, only one people who have knowledge of the manners and customs of these nations, who are capable of trading with them, to whom firmness and resolution are also extremely necessary.

I myself again attended on this occasion, to the end of appeasing this little difference between the savages, and I effected their reconciliation, which was the reason that their chief protested to me afresh in calling me "Porcupine's Head," which is the name that they have given me among them, that he would always come to me to trade and that, whereas I had seen him but with a hundred of his young men, he would bring with him 13 different nations and that he wanted nothing in his country, neither men nor beaver skins, for my service. After which, they left us, and we dispersed ourselves to go and take possession of the house of my nephew in the manner that I had arranged with him for it.

With this in view I parted with the governor, Captain Gazer, and our people to go by land as far as the place where we had left one of our canoes upon the River Hayes, whilst the other party went by sea with the shallop, *The Adventure*, to round the point. We had the pleasure of contemplating at our ease the beauty of the country and of its shores, with which the governor was charmed by the difference that there was in the places that he had seen upon Nelson's river.

We embarked ourselves then in the canoe just at the place where the French had built their new house, where we found those who were left much advanced in the work that I had ordered them to do, but, however, very inquiet on account of having no news from my nephew, their commandant, nor of me. They had carried all the beaver skins from the wood into the house and punctually executed my all other orders. Having then seen myself master of all things without having been obliged to come to any extremity for it, the French being in the disposition of continuing their allegiance to me, I made them take an inventory of all that was in the house, where I found 239 packages of beaver skins, to the number of 12,000 skins, and some merchandise for trading yet for 7 or 8,000 more, which gave me much satisfaction.

Then I told my nephew to give a command in my name to

these same Frenchmen to bring down the beaver skins as far
as the place where they should be embarked, to transport them
to the ships, which was executed with so much diligence that in
6 days eight or ten men did (in spite of difficulties which hindered
them that we could go in that place but by canoes because of the
rapidity and want of water that they had in the river) what others
would have had trouble in doing in 6 months, without any exaggeration. My nephew had in my absence chosen this place where he
built the new house — that was, so to speak, inaccessible — to the
end of guaranteeing himself from the attacks that they would be
able to make against him; and it was that same thing which re-
strained the liberty of going and coming there freely and easily.

The savages with whom we had made the trading, not having
made so much diligence on their route as we for returning themselves into their country, having found out that I was in our
house, came to me there to demand some tobacco because I had
not given them any of that which was in the ships (because it
was not good), making as an excuse that it was at the bottom of
the cellar. I made them a present of some that my nephew had
to spare, of which they were satisfied. But I was surprised on
seeing upon the sands, in my walk around the house with the
governor, rejected quantities of another tobacco, which had been,
according to appearances, thus thrown away through indignation.
I turned over in my mind what could have possibly given occasion for this, when the great chief and captain of the savages came
to tell me that some young men of the band, irritated by the recollection of that which the English had said to them — that my
brother, Des Groseilliers, was dead, that I was a prisoner, that
they were come to make all the other Frenchmen perish, as well
as some reports of cannon that they had fired with ball in the
wood the day that I was arrived — and [the savages had] thus
thrown away this tobacco which had come from the English by
mistake, not wishing to smoke any of it. He assured me also that
the young men had wicked designs upon the English, that he had
diverted them from it by hindering them from going out of the
house. The governor, who had difficulty in believing that this
tobacco thrown upon the sands was the omen of some grievous
enterprise, was nevertheless convinced of it by the discourse of
the savage. I begged him to come with me into the house and to
go out from it no more with the other English for some time,
assuring them, nevertheless, that they had nothing to fear and

that all the French and myself would perish rather than suffer that one of them should be in the least insulted. After which, I ordered my nephew to make all those savages embark immediately, so as to continue their journey as far as their own country, which was done. Thus we were delivered from all kinds of apprehension, and free to work at our business.

In the meanwhile I could not admire enough the contancy of my nephew and of his men in that in which they themselves labored to dispossess themselves of any but good in favor of the English, their old enemies, for whom they had just pretensions, without having any other assurances of their satisfaction but the confidence that they had in my promises. Besides, I could not prevent myself from showing the pleasure that I experienced in having succeeded in my enterprise and in seeing that, in commencing to give some proofs of my zeal for the service of the English Company, I made it profit them by an advantage very considerable, which gave them for the future assurances of my fidelity and obliged them to have care of my interests in giving me that which belonged to me legitimately and [in] acquitting me towards my nephew and the other French of that which I had promised them and that a long and laborious work had gained for them.

After that, that is to say, during the 3 days that we rested in that house, I wished to inform myself exactly from my nephew, in the presence of the Englishmen, of all that which had passed between them since I had departed from the country and know in what manner he had killed two Englishmen there. Upon which, my nephew began to speak in these words:

"Some days after your departure, in the year 1683, the 27th of July, the number of reports of cannon shots that we heard fired on the side of the great river made us believe that they came from some English ship that had arrived. In fact, having sent 3 of my men to know and endeavor to understand their design, I learned from them on their return that it was 2 English ships and that they had encountered 3 men of that nation a league from these vessels, but that they had not spoken to them, having contented themselves with saluting both. As my principal design was to discover the English ones, and that my men had done nothing in it, I sent back 3 others of them to inform themselves of all that passed. These 3 last, having arrived at the point which is between the 2 rivers of Nelson and Hayes, they met 14 or 15 savages loaded with merchandise, to whom, having demanded

222

from whence they were and from whence they had come, they had replied that their nation lived along the river called Neno-savern, which was at the south of that of Hayes, and that they came to trade with their brothers who were established at the bottom of the bay. After which, my men told them who they were and where they lived, in begging them to come smoke with them some tobacco, the most esteemed in the country; to which they freely consented, in making it appear to them that they were much chagrined in not having known sooner that we were established near them, giving evidence that they would have been well pleased to have made their trade with us. In continuing to converse upon several things touching trade, they arrived together in our house, reserving each time that but one of them should enter at once.

"Under a pretext of having forgotten something, one had returned upon his steps, saying to his comrades that they had leave to wait for him at the house of the French, where [he] arrived 2 days after, to be the witness of the good reception that I made to his brothers, whom I made also participants in giving to him some tobacco. But I discovered that this savage had had quite another design than of going to seek that which he had lost, having learned that he had been heard telling the other savages that he had been to find the English and that he was charged by them of making some enterprise against us. In fact, this villain, having seen me alone and without any defense, must set himself to execute his wicked design. He seized me by the hand, and in telling me that I was of no value, since I loved not the English, and that I had not paid him by a present for the possession of the country that I lived in (to him who was the chief of all the nations and the friend of the English at the bottom of the bay), he let fall the robe which covered him and, standing all naked, he struck me a blow with his poniard, which I luckily parried with the hand, where I received a light wound, which did not hinder me from seizing him by a necklace that he had around his neck and of throwing him to the ground, which having given me the leisure of taking my sword and looking about, I perceived that the other savages had also poniards in their hands, with the exception of one who cried out, 'Do not kill the French, for their death will be avenged by all the nations from above upon all our families!' The movement that I had made to take my sword did not prevent me from holding my foot upon the throat of my enemy, and [I] knew that

that posture on my sword had frightened the other conspirators. There was none of them there who dared approach; on the contrary, they all went out of the house, armed with their poniards.

"But some Frenchmen who were near to us, having perceived things thus, they ran in a fury right to the house, where having entered, the savages threw their poniards upon the ground, saying to us that the English had promised to their chief a barrel of powder and other merchandise to kill all the French, but that their chief being dead (for they believed in fact that he was so), we had nothing more to fear because they were men of courage, abhorring wicked actions. My people, having seen that I was wounded, put themselves into a state to lay violent hands on the savages, but I prevented any disturbance, wishing by that generosity, and in sparing his life to the chief, to give some proofs of my courage and that I did not fear neither the English there nor themselves. After which, they left us, and we resolved to put ourselves better upon our guard in the future and of making come to our relief the savages, our allies.

"Some days after, these savages [our allies], by the smoke of our fires, which were our ordinary signals, arrived at our house. According to their custom, they, having been appraised of my adventure, without saying anthing to us, marched upon the track of the other savages and, having overtaken them, they invited them to a feast in order to know from the truth of the things; of which having been informed, the one among them who was my adopted brother-in-law spoke to the chief who had wished to assassinate me thus, as has been reported to me by him, 'Thou art not a man because, having about thee 15 of thy people, thou hast tried to accomplish the end of killing a single man.' To which the other replied haughtily and with impudence, 'It is true. But if I have missed him this autumn with the fifteen men, he shall not escape in the spring by my own hand alone.' 'It is necessary,' then replied my adopted brother-in-law, 'that thou makes me die first, for without that I shall hinder thy wicked design.' Upon which, having come within reach, the chief whose life I had spared received a blow of a bayonet in the stomach and another of a hatchet upon the head; upon which he fell dead upon the spot. In respect to the others, they did not retaliate with any kind of bad treatment, and they allowed them to retire with all liberty, saying to them that if they were in the design of revenging the death of their chief they had only to speak, and they would declare war upon them. After that expedition these same savages, our allies, divided into two parties and, without telling us their design, descended to the place where the English made their establishment. They attacked them and killed some of them. Of which they then came to inform me, telling me that they had killed a great number of my enemies to avenge me of the conspiracy that they had done me and my brother, and that they were ready to sacrifice their lives for my service.

"In recognition of which I thanked them and made them a feast, begging them not to kill any more of them and to await the return of my father and my uncle, who would revenge upon the English the insult which they had made me, without their tarnishing the glory that they had merited in chastising the English and the savages, their friends, of their perfidy.

"We were nevertheless always upon the defensive, and we apprehended being surprised at the place where we were, as much on the part of the English as of those of the savages, their friends. That is why we resolved of coming to establish ourselves in the place where we are at present, and which is, as you see, difficult enough of access for all those who have not been enslaved as we are amongst the savages. We built there this house in a few days with the assistance of the savages, and for still greater security we obliged several among them to pass the winter with us on the condition of our feeding them, which was the reason that our young men parted in the summer, having almost consumed all our provisions. During the winter nothing worthy of mention passed, except that some savages made several juggles to know from our Manitou, who is their familiar spirit among them, if my father and my uncle would return in the spring, who answered them that they would not be missing there and that they would bring with them all kinds of merchandise and of that which would avenge them on their enemies.

"At the beginning of April, 1684, some savages from the south coast arrived at our new house to trade for guns, but as we had none of them they went to the English, who had, as I afterwards learned, made them some presents and promised them many other things if they would undertake to kill me with the one of my men whom you saw still wounded, who spoke plainly the language of the country. These savages, encouraged by the hope of gain, accepted the proposition and promised to execute it. For that means they found an opportunity of gaining over one of the savages who was among us, who served them as a spy and informed them of all that we did. Nevertheless, they dared not attack us with open force because they feared us, and that was the reason why they proceeded otherwise in it, and this is how it was to be done:

"The Frenchman that you saw wounded, having gone by my orders with one of his comrades to the place where these savages, our friends, made some smoked stag meat that they had killed, to tell them to bring me some of it, fell, in chasing a stag, upon the barrel of his gun and bent it in such a manner that he could not kill anything with it without before having frightened it. Which having done, after having arrived at the place where the savages were, he wished to make a test of it, firing blank at some distance from their cabin, but whilst he disposed himself to that, one of the savages who had promised to the English his death and mine, who was unknown to several of his comrades amongst the others, fired a shot at him with his gun, which pierced his shoulder with a ball. He cried out directly that they had killed him, and that it was for the men who loved the French to avenge his death. Which the savages who were our friends having heard, [they] went out of their cabins and followed the culprit without his adherents daring to declare themselves. But the pursuit was useless, for he saved himself in the wood after having thrown away his gun, and taken in its place his bow and his quiver. This behavior surprised our allies, the savages, exceedingly and obliged them to swear, in their manner, vengeance for it, as much against that savage nation as against the English, but not having enough guns for that enterprise, they resolved to wait until my father and uncle had arrived.

"In the meantime, they sent to entreat all the nations who had sworn friendship to my father and my uncle to come to make war upon the English and the savages on the southern coast, representing to them that they were obliged to take our side because that they had at other times accepted our presents in token of peace and of good will; that as to the rest, we were always men of courage and their brothers. As soon as these other nations had received intelligence of the condition in which we were, they resolved to assist us with all their forces and, in waiting the return of my father or my uncle, to send hostages for it to give a token of their courage, in the persons of two of their young men.

"One of the most considerable chiefs among these nations was deputed to conduct them. I received them as I ought. This chief was the adopted father of my uncle and one of the best friends of the French, whom I found adapted to serve me to procure an interview with the English, to the end of knowing what could possibly be their resolution. For that purpose I deputed this chief savage towards the English, to persuade them to allow that I should visit them and take their word that they would not make me any insult, neither whilst with them nor along the route there, for which this chief stood security. The English accepted the proposition.

"I made them a visit with one of the French, who carried the present that I had sent to make them, in the manner of the savages, and who received it on their part for me, according to custom. We traded nothing in that interview regarding our business because I remembered that the English attributed directly that which had been done against them to the savages. All the advantage that I received in that step was of making a trade for the savages, my friends, of guns which I wanted, although they cost me dear by the gratuity which I was obliged to make to those who I employed there. But it was important that I had in fact hindered the savages from it who came down from the country to trade, of passing on as far as the English. The end of that invitation and that visit was that I promised to the solicitation of the governor of the English of visiting there once again with my chief.

"After which, we retired to our house, where I was informed by some discontented savages not to go any more to see the English because they had resolved either to arrest me prisoner or of killing me. Which my chief having also learned, he told me that he wished no more to be security with his word with a nation who had none of it, which obliged us to remain at home, keeping up a very strict guard.

"At the same time, the River Hayes having become free, several detachments of the nations who were our allies arrived to assist us. The Asenipoetes[3] alone made more than 400 men. They were the descendants of the great Christinos of the old acquaintance of my uncle, and all ready to make war with the English. But I did not find it desirable to interest them in it directly nor indirectly because I did not wish to be held on the defensive in awaiting the return of my father or of my uncle, and besides, I knew that several other nations loved the French—more particu-

227

larly, those who would come to our relief at the least signal. In the meantime, the chief of the Asenipoetes did not wish us to leave his camp around our house, resolved to await up to the last moment the return of my uncle, of which he always spoke, making himself break forth with the joy that he would have in seeing him by a thousand postures, and he often repeated that he wished to make it appear that he had been worthy of the presents that the governor of Canada had made to him formerly in giving tokens of his zeal to serve the French.

"The necessity for stores which should arrive in their camp partly hindered the effects of that praiseworthy resolution and obliged the chief of the Asenipoetes to send back into his country 40 canoes, in which he embarked 200 men of the most feeble and of the least resolute. He kept with him a like number of them more robust and those who were able to endure fatigue and hunger, and determined having them to content themselves with certain small fruits, which commenced to ripen, for their subsistence, in order to await the new moon, in which the spirit of the other savages had predicted the arrival of my uncle, which they believed infallible because their superstitious custom is of giving faith to all which their Manitou predicts. They remained in that state until the end of the first quarter of the moon, during which their oracles had assured them that my uncle would arrive.

"But the time having expired, they believed their Manitou had deceived them, and it was determined between them to join themselves with us and of separating in 2 bodies, so as to go attack the English and the savages at the south; resolved, in case that the enterprise had the success that they expected, of passing the winter with us [in order] to burn the English ships, in order to remove the means of defending themselves in the spring and of effecting their return. That which contributed much to that deliberation was some information which was given to them that the English had formed a design of coming to seek the French to attack them, which they wished to prevent. These menaces on the part of the English were capable of producing bad effects, the genius of the savages being of never awaiting their enemies, but on the contrary of going to seek them. In this design the chief of the Asenipoetes disposed himself to march against the English with a party of his people. When 10 or 12 persons were seen on the northern side of the Hayes river seeking for these same fruits on which the savages had lived for some time, he believed that they were the advance guard of the English and of the savages from the south, whom he supposed united, who came to attack us, which obliged him to make all his men take their bows and arrows; after which he ranged them in order of battle and made his address in our presence: 'My design is to pass the river with 2 of the most courageous among you to go attack the enemy, and of disposing of you in a manner that you may be in a condition of relieving me or of receiving me, whilst the French will form the corps of reserve. Our women will load in our canoes all our effects, which they are to throw over in case necssity requires it. But before undertaking this expedition, I wish that you make choice of a chief to command you in my absence or in case of my death.' Which having been done at the moment, this brave chief addressing us said: 'We camp ourselves upon the edge of the wood with our guns, so as to hinder the approach of the enemy. And then it would be necessary to march the men upon the edge of the water, to the end that they should be in a condition to pass to support or to receive him, according to the necessity.'

"After that, he passes the river with 2 men of the most hardihood of his troops, who had greased themselves, like himself, from the feet up to the head. Having each only 2 poniards for arms, their design was to go right to the chief of the English, present to him a pipe of tobacco as a mark of union, and then, if he refused it, endeavor to kill him and make for themselves a passage through his people with their poniards as far as the place where they would be able to pass the river to be supported by their men. But after having marched as far as the place where the persons were who they had seen, they recognized that it was some women; to whom having spoken, they returned upon their steps and said to us that there was nothing to fear and that it was a false alarm. This general proceeding on their part gave us proofs of their courage and of their amity in a manner that the confidence that we had placed in their help had put us in a condition of fearing nothing on the part of the English nor or those there of the savages of the south.

"We were in that state when God, Who is the Author of all things and Who disposes of them according to His good pleasure, gave me the grace of my uncle's arrival in this country to arrest the course of the disorders, who could come and work for our reconciliation. That work so much desired on both sides is accomplished. It depends not upon me that it may not be permanent. Live henceforth like brothers, in good union and without jealousy. As to myself, I am resolved, if the time should arrive, of sacrificing my life for the glory of the King of Great Britain, for the interest of the nation, and the advantage of the Hudson's Bay Company, and of obeying in all things my uncle."

I found this with regard to repeating the recital that my nephew made us, concerning what had passed between him and the English and the savages, their allies: that although he had appraised me of the true state in which the 2 parties were at the time of my arrival, yet I also saw plainly the need that the English had of being succored and the neccessity that the French had for provisions, of merchandise, and especially of guns, which could not come to them but by my means.

But it is time to resume the care of affairs and to continue to render an account of our conduct. Our people worked always with great application to transport the beaver skins a half-league across the wood, for it was the road that it was necessary to make from the house as far as the place where the shallops were, and they carried them to the little frigate, which discharged them upon the ships. I was always present at the work for the purpose of animating all our men, who gave themselves in this work no rest until it was done, and that against the experience of the captains of our ships, whom some had made believe that the business would drag at length; but having gone to them, I assured them that if they were ready to do so they could raise the anchor tomorrow.

These things thus disposed of, it only disturbed me yet more to execute a secret order that the Company had given me, leaving it, however, to my prudence and discretion. It was of retaining in its service my nephew and some other Frenchmen, and above all the one who spoke the savage dialect, who was the wounded one, to remain in the country in my absence, which I dared not promise myself. In the meantime, I resolved to make the proposition to my nephew, believing that after gaining him I should be able easily to add the others also. I caused to assemble for that end 5 or 6 of the savages of the most consideration in the country, with the [English] governor, and in their presence I said to him [the nephew] that for the glory of the King and for the advantage of the Company it was necessary that he should remain in the country. To which he was averse at first, but the governor having

230

assured him that he would trust him as his own nephew and that he would divide the authority that he had with him, and myself on my part having reproached him that he was not loyal to the oath of allegiance that he had sworn to me, these reasons obliged him to determine, and he assured me that he was ready to do all that I wished of him. What contributed much was the discourse that the savages made to him, telling him that I left him amongst them to receive in my absence the marks of amity that they had sworn to me and that they regarded him as the nephew of the one who had brought peace to the nations and made the union of the English and French in making by the same means the brothers of both.

This last success in my affairs was proof to me of the authority that I had over the French and the savages, for my nephew had no sooner declared that he submitted himself to do what I wished than all the other Frenchmen offered themselves to risk the ennui of remaining in the country, although my design was only to leave but two of them, and the savages on their part burst out in cries of joy in such a manner that I no more considered after that but to put an end of all things.

All our beaver skins having been embarked, I resolved, after having put everything into tranquil and assured state for my return into England, where my presence was absolutely necessary, to make known to the Company in what manner it was necessary to act to profit advantageously the solid establishment that I came to do, and the things which were of indispensible necessity in the country to facilitate the trade with the savages and hindering them from making any of it with foreigners, that is to say, with the French of Canada.

I was then for the last time with my nephew at the house of our Frenchmen, to the end of leaving there some Englishmen. I found there a number of savages arrived to visit me, who called my nephew and myself into one of their cabins, where a venerable old man spoke to me in these terms: "Porcupine's Head, thy heart is good and thou has great courage, having made peace with the English for the love of us. Behold, we have come towards thee, old and young, wives and daughters and little children, to thank thee for it and to recognize thee for our father. We wish to be thy children and adopt for our son thy nephew that thou lovest so much, and in fine to give thee an eternal mark of the obligation that we have to thee. We weep no more henceforth, except for the memory of those of whom thou bearest the name." After which, having told one of the young people to speak, he fell like as if in a swoon, and the other spoke after that same manner: "Men and women, young men and children, even those who are at the breast, remember this one here for your father. He is better than the sun who warms you. You will find always in him a protector who will help you in your needs and console you in your afflictions. Men, remember that he gave you guns during the course of the year for you to defend yourselves against your enemies and to kill the beasts who nourish you and your families. Wives, consider that he gave you hatchets and knives with which you banish hunger from your country. Daughters and children, fear nothing more, since the one who is your father loves you always, and [remember] that he gave you from time to time all that is necessary for you to have your subsistance. We all together weep no more; on the contrary, give evidence by cries of our mirth that we have beheld the man of courage." And at the same time they set themselves to cry with all their might, weeping bitterly for the last time, in saying, "We have lost our father.* We have lost our children."**

After that pitiful music they all came to be acknowledged — to be acknowledged by our adoption with some presents — and covering us with robes of white beaver skins, giving us quantities of beavers' tails, some bladders of stag's marrow, several tongues of the same animal smoked, that which is the most exquisite to eat among them. They also presented us two great copper boilers full of smoked and boiled flesh, of which we ate all together — they, the English, and ourselves — and it is what is called a feast among these nations.

After that I said adieu to them, and having given charge in the house what should be embarked in the ship, I went down to the mouth of the river, where Captain Gazer worked to build a fort in the same place where the preceding year Sieur Bridgar had made to be constructed his shallop. It was the most advantageous situation that he had been able to find, and I advised that he should make all the diligence possible, but he had some

---

*"But here is one that you adopted for your father." [Note by Radisson; apparently this is what he said to the Indians.]

**"Here is the nephew of your father, who will be your son. He remains with you and he will have care of his mothers." [Note by Radisson.]

men who by their delicacy were incapable of responding to his vigilance. I made this observation because I hold it for a maxim that one should only employ men robust, skillful, and capable of serving, and that those who are of a complexion feeble, or who flatter themselves of having protection and favor, ought to be dismissed.

Then we passed to the place where the ships were, because my design was to oblige by my presence the captains to return to their ships, ready to make sail. But I was no sooner arrived there than a savage came to inform me that my adopted father, whom I had not seen because that he was at the wars, waited for me at the place where Captain Gazer was building the fort of which I came to speak. That is why I resolved to go there, and I expressed the same hope to the savage, whom I sent back to give information to my father that the governor would come with me to make some friendship to him and protect him in my absence. It was with the consent of the governor and upon his parole that I had told him that; nevertheless, he did not wish to come, and I was for the first time found a liar among the savages, which is of a dangerous consequence, for these nations have in abomination this vice. He came to me, however, in no wise angry in that interview, and I received not even a reproach from him.

When I was at the rendezvous they told me that my adopted father was gone away from it because I had annoyed a savage, for he had been informed that I had arrived to see him. This savage, having remembered the obligation to return (although very sad on account of some news that he had learned upon the road, which was that the chief of the nation who inhabited the height above the River Neosaverne, named The Bearded, and one of his sons, who were of his relations, had been killed in going to insult those among the savages who were set to the duty of taking care of the Frenchman who had been wounded by a savage gained over by the English), after he had embraced me and he had informed me of the circumstance of that affair, and the number of people he had as followers, I wrote to the governor to come to me in the place where we were, to make him know in effect that he must after my departure prevent the continuation of these disorders, in virtue of the treaty of peace and of union that I had made in presence of the savages between the French and the English.

The governor having arrived, I presented to him my adopted

father and said to him that, as it was the chief who commanded the nation that inhabited in the place where they built the fort, I had made him some little presents by Captain Gazer and that it was also desirable that he make some to him, because I had promised some the preceding year that I had not given. Which the governor found very bad, and he became irritated even against this chief without any cause for it, except that it might be because he was my adopted father, and I have learned since that he was angry that when I had arrived I had not given any present to a simple savage who served as a spy, who was the son of that chief called The Bearded. That was a horrible extravagance, for this governor was inferior to me, and I was not under any obligation to recognize his favor; besides, I had never made any presents but to the chiefs of the nations. Moreover, it was not for our governor to censure my conduct; I had received some independent orders, which had been given me on account of the outrage that he had committed; but, acting for the service of my King and for those of the Company, I passed it over in silence. I saw that it would be imprudent if I should speak my sentiments openly to a man who after my departure should command all those who remained in the country.* I contented myself then with letting him know the inconveniences which would happen from the indifference that he affected to have for the chief of the savage nations, and I exhorted him also to change at once his policy in regard to my adopted father; not by that consideration, but because that he was, as I said to him, the chief of the nations which inhabited the place where they built the fort, which he promised me of undoing. After that I went on board our ship.

My nephew, who remained in the fort with the governor, having learned that the ships were ready to leave, kept himself near me, with the French whom I had resolved to leave in Canada, to say adieu to me, and it was in the company of this governor that they made the journey, during which, as I have since learned from my nephew, he showed to them more good will than he had yet done, assuring them that they should never want anything and, in consideration of me, they would receive the same treatment as myself. The behavior that my nephew and the other Frenchmen had shown gave no reason for doubting the sincerty of their pro-

---

*That would have perhaps drawn upon him some contempt. [Note by Radisson.]

234

testations. They no longer believed that anyone could have any mistrust of them. My nephew and his interpreter had been solicited to remain in the country to serve the Company, and they had consented to it without a murmur because I had charged myself with the care of their interests in England. All that passed in the presence and by the persuasions of the governor.

Nevertheless, behold a surprising change which came to pass by the inconstancy, the caprice, and the wicked behavior of this same governor. I disposed myself to part with the other Frenchmen, when the governor, having come aboard of the little frigate, caused a signal to be made to hold a council of war. Upon this the captains of the ships and myself rendered ourselves on board, where my nephew followed us, remaining upon the poop, whilst the officers and myself were in the room where this governor demanded of us, at first, if we had any valid reasons why he should not send back in the ships all the Frenchmen who were in the country.

To all which the others having said nothing, I was obliged to speak in these terms: "At my departure from England I received a verbal order from the Company, in particular from Sir James Hayes, to leave in the country where we are as many of Frenchmen as I should find desirable for the good and advantage of the Company. I have upon that resolved to engage my nephew and his interpreter to remain in it, and I have come for that end, by my attendance, for the consent of the governor, who demands today that they may be sent back as people who apparently are known to him as suspected. I have always believed, and I believe it still, that their presence is useful in this country and also necessary to the Company, and it was difficult to be able to overlook [these] two, because they are known to all the nations. It is also upon them that I have relied for the security of the merchandises which are left behind at the houses of the French, because without their assistance or their presence they would be exposed to pillage. Nevertheless, I do not pretend to oppose myself to the design that the governor has put in execution and the proposition that he proposes making. He is free to undo what he pleases, but he cannot make me subscribe to his resolutions because I see that they are directly opposed to those of the Company, to my instructions, and to my experience. On the contrary, I will protest before God and before men against all that he does because, after what he has said to you, he is incapable of doing what is advantageous for his masters. It is in vain that one should give him good counsels (for he has not the spirit to understand them) that he may again deal a blow to which he would wish I opposed nothing."

This declaration had without doubt made some impression upon a spirit not anticipated in an imaginary capacity of governor; but this one here, on the contrary, fortified himself in his resolution and begged me to tell the French to embark themselves, without considering that my nephew had not time enough to go seek his clothes nor several bonds that were due to him in Canada, which remained in the house of the French and that I had abandoned to him to yield whatever I was in a condition of giving satisfaction to him, and that in the hope that the Company would set up for him the way exclusively.

The council after that broke up. But the governor, apprehending that the Frenchmen would not obey, wished to give an order to the captains to seize upon them and put them on board. He had even the insolence of putting me first on the lists (as if I was suspected or guilty of something), for which Captain Bond, having perceived, said to him that he should not make a charge of that kind, as I must be excepted from it because he remembered nothing in me but much of attachment for the service of his masters and that they should take care of the establishment that we had made and of the advantages that would accrue to the Company. They obliged the governor to make another list, and thus finished the council of war held against the interests of those who had given power to assemble them.

The persons who had any knowlege of these savages of the North would be able to judge of the prejudice which the conduct of this imprudent governor would, without contradiction, have caused the Company. Many would attribute his proceeding to his little experience or to some particular hatred that he had conceived against the French. Be it as it may, I was not of his way of thinking, and I believed that his timidity and want of courage had prompted him to do all that he had done, by the apprehension that he had of the French undertaking something against him, and what confirmed me in that thought was the precaution that he had taken for preventing the French from speaking to any person since the day of the council, for he put them away from the moment that he went away from them. I made out also that he had wanted but the the occasion of putting to the sword my nephew if he had had the least pretext.

But, knowing his wicked designs, I made him understand, as well as the other Frenchmen, that we were to go to England and that he must not leave the ship because we were at any moment ready to depart. Although this change surprised my nephew and his interpreter, nevertheless they appeared not discontented with it, especially when I had assured them, as well as the other Frenchmen, that they would receive all kinds of good treatment in England and that it would do them no harm in their persons nor in their pretensions.

I left them then in the ship, and having embarked myself in the frigate, we were put ashore two leagues from the place where they were at anchor, to take on board some goods that remained on the shore, with more diligence than we had been able to make with the ships; which having succeeded in happily doing, we went to rejoin the ships at the place where they were at anchor, in one of which my nephew and the other Frenchmen were staying during this time without having taken the least step, although they were in a condition for any enterprise because they could easily render themselves masters of the two ships and burn them, having there for both but two men and one boy in each; after which they could also, without danger, go on shore on the south side with the canoes of the savages, who were from the North, and then make themselves masters of their houses and their merchandise, which were guarded but by two men. But to go there to them, he [would have] made doubts of all that I had told him, and it would be ill-intentioned to the service of the Company, as it was to the governor. That is why they were not capable, neither those nor the others, after having submitted themselves and and having taken the oath of fidelity as they had done.

At length, after having suffered in my honor and in my probity many things on the part of the governor, and much fatigue and indisposition of trouble and of care in my person, to come to the end of my design, having happily succeeded, and all that was to be embarked in the ships being on board, we made sail the 4th day of September, 1684, and we arrived at the Downs, [England,] without anything passing worth mentioning, the 23rd of October of the same year.

The impatience that I had of informing the gentlemen of the Hudson's Bay Company of the happy success of my voyage and our return, and that I had acquitted myself for the service of the King and their own interest in all the engagements into which I had entered, obliged me to mount a horse the same day, to present myself in London, where I arrived at midnight. All [of] which did not hinder me, so the Sieur Ecuyer Young was informed, who was one of those interested, who having come to me on the morrow morning to take me, did me the honor to present me to His Majesty and to His Royal Highness, to whom I rendered an account of all which had been done, and I had the consolation of receiving some marks of the satisfaction of these great princes, who in token gave order to the Sieur Ecuyer Young to tell the Company to have care of my interests and to remember my services.

Some days after, I went before the committee of the Hudson's Bay Company to render to it an account of my conduct, hoping to receive their approbation of my proceeding as the first fruits of the just satisfaction and recompence which was my due. But in place of that I found the members of the committee for the most part offended because I had had the honor of making my reverence to the King and to His Royal Highness, and these same persons continued even their bad intention to injure me, and under pretext of refusing me the justice which is due to me, they oppose themselves also to the solid and useful resolutions that are necessary for the glory of His Majesty and the advantage of the nation and their own interest.

FINIS

A THEORY[1]

As STATED in the Foreword, a journey was made by two un-named Frenchmen during the years 1654-56, and many writers believe that this journey was the Mississippi voyage of Radisson and Groseilliers. After critically analyzing Radisson's narrative and carefully studying the conclusions of these scholars, the writer ventures to formulate a theory which, if correct, goes far toward the solution of the many problems that have developed since the original publication of his chronicle. This theory may be stated as follows:

> Radisson and Groseilliers made both the Unwritten and Mississippi voyages, and Radisson's narrative of the Mississippi voyage is a *composite* record of the two.

Before proceeding to offer evidence in support of this theory it will be well to lay a foundation to determine the possiblity and plausibility of this proposition. It must first be understood that these two journeys were of the same duration and covered virtu-ally the same territory. It should also be known that the journeys were separated by a period of four years and that the narrative of the second journey was written ten years later. We are now prepared to consider a hypothetical case which will very likely prove to have been an experience of every reader:

> SUPPOSE that some years ago a vacation was spent in visiting a distant region. A few years later a similar journey was made to the same locality for a similar pur-pose. Now, after the lapse of say ten years, an attempt is made to write a detailed account of the later trip.

Is it not probable that incidents experienced during the first journey will unavoidably and unconsciously creep into the narra-tive of the second? This proposition and question have been put to numerous persons who have given invariably affirmative answers.

Not only this, but the earlier incidents will appear as having occurred during the second trip and the narrative will seem to be that of a single journey. The account will thus be composite in character. It is upon the truth of this assumption that the theory above stated is predicated. We shall now consider some of the evidences that appear to sustain this view.

1. *No inconsistent record.*

The first point to be noted is negative in character. There is no record, so far as known, either in Radisson's writings or elsewhere, in conflict with this theory. In regard to Radisson, his own journal is completely blank as to the years 1654 to 1657, while his name is not mentioned in the *Jesuit Relations* or *Jesuit Journal*. As to Groseilliers, a few items of record are found for the year 1657, but for the years 1654 to 1656 his doings and whereabouts are as completely eclipsed as are those of Radisson. As a matter of record, therefore, it is entirely possible that these two Frenchmen could have made the journey of 1654-56.

It is pertinent now to ask: where were they and what were they doing during this blank period of two years? It is reasonable to infer that they were not idle. Their later lives and activities prove that they were men of great energy, hardihood, and ambition. They were interested in the fur trade, and Groseilliers had already visited the Ottawa country; hence their interests would naturally direct them toward the North and West. Since Radisson himself records that their first journey to the North (Hudson Bay) was during the Superior voyage of 1661-63, it seems probable that these two years were spent in exploration in the West.

2. *Relation of 1656.*

The first positive evidence bearing on the mooted subject is found in the *Jesuit Relations* for the year 1656.[2] Here we find a more or less detailed account of a two years' journey to the West made by the two Frenchmen whose names are not stated. This record of the Jesuits, the reliability of which is not questioned, has so much in common with Radisson's narrative of the Mississippi voyage that many authors are fully convinced that the two accounts refer to one and the same journey and that the two unnamed Frenchmen of the *Jesuit Relations* are no other than Radisson and Groseilliers. The resemblance is particularly striking in the accounts of the departure for the West. This may be shown by the following parallel:

240

Departure

Jesuit Relations	Mississippi Voyage
1. Left August 6, 1654.	1. "About the middle of June . . . at last."
2. Two young Frenchmen.	
3. Full of courage.	2. Radisson and Groseilliers (aged 18 and 34 yrs.).
4. Permission of the governor.	
5. Embark with people who came down to the French settlements.	3. "Finish that voyage or die by the way."
	4. "Resolution of the governor."
6. 500 leagues' journey.	5. Embark with Hurons and Ottawas.
7. Gondolas of bark.	
8. Expected to return 1655.	6. As far as the Mississippi river.
	7. Indian canoes.
	8. Expected to return the next year.

The incidents recorded in the two accounts relative to the return of the voyageurs are also remarkably similar, as indicated in the parallel following:

Return

Jesuit Relations	Mississippi Voyage
1. Toward the end of August.	1. At end of two years (August 22nd?).
2. Universal joy.	
3. Accompanied by 50 canoes of goods.	2. Montreal overjoyed.
	3. Great Store of castors' skins.
4. French came to this end of the world for furs in ships.	4. Three F r e n c h ships at anchor.
5. Fleet rode in state on our mighty river.	5. Well treated five days in Quebec.
6. Noise of cannon.	6. Saluted with thundering of guns and batteries.
7. Built their t e m p o r a r y dwellings.	7. Indians pitched their tents.
8. Salute governor, speeches, two presents.	8. Governor made gifts.

The Jesuit writer seeks to "learn some news from the two French pilgrims and their hosts," and Radisson's account in the Mississippi narrative affords the information obtained as shown below:

Body of the Narrative

Jesuit Relations	Mississippi Voyage
1. Great territorial extent of Indian languages.	1. Learned of neighboring nations — Southern and hunting journeys.
2. Great fresh water l a k e , large as Caspean Sea.	2. Lake Superior.
3. Names of Indian nations: W i n n e b a g o e s, Illinois Sioux, Crees.	3. Winnebagoes, Potawatomies, C r e e s , Mascoutens, Sioux.
4. Baptized Indian children.	4. Groseilliers baptized children at Prairie island.

3. *Relation of 1658.*

In the *Relation* of 1658 the Jesuit writer obtained his information about the West chiefly from Father Druillettes, but "partly from two Frenchmen who have made their way far inland" and "who say that these people [Indians west of Lake Michigan] are of a very gentle disposition."[3] These two Frenchmen are regarded by high authority as Radisson and Groseilliers. If so, the reference must be to a journey prior to the Mississippi voyage of 1658-60, and therefore to the Unwritten voyaage of 1654-56.

4. *Relation of 1660.*

In the *Relation* for August, 1660, reference is again made to two Frenchmen "who had but just arrived from these upper countries with three hundred Algonquins, in sixty canoes loaded with furs."[4] It is quite certain that the two Frenchmen referred to here are Radisson and Groseilliers, since an entry in the *Jesuit Journal* of the same date mentions the name of Groseilliers twice. It states that he was in the company of the three hundred Ottawas that had just returned from the West on August 19th, and also states that "des Groseillers wintered with the nation of the ox [Sioux]."[5]

The important point to be noted here is that the *Relation* of 1660 refers to the voyage of 1658-60. It states that "they passed the winter on the shores of Lake Superior."[6] By referring to the text of the Mississippi voyage it will be seen that prior to their fifty league snowshoe trek to the riverside in the early spring, they were among the Saulteurs, whose habitat at that time was on the south side of Lake Superior in upper Michigan or Wisconsin.[7] The latterly mentioned *Relation* also states that "they saw six days' journey beyond the lake toward the Southwest, a tribe composed of the Hurons of the Tobacco Nation, who . . . fortunately encountered a beautiful River, large, wide, deep, and worthy of comparison, they say, with our great river St. Lawrence." By comparing these words with the text of Radisson's narration from the beginning of the snowshoe journey (six days' journey of the *Relation)* to the landing isle paragraph,[8] it will be difficult to escape the conclusion that "the riverside" of Radisson and the "beautiful river" of the *Relation* are identical and that this *Relation* refers to the Mississippi voyage which ended in 1660.

Since the *Relations* of 1656 and 1658 necessarily refer to the earlier, or Unwritten, voyage and the *Relation* of 1660 certainly refers to the Mississippi voyage, it follows that all three of these Jesuit accounts, considered collectively, afford strong evidence that Radisson's account of the Mississippi voyage is, in reality, a composite narrative describing both that and the Unwritten voyage.

5. *Battle of August 30th, 1656.*

The closing sentences of the Mississippi narrative, describing the return to Quebec, have been shown to correspond closely with an account of the Unwritten voyage in the *Jesuit Relation* of 1656. Immediately following the description of their return, Radisson continues his narrative with an account of a battle between the Iroquois on one side and the French and returning Ottawas and other Western Indians on the other.[9] It will now be shown that this battle was the same as that described in the *Jesuit Relation* as occurring on August 30th, 1656,[10] and therefore that this part of Radisson's narrative refers to the Unwritten voyage.

As to the details recorded in the two accounts, there is little in common, owing chiefly to the unusual ambiguity of Radisson's language in this part of his record. There are three essentials, however, which, if found to be in accord, will tend to prove the identity of the two records. These essentials are: time, place, and combatants.

a. Time.

The date of the battle of the Jesuit account is definitely stated as August 30th, 1656. The only clue we have in Radisson's narrative to the date of the battle he describes is the inference that it occurred eight days after their arrival at Quebec. He says they were well treated for five days at Quebec. They were then taken to Three Rivers in brigantines, and arrived there the second day.

243

The next day the battle was fought; thus making eight days after their return to Quebec. It is stated in the *Relation* that the two Frenchmen returned "toward the end of August." Now if the battle of Radisson's acount is the same as that of the Jesuit's, it occurred on August 30th. Their arrival at Quebec, then, would have been eight days before, or August 22nd, which would reasonably accord with the Jesuit's "toward the end of August." Thus we see that the time (month and day) of the battle in each of the accounts is virtually the same. While this is not definite proof, the probability is strong that the two accounts refer to one and the same battle.

b. Place.

The place of the battle, according to the *Jesuit Relation,* seems to be in the St. Lawrence river just above the town of Three Rivers. By reading this chapter closely, it will be noticed that the phrase "the great river" is used three times. The first use of it necessarily refers to the St. Lawrence, since, quoting from the *Relation,* "scarcely had this Fleet of more than sixty Vessels accomplished one day's voyage on the great river when it met two French souldiers in a Canoe, who had been sent by the Governor of Three Rivers to give warning. . . . Our men . . . passed swiftly in the darkness without being seen, and arrived safe and sound at the Village of Three Rivers."[11] Their journey thus far was between Quebec and Three Rivers, therefore on the St. Lawrence. The account then shows the French and Ottawas proceeding in canoes by night to elude the Iroquois, but the enemy succeeded in passing them on land and "went ahead and seized a very advantageous position on the great River, in the path of the Algonquins. . . . The Sentinels, posted very advantageously for commanding a long view of the great river, gave their Captain warning when the fleet appeared."[12] It was at this point where the battle occurred. It is reasonable to assume that the two later references to the great river mean the St. Lawrence as well as does the first, and thus it appears that the battle described by the Jesuit took place in the St. Lawrence between Three Rivers and Montreal.[13]

It now becomes necessary to locate the battle of Radisson's narrative. By turning to his text we read: "The governor made gifts and sent two brigantines to bring us to Three Rivers, where we arrived the second day, and the fourth day they went away . . . . So [the Iroquois] came the next day after our arrival to make a discovery [at] Three Rivers, where, being perceived, there is care taken to receive them." Following this quotation Radisson proceeds with the description of the battle. It appears that the battle was fought on the same day that the Iroquois came to Three Rivers "to make a discovery." It is evident that the battle could not have been far distant from Three Rivers, and doubtless was up the St. Lawrence toward Montreal. The conclusion is that the battle described by Radisson and that described by the Jesuit occurred at practically the same place and that it was one and the same battle.

While the time and place in each account appear to be substantially identical, the time of the battle as above shown refers only to the month and day with reference to Radisson's account. It is still possible that there were two battles separated by one or more years. This brings us to the consideration of the third essential phase of the two battle descriptions, namely, the combatants.

c. Combatants.

In all Indian battles of those times the Iroquois, of course, were on one side. In the battle recorded in each of the accounts under consideration it is important to understand clearly that the belligerents opposed to the Iroquois consisted mainly of the Western Indians who had recently come down to the French settlements with furs and *were now returning*. It must also be understood that the battle Radisson describes occurred either in the year 1656 or 1660. If we turn now to the *Jesuit Relation* for 1660 we find two brief notices of the *return* of the three hundred Ottawas who came down that year from the West. The first of these entries is here quoted:

"This year, one thousand six hundred and sixty, another fleet manned by the same Algonkins [as those of 1656], sixty canoes in number, having arrived, two of our Fathers again joined them, in order to leave no way untried. But one of them could not go beyond Montreal, owing to the whim of a Savage, who would not allow him in his canoe, while the other, Father Rene Menard, passed that place indeed, but we do not know whether some accident, similar to that which befell Father Gareau, has not overtaken him. For we have learned that a band of a hundred Onnontagueronnons was to lie in wait for them above Montreal, for the purpose of attacking them in some narrow pass, or else assaulting them in some rapids, where one has enough to do to contend with currents and rocks, without having other enemies on his hands. We know not what success the enterprise of the Iroquois may have had, but fear that they will strangle that poor Mission in its cradle, as they have done once already."[14]

After obtaining later news, the following account was entered in the *Relation:*

"The three hundred Outawaks who came this year to trade with us, and with whom Father Menard went back to their country to labor at their conversion, encountered a hundred Onnontagueronnons stationed below the great falls, but lost only three men, who, advancing too far ahead of the main body of the canoes, were captured by the Iroquois. All the rest, however, passed in safety, the Onnontagueronnon finding himself too weak to sustain a conflict."[15]

It is clear that the "encounter" here mentioned cannot refer to the battle of Radisson's narrative. There was no battle at all and, furthermore, the encounter took place in the Ottawa river above Montreal and not in the St. Lawrence above Three Rivers. Our conclusion is, that if the battle of Radisson's account is the same as that of the *Jesuit Relation,* it must have been the battle of August 30th, 1656. We are now to determine the identity of the combatants in Radisson's account and in that of the *Relation* of 1656.

The people fighting the Iroquois are, beyond any doubt, the same in both accounts; namely, the newly organized expedition of French and Algonquins (including the Hurons and Ottawas who have recently come down from the West with the two French explorers) who are just commencing their long *return* journey to the West, and whose advance it is the purpose of the Iroquois to intercept. This is perfectly clear in the Jesuit account. Radisson uses the following language, which evidently refers to the same group of people. "The enemy that had discovered us in our going down [from Montreal to Quebec] got more company, as many as they could, to come to the passages, and there to wait for the return of those people, knowing well that they could not stay there long because the season of the year was almost spent."[16]

The conclusion to be drawn from the consideration of these three essentials — time, place, and combatants — is that the accounts in Radisson's narrative and in the *Jesuit Relation* for 1656 refer to one and the same battle and, therefore, that this part of the Mississippi voyage has reference to the Unwritten journey of 1654-56, and thus tends to prove the compositeness of the Mississippi narrative.

It may be added here that, in view of Radisson's confusion in locating the Dollard massacre story in the wrong voyage, there is nothing inconsistent or unreasonable in assuming that he was similarly confused in misplacing the description of this battle.

It may be interesting to see how Radisson, at the end of his description of this battle of 1656, gets back in his narrative to the year 1660. The transition is abrupt, but the leap across four years is made so smoothly that it challenges detection.

Immediately following the battle description in this sentence: "They went away the next day, and we stayed at home at rest that year."[17] The first clause of this sentence, "They went away the next day," refers to the two brigantines (or possibly to the Iroquois or Western Indians) and closes the story of the battle which we have found occurred in 1656. The second clause, "we stayed at home at rest that year," must refer to the year 1660, when the Mississippi voyage came to an end. This fact is clearly shown in the opening sentences of the Superior voyage, which began in 1661.

Having compared the narrative of Radisson's Mississippi voyage with certain parts of the *Jesuit Relations,* we shall now pass to a consideration of some of the evidences of compositeness found in the context of Radisson's own writing.

6. *Three Years' Voyage.*

One of the inconsistencies which has made the interpretation of the Mississippi narrative difficult is Radisson's repeated assertions and implications that it continued three years. In one place he says: "In our voyage we proceeded three years."[18] In another, "This is the end of our three years' voyage and [a] few months."[19] After describing the Mascoutens he says: "In the last voyage that we made, I will let you only know what course we runned in three years' time."[20] Just before the snowshoe trek of fifty leagues we find: "Two years were expired."[21] A month or two later, upon the refusal of the Indians on the landing isle to return to Canada with them, Radisson says: "Our journey was broken till the next year, and must per force."[22] This sentence surely implies an added year to the two years already expired, thus making three years. This is corroborated by the next paragraph, which describes the sojourn on the landing isle, where they had arrived in early spring. Here we read: "The winter passes away in good correspondence one with another . . . which rejoiced them the more and made us pass that year with a greater pleasure."

247

From these quotations there seems to be little doubt that Radisson believed that the Mississippi voyage was of three years' duration. In view of historic facts and the context of his narrative, however, it is impossible for this voyage to be more than two years. How does he get the idea of three years? It appears that the solution to this puzzle is to be found in that short paragraph dealing with the sojourn on the landing isle.

When the hunting story is transferred to its proper place, immediately after this landing isle paragraph, it follows that the time spent at the landing isle by Groseilliers *must be coincident with* the time spent by Radisson on the hunting trip, and this, according to the narrative, was four months comprising the spring and early summer. What, then, does Radisson mean by the words "winter" and "that year" in this paragraph? It looks very much as if he thought they spent a year there, and in the light of this theory that is precisely what they did; since both context and historic facts make it impossible for them to spend a year there during the Mississippi voyage, the inference seems to be that this period of time was spent there during a previous journey.

The question may now be asked: if Radisson and Groseilliers made the Unwritten voyage, how did they spend the two years' time? In the Mississippi voyage the two years may be divided approximately as follows: seven months from Three Rivers to the Mascoutens, one year from the beginning of the Southern journey to the landing isle, four months or a little less at the landing isle, and a month or a little more returning to Three Rivers. We can only conjecture the divisions of time in the Unwritten voyage and the manner in which these divisions were occupied. We can be sure, however, that a definite part would be required to go out and to return, and this time may be fairly estimated as the greater part of one year. How and where did they spend the other year?

To this question we have Radisson's own answer in the landing isle paragraph. The passing of a "winter" and of a "year" there surely cannot be interpreted as a spring and a summer, and must imply a longer period than "four months." Since this period of one year on the landing isle could not be a part of the Mississippi voyage it must be referred to the previous or Unwritten voyage.

7. *Brevity of the Landing Isle Paragraph.*

A significant question arises here: why is the landing isle paragraph so brief? In the light of our theory the answer does not seem difficult. A casual reading of these two or three sentences will show this part of Radisson's narrative to be very ambiguous and inadequate, and at this point we may observe a distinct characteristic running through all of Radisson's writing; namely, descriptions of *journeys* from place to place are usually very meagre,[23] while *localities* are described with considerable fullness and frequently in much detail.[24] In ivew of this peculiarity it seems hardly probable that Radisson would dismiss in five or six lines the experiences and activities of both men at the landing isle during a period of more than one year.

This curious lapse is partially accounted for by the fact that the "annotations" made by Groseilliers on the earlier voyage were lost[25] and therefore not available to Radisson in writing his narrative of the Mississippi voyage. It may also be observed that if notes were made on the Mississippi voyage, as doubtless they were, they would be Groseilliers' notes. At least this would be true with respect to the sojourn on the landing isle, since Radisson was not there during that four months' period, but off on his hunting trip. The primary purpose of the notes would doubtless be to refresh the memory, but Radisson, not being a witness to the incidents and events noted by Groseilliers, would have no memory regarding the landing isle doings to refresh. These notes would therefore be of little aid to Radisson in writing his narrative of the Mississippi voyage, and hence the brevity and ambiguity of his account of the period spent at the landing isle.

The result of the observations made in this and in the preceding topic may be summarized as follows: Radisson knew the time occupied on the various divisions of the Mississippi voyage, i.e., he knew the duraton of the outward journey, the Southern journey, the hunting trip, and the return journey. These aggregated two years, but in writing his narrative he apparently recalls, as a part of this journey, the one year spent on the landing isle during the earlier or Unwritten voyage. Hence this one year, added to the necessary two years for the Mississippi voyage, gives a total of three years, as it appears to him, and he so records it.

8. *Was the Landing Isle their Destination?*

The evidence seems to be almost conclusive that the voyageurs had visited the first landing isle on a previous occasion and that it was their destination on this voyage. In his narrative of the Southern journey Radisson states: "We had not as yet seen the nation Nadoueceronons. We had Hurons with us; we persuaded them to come along to see their own nation that fled there."[26] It is definitely known that some of the Hurons and Ottawas who were driven from their homes in the East by the Iroquois fled as far west as the Mississippi river and, for a few years, occupied Prairie island between Red Wing and Hastings.[27] In view of this well authenticated fact, the conclusion can hardly be avoided that the above quotation refers to Prairie island and that the voyageurs were on their way to visit that place, and the inference seems equally clear that they had been there before.

Again, upon their reaching the "riverside" at the end of their long snowshoe journey, Radisson says they "made feasts at a high rate," and they refreshed themselves from their labors. When they saw buds begin to spring they made more haste to be gone, and on going up the river eight days they obtained corn and meal, which lasted them till they came to the first landing isle.[28] Why the feasts at a high rate? Why the rest from their labors? Apparently they had reached a well known landmark on their journey — a highway that gave them reason to rejoice and celebrate. Upon noticing the approach of spring, why did they make haste to be gone? Since they expected to return to Canada that summer, they must have known where they were going and that to accomplish their ends they must hurry along. When they had canoed up the river eight days they procured corn and meal. How much? Enough and only enough to last till they reached their destination. They must have known the approximate distance yet to be traveled.

When they arrived at the landing isle we read: "There we were well received again." The word "again" might suggest that this was only another instance of being well received, which seemed to be their experience everywhere. In view of all the other evidence, however, the alternative meaning that it was another visit to the same place seems to be more probable.

Radisson also states that the Indians they found on the landing isle "made no great harvest, being but newly there." It is sufficiently clear that these Indians were refugee Hurons and Ottawas who had fled from the Iroquois at the time of their great dispersion in 1649.[29] The sentence here quoted indicates that they had not been there long. Our question now is: to which voyage does this statement refer, the Unwritten or Mississippi voyage? If to the Unwritten voyage, the explorers arrived here in the spring of

250

1655, but if it refers to the Mississippi voyage they arrived in the spring of 1660. What length of time would be required for these fleeing fugitives to reach the Mississippi river? They would apparently have time to reach Prairie island and yet be "newly" there in 1655, but if the reference be to the Mississippi voyage and their arrival were in 1660 it would hardly be said that these fugitives were newly there ten or eleven years after their flight. It appears then, that this statement has reference to the earlier or Unwritten voyage.

9. *Three Year Gap in the Onondaga Voyage*

If the theory be accepted that the Mississippi voyage is a composite narrative of the two journeys, 1654-56 and 1658-60, some light may be thrown upon the peculiar manner in which Radisson passes, in his record, from the Captivity to the Onondaga voyage.

The reader is here directed to turn to the last paragraph of the Captivity voyage and the first of the Onondage voyage and observe a very curious fact. Note this passage: "In my absence, peace was made between the French and the Iroquois, which was the reason I stayed not long in a place. The year before, the French began a new plantation in the upper country of the Iroquois."[30] Between these two sentences Radisson leaps across a period of three years. In the first sentence the word "peace" must refer to the peace of November, 1653,[31] since his absence extended from May, 1652, to May, 1654. In the second sentence the world "plantation" must refer to the Jesuit mission which was founded among the Onondagas in July, 1656.[32] Since it is well known that the Onondaga voyage began in 1657 the words "the year before" must refer to the year 1656. The most curious feature about this is that Radisson passes over this three year period in his narrative without noticing, apparently, this outstanding error. In the original manuscript, Radisson put what in this volume is the last paragraph of the Captivity voyage at the beginning of the Onondaga. The sentence commencing "The year before" is, in reality, the beginning of the Onondaga voyage (and has been so made). In other words, the pause between these two sentences is truly the division point between the Captivity and Onondaga voyages, and a period of three years intervenes between them.

Turning now to the beginning of the Mississippi voyage, we find this expression: "So my brother seeing me back from those two dangerous voyages . . . he thought I was fitter and more faithful for the discovery that he was to make."[33] Why does Radisson connect these two voyages among the Iroquois without recognizing or intimating the fact that they were separated by three years, and knowing also that during two of those years he and his brother-in-law were so intimately associated in the West? It seems plain that Radisson looks upon these two Iroquois voyages as occurring in sequence, and the manner of passing, in the narrative, from the Captivity to the Onondage voyage seems to support this view. A cause for this anomaly may be suggested.

Keep in mind that Radisson wrote the narrative of his early voyages some ten to fifteen years after the Unwritten and Mississippi voyages took place,[34] and that the notes made while on the former voyage had been lost. Owing to his lapse of time, the loss of the notes, the remarkable similarity of the two voyages, and the continued and constant activity of Radisson's mind in other absorbing enterprises, it may be conjectured that in his memory the Unwritten voyage virtually became absorbed or merged in the Mississippi voyage, thus completely dropping out of his mind. The two voyages became one to him, and that one was the Mississippi voyage of 1658-60. This disappearance of the Unwritten voyage naturally removed the connecting link and closes the gap of three years between the two Iroquois voyages, and thus, after many years, they are recalled and recorded as taking place in close succession.

Conversely, the original manner of transition from the Captivity to the Onondaga voyage is evidence of his lapse of memory as to the intervening years, and that the events of that period, insofar as they were subconsciously recalled, were associated with similar events and experiences occurring during their voyage of four years later.

10. *Loss of Annotations.*

Another evidence of the composite character of the Mississippi voyage is found near the end of that narrative, where Radisson describes their passage through the Long Sault in the Ottawa on their return home. In the swift current Groseilliers' boat overturns and he loses his notebook. This incident is described in the following significant sentence: "My brother lost his book of annotations of the last year of our being in these foreign nations."[35] Our problem here is to interpret the words "the last year."

If we are to assume that the Mississippi voyage was the first

Western voyage, it is difficult to understand the meaning of these words. It would seem that the word "year" refers to the entire voyage rather than literally to a twelve-month, since it is hardly probable, under the circumstances, that a notebook would be made up in parts or divisions according to the calendar. With this interpretation of the word "year," the word "last" would not likely be used to denote the present voyage, which was still in progress at the time the notes were lost. If the words "last year" refer to the present voyage, one might inquire how this voyage could have been written up ten years later. Radisson must have had notes on this voyage in order to write his narrative as well (or poorly) as he did; hence those notes were not lost. The lost notes must have been made on the previous voyage and the fact that it was not written up is largely explained by the loss of the notes.

It is implied that two notebooks were made, one on each voyage, and the lost notes were taken along on the second journey for the purpose of guidance. During Groseilliers' apprenticeship to the Jesuit Fathers among the Hurons, he doubtless observed their practice of making notes which were later used in compiling their *Journal* and the *Relations*. It is indeed probable that he acquired the habit of making personal notes, and continued this useful practice on their Western voyages.

11. *Sickness Due to Idleness.*

An interesting evidence of the compositeness of the Mississippi voyage is shown in Radisson's two references to sickness due to idleness. On passing from Manitoulin island into the Lake of "the Staring Hairs" he says: "The season began to invite the lustiest to hunting. We neither desire to be idle in any place, having learned by experience that idleness is the mother of all evil, for it breeds most part of all sickness in those parts where the air is the most delightful."[36] Where and when did they experience this idleness and the resulting sickness? Surely not during the Captivity and Onondaga voyages among the Iroquois, when Radisson and Groseilliers were not associated. Nor has there been any indivation of sickness or idleness on this Mississippi voyage, up to this point in their journey. The plain assertion of this experience points to some other and previous voyage. If now we turn to the landing isle paragraph, we find a significant expression alluding to idleness and sickness. Radisson says they passed "that year with greater pleasure, saving that my brother fell into the falling sickness, and many were sorry for it. That [the sickness] proceeded only by a long stay in a new discovered country, and the idleness contributes much to it."[37]

While this particular attack of epilepsy on Groseilliers appears to have occurred during the Mississippi voyage, Radisson's comment indicates a long period of idleness, which does not square with the probable conditions and activities there during the sojourn of four months. While Radisson was off on his hunting trip, Groseilliers could hardy have been idle, in view of his successful efforts in putting up corn and gathering other necessary food and equipment for the return journey to Canada when Radisson came back. Not the least of Groseilliers' activities was his conversion of several hundred Indians from a positive refusal to a desire to go to Canada that summer. It is also probable that he spent much time and effort in converting the Indians to Christianity and in baptizing the children. It seems evident, therefore, that his sickness on this occasion did not proceed from prolonged idleness, and the "long stay in a new discovered country" must refer to a previous voyage.

This conclusion is entirely consistent, since the intermittent and constantly recurring character of epilepsy is well known, and Groseilliers no doubt suffered from this malady on both voyages, in fact during all his life.

12. *Allusions to Other Voyages.*

It may be suggested that if Radisson and Groseilliers made the Unwritten voyage there would be frequent references to it in the narrative of the Mississippi voyage. This seems very plausible, but if this narrative is composite, as here contended, specific reference to incidents occurring on the previous journey could hardly be expected, since such incidents would be regarded as parts of, and as merged into, the present voyage and would so appear in the narrative.

There are, however, definite allusions to other voyages, and apparentley they do not refer to the present one. For example, after describing the Mascoutens, Radisson says: "In the last voyage that we made, I will let you only know what course we runned in three years' time."[38] This expression seems to be wholly parenthetical. It surely cannot refer to the present or Mississippi voyage, and likewise it cannot allude to the Superior voyage, since Radisson states elsewhere that that voyage was "less than two years."[39]

It is hard to determine the meaning of this statement, although some previous journey seems to be implied.

Again, at the end of the Southern journey, he says: "I will speak of their manners in my last voyage which I made."[40] This also appears to be parenthetical and might be omitted. This allusion to some other voyage is the only connecting link in the narrative between their presence in a country "mighty hot" and their appearance at Green Bay in October. This fact indicates that something is omitted, and thus renders the identification of this voyage difficult. The word "last" would apparently refer to the Superior voyage. If so, however, one would expect to find some reference to the manners of the Southern Indians in that narrative, but such reference is not made.

There are still other instances where some other voyages seem to be involved. Note the following: in describing Lake Huron Radisson refers to "the great Lake of the Hurons — which is near two hundred leagues in length and sixty in breadth (as I guess), for I have [journeyed] round about it."[41] The accuracy of his guess seems to warrant his assertion, but the context clearly shows that this circuit could not have been made on this journey.

Regarding the Ottawas he says: "But since the destruction of many neighboring nations, they retired themselves to the height of the lake. We knowed those people well; we went to them almost yearly."[42] There is no doubt that Groseilliers visited them perhaps annually, but the inclusion of Radisson by the use of the pronoun "we" suggests his visit to the Sault Ste. Marie or one or more previous journeys.

After the division of their party on entering Georgian Bay, they experience difficulty in navigation because of high winds and "the impetuosity of the waves, which is the reason that our voyages are so long and tedious."[43] The pronoun "our" and the plurality and length of voyages suggest a previous journey of similar character.

Near the commencement of this narrative we read: "The French were together in order, the wildmen also. Saving my brother and I, that were accustomed to such like voyages, [not one of them] have foreseen what happened afterwards."[44] What happened afterward was a battle with the Iroquois in which they "wandered all asunder" and were "all put to it; none knows where he is, they are put to such a confusion." No previously recorded voyage in which either Radisson or Groseilliers took a part has any resemblance to this one or even suggests a "such like" voyage. During the Superior voyage, which came afterward, they doubtless had similar experiences, but in this instance the context seems to indicate a previous voyage of a similar nature.

13. *Ambiguity and Confusion.*

Perhaps one of the best evidences of the compositeness of the Mississippi voyage is the ambiguity and confusion which prevails in large degree throughout the narrative, and for this assertion corroboration is found in Radisson's own recognition of this significant fact. While among the Mascoutens he seeks information about "their neighboring nations" and says: "They gave us the names, which I hope to describe in the end of this most imperfect discourse, at least those that I can remember."[45]

The first thing to be noticed is that Radisson himself recognizes the imperfections in this narrative, and this recognition has a direct bearing on our theory. If he were writing up only one voyage, even ten years afterward, and had the notes of that voyage before him, there would seem to be little reason for his writing a "most imperfect discourse." For some cause, however, Radisson's mind was much confused while writing this narrative, and though he was aware of it he evidently did not recognize the disturbing cause. Any number of causes might be conjectured for the manifest imperfections in his writing, but the theory under consideration offers a plausible explanation for its "most imperfect" character.

Recall the hypothesis at the beginning of this monograph. What would be the effect of the incidents of the former journey, lying subconsciously in the memory, on the product of the present effort? Would they not naturally cause some interference in the operation of the mental faculties? Would not those dormant and subconscious ideas assert themselves to some extent and thus, by their influence, give rise to a confused expression? The causes resulting in a product so unsatisfactory might not be recalled or understood by the writer of the narrative, but the effect would be readily seen in the production of a "most imperfect discourse."

Another evidence of Radisson's confusion is found in the above quotation. He says he hopes "to describe their names in the end of this most imperfect discourse." One would expect to find this list of names appended to the Mississippi voyage, but the names are not there. If, however, we turn to the end of the Superior voyage we find a list of seventy-two names of Indian nations and a reference to eight or nine others whom he met later.[46] No allusion is made to these names in the Superior voyage; hence we may assume that these are the names to which he refers in this quotation.

Looking at the Mississippi narrative as a whole, it may be observed that the greater part of the confusion and ambiguity is found in the few pages preceding the return journey to Canada. Following the description of the Mascoutens[47] is a page of vague information about the Sioux and the Christinos. Then follows the very uncertain story of the Southern journey, at the end of which occurs the curious reference to "my last voyage which I made." At this point there is almost certainly an omission since, from the country "might hot," without a connecting word, the voyageurs next appear at Green Bay. From here it is impossible to trace their wanderings to the point where they commenced their snowshoe trek from the country of the Saulteurs in northern Wisconsin or Michigan. From here to the riverside, and thence to the first landing isle, their route seems to be clear, but the landing isle paragraph is very confusing.

It would be impossible to go through the entire narrative of the Mississippi voyage and single out definite sentences and paragraphs and assign them respectively to the one or the other voyage. For convenience, however, we may partially sumarize the conclusions derived from the foregoing arguments as follows: (1) The departure at the commencement of the voyage,[48] the arrival at the end,[49] the landing isle paragraph,[50] and the battle following their return[51] should apparently be assigned to the Unwritten voyage, 1654-56. (2) The first few sentences of the narrative,[52] the hunting story,[53] the return journey,[54] the battle in the Ottawa rapids on their return,[55] the loss of Groseilliers' notes,[56] and the last few sentences following the battle description at the end[57] seem to belong to the Mississippi voyage, 1658-60. (3) The few sentences following their arrival at the first landing isle[58] appear to refer indifferently to either voyage.

Perhaps Radisson's greatest confusion occurs within the last two or three pages of the Mississippi narrative and involves all three Western voyages.[59] (1) The story of the hunting journey is misplaced in the original manuscript and should be (and has been) set back in the narrative. (2) The Dollard massacre story, in the manuscript of the Superior voyage, 1663, should me (and has been) inserted in the Mississippi voyage, 1660. (3) The battle at the end of the Mississippi voyage actually occurred at the end of the Unwritten voyage, 1656.

It is not to be presumed that Radisson purposely or consciously vacillated from one voyage to the other. He wrote the narrative of the Mississippi voyage as *one* voyage, and the incidents of the previous journey crept in unwittingly; hence we must not expect to find sharp and abrupt transitions from one voyage to the other. Since all the events described and referred to are recalled by him as occurring during the one journey, he passes from one to the other as freely and readily in the midst of a sentence[60] as he would do consciously or purposely at the end of a chapter.

NOTES FOR THE BIOGRAPHICAL SKETCH

1. The data for this sketch has been taken chiefly from Scull's "Introduction" to the Prince Society edition of the *Voyages of Peter Esprit Radisson* (Boston, 1885) and George Bryce's *The Remarkable History of the Hudson's Bay Company* (Toronto, 1900).
2. "Radisson's Journal: Its Value in History," *Proceedings of Wisconsin Historical Society,* for 1895 (Madison, Wisconsin), p. 89.
3. *Bureau of Ethnology,* bulletin no. 69, p. 51.
4. Supra, p. 239.
5. Reuben Gold Thwaites (ed.), *Jesuit Relations* (Cleveland, 1896-1901; 73 vols.), vol. 44, pp. 175, 311. (Hereafter referred to as *Jesuit Relations.*)
6. Francis Parkman, *The Old Regime in Canada* (Centenary Edition), p. 63.
7. Douglas Brymner, in *Canadian Archives,* Report for 1895, p. xxii.
8. *History of Minnesota* (Minneapolis, 1882), p. 803.
9. Supra, p. 96, n. 87.
10. Supra, p. 119, n. 4.
11. Supra, p. 136, n. 77.
12. Bryce, op. cit., pp. 35-38.
13. Ibid., p. 39.
14. Ibid., pp. 43-44.
15. Ibid., pp. 44-45.

NOTES FOR THE FOREWORD

1. Supra, pp. viii; 159, n. 166.
2. This motive for writing the first four voyages seems to be doubtful. The inclusion of the two Iroquois voyages is inconsistent with it, and only a few casual references are made to the beaver as a commercial element.
3. Gideon D. Scull (ed.), *Voyages of Peter Esprit Radisson* (Publications of the Prince Society: Boston, 1885).
4. Supra, p. 2, n. 6.
5. *Jesuit Relations,* vol. 44, p. 175.
6. Supra, p. 73.
7. Supra, p. 247, topic no. 6.
8. *Jesuit Relations,* vol. 42, p. 219 and all of ch. 14.
9. Supra, p. xx, n. 24.
10. *Jesuit Relations,* vol. 45, pp. 245-61. Also Pierre Francois Xavier De Charlevoix, trans. John G. Shea, *History and General Description of New France* (New York, 1863), vol. 3, p. 33, n.
11. Supra, pp. 240-42, topic no. 2.
12. Supra, pp. 155-56.
13. There is no reference to this lawsuit in the early records at Boston. Radisson's own statement seems to be the only source authority on the matter.
14. Supra, p. 158. Also Adam Shortt, A. G. Doughty (eds.), *Canada and Its Provinces* (Toronto, 1914; 23 vols.), vol. I, p. 161.
15. J. H. Larned, "London 1665," *The New Larned History for Ready Reference* . . . (Springfield, Mass., 1922-24; 12 vols.).
16. Ibid., "Netherlands."
17. Ibid.
18. Short and Doughty, op. cit., pp. 159-65.
19. Supra, p. 112.
20. Supra, p. 155.
21. Francois J. Audet, *Canadian Historical Dates and Events* (Ottowa, 1917), p. 32.
22. Ibid.
23. Jacob Abbot, *Louis XIV,* (Makers of History series, n.p., n.d.).
24. Now supra, p. 104, n. 120. In the original ms. the Dollard massacre story occurs supra, p. 151, immediately following n. 135.

25. Now supra, p. 97, immediately following n. 93. In the original ms. the hunting story occurs on supra, p. 104, immediately following n. 119.
26. Supra, p. 98.
27. Supra, p. 98.
28. *Bouvier's Law Dictionary,* "Interpretation."
29. Supra, p. 12.
30. Supra, p. 37.
31. Supra, p. 50.
32. Supra, p. 106.
33. Supra, p. 155.
34. Supra, p. 151.
35. Supra, p. xvi, n. 10.
36. *Jesuit Relations,* vol. 45, p. 161.
37. Supra, p. 98.
38. Benjamin Sulte, in Jacob V. Brower's *Memoirs* (St. Paul, 1900), vol. VI, p. 81.
39. Supra, p. 151; also supra, p. 125, for the end of the Dollard massacre, which in the original ms. contains the description of the fort and which precedes the quotation in question.
40. Supra, p. 106.
41. Supra, p. 96.
42. Supra, pp. 99-101.
43. Supra, p. 151, where, on the Superior voyage at about the same season of the year, they experience favorable weather.
44. *Jesuit Relations,* vol. 44, pp. 239, 241, 243. See also Paul Kane, *Wanderings of an Artist,* ch. IV, in which canoeing distance is stated at the end of each day.
45. Supra, pp. 19-22.
46. Supra, pp. 73-76.
47. Supra, pp. 99-101.
48. Supra, pp. 135-141.
49. Supra, p. 41, where Radisson, yet a boy of seventeen, sought "a piece of paper and ink and pen" with which to write an important letter to the governor.
50. Supra, p. 139. In the original ms. see p. 104, lines 26 and 27.
51. Supra, p. 104.
52. Supra, p. 42, n. 71.
53. Supra, p. 79.
54. Supra, p. 109.
55. Supra, p. 79, n. 1.

NOTES FOR THE CAPTIVITY VOYAGE

1. In Radisson's ms. the several voyages are untitled. The titles were chosen by Mr. Adams. Δ

2. Dates are seldom mentioned in the narratives. In only three instances is the year stated, and in two of these there is an error of ten years. The date of Radisson's arrival in Canada, however, is not questioned, and it may be assumed that he was captured in 1652, at the age of sixteen.

3. The terms "cottage," "cabin," "dwelling," and "habitation," which are used throughout the chronicle, seem to apply indifferently to any sort of house or shelter.

4. The home town of Radisson and Groseilliers on the St. Lawrence river between Quebec and Montreal.

5. The term "barbarians," spelled "barbars" in the ms., generally refers to the Iroquois, while other Indians are usually called "wildmen."

6. From this remark and the date of his escape, Oct. 29, 1653, it may be inferred that Radisson's capture occurred about April or May, 1652.

7. The French league was 2.76 miles.

8. Probably Nicolet river.

9. Three Rivers. The word 'fort" is frequently used, and applies to any kind of protection against enemies or the elements. A "fort" could be made of brush, rocks, fallen trees, etc., as well as standard building materials.

10. Supra, p. 49, n. 18.

11. Menada: Manhattan, the present New York City. Fort Orange: the present Albany.

12. Probably Lake Champlain.

13. Caribou.

14. Salt seems to have been a rarity and luxury among the Iroquois, although they occupied a region noted for salt production in later days.

15. Radisson frequently refers to the time of day by the clock, suggesting that either he carried a timepiece in his bag or was a close observer of the sun.

16. Probably Lake Champlain.

17. Fir or pine.

18. The vapor bath was a universal custom among the American Indians; Eastman, *The Soul of the Indian,* p. 78. Father Louis

Hennepin was given this treatment at Mille Lacs; *Minnesota Historical Society Collections,* vol. I, p. 254.

19. Part of the stomach wall of certain animals used as food.

20. This was doubtless the chief village of the Mohawks, where Radisson was held during the greater part of his captivity. It is supposed to have been at Auriesville, near the present city of Fonda. It may have been on or near the Mohawk river west of Albany. For distance see supra, p. 39, n. 63, and p. 40, n. 66.

21. Ordered to run the gauntlet.

22. The Indians' "ho" or "ho ho ho" indicated approval.

23. Gabbling? (But it is also close to the French "habler," meaning "to boast." Δ)

24. Beads or wampum.

25. An Indian food made chiefly of pounded Indian corn, boiled with bits of meat and fish.

26. French name for the Canada moose.

27. Beaver

28. Reintroductory phrase; see supra, p. xxi.

29. Bark.

30. Mosquitoes.

31. Jesuit Fathers.

32. Lake St. Peter.

33. Heads placed on the ends of poles.

34. Probably the village of Radisson's captivity.

35. Gauntlet.

36. Father Ponset experienced similar torture at the hands of a child five years old; *Jesuit Relations,* vol. 40, pp. 131-33.

37. Peace pipe.

38. Medicine pouches or bags.

39. Dutch or Hollanders at Fort Orange.

40. In the ms. Radisson says "four males, and five femals." Context shows that he was confused. Δ

41. Mascoutens, nation of the Fire.

42. Probably Lake Michigan.

43. Oneida.

44. Onondaga.

45. Seneca.

46. Cayuga.

47. Snowshoe.

48. Genesee? Niagara?

49. Lake Ontario.
50. Oswego?
51. Branch of the Oswego?
52. Lake Onondaga?
53. Henry Colin Campbell, in an address before the Historical Society of Wisconsin, Dec. 12, 1895, criticized Radisson as follows: "I am convinced that Radisson, in his journal, is guilty of gross exaggeration and downright falsehood in regard to the exploration of the territory in and around Wisconsin. He often allows his imagination to run riot. In one place, for instance, Radisson speaks of a little convention of three hundred bears [supra, p. 36]. In another place he minutely describes a reptile that nobody has ever seen on land or sea, a reptile that is absolutely unknown to science [supra, p. 31]. He calmly records the killing, during one trip, of six hundred elk by himself, Groseilliers and one Indian [supra, p. 143]. He tells us, moreover, of the shifting by the wind, within a day, of fifty small sand-mountains from one side of Lake Superior to the other, the scene of this remarkable occurrence being not far from Sault Ste. Marie [supra, p. 122]. And, to our still greater astonishment, he tells of sea-serpents in our great lakes [supra, p. 92]. Under the circumstances, I trust I may not seem too severe a critic when I accuse Radisson of drawing the long bow."

    As to this reptile, it may be necessary to grant Radisson some latitude in his minutely detailed description. He does not come far amiss, however, in describing the iguana, a species of lizard, some of which have their habitat as far north as the middle states. See *Americana Encyclopedia,* "Iguana."

54. Radisson often applies the term "great" to rivers of slight significance, while he refers to the Mississippi merely as a "riverside." See supra, p. 96.
55. This desire was to take their enemies alive and hold them as prisoners for torture.
56. Death song or fatal song?
57. Headdress.
58. Possibly Mincees, called Sanhikans by the Dutch. They lived west of the Hudson river.
59. Lake Champlain.
60. Sunflower. Δ
61. This reference to other voyages occupying a period of ten

years has a bearing on the time the Superior voyage terminated. Since the present time is 1653 (near the end of the captivity), it appears that the last voyage would end ten years later, or 1663. See supra, p. xvii, ff.

62. Albany.

63. Two days' journey for a large group of Indians suggests the probably distance from the Mohawk village to Albany as about 50 miles.

64. In the ms. the sentence reads: "The great effect yt ye flemings shewed and the little space was from there can I make that Journey one day." Δ

65. In the ms.: "29th 8bre, 1663"; this error of ten years was probably due to absent-mindedness.

66. The duration of the journey (8 a.m. to 4 p.m. the following day), traveling alone day and night on foot, suggests a distance of somewhat less than 100 miles.

67. Value. In the ms. the French word is spelled "vallor."

68. Father Ponset. See *Jesuit Relations,* vol. 40, p. 143.

69. The ms. reads: "4/7 of January, 1664." The error of ten years, again, was probably due to absent-mindedness.

70. In the ms. the Captivity voyage ends at this point. What now follows in the Captivity voyage has been transposed from what is the beginning of the Onondaga voyage in the ms. See supra, p. 251, topic no. 9, for the reason for the editor's transposition.

71. The ms. reads: "The 15th day of Mar May . . . ." It is clear from the discrepancy in these two dates that only one, if either, can be correct. Benjamin Sulte says: "This is a manifest contradiction" and assumes that Radisson left France on May 15th. By approximating the time for the voyage across the Atlantic as seven weeks, Mr. Sulte asserts that Radisson's statement "must read 7th July." His reason for this conclusion is that "in those days, the vessels from France never reached Quebec before the 20th of June and not often before the 1st of July." In answer to this it may be observed that Radisson sailed in a "fisher boat" for Percé island, and not in a "vessel" (merchantman) for Quebec, nearly 400 miles farther west. If the date of arrival May 7th be correct, Radisson must have left France seven weeks earlier, or March 15th. This seems more probable, since fishermen would start early enough to arrive at Percé island at the beginning of the fishing season, which, according to LaHontan, "commences in the beginning

of June and is at an end about the middle of August."
Jacob V. Brower, *Memoirs,* vol. VI, p. 76.
Baron De LaHontan (Chicago, 1905; 2 vols.), col. I, p. 337.
For peculiarity in the original ms., see supra, p. xxviii.

72. Peace of Nov., 1653. See supra, p. xiv and p. 251, topic no. 9.
73. The Captivity voyage properly ends at this point. See supra, p. 251, topic no. 9.

NOTES FOR THE ONONDAGA VOYAGE

1. Onondaga mission, founded in 1656. See Edna Kenton, *The Jesuit Relations and Allied Documents* . . . . (New York, 1925), p. 264.
2. Radisson distinguishes the "upper" from the "lower" Iroquois, and his estimate of distance between this mission (near Syracuse) and the village of his captivity (probably near Fonda) is somewhat exaggerated, the actual distance being about 100 miles. See Kenton, op. cit.
3. The two great divisions of the Eastern Indians were the Iroquois and the Algonquins. The Hurons were of the Iroquois stock and were also their ancient enemies.
4. Lake Huron.
5. Supra, p. 50, n. 20.
6. Mascoutens. Supra, p. 89, n. 42; also see pp. 58-59.
7. St. Lawrence.
8. Probably Moose river.
9. Hudson Bay.
10. Golden arm?
11. Coast of Labrador.
12. Lake Nipissing.
13. Probably Assiniboines. Supra, p. 144, n. 108. ∆
14. A river emptying into the St. Lawrence a few miles above Quebec.
15. Lake Huron.
16. Andastes, also called Susquehannas, south of the Iroquois.
17. Hurons, north of Lake Erie.
18. The Dutch furnished firearms to the Iroquois as early as 1630. See *Americana Ency.,* "Iroquois League."
19. Old French monetary unit equal to about nineteen cents.
20. During the long continued warfare between the Iroquois and the Hurons, it was not unusual for some of the latter, in case of capture, to turn traitor and join the Iroquois in the wars against their own people. See Parkmen, *The Old Regime in Canada,* p. 134.
21. Montreal.
22. This other design of the Iroquois was to entice the Hurons, along with the French, into their country and at an opportune time to massacre all of them. The French and Hurons became suspicious of this before they were long on their way. See Parkman, *The Old Regime in Canada,* p. 89.

23. This fort was the stockade and building at the Onondaga mission, which was their destination on this voyage.
24. Fathers Paul Ragueneau and Joseph Dupéron. Grace Lee Nute, *Caesars of the Wilderness* (New York, 1943), p. 50.
25. Route, trail.
26. Baggage.
27. St. Lawrence and Ottawa.
28. In fact from the southwest.
29. Lake St. Louis.
30. Portage. Radisson also uses the words "drawage," "trainage," "wainage" where navigation is difficult.
31. An iron with the ends bent for holding objects together.
32. St. Lawrence.
33. Supra, p. 45, n. 2.
34. St. Lawrence.
35. Supra, p. i.
36. Supra, p. 31, n. 53 (Campbell's criticism). This "little convention of three hundred bears" was observed by Radisson and his wild companions in the darkness, and their number was estimated only by the noise they made in the brush. Even if the number of bears were large, they doubtless came together under unusual circumstances, since the wildmen "never heard their father speak of so many together."
37. Supra, p. 97, n. 95. Believed to be the confluence of the Mississippi and the Missouri.
38. Mascoutens. Supra, p. 89, n. 42.
39. Hurons, also called "Standing Hairs."
40. On p. 107 of the Prince Society edition of *Radisson's Voyages* is the following note: "In O'Callaghan's *Documentary History of New York,* Vol. IV, p. 77, 1851, is given an engraving of this animal, with the title, 'Wild Animals of New Netherlands,' taken from a Dutch work published in Amsterdam in 1671. In this work it is thus described: 'On the borders of Canada animals are now and again seen somewhat resembling a horse; they have cloven hoofs, shaggy manes, a horn right out of the forehead, a tail like that of a wild hog, black eyes, a stag's neck, and love the gloomiest wildernesses, are shy of each other, so that the male never feeds with the female except when they associate for the purpose of increase. Then they lay aside their ferocity. As soon as the rutting season is past, they again not only become wild but even attack their own.' "

41. St. Lawrence above Ogdensburg?
42. Wisest.
43. Cape.
44. Supra, p. 53, n. 30.
45. They are forced downstream in the Lachine rapids.
46. Thousand Islands.
47. Eries.
48. A Huron, called elsewhere in the narratives "Staring Hairs."
49. Lake Ontario.
50. A cape or blanket.
51. Whitecaps.
52. Armpits.
53. Oswego.
54. Meriwether Lewis and William Clark, *History of the Expedition Under Lewis and Clark* (London, 1815; 3 vols.), vol. II, p. 112.
55. Stockade at Onondaga mission.
56. Branch of Oswego.
57. Lake Onondaga.
58. The buildings and stockade of the Jesuit mission.
59. Pumpkin.
60. Many strange stories are told about toads. For example, it was claimed in 1928 that a toad was taken from the corner stone of a wrecked building in Texas after thirty-five years and was alive. For live toads in Oklahoma, alive after being buried for three centuries, see Minneapolis *Tribune*, Sept. 30, 1930.
61. This feigned accident is not mentioned in other accounts.
62. A stringed musical instrument.
63. Probably a reference to a drum used for taps. (However, on p. 129 of the Prince edition of *Radisson's Voyages* is found the following note: " 'To beat the gien,' probably meaning the guitar, as Charlevoix mentions that at the feast of the Indians one of the French young men played upon that instrument for their amusement." Such a statement seems to imply that the guitar, if such it was, would not furnish wild enough music. Δ) See Parkman, *The Old Regime in Canada*, p. 90, re custom of *eating all* at a feast.
64. This device is not mentioned in other accounts.
65. Radisson believed in getting the jump on his adversaries. Supra, p. 162.

66. On p. 130 of the Prince edition of *Radisson's Voyages* is found this note: "The new Governor, Viscount d'Argenson, who arrived in Canada a few months after, disapproved of the evacuation of Onondaga. 'The location of this fortification was probably about three quarter of a mile below Green Point, on a farm now occupied [in 1849] by Mr. Myrick Bradley, in the town of Salina, where the embankment and outlines were plain to be seen fifty years ago.' *History of Onondaga,* by J. V. H. Clarke, Vol. I, p. 161, n., 1849." △
67. Genesee.
68. Upper branch of the Genesee.
69. Waterfall.
70. St. Lawrence.
71. Father Ragueneau gives April 3rd as the date of arrival at Montreal. For his account of this journey see *Jesuit Relations,* vol. 44, pp. 175 ff., 311.
72. Medard Chouart, Sieur Des Groseilliers. This is Radisson's first mention of his brother-in-law and future companion in travel and enterprise for many years.
73. Supra, p. 247, topic no. 6.

NOTES FOR THE MISSISSIPPI VOYAGE

1. The meaning of this title and its variant form at the end of this voyage has perplexed students of Radisson's chronicle ever since its original publication. The enigma was solved, however, by Mr. Edward C. Gale, of Minneapolis, in the following manner: the prefix "aux" is the French word meaning "to the," and the remainder of the word in each of the forms is an imperfect spelling of the name "Ottawa," the combined form meaning, therefore, "to the Ottawa." The following simple experiments by the reader will make this solution very clear: write the word "Otiuat" (one of many spellings) in bold script. Now curve slightly the first downward stroke of the "u"; place a dot over the second downward stroke; and prefix the "aux." The result is "auxoticiat." Again, write the word "Otawac" (another spelling). Now modify the letter "w" thus: curve slightly the first downward stroke as before; place a dot over the second downward stroke; strengthen or exaggerate the final stroke into the form of a small "c"; and prefix the "aux." The result is "auxotacicac."

    In the original ms. the word "auxotacicac" is somewhat mutilated, the "a" following "t" having been first written as "i."

    See *Minnesota History,* vol. VII (Dec., 1926), p. 340. For more than 150 forms of spelling the name "Ottawa" see Frederick W. Hodge (ed.), *Handbook of American Indians* (Washington, 1907, 1910; 2 vols.), vol. II, p. 171.
2. 1657. Groseilliers spent a number of years at the Huron mission as a lay helper to the Jesuits. Supra, p. iii.
3. Probably a reference to Lake Superior.
4. Captivity and Onondaga voyages. Supra, p. 251, topic no. 9.
5. See the Superior voyage, supra, p. 130, where they separated into small groups for the same reason.
6. It was intended and believed that this voyage would continue for one year only. Supra, pp. 92, 96.
7. A reference to furs.
8. Both the civil and clerical authorities were apparently interested in this voyage, but no record of it is found in the *Jesuit Relations,* and the names of the two Fathers are unknown.
9. Some writers have assumed that the middle of June was the date of departure of this expedition. Owing to the fact, how-

ever, that one of Groseilliers' children was born on April 15, 1659, they could not have left prior to about July 15, 1658. Also supra, p. 85, n. 21.

10. Happy-go-lucky, irresponsible adventurers.
11. The words "at last" suggest a period of preparation following the "middle of June."
12. Supra, p. 254, topic no. 12.
13. Ottawa.
14. Radisson, as the reader will have noticed by now, sometimes uses the present or future tense to denote the past.
15. A breechclout.
16. Domineering fellows; might also refer to the Greek hero.
17. To call an Indian a woman is to bestow on him a most loathsome epithet.
18. For consideration of this battle, see supra, p. 239, n. 1.
19. Tripe des roche, a species of lichen.
20. Supra, p. 8, n. 19.
21. In the latitude of the Ottawa river gooseberries do not ripen before the 1st of August. It may be inferred, therefore, that they left Three Rivers probably during the latter part of July. Supra, p. 80, n. 9.
22. Result of overeating.
23. Lake Nipissing.
24. Probably a cache of some food, but they found it was not needed now, owing to the abundance of fish.
25. Chaudiere falls near Ottawa.
26. French river.
27. Georgian Bay.
28. There were both Ottawas and Hurons in this expedition. It is probable that the Ottawas went in the seven boats to their village on Manitoulin island, and the Hurons went south with the Frenchmen and skirted the shores of Georgian Bay.
29. Site of the destroyed Huron mission near the River Wye at the south end of the bay.
30. St. Lawrence.
31. Supra, p. 254, topic no. 12.
32. Manitoulin island and the Ottawa village.

There is some difference of opinion as to the identity of this "large island," some writers holding that it is Bois Blanc. It is a well established fact that the Ottawas were located on Manitoulin island before and at the time of the Mississippi voyage, and the context clearly points to this island as the place of their arrival. In Radisson's next sentence, however, he says they "passed a strait some three leagues beyond that place." This would seem to be the Strait of Mackinac, but that point is about thirty leagues distant. Although the distance from Bois Blanc island to that strait is about three leagues, there is no evidence or authority that this island was ever occupied by the Ottawas.

It may be conjectured that in passing from Manitoulin to the Strait of Mackinac the party made a temporary stop at Bois Blanc and that this is the "place" referred to in the phrase quoted. It seems hardly probable or even possible, as some contend, that they skirted the entire shore of Lake Huron, including Georgian Bay, which would be a distance of approximately 1,000 miles.

33. Lake Michigan.
34. A probable reference to the region north of Lake Superior, seen on the way to Hudson Bay when on the Superior voyage.
35. Supra, 253, topic no. 11.
36. Hurons.
37. Supra, p. 50, n. 20.
38. Manitoulin.
39. Ottawas at Green Bay.
40. Firearms.
41. Potawatomies.
42. These Indians were doubtless the Mascoutens. The Chippewa name was "Mashcodens," which meant "Little Prairie People." The Hurons called them the "Fire People," or nation of the Fire, and in the Chippewa dialect the word for fire is "ishkote." Owing to Radisson's defective English it is not surprising that he used the name "Escotecke."

Some difference of opinion prevails as to the location of the Mascoutens at the time of Radisson's visit. The preponderance of authority leaves little doubt, however, that their habitat was about the Fox river in southern Wisconsin, near the Potawatomies. Some writers contend that they were on the Missouri river and that Radisson and Groseilliers visited them there.

See Bulletin 30, *Bureau of American Ethnology,* "Mascoutens."

Agnes C. Laut, *Pathfinders of the West* (New York, 1914), p. 86, n. 1; p. 365.

Campbell, "Radisson's Journal: Its Value in History," *Proceedings of the State Historical Society of Wisconsin,* for 1895, p. 99, n. 2.

Supra, p. 96, n. 86 and n. 87.

43. Supra, p. 247, topic no. 6.
44. Supra, p. 256, topic no. 13.
45. One of the numerous variations of the name applied to the Sioux nation. Jonathan Carver refers to them as Naudowessies, but the most common form of the name is Nadouesioux. The prefix "Nadoue" is a Chippewa word meaning adder, snake, or enemy, and "Sioux" is a later contraction of the name. W. W. Folwell, *History of Minnesota* (St. Paul, 1921), vol. I, p. 79, n. 16. Also *Minnesota Historical Society Collections,* vol. V, p. 83.
46. Crees of the Hudson Bay region.
47. Green Bay.
48. The "coming-in" of the lake is Sault Ste. Marie.
49. Western end?
50. Supra, p. 254, topic no. 12.
51. Ottawas.
52. The place of the Christinos, or Crees, on Hudson Bay.
53. Region of Green Bay and Fox river.
54. Lake Michigan. The Southern journey, which commences at this point, extended apparently into the South "where it never snows nor freezes there but mighty hot."
55. Reference to the land of Cockaigne. See Ebenezer Brewer, *Dictionary of Phrase and Fable* (New York, 1923), "Cockaigne."
56. Probably Lake Michigan, possibly the Gulf of Mexico.
57. Gulf of Mexico.
58. Prairie Sioux. In the original ms. this name is incorrectly written "Tatarga" and is so printed in the Prince edition.
59. Lake Superior is between the Sioux and the Crees.
60. An apparent reference to the fugitive Hurons who had settled at Prairie island in the Mississippi within Sioux territory. Supra, p. 96, n. 87.
61. Supra, p. 80, n. 6.
62. Lake Michigan.
63. Probably the prong-horned antelope "which inhabits the drier portions of the North American continent west of the Mississippi." See *Johnson's Universal Cyclopedia* (New York, 1898), "Antilocapra."

64. Poisonous water snake. Supra, p. 31, n. 53 (Campbell's criticism).

Mr. Campbell's "great astonishment" seems to imply that "sea serpent" means "sea monster." Shortly after this reference to sea serpents Radisson says: "In that [lake] of the Staring Hairs I saw [a] young boy [who] was bitten. He takes immediately his stony knife and a pointed stick and cuts off the whole wound, being no other remedy for it." Imagine the huge form of this (Campbell's) sea monster rising out of Lake Michigan and biting this little boy so severely that he must cut out the wound with his stone knife.

65. A reference to the calument. Supra, p. 134.

66. Lake Michigan and sand dunes.

67. Supra, p. 254, topic no. 12.

68. This passage refers to the Strait of Mackinac, Green Bay, Lake Michigan, and Lake Superior. There appears to be an omission at this point, since the narrative passes from the end of the Southern journey (wherever that may have been) to the region of Green Bay and Lake Superior.

In the original ms. there appears to be a faint period after the word "October," thus attaching the phrase "in October" to the end of the preceding sentence. If this had been allowed (and it has not been), that sentence would clearly refer to some other voyage during the month of October, which does not accord with any of the principal or subsidiary voyages. If this period is arbitrarily placed after "made" (as has been done), the sentence probably refers to the Superior voyage, and the word "October" indicates the time of their return from the Southern journey to the Green Bay region.

It will be observed that Radisson's narrative of the entire Southern journey is very ambiguous, and it is difficult even to conjecture their itinerary. The whole story is largely hearsay, and there is nothing to determine positively that they went far beyond Lake Michigan, though it may be inferred that they did reach a country "mighty hot."

69. Hurons, Ottawas, and Mascoutens.

70. In the ms. the word is "contended."

71. This indicates that they were then some distance west of the Sault Ste. Marie, or somewhere in northern Michigan or Wisconsin.

72. For an account of this war see Nicolas Perrot, *Minnesota*

xlvii

Historical Society Collections, vol. II, pp. 208-9. Also in Emma Blair (ed.), *Indian Tribes of the Upper Mississippi Valley* (Cleveland, 1911; 2 vols.), vol. I, pp. 163-65.
73. Supra, p. 89, n. 45.
74. Northern Wisconsin, probably Chequamegon bay.
75. These Frenchmen were probably of the group that went back after the battle at the beginning of this expedition and made a more successful venture into the West a year later.
76. The Christinos.
77. On the south side of Lake Superior. *Jesuit Relations,* vol. 45, pp. 233-39.
78. Moose.
79. Caribou.
80. Canada moose.
81. Sioux.
82. About one and a half years (Aug., 1658, to about Feb., 1660).
83. Supra, p. 80, n. 6.
84. In view of the divergence of opinion as to the following part of Radisson's narrative, it is important to note that this departure of the Frenchmen from the Saulteurs and Christinos took place in the country of the Salteurs in *northern Michigan or Wisconsin.* Supra, p. 96, n. 87.
85. Mississippi river. Supra, p. 92, n. 60.
86. Probably renegade bands of Potawatomies and Menominees. The name "Matouenock" can hardly mean Mascoutens, since these have already been named "Escoteke." Supra, p. 89, n. 42.
87. The location of this island has been the subject of much speculation. Two eminent scholars, Mr. H. C. Campbell and Dr. Warren Upham, have identified Prairie island, in the Mississippi river between Hastings and Red Wing as "the first landing isle." There are two substantial grounds for this conclusion, one historical and the other geographical. The historical basis is an assertion by Nicolas Perrot, a contemporary of Radisson and for many years associated with the Indians of the Northwest. In referring to the Hurons and Ottawas on Prairie island, Perrot wrote: "The Sioux made a thousand expressions of affection to the Hurons and Ottawas everywhere they were. . . . The Ottawas decided finally to choose the island named Pelee for their settlement, where they were some years in peace. They there received often the visits of

xlviii

the Sioux." Pelee was the French name for Bald island, which is today known as Prairie island.

It is clear from Radisson's narrative that they had Hurons and Ottawas with them and it is equally certain that the Indians they found on the first landing isle were Huron and Ottawa refugees from the aggressive Iroquois. The fact that they were "newly there" is in accord with the historic fact of their dispersion by the Iroquois in 1649.

The geographic evidence involves the identification of the "riverside" which was the termination of their fifty-league snowshoe trek. It should be remembered that they started from the land of the Saulteurs, or Chippewas, in northern Michigan or Wisconsin, a country with which they had become somewhat familiar. The season of the year indicates that the ice was yet in the rivers, at least the smaller ones, since the snow was still on the ground. When they came to the riverside they apparently found this river open for canoe navigation, as suggested by the making of boats. They traveled up the river for several days, perhaps two weeks. Their arrival at the *first* landing isle suggests that there were more islands in the river farther up, all of which implies that this was a stream of considerable size.

It is evident that this river was either the Mississippi or some tributary flowing into it from the east. Among these are the Rock, Wisconsin, Black, Chippewa, and St. Croix. Had they come to any one of these they could hardly have navigated for eight days and more *upstream* at this season of the year, when those rivers would have been filled with ice. Even if they had been open the voyageurs would have returned to the country from which they had come and in which they had already spent the larger part of two winters, becoming well acquainted with the Saulteurs, Potawatomies, Winnebagoes, Mascoutens, and in fact all the Indians of that region. Since this river could not have been any of these eastern tributaries, it must have been the Mississippi and the first landing isle must have been an island in that river. The unimpeachable testimony of Perrot is amply sufficient to prove that such island was no other than Prairie island.

It has been suggested that the Matouenock, the Indians met with on the way up the river to the first landing isle, were the Mandans on the Missouri, and that the first landing isle, therefore, was in that river. There are several outstanding

xlix

objections to this theory. First, there is no similarity in the names, and no other name designating the Mandans has any resemblance to "Matouenock." Second, there is no historical evidence that the fugitive Hurons and Ottawas ever went beyond the Mississippi. Third, it would not be possible to reach the Missouri river at its mouth on snowshoes because of the temperate climate. Fourth, to reach the Missouri at any point would involve crossing the Mississippi and require an overland journey far in excess of the stated fifty leagues.

See Warren Upham, *Minnesota Historical Society Collections,* vol. X, p. 462. Supra, p. 89, n. 42 and references.

See also the Sulte Studies in Brower's *Memoirs,* vol. VI, pp. 74-84, where Mr. Sulte interprets this part of Radisson's narrative in the following language: "They left the Sioux country on snowshoes (racketts) undoubtedly in March, 1660, and reached Lake Superior, where they remained three weeks building canoes, after which they navigated eight days on a river [upstream?] which conducted them to Green Bay." Supra, p. 42, n. 71 for another Sulte interpretation.

88. Ottawa river.

89. Supra, p. 96, n. 87.

90. Their journey was not "broken" on this voyage. They remained here four months and returned in about July. Supra, p. 247, topic no. 6.

91. Epilepsy.

92. Supra, p. 253, topic no. 11.

93. The lines commencing "That summer I went ahunting" constitute the "landing isle paragraph." Supra, p. xx; also p. 248, topic no. 7.

94. Beginning of the hunting story. Supra, p. xx. Like the Southern journey, this story is largely hearsay, and the itinerary is difficult to determine.

95. Believed to be the confluence of the Mississippi and Missouri.

96. This may also refer to the Mississippi or Missouri.

97. Rosary.

98. Tawny. ("Tany" apparently is a phonetic spelling in English of the French "tanné." Δ)

99. Pumpkins.

1

100. Calument or peace pipe.
101. Reference to Groseilliers' epilepsy, mentioned at the end of the landing isle paragraph. Supra, p. 97.
102. End of the hunting story.
103. The Dollard massacre at the Long Sault, May 21, 1660.
104. From this it appears that Groseilliers baptized children at the landing isle.
105. Supplies exhausted.
106. This remarkable convocation was one of the most notable events recorded in the aboriginal history of the region.
107. This was about the middle of July, 1660.
108. They went south on the Mississippi to the mouth of the Wisconsin, thence north up that river, down the Fox river and through Green Bay and the Great Lakes.
109. Green Bay (Lake of the Stinkings).
110. Lakes Michigan and Huron and probably lake Nipissing.
111. A rapids in the Ottawa river.
112. About 275 miles above Montreal.
113. Caribou.
114. Guns.
115. Hurons, Algonquins, Ottawas, Chippewas, Beavers, Sioux, and Kiskakons.
116. A rapids in the Ottawa river, forty miles above Montreal.
117. A reference to the murder of the three Iroquois on the Captivity voyage.
118. Attempted to shoot the rapids.
119. Supra, p. 252, topic no. 10.
120. Beginning of the Dollard massacre story. Supra, p. xx, n. 24.
121. A rapids in the Ottawa river, forty miles above Montreal.
122. This tactic was also used by Radisson and company on the Superior voyage. Supra, p. 117.
123. At this point in the original ms. the handwriting changes. It is more shaded, coarser, with less flourish and a distinct change in the form of certain letters. Supra, p. xxiii.
124. Supra, p. xxiii.
125. End of Dollard massacre story.
126. Back from a visit to the scene of the Dollard massacre. Supra, p. xx, ff.
127. Supra, p. 240, topic no. 2.
128. Supra, p. 247, topic no. 6.
129. Groseilliers.

130. Radisson.
131. Beginning of the ambiguous description of the battle described in the *Jesuit Relations,* vol. 42, pp. 225-33. See Supra, p. 243, topic no. 5; and p. 239, n. 1.
132. Ottawas.
133. "They" probably alludes to the two brigantines on which Radisson and company came to Three Rivers, but it might also allude to the Iroquois or even to the Western Indians.
134. The first half of this compound sentence refers to the year 1656. The second half refers to the year 1660. Supra, p. 243, topic no. 5.
135. Supra, p. 79, n. 1.

NOTES FOR THE SUPERIOR VOYAGE

1. Following their return from the West in August, 1660.
2. The Porc-épics (Porcupines) and Montagnais occupied territory about the St. Lawrence and Saguenay rivers. From context, the Squirrels seem to have been in the same region.
3. Saguenay.
4. This reference to the Jesuit Fathers going to Hudson Bay by way of the Saguenay has an important bearing on the time and order of the voyages. As stated in the "Foreword" the Superior voyage took place during the official term of Governor D'Avaugour, that is, from 1661 to 1663. This assertion is contradicted by many scholars upon the authority of an entry in the *Journal of the Jesuits* (included in *Jesuit Relations*), under date of May 3, 1662, which runs as follows: "I left Quebec on the 3rd for 3 rivers. On the way I met Des Groseillers, who was going to the North sea. He passed Quebec during the night, with 10 men; and when he reached Cap Tourmente he wrote about it to monsieur the Governor."

   If the Superior voyage extended from 1661 to 1663 Groseilliers must have been in the vicinity of Lake Superior in May, 1662, and therefore the Jesuit record above quoted must be erroneous. The view that the year 1662 is an error and should be 1661 is substantially corroborated by both Radisson and the *Journal of the Jesuits*.

   In the *Journal of the Jesuits* for the summer of 1662 there is no reference to any activity on the part of the Fathers in going or attempting to go to Hudson Bay by any route. But for the summer of 1661 it is recorded that Fathers Dablon and Druillettes and other French and numerous Algonquins made such an attempt by way of Tadousac and the Saguenay river on June 1st or 2nd (ovl. 46, p. 173) but returned July 27th (vol. 46, p. 181). They failed because of opposition by the Iroquois.

   At the beginning of Radisson's narrative of the Superior voyage, which commenced in 1661, we find that the Fathers made the attempt by way of the Saguenay. They also tried to induce Radisson and Groseilliers to go with them. Radisson says: "They were very earnest with me to engage myself in that voyage, to the end that my brother would give over his, which I utterly denied them, knowing that they could never bring it about . . . because . . . the wildmen . . . would have hindered them."

We may now interpret Radisson's ambiguous language in the light of the above facts. It will be noticed that the Fathers were very earnest with Radisson and that he denied them (he does not say "we"). What does he mean by the words "to the end that my brother would give over his"? Apparently the Fathers had already talked with and convinced Groseilliers, and that he had consented to go, hence their earnestness with Radisson to whom they virtually said: "Will you go since your brother has consented to go?"

It seems entirely plausible that Groseilliers actually did go with the Fathers. Radisson says, a little farther on in his narrative, that "Nevertheless the Fathers are gone with the governor's son of the Three Rivers, and six other French and twelve wildmen." This party must have left sometime in May, since they "left Tadousac" June 1st or 2nd. According to Radisson, he and Groseilliers "stayed at home at rest that years [August, 1660, to September, 1661]," hence it was possible for Groseilliers to go with the Fathers in May, 1661, and return in July.

Since this expedition traveled down the St. Lawrence in a number of canoes it is probable that the Jesuit writer made note only of the one canoe in which he saw Groseilliers and ten men, or the canoes may have been scattered and thus only the canoe of Groseilliers observed.

Jesuit Relations, vol. 47, p. 279.

Ibid., vol. 46, pp. 173, 179, 181.

Campbell, in *Parkman Club Papers* (No. 2, 1896), p. 22.

Grace Lee Nute, *Caesars of the Wilderness* (New York, 1943), p. 78, n. 9, where it says Marguérite Hayet "femme de Medard Chouar Sr desgrosillers absen" sued the Sieur de St. Quentin for a pig that was killed. Court record at Three Rivers. Absent where? To the North with Dablon and Druillettes.

5. Supra, p. xix.
6. Chippewas.
7. When did they go? It has been shown supra, p. xix that the Superior voyage comenced after the arrival of Governor D'Avaugour, August 31st. The new governor went to Three Rivers the next day, and therefore their trouble occurred shortly after, and the expedition started early in September.

At this point there should be noticed a discrepancy between Radisson's narrative and the *Journal of the Jesuits* (included in *Jesuit Relations*). According to Radisson the Saulteurs, or Chippewas, seem to have arrived in August (no assertion, however). The answer they received from Quebec required that they remain until the return of the two Fathers (Dablon and Druillettes) from Tadousac, but these Fathers had already returned on July 27th, according to the *Journal of the Jesuits*. See *Jesuit Relations*, vol. 46, p. 181.

8. Forbids them to go.
9. Nipissings.
10. Mascoutens.
11. River of the Meadows.
12. Reference to the battle at the beginning of the Mississippi voyage, supra, pp. 81-84.
13. Remains of boats burned?
14. Ottawa.
15. An indication of a late start.
16. Enemy.
17. A similar ruse was employed by Le Sueur when going up the Mississippi. *Minnesota Historical Society Collections*, vol. I, p. 267.
18. For a similar strategy see *Jesuit Relations*, vol. 42, p. 234.
19. Chaudierre falls. Supra, p. 85.
20. Lake Nipissing.
21. French river.
22. Georgian Bay.
23. St. Mary's river?
24. Sault Ste. Marie or fall of St. Mary's.
25. Saulteurs, Chippewas.
26. The well known Lake Superior whitefish.
27. The word "kinakouir" seems to suggest prayers or thanksgiving, since they have enjoyed abundance and variety of food since arriving at Whitefish bay. They all give thanks to their various conceptions of deity: "In a word, there is nothing but kinakouir of all sorts. . . ." This word might be a variant of "kinnikinic," the bark of willow or sumac used for ceremonial burning. The words which follow it—"the encens of our encens is not spared"—seem to indicate that they used up or consumed all the incense they carried with them. The first "encens" is probably an antecedent repetition (supra, p. xxvi) and should be "supply" or another word of similar import.

28. Whitefish bay.

29. Some small island west of Whitefish bay.

30. A small river flowing into Lake Superior east of Pictured Rocks.

31. Sand dunes on south shore of Lake Superior, near Point Au Sable.

32. Supra, p. 31, n. 53 (Campbell's criticism). To interpret these words of description as meaning that "fifty small mountains" moved from one side of Lake Superior to the other would seem to place an unusual strain upon the imagination. Any observer of the action of wind on a broad expanse of fine dry sand knows how ripples or ridges form and creep forward with the wind and reverse their direction when the wind changes. This seems a fair and reasonable interpretation of Radisson's description.

33. From this statement some writers have inferred that Radisson had visited Turkey, probably on a sailing vessel when a boy, before coming to Canada.

34. This suggests a late start on this voyage. They reached Georgian Bay in twenty-two days (supra, p. 120). Perhaps two or three more weeks brought them to this place—east of Pictured Rocks. Assuming that freezing would occur about the latter part of October, it may be inferred that they left Three Rivers about the early part of September. Supra, p. xix.

35. A band they had doubtless seen on their Southern journey during the Mississippi voyage.

36. The scalp dance.

37. Grand Portal, Arched Rock.

38. Gulls.

39. Radisson's given name was Pierre (Peter). These rocks had been seen before, but Radisson may not have known it.

40. Huron islands.

41. They had come to Keweenaw peninsula and they portaged across.

42. Manitou island.

43. Isle Royal.

44. Sixscore and ten leagues equal 130 leagues or about 350 miles. From sunrise to the following morning is twenty-four hours, or may be reckoned as two days. Twenty leagues a day would be forty leagues, or about 110 miles, which is about the distance from Manitou island to the Canadian shore be-

yond Isle Royal. Radisson may have meant miles instead of leagues.

45. Supra, p. 96.
46. Probably Montreal river.
47. "Their nation" was the group of fugitive Hurons who had located some years before at Prairie island in the Mississippi and were later driven out by the Sioux, and were now encamped at a point near the headwaters of the Chippewa river in northern Wisconsin. See Perrot in Minnesota *Historical Society Collections,* vol. II, pp. 208-9.
48. A long sand bar projecting toward Madeline island and separating Chequamegon bay from the main body of Lake Superior. It is now disjoined from Chequamegon point and forms Long island.
49. Chequamegon bay.
50. Houghton point, or possibly La Pointe on Madeline island, or Van Tassell's point.
51. Supra, p. 143.
52. Not far from the mouth of Wittlesey creek. Now marked by a tablet.
53. Reference to themselves, Radisson and Groseilliers.
54. It is probable that Radisson did the more arduous work, being younger, while Groseilliers did the lighter work, being subject to the malady of epilepsy. Supra, p. 97.
55. The brook was probably Fish creek, which flows through swamps and meadows into the bay near Ashland. Even in late years great flocks of wild geese and swans have come to these swamps and marshes in proper season.
56. Breechclout.
57. In the ms. "faithlesse."
58. A reference to the entry of Louis XIV and his bride, Maria Theresa of Spain, into Paris after their marriage in June, 1660.
59. This lake has been identified by Father Chrysostom Verwyst as Lac Courte Orielle, Sawyer county, Wisconsin. *Parkman Club Papers* (No. 11), vol. II, pp. 1-24.
60. When the writer of this note visited the site of this transitory village, which is now the Chippewa village of Reserve, Mr. John Bracelin, an Ojibwa of about 60 years, indicated on a road map the ancient trail from Chequamegon bay to this point. The trail ended on the north side of the lake, and Mr. Bracelin stated that it is traditional that the Indians left the

trail and came across the lake on the ice or in canoes to the village here. This accords well with Radisson's narrative.

61. The feast of the dead. See *Jesuit Relations,* vol. 10, pp. 279-311. Also in Newton H. Winchell, *The Aborigines of Minnesota* (St. Paul, 1911), p. 732.

62. Mug, drinking cup.

63. Supra, p. 122, n. 36.

64. This suggests the time as late November.

65. Five moons probably means here both light and dark moons, which would equal two and a half months.

66. Supra, p. 144, n. 108 (Bryce criticism).

67. Catamount, panther, or mountain lion.

68. Radisson seems to be confused. Since leaving Chequamegon bay, the voyageurs were accompanied only by Hurons. There were no Ottawas with them on the Superior voyage at any time. The entire passage in parenthesis is very unclear.

69. An island at the mouth of Green Bay.

70. Radisson was twenty-six or twenty-seven years old at this time.

71. The voyageurs apparently have crossed the St. Croix and are within the limits of the present state of Minnesota. The habitat of the Nadoueceronons, or Sioux proper, never extended east of Minnesota, except for the Winnebagoes.

72. This reference to the "rendezvous" is too ambiguous to throw any light on its location.

73. Feast of the dead. Supra, p. 129, n. 61.

74. Nation of the Buffalo: Sioux.

75. This weeping and shedding of tears to obtain favors was a custom of the Sioux. It was experienced by Father Hennepin at Lake Pepin. *Minnesota Historical Society Collections,* vol. I, p. 252.

76. About a quarter of a mile square.

77. The foregoing passage commencing "The time now was nigh" and ending "In two days this was finished" is a somewhat detailed description of the "fort" and rendezvous or meeting place which was designated when they left the Huron village at Lac Courte Orielle. The events which occurred here during the spring of 1662 make this place one of the most significant historic sites within the area of the entire Northwest. The identification of this site has been the desire of many students of Radisson's journal, and the writer of this note acquired a similar ambition after a "voyage" through the heart of the "Sioux country" from Minneapolis to Duluth in 1922.

The site had already been located in a general way by a number of scholars as somewhere between Mille Lacs and the St. Croix river. Campbell placed it within "Minnesota"; Sulte "somewhere near the site of St. Paul"; Hill "between Kettle and Snake rivers in eastern Minnesota"; Upham "near Knife lake"; and Winchell "in the vicinity of Ann river and Fish lake in Kanabec county." The writer desired to locate the site definitively, if possible, and adopted a method of procedure briefly outlined as follows:

Upon reading Radisson's description carefully it will be observed that there were six distinct elements characterizing the place, namely: (1) It was *elevated* since the "fort" could be seen afar off. (2) A *brook* flowed by it. (3) This brook came from "the lake." (4) The brook emptied into a *meadow*. (5) The "fort" was *betwixt* the lake and meadow. (6) The place must have been *well known* to all the Indians in this extensive region. With this data the problem was to find a spot within the general area of eastern Minnesota wherein *all* of these six elements were present. The most important and essential one seemed to be the last, that is, the use of the spot as a permanent and general council-meeting place of the Indians.

In order to locate such a place two hypotheses were assumed:

1. The spot must have been well known to the Indians at that time, 1660.

2. Such a general meeting place would continue to be so used down to the days of our pioneers, a time within the memory of men now living.

The first step taken was to find "the oldest inhabitant" who was familiar with the region between Mille Lacs and the St. Croix in the early pioneer days. Mr. Julius Dosey of Pine City, an early timber "cruiser" for the lumber companies, fulfilled the requirement. He indicated on several county maps covering the region eight or nine village sites and meeting places known to him during his early residence there. All of these, except one, were located on the shores of lakes. These were all eliminated at once, since Radisson's description required that it be *betwixt* a lake and meadow and therefore not *on* a lake.

It now remained to visit and examine the other spot marked

on the map, which is known as Spring Brook hill near the confluence of the Snake and Ann rivers two miles south of Mora, Kanabec county. Not only is this place traditionally known to have been a notable gathering place of the Indians in early times, but the presence of a large burying ground, scores of mounds, its proximity to notable trail and water routes, and the abundant supply of food and spring water all point to the truth of the two hypotheses above stated.

Upon thorough investigation it was found that this spot complied with Radisson's description in all of the remaining five physical elements. (1) It is *elevated* and affords a distant view up the valleys of the Snake and Ann rivers. (2) Spring *Brook* flows by the place. (3) Spring Brook (the upper part is now dry because of artificial drainage) took its rise in a small *lake* about four miles northeast of Mora. The bed of this former lake is clearly marked by beaches and shore line. (4) The brook empties in Snake river. At the time of the visit, however, the level valleys of the two rivers, being filled with wild rice, were frozen over and covered with snow, thus giving the *appearance of a meadow*. (5) The hill is *between* the lake and the valleys of the two rivers.

The identification of Spring Brook hill as the site of the "fort" and rendezvous of Radisson and Groseilliers is based wholly upon the accord between the actual conditions there and Radisson's description, there being no "remains" of any sort whatsoever. The deduction reached could be derived only through a course of "ratiocinative reasoning" and the identification cannot be regarded as conclusive.

It may be added, however, that if a place is described as having one characteristic feature, such as elevation, many such sites might be located. If a second characteristic be added, such as a near by brook, the number of possible sites would be much reduced. When these features mount to six it would be difficult, probably impossible, to find two such places within the area involved or even within the whole country. But if *one* such site *is found* as in the case of Spring Brook hill, the probability becomes very strong that the object of the search has been attained.

Henry Colin Campbell, in *Proceedings of the Historical Society of Wisconsin,* for 1895, p. 102.

Benjamin Sulte, in Jacob Brower's *Memoirs,* vol. VI, pp. 74-84.

Alfred Hill, in *Minnesota Historical Society Collections,* vol. VII, p. 56, n.

Warren Upham, ibid., vol. X, p. 495.

Newton H. Winchell, *The Aborigines of Minnesota* (St. Paul, 1911), p. 339.

Minnesota History Bulletin, vol. V (May, 1923), p. 118.

Minneapolis Journal, editorial section, Jan. 14, 1923.

78. Framework for teepees?
79. The event alluded to remains obscure.
80. In the ms. "Turkey stones."
81. Lacework?
82. Medicine bag or pouch, possessing magic powers and used only by the medicine men.
83. Wild rice. Supra, pp. xxvii-xxviii.
84. Atlantic ocean.
85. Nations about Hudson Bay.
86. The distance from the rendezvous to the Christinos' camp was not great, since the line separating the Sioux from the Algonquins was about the latitude of Leech lake, Minnesota, and the Christinos were of Algonquin stock. See J. W. Powell, "Indians of North America" (map), *Johnson's Universal Cyclopedia* (1897).
87. The thought expressed in this sentence seems to have occurred to Radisson at the time of writing, which was probably 1668 while in London, and after having left the service of France.
88. Probably Mille Lacs.
89. Probably Sioux and Christinos.
90. Peace was accomplished, and their battles were sham.
91. Probably somewhere in southeastern Minnesota, seven days' journey from the rendezvous.
92. North side of Lake Superior.
93. For corroboration see *Jesuit Relations,* vols. 44 and 45, pp. 237-45 and 233-39 respectively.
94. Elevated platforms for burial?
95. This suggests the vicinity of Galena, Illinois.
96. Probably a reference to the Pipestone country in southwestern Minnesota. The red pipestone is "tender" and carves easily into pipes and other articles.
97. According to this, the beaver fur in the latitude of Lake Superior is better than that farther north.
98. Supra, p. 31, n. 53 (Campbell's criticism). The "one trip" to

which Mr. Campbell refers is this Buffalo Sioux journey, which occupied about seven weeks. During this period of about fifty days 600 elk were killed by three men. A simple calculation will show their quarry to be four animals each per day; not an extraordinary feat for these expert hunters in view of the multitudes of large game in these regions at that time.

99. Chequamegon bay.
100. This "fort" was probably at the south end of the bay, on the site of the previous fort. Supra, p. 125, n. 52.
101. Supra, p. 127.
102. Probably Houghton point. Supra, p. 125, n. 50.
103. During a hard winter the ice becomes very thick in Chequamegon bay, and in the spring the sun thaws the surface. Later falls of snow and continued thawing cause a deep slush to form before the solid ice beneath goes out.
104. Radisson must mean miles, which would correspond fairly well with fact. He usually states distances in leagues, but occasionally in miles.
105. The nature of the injury cannot well be determined. From this it would appear to be a sprain, but later the "sore breaks out again."
106. The Ottawa village or camp was probably at La Pointe at the south end of Madeline island, or at the north end of the present Long island.
107. Probably Assiniboines, whose habitat was in the vicinity of Lake Winnipeg.
108. The Hudson Bay journey begins at this point.

This side journey of Radisson and Groseilliers to the Bay of the North, or Hudson Bay, has been the subject of much doubt and controversy, some authorities discarding the story entirely while others believe they went to Lake Winnipeg.

Some of the latter group regard these "new wildmen" as Assiniboines, probably because they were fish-eaters, and since Radisson includes them in his list at the end of this voyage they assume that he visited that country. This deduction seems doubtful, however, and some light may be thrown upon this point by Radisson's own language. He says that these new wildmen came "to seek a nation in that land for a weighty business." This would seem to mean that this "great company" was a war party in search of their enemies outside of their own country. Hence the meeting with this transient and fast-moving band does not imply a journey to their country about Lake of the Woods and Lake Winnipeg.

A consideration of the state of geographical knowledge at that time, together with a careful glance at a modern map of British America, will disclose a decided probability that the two explorers reached Hudson Bay rather than Lake Winnipeg. At the time this voyage commenced, 1661, it was generally known that Hudson Bay was northwest of Quebec some 400 or 500 miles. When they reached the west end of Lake Superior Radisson must have known, from the latitude, that they were about due west of Quebec, and, owing to his careful and accurate observation, he knew that the distance was approximately 800 or 900 miles. Now, since they desired and intended to go to Hudson Bay, it seems entirely reasonable and logical that they would go northeast, and not northwest to Lake Winnipeg. Radisson's narrative a little farther on amply corroborates this view.

Supra, p. 148, n. 126. Bryce, *The Remarkable History of the Hudson's Bay Company,* pp. 3-11 and all of Ch. V. *Minnesota Historical Society Collections,* vol. X, p. 508.

109. The Assiniboines were also known as Hohay, or Hohe; that is, Fish-catchers. *Wisconsin Historical Society Collections,* vol. XVIII, p. 188, n. 41. Also Hodge, *Handbook of American Indians,* vol. I, p. 105.

110. Groseilliers must have gone ahead while Radisson was convalescing at the camp of the Ottawas at La Pointe or Chequamegon point.

111. Probably Thunder bay.

112. Promise fulfilled. Supra, p. 96.

113. Probably Albany river.

114. James bay, the south end of Hudson Bay.

115. The house battered with bullets and the reference to Europeans by the Indians is very strong evidence that other white men had been there before.

116. James bay is dotted with many islands.

117. Caribou.

118. The "place" where they were to pass the summer (first written "winter" in the original ms. and then crossed out) may have been at the mouth of Rupert river, which was formerly occupied by Hudson and later chosen by the English as a suitable spot for a trading post. This river has

its source in Lake Mistassini, but no river from that lake empties into the Saguenay, although it is not far across the height of land to the river. This passage commencing "We went further" (two sentences previous) is very ambiguous. It is difficult, in fact, to interpret large parts of the Hudson Bay narrative because of Radisson's defective English.

119. It has been said by an eminent authority that this statement "brands the whole story of the travel to Hudson Bay as false." Radisson is amply supported, however, by other authorities. Referring to the polar regions, Jean-Henri Fabre says: "In this season of the longest days the sun's heat steadily accumulates because each day's increase is not dissipated by the nightly cooling-off that follows, the night being too short to use up the supply, so that the temperature mounts as the season advances . . . During those long days [beyond the polar circles], when the sun circles about the spectator without setting, visible at midnight no less than at midday—during these long days, a single one of which amounts to many of ours, or even to weeks or months, according to the position, the heat from the sun's rays, oblique though those rays are, accumulates so as to be at last hardly endurable. In some sheltered bays navigators have even seen the tar of their vessels melt and run, under the heat of this continuous sun."

Fabre, *This Earth Of Ours* (New York, 1923), pp. 67-69.

Warren Upham, in *Minnesota Historical Society Collections,* vol. X, p. 511.

Vilhjalmur Stefansson, *The Friendly Arctic* (New York, 1921), p. 15.

Jesuit Relations, vol. 46, p. 279.

120. Possibly Moose river, but more likely Albany river to some other branch of it, then to Lake Superior. They desired to return to Chequamegon bay, and Moose river would have taken them far east. This is the end of the Hudson Bay journey.

121. Fort at Chequamegon bay.

122. Possibly a reference to a place where Europeans had been. James bay?

123. Christinos? Assiniboines?

124. Hudson Bay? Lake Winnipeg?

125. Radisson usually employs the word "trade" when he refers

to trinkets, beads, and other articles of barter. "Merchandise" usually refers to furs.

126. Lake Winnipeg. The statement clearly shows that the side journey to the Bay of the North was not to Lake Winnipeg. The information obtained was hearsay. Supra, p. 144, n. 108.

127. It has been urged that the return journey must have started from the north side of Lake Superior, for the reason that the Christinos would not be likely to cross the lake in so many boats loaded with beaver skins. While it may appear improbable that the Christinos would cross to the south side of the lake, it is not impossible. They came to the celebration after the feast of the dead at the rendezvous, and they were also on the south side with the Saulteurs at the time of the snowshoe trek on the Mississippi voyage.

128. In northern Michigan, a little west of Keweenaw peninsula.

129. Probably a thousand is meant. "Mille" is French for "thousand."

130. Keweenaw peninsula. Supra. p. 123.

131. Sault Ste. Marie.

132. Vapor bath. Supra, p. 8, n. 18.

133. Lake Huron and Georgian Bay.

134. Supra, p. 104.

135. In the ms. the Dollard massacre is described immediately following this note. The description has been transposed to the appropriate place in the Mississippi voyage, supra, p. 104, n. 120. The transposition is explained supra, "Foreword," passim, esp., p. xxi, ff.

136. About eighty-three miles. The actual distance is about forty miles.

137. This kind of "delayed reaction" comment is typical of Radisson.

138. Since the voyageurs returned prior to the departure of Governor D'Avaugour, July 23rd, this reference to August indicates Radisson's confusion of this voyage with their return from the Mississippi voyage.

139. Governor D'Avaugour.

140. Supra, p. xix.

141. Supra, p. 112.

142. Bugger, blackguard.

143. Old Spanish gold coin equal to $3.92, or any of a variety of obsolete gold coins having about that value.

144. Old French monetary unit equal to about nineteen cents.
145. About July, 1663.
146. Spring of 1664.
147. Anticosti.
148. "Cadis" remains obscure.
149. Spelled "Denier" in the ms.
150. Radisson's language is conflicting here. The time must be late summer. See Adam Short, A. G. Doughty (eds.) *Canada and Its Provinces,* vol. I, pp. 159-65.
151. Captain Zacharia Gillam and the ship *Nonsuch*. Ibid.
152. Icebergs.
153. Winter of 1664-5.
154. Spring or early summer of 1665.
155. Summer of 1665. Supra, p. xviii, n. 13.
156. Summer of 1665. These four commissioners had come over on business regarding the transfer of New Netherlands to the English as a result of the war with Holland. See Adam Short, A. G. Doughty, *Canada and Its Provinces,* vol. I, p. 161.
157. This expression has led some writers to believe that Radisson wrote this part of his narrative while crossing the Atlantic. The inference is not fully justified in view of Radisson's frequent use of the wrong tense.
158. Spelled "Carteret" in the ms.
159. Summer or autumn of 1665. The London plague was at its height, and the war with Holland was still in progress.
160. Winter of 1665-6.
161. The Dutch stopped the passage of the Thames in 1666. See any history of England.
162. 1667.
163. 1668
164. *The Nonsuch* and the *Eaglet. Canada and Its Provinces,* vol. I, pp. 162-3.
165. Groseilliers continued his voyage in the *Nonsuch* and reached the mouth of Rupert river in James bay.
166. Radisson was forced to spend some time in London alone and probably wrote his narratives of the first four voyages during this period.

NOTES FOR THE FIFTH VOYAGE

1. The text for the Fifth voyage has been taken from the Prince Society edition of the *Voyages of Peter Esprit Radisson*. There have been a few changes made in spelling, punctuation, and paragraphing. Mr. Scull, the editor of the Prince volume, took his text from a ms. in English in the British Museum. This ms. is a translation from the French, and the original French ms. may be found in the archives of the Hudson's Bay Company. The records of the British Museum do not indicate who the translator might have been. The voyage in the French has been printed in *Canadian Archives,* Report for 1895. Δ

2. From the Prince edition, p. 250, n.: "He married, between 1666 and 1673, for his second wife, the daughter of Sir John Kirke. He [Kirke] was one of the original founders of the Hudson's Bay Company, having subscribed L300 to the common stock in 1670. He was one of the seven members on the Committee of management for the Company, and was no doubt instrumental in securing Radisson a permanent pension of 1,200 livres a year, after he left the service of France. In all probability, Radisson emigrated to Canada with his family in 1694, for in that year his son's name thus appears as holding a land patent: '1695. Another patent of confirmation to "Sieur Etienne Volant Radisson" of the concession made to him the 19th of October, 1694, of the isles, islets, and "bastures" not granted, that are to be found across Lake St. Peter, above the islands granted to the "Sieur Sorel," from the edge of the north channel, as far as the great middle channel, called the channel of Platte Island,' etc., etc. As Peter Radisson's will can nowhere be found at Somerset House, London, he probably died in Canada."

3. From the Prince edition, p. 251, n.: "This expedition was commanded by Jean, Count d'Estrees. He reduced the Island of Tobaga. He was made a Marshal of France, and sent out, 1 August, 1687, as Viceroy over America."

4. Jean Baptiste Colbert, Minister of Finance under Louis XIV, was a promoter of industry, commerce, art, science, and literature; he reformed the finances of France through strict regulation. Because of his cold nature, he was known by his friends as the "man of marble." *The New International Encyclopedia* (New York, 1926). Δ

5. From the Prince edition, p. 254, n.: "John Kirke and his elder brother, Sir David, Sir Lewis, and others, held a large claim against Canada, or rather France, dating back to 1633, which amounted in 1654, including principal and interest, to over L34,000."

6. Father Francois Bellizani was Colbert's right hand man in matters of trade. Nute, *Caesars of the Wilderness*, p. 176. ∆

7. Spelled "De La Chesnay" in the Prince edition. The spelling herein is a compromise between that and the "la Chenaye" used by Miss Nute.

   In addition, there seems to be some confusion as to the identity of the man. Scull in the Prince edition (p. 255) notes his name thus: "M. Du Chesneau was appointed 30 May, 1675, Intendant of Justice, Police, and Finance of Canada, Acadia, and Isles of Newfoundland." Scull apparently believed that De La Chesnaye and Du Chesneau were the same person. Miss Nute, however, who is the foremost biographer of Radisson and Groseilliers, applies the names of different persons. She says "De la Chenaye" was the director of the beaver trade in New France, and that "Duchesneau" was the intendant (in this sentence I have used the spellings found in *Caesars of the Wilderness*). ∆

8. Radisson is confused. Should read 1883.

9. Hayes river. ∆

10. Nelson river. ∆

11. From the Prince edition, p. 282, n.: "The Company's early standard for trading was: 'For 1 Gun, one with another, 10 goods skins, that is, winter beavor; 12 skins for the biggest sort, 10 for the mean, and 8 for the smallest. Powder, a beaver for ½ a lb. A beaver for 4 lb. of shot. A beaver for a great and little hatchet. A beaver for 6 great knives or 8 jack-knives. Beads, a beaver for ½ lb. Six beavers for one good laced coat. Five beavers for one red plain coat. Coats for women, laced, two yards, six beavers. Coats for women, plain, Five beavers. Tobacco, a beaver for 1 lb. Powder-horns, a beaver for a large one and two small ones. Kettles, a beaver for one 1 lb. of Kettle. Looking-glasses and combs, 2 skins.'"

12. From the Prince edition, p. 312, n.: "This restoration did not meet with the approval of Monsr de Seignelay, for he wrote to Govr De la Barre, 10th April, 1684: 'It is impossible to imagine what you meant, when of our own authority, without

calling on the Intendant, and without carrying the affair before the Sovereign council, you caused to be given up to one Guillin, a vessel captured by the men named Radisson and des Grozelliers, and in truth you ought to prevent the appearance before his Majesty's eyes of this kind of proceeding, in which there is not a shadow of reason, and whereby you have furnished the English with matter of which they will take advantage; for by yr ordinance you have caused a vessel to be restored that according to law ought to be considered a Pirate, having no commission, and the English will not fail to say that you had so fully acknowledged the vessel to have been provided with requisite papers, that you had it surrendered to the owners; and will thence pretend to establish their legitimate possession of Nelson's river, before the said Radisson and des Grozeliers had been there.' *New York Colonial MSS.*, Vol. IX. p. 221."

13. From the Prince edition, p. 314, n.: "Louis XIV. to De la Barre, 10 April, 1684: 'The King of England has authorized his ambassador to speak to me respecting what occurred in the river Nelson between the English and Radisson and des Grozelliers, whereupon I am happy to inform you that, as I am unwilling to afford the King of England any cause of complaint, & as I think it important, nevertheless, to prevent the English establishing themselves on that river, it would be well for you to have a proposal made to the commandant at Hudson's Bay that neither the French nor the English should have power to make any new establishments; to which I am persuaded he will give his consent the more readily, as he is not in a position to prevent those which my subjects wish to form in said Nelson's river.' "

NOTES FOR THE SIXTH VOYAGE

1. The text for the Sixth voyage has been taken from the Prince edition, with a few corrections and changes in spelling, punctuation, and paragraphing. The original ms. in French for this voyage is in the British Museum. Presumably, though not certainly, the version herein presented was translated from the French by Gideon Scull, the editor of the Prince edition; the doubt enters in because Scull did not specify that he did the translating, only that he did the editing.

   Unlike the Fifth voyage, for which an English translation existed before Scull did his work, the Sixth appeared prior to the Prince edition only in French. The French text has been printed in *Canadian Archives,* Report for 1895. ∆

2. From the Prince edition, p. 360, n.: " 'Before Radisson's arrival, Capt. John Abraham had been to Port Nelson with supplies of stores, & finding Mr. Bridgar was gone, he staid himself, & was continued Governor by the Company in 1684.' Oldmixon."

3. From the Prince edition, p. 345, n.: *"Asenipoetes, Assinipoueles, Assenipoulacs,* and, according to Dr. O'Callaghan, *Assiniboins,* or 'Sioux of the Rocks.' "

NOTES FOR "A THEORY"

1. A theory purporting to explain the discrepancies in Radisson's narratives as to the order and duration of the voyages has been advanced by Miss Louise Phelps Kellogg, research associate of the Wisconsin Historical Society.

   This theory is based upon the similarity of the two descriptions of an Indian battle. One of these is found in *Jesuit Relations,* vol. 42, p. 237, where it is stated that the battle occurred on August 30, 1656. The other description is near the beginning of Radisson's Mississippi voyage, in which a conflict with the Iroquois took place shortly after leaving on this journey. It is assumed that these descriptions refer to the same battle—that of August 30, 1656.

   Miss Kellogg accepts the conclusion of many writers that Groseilliers was one of the two Frenchmen sent by Governor Lauzon on the Unwritten voyage, and returned in August, 1656. She then conjectures that Radisson joined him on another voyage of one year over the same ground, returning in 1657 in time for Radisson to accompany the Jesuits on the Onondaga voyage. The Mississippi voyage is thus made to cover both voyages and accounts for three years' time.

   The supposition that the battle described by Radisson at the beginning of this voyage was the same as that of the Jesuit account necessitates their starting on their journey prior to August 30, 1656.

   This theory appears to be untenable for several reasons, but conclusively so because of the fact that one of Groseilliers' children was born on August 7, 1657; therefore they could not have left for a year's journey in the West prior to about November 7, 1656.

   Kellogg, in *Wisconsin Magazine of History,* vol. V (June, 1922), p. 348. Also in her *The French Regime in Wisconsin* (Madison, 1925), p. 106.

   L'Abbe Cyprien Tanguay, "Chouart," in his *Genealogical Dictionary of Canadian Families* (Montreal, 1871), vol. I, p. 129.

   See also "The Radisson Problem," *Minnesota History,* for Sept., 1934.

2. *Jesuit Relations,* vol. 42, p. 219 ff.
3. Ibid., vol. 44, pp. 237, 247.
4. Ibid., vol. 45, 235.

5. Ibid., p. 163.
6. Ibid., p. 233.
7. Supra, p. 96. See map in *Indian Tribes of the Upper Mississippi.*
8. Supra, p. 96 for snowshoe journey, p. 97 for landing isle.
9. Supra, pp. 107-109.
10. *Jesuit Relations,* vol. 42, p. 237.
11. Ibid., pp. 225, 227.
12. Ibid., p. 229.
13. Some authorities locate this battle at the Long Sault in the Ottawa river. Parkman, *The Old Regime in Canada,* p. 85. William Kingsford, *The History of Canada* (Toronto, 1887-98), vol. I, pp. 237-8.
14. *Jesuit Relations,* vol. 46, p. 75.
15. Ibid., pp. 119, 121.
16. Supra, p. 107.
17. Supra, p. 109.
18. Supra, p. 78.
19. Supra, p. 107.
20. Supra, p. 89.
21. Supra, p. 96.
22. Supra, p. 97.
23. Supra, p. 93, from land "mighty hot" to Green Bay; p. 142, from rendezvous to Buffalo Sioux country; pp. 145-146, from Lake Superior to Hudson Bay.
24. Supra, pp. 73-76, escape from Onondaga mission; pp. 131-134, famine; pp. 135-141, feast and celebration.
25. Supra, p. 104; also p. 252, topic no. 10.
26. Supra, p. 92.
27. Emma Blair, *Indian Tribes of the Upper Mississippi Valley* . . . ., vol. I, pp.163-5. Also in *Minnesota Historical Society Collections,* vol. II, p. 208. Supra, p. 96, n. 87.
28. Supra, p. 96.
29. Parkman, *The Jesuits in North America,* ch. I. Also Edna Kenton, *The Jesuit Relations and Allied Documents* . . . ., p. 225.
30. Supra, pp. 43 and 45.
31. *Jesuit Relations,* vol. 40, pp. 157-193.
32. Supra, p. 45, n. 1. Kenton, op. cit., p. 280.
33. Supra, p. 79.
34. Supra, p. xiii, n. 1.

35. Supra, p. 104.
36. Supra, p. 88.
37. Supra, p. 97.
38. Supra, p. 89.
39. Supra, p. 156.
40. Supra, p. 93, n. 68.
41. Supra, p. 87.
42. Supra, p. 90.
43. Supra, p. 87.
44. Supra, p. 80.
45. Supra, p. 89.
46. Supra, pp. 159-160.
47. Supra, p. 89.
48. Supra, p. 81.
49. Supra, p. 106.
50. Supra, p. 97.
51. Supra, pp. 107-109.
52. Supra, p. 79.
53. Supra, pp. 97-98.
54. Supra, p. 98, ff.
55. Supra, pp. 103-104.
56. Supra, p. 104.
57. Supra, p. 109.
58. Supra, p. 97.
59. Supra, pp. 107-109.
60. Supra, p. 43, n. 73, passing from the Captivity to the Onon-
    daga voyage; p. 109, n. 134, passing from the battle of 1656
    to the year "at home at rest."

BIBLIOGRAPHY

ADAMS, A. T., "A New Interpretation of the Voyages of Radisson," *Minnesota History*, vol. VI (Dec., 1925), pp. 317-29.

ADAMS, A. T., "The Radisson Problem," *Minnesota History*, vol. XV (Sept., 1934), pp. 317-27.

BEGG, ALEXANDER, *History of the North-West* (Toronto, 1894-5), vol. I, pp. 71-4. Also vol. III, p. 479.

BLAKELY, CAPT. RUSSELL, in *Minnesota Historical Society Collections*, vol. VIII, pp. 303-62.

BRADLEY, A. G., in *MacMillan's Magazine*, vol. LXXXIII (Jan., 1901), p. 231.

BROWER, JACOB V., *Memoirs*, vol. VI, entitled *Minnesota* (St. Paul, 1900); also vols. III, IV, V.

BROWER, JACOB V., in *Minnesota Historical Society Collections*, vol. VII, pp. 47-57.

BROWER, JACOB V., in *Journal of the Manchester Geographical Society* (Manchester, England), vol. XI, pp. 1-80.

BROWER, JACOB V., contributions to *The Aborigines of Minnesota* (St. Paul, 1911), by Newton H. Winchell.

BRYCE, GEORGE, *The Remarkable History of the Hudson's Bay Company* (Toronto, 1900).

BRYCE, GEORGE, in *Proceedings and Transactions of the Royal Society of Canada* (second series), vol. IV, section ii, pp. 53-66.

BRYMNER, DOUGLAS (archivist), in *Canadian Archives*, report for 1883, note C, pp. 173-201; report for 1895, note A, pp. 1-83.

CAMPBELL, HENRY COLIN, "Radisson's Journal: Its Value in History," *Proceedings of the State Historical Society of Wisconsin* (Madison, 1896), 43rd annual meeting, Dec. 12, 1895, pp. 88-116.

CAMPBELL, HENRY COLIN, "Radisson and Groseilliers," *The American Historical Review*, vol. I (Jan., 1896), pp. 226-37.

CAMPBELL, HENRY COLIN, "Exploration of Lake Superior," *Parkman Club Publications*, no. 2, vol. I, pp. 17-35.

CAMPBELL, HENRY COLIN, "Pere Rene Menard," *Parkman Club Publications*, no. 11, vol. II, pp. 1-24.

CAMPBELL, T. J., "Pierre Esprit Radisson," *U. S. Catholic Historical Society, Historical Records and Studies*, vol. VI (Feb., 1911), pp. 7-35.

CAMPBELL, T. J., *Pioneer Laymen of North America* (New York, 1915), vol. I.

CHARLEVOIX, PIERRE FRANCOIS DE (trans. by John G. Shea), *History and General Description of New France* (New York, 1863), vol. III, pp. 230-7, 261.

COYNE, JAMES H. (trans. and ed.), *Exploration of the Great Lakes*, by de Casson and de Galinee, Ontario Historical Society Papers and Records, vol. LV (Toronto, 1903).

DAVIDSON, JOHN NELSON, in *Wisconsin Historical Collections,* vol. XII, pp. 434-5.

DAVIDSON, JOHN NELSON, *In Unnamed Wisconsin* (Milwaukee, 1895), passim.

DE TREMANDAN, A. H., *Le Sang Francais* (Winnipeg), chapter entitled "Decouverte de la baie d'Hudson par terre."

DIONNE, NARCISSE E., *Chouart et Radisson; Odyssee de deux Canadiens-Francais au XVII siecle* (Quebec, 1910).

DIONNE, NARCISSE E., in *Proceedings and Transactions of the Royal Society of Canada,* vol. XI, section i, pp. 115-35; vol. XII, section i, pp. 29-48.

DUGAS, L'ABBE G., *L'Ouest canadien* (Montreal, 1896).

ELLIS, HENRY, *A Voyage to Hudson's Bay* (London, 1748), pp. XXVIII, 336.

FOLWELL, WILLIAM WATTS, *History of Minnesota* (St. Paul, 1921), vol. I, pp. 7-14.

GARNEAU, FRANCOIS ZAVIER (trans. by Andrew Bell), *History of Canada* (Montreal, 1866).

GALE, E. C., "Radisson Manuscript," *Minnesota History,* vol. VII (Dec., 1926), pp. 340-2.

GARY, GEORGE, *Studies in the Early History of the Fox River Valley* (Oshkosh, 1901).

HAWORTH, P. L., *Trailmakers of the Northwest* (New York, 1921).

HEBBARD, S. S., *History of Wisconsin under the Dominion of France* (Madison, 1890).

HILL, ALFRED J., "The Geography of Perrot," *Minnesota Historical Society Collections,* vol. II, p. 200.

HILL, ALFRED J., associated with Brower in *Minnesota Historical Society Collections,* vol. VII.

HILL, ALFRED J., contributions to Winchell's *The Aborigines of Minnesota.*

INCARNATION, MARIE, letters, *Magazine of Western History,* vol. VII (Feb., 1888), p. 418.

JEREMIE, NOEL, *Relation du Detroit et de la Baie d'Hudson* (Amsterdam, 1710).

JOHNSTON, C. H., *Famous Discoverers and Explorers of America* (Boston, 1917), chapter on Radisson.

KELLOG, LOUISE PHELPS, *Early Narratives of the Northwest, 1634-1699* (New York, 1917).

KELLOG, LOUISE PHELPS, *The French Regime in Canada* (Madison, 1925), Chapter VII, pp. 104-14.

KELLOG, LOUISE PHELPS, in *Wisconsin Magazine of History,* vol. V (June, 1922), p. 348.

KERR, ROBERT F., "Voyages of Radisson and Groseilliers," *South Dakota Historical Society Collections,* vol. I (1902), pp. 163-78.

KEYES, C. R., "Earliest Explorations of Iowa-land," *Annals of Iowa,* 3rd series, vol. X, pp. 265-72.

KINGSFORD, WILLIAM, *The History of Canada* (Toronto, 1887-98), vol. III, pp. 1-12 and 45-9.

LAHONTAN, BARON DE, *New Voyages to North America* (Chicago, 1905), vol. I, p. 312.

LAUT, AGNES C., *The Conquest of the Great Northwest* (New York, 1918).

LAUT, AGNES C., *Pathfinders of the West* (New York, 1914), pp. 1-192.

LAUT, AGNES C., in *Leslie's Monthly Magazine,* vol. LVIII (July, 1904), pp. 275-83; vol. LVII (April, 1904), pp. 667-78.

LEGLER, HENRY E., *Leading Events of Wisconsin History* (Milwaukee, 1898).

LONG, LILY A., *Radisson, the Voyageur* (New York, 1914).

LONG, M. H., *Knights Errant of the Wilderness* (Toronto, 1920).

LUCAS, C. P., *A Historical Geography of the British Colonies* (Oxford, England, 1901), vol. V, entitled *Canada.*

McCORMICK, ROBERT LAIRD, *Press History of Sawyer County, Wisconsin* (Hayward, Wisconsin, 1898).

MOORE CHARLES, *The Northwest under Three Flags, 1635-1796* (New York, 1900).

MOORE, CHARLES, "The Discoverers of Lake Superior," *Publications of the Michigan Political Science Association,* vol. II, pp. 199-211.

NEILL, EDWARD D., *Explorers and Pioneers of Minnesota* (Minneapolis, 1881-82).

NEILL, EDWARD D., *History of Minnesota* (Minneapolis, 1882).

NEILL, EDWARD D., in *Minnesota Historical Society Collections,* vol. V, pp. 401-4.

NEILL, EDWARD D., "The First Explorers of Lake Superior and the State of Minnesota," *Magazine of Western History,* vol. VII (Feb., 1888), pp. 412-21.

NEILL, EDWARD D., in *Wisconsin Historical Society Collections,* vol. X, pp. 292-7.

NEILL, EDWARD D., in *Macalester College Contributions,* first series (St. Paul, 1890), pp. 86-94, 223-4; *Macalester College Contributions,* second series, 1892, pp. 152-8.

NEVILLE, ELLA HOES, et al., *Historic Green Bay, 1634-1840* (Green Bay, Wisconsin, 1893).

NUTE, GRACE LEE, *Caesars of the Wilderness* (New York, 1943).

O'CALLIGHAN, E. B. (ed.), *Documents Relative to the Colonial History of the State of New York* (Albany, New York, 1853-8; 10 vols.).

OGG, FREDERIC AUSTIN, *The Opening of the Mississippi* (New York, 1904).

OLDMIXON, JOHN, The *British Empire in America* (2nd ed.; London, 1741).

PARKER, GILBERT, *The Trail of the Sword* (New York, 1894).

PARKMAN, FRANCIS, *The Old Regime in Canada* (any edition). Also *La Salle and the Discovery of the Great West* (any edition).

PERROT, NICOLAS, in Emma Blair (ed.), *Indian Tribes of the Upper Mississippi Valley and Region of the Great Lakes* (Cleveland, 1911).

POTHERIE, DE BASQUEVILLE DE LA, in ibid.

PRUD'HOMME, L. A., *Notes Historiques sur la Vie de P. E. de Radisson* (St. Boniface, Manitoba, 1892).

RADISSON, PIERRE ESPRIT, *Voyages of Pierre Esprit Radisson* (Boston, 1885).

ROBINSON, DOANE, in *South Dakota Historical Society Collections,* vol. II, part i, p. 87; also part ii, p. 21.

ROBSON, JOSEPH, *Six Years Residence in Hudson's Bay* (London, 1752).

SULTE, BENJAMIN, *Chronique Trifluvienne* (Montreal, 1879).

SULTE, BENJAMIN, *Histoire des Canadiens-Francais* (Montreal, 1882-84).

SULTE, BENJAMIN, *Pages d'Histoire de Canada* (Montreal, 1891).

SULTE, BENJAMIN, *Le Pays des Grande Lacs* (Quebec, 1889).

SULTE, BENJAMIN, "Le Pere Menard," *Quebec Bulletin,* vol. 12 (July, 1918), pp. 195-9.

SULTE, BENJAMIN (ed. by G. Ducharme), *Melanges historiques; etudes eparses et inedites de Benjamin Sulte,* vol. I, chapter on "Chouart et Radisson à Londres."

SULTE, BENJAMIN, articles in *Le Canadien,* St. Paul, Jan. 21 to Sept. 30, 1897. Also articles in *Echo de l'Quest,* Minneapolis, April 11 to Aug. 15, 1902.

SULTE, BENJAMIN, in *Memoirs of the Royal Society of Canada,* vol. IX (1893), section i, pp. 3-44.

SULTE, BENJAMIN, contributions to Brower's *Memoirs,* vol. VI.

TANGUAY, L'ABBE CYPRIEN, *Genealogical Dictionary of Canadian Families* (Montreal, 1871).

THWAITES, REUBEN GOLD, *Father Marquette* (New York, 1902).

THWAITES, REUBEN GOLD, *The Story of Wisconsin* (Boston, 1891).

THWAITES, REUBEN GOLD, "Radisson and Groseilliers in Wisconsin," *Wisconsin Historical Society Collections,* vol. XI, p. 64. "Story of Chequamegon Bay," same publication, vol. XIII, p. 397.

THWAITES, REUBEN GOLD (ed.), *Jesuit Relations,* which includes *Journal of the Jesuits,* (Cleveland, 1896-1901; 73 vols.).

TURNER, FREDERICK J., in *Proceedings of the State Historical Society of Wisconsin,* 36th annual meeting, 1889, pp. 52-98.

BIBLIOGRAPHY

UPHAM, WARREN, in *Minnesota Historical Society Collections,* vol. X, part 2, pp. 449-594.

UPHAM, WARREN, in *Minnesota in Three Centuries* (New York, 1908), vol. I, pp. 127-203. Put out by the Publishing Society of Minnesota.

UPHAM, WARREN, contributions to Brower's *Memoirs,* vol. VI.

VERWYST, CHRYSOSTEM, *Missionary Labors of Fathers Marquette, Menard and Allouez, in the Lake Superior Region* (Milwaukee, 1886).

WILSON, BECKLES, *The Great Company* (Toronto, 1889).

WILSON, BECKLES, "Pierre Radisson, Bushranger," *Canadian Magazine,* vol. XIII (June, 1899), p. 117.

WINCHELL, NEWTON H., *The Aborigines of Minnesota* (St. Paul, 1911).

WINCHELL, NEWTON H., *Geological Survey of Minnesota* (Minneapolis, 1884), vol. I.

WINSOR, JUSTIN, *Cartier to Frontenac, 1534-1700* (Boston, 1895).

WINSOR, JUSTIN, *Narrative and Critical History of America* (Boston, 1884-9).